"*Soundings in the Christian Mystical Tradition* provides strong nourishment for those who are just beginning or have long journeys to take. Based on fifty years of classroom experience in teaching mysticism, Egan casts a wider net—more than seventy entries—than is usual in surveys of this kind. His effort is an important contribution to the burgeoning interest in mysticism."

—Paul Lachance, OFM
Adjunct Professor of Spirituality
Catholic Theological Union

"This book is a fitting culmination ⌐⌐ reading, writing, and lecturing about lue of the work is his inclusion of not on hose whom he has found to be undeserve *'ings* will surely be drawn to read the ful so let themselves be 'sounded' in ret

—James A. Wiseman, OSB
Professor of Theology and Religious
Studies
The Catholic University of America
Monk of St. Anselm's Abbey
in Washington, DC

"*Soundings* comes together here to offer an overview of Christian spiritualities ranging from the Old Testament to Mother Teresa. Several dozen well-known and less-known theologians of mystical communion take the reader on a journey through approaches to Christian life and prayer. Locating them concretely in their own times and cultures, Harvey Egan presents these men and women with vitality and insight."

—Thomas O'Meara, OP
Warren Professor Emeritus
University of Notre Dame

"This is one of the finest books I have ever read on Christian mysticism. Harvey Egan, SJ, with his usual careful scholarship and clear writing style, leads us through the lives of the great Christian mystics in a way that makes mysticism and prayer accessible and inviting even to the most non-saintly among us. Father Egan, a master of the spiritual masters, brings to bear a lifetime of experience and erudition to a topic that can seem far removed from our daily lives, but is in fact at its heart: the way we relate to God. I can think of no better introduction to the Christian mystic tradition than *Soundings*."

—James Martin, SJ
Author of *The Jesuit Guide to Almost
Everything*
Culture Editor, *America Magazine*

"Harvey Egan's *Soundings* are the distillation of a lifetime of theological research into the deeper reaches of Christian experience. His book, in style, format, and content, is a perfect resource for theological teachers and students eager to make their own the deep creativity and catholicity of Christian faith. Professor Egan has made a wide-ranging selection of the long-recognized (Gregory of Nyssa, Teresa of Avila), too little appreciated (Thomas Aquinas, Ignatius of Loyola), and of the sometimes all-but-forgotten (Guigo Ii, Ramon Llull, Christina of St Trond), remarkable men and women who have been living witnesses to the mystical depth of Christian life. There is a benign provocation in this: readers will inevitably ask, How can you leave out this or that radiant mystical presence? But that is a good problem to have: the cloud of witnesses—over seventy, in fact, here presented—that will keep reminding us that there is so much in need of discovery, recovery, and celebration in the life of the Church itself, and in its growing dialogue with the great religious traditions of humankind. A wise book, deeply theological, methodologically alert (Rahner and Lonergan), spiritually inspiring, and widely attractive to any reader in search of the sacred heart of the Christian tradition."

—Anthony J. Kelly, CSsR
Professor of Theology
Australian Catholic University
Member of the International
Theological Commission

"Harvey Egan is an eminent scholar of Christian mysticism. This present volume reflects fifty years of engagement with those major figures who have experienced, in the words of Saint John of the Cross, that 'hidden wisdom which comes through love.' This eminently readable book would be of enormous value both for the individual reader and for use in a classroom setting. I highly recommend it to both audiences."

—Lawrence S. Cunningham
John A. O'Brien Professor of
Theology
University of Notre Dame

# Soundings in the Christian Mystical Tradition

*Harvey D. Egan, S.J.*

A Michael Glazier Book

**LITURGICAL PRESS**
Collegeville, Minnesota

www.litpress.org

A Michael Glazier Book published by Liturgical Press

Cover design by David Manahan, O.S.B. Photo courtesy of Photos.com.

1    2    3    4    5    6    7    8    9

**Library of Congress Cataloging-in-Publication Data**

Egan, Harvey D.
    Soundings in the Christian mystical tradition / Harvey D. Egan.
        p. cm.
    "A Michael Glazier Book."
    Includes bibliographical references (p.        ) and index.
    ISBN 978-0-8146-5613-6 — ISBN 978-0-8146-8003-2 (e-book)
    1. Mysticism.    2. Mystics.    I. Title.

BV5082.3.E36    2010
248.2'2—dc22                                                    2010020551

*To*
*Joyce, David, Donna, Denise,*
*Brian, Erin, Wrangler, Odis—*
*and in memory of my mother and father.*

# Contents

# Preface

In a survey taken in the United States many years ago, a simple question was asked: "Who are you?" As expected, some responded with their name or profession; others became angry or laughed; still others just walked away. However, a small percentage replied, "I am a child of God." When this question was asked in an undergraduate class here at Boston College, a perceptive student offered a remarkable answer: "Isn't that the question Moses asked God and to which only God can say, 'I AM'?"

The Christian mystics raise the question of human identity in a striking manner and receive an arresting response. In a variety of ways, they not only know but also experience that the human person is made in God's image, an image that contains what it images. They also experience themselves as an infinite question to which only God is the answer; an immense longing that only Love can quench; an endless desire that finds "dissatisfied satisfaction" only in God's incomprehensible Mystery; a nothing in the face of the No-thing; and an abyss whose bottom is the Abyss, into which "even the soul of Christ vanishes." These God-haunted, God-possessed, God-illuminated, and God-transformed persons—"theologians," in the profoundest sense of the word—know that human identity is rooted in God.

Plunged into the Father's Mystery, addressed and illuminated by the Father's Word, and burning with the fire of the Holy Spirit, many mystics stress the trinitarian dimension of their identity. Others, on the other hand, emphasize their identity in relationship to Christ, as sons or daughters in the Son, redeemed sinners, who are called to share eternally in divine life because of Christ's life, death, and resurrection. Many sought to hang with Christ on the cross for the world's redemption and were explicitly conscious as "hiding in Christ's wounds" and as having his wounds engraved on both spirit and body.

Alert to the least prompting of the Holy Spirit, many mystics discovered their identity through a contemplation in apostolic action. More recent mystics were conscious of themselves as "living cells" in the cosmic Christ—the Alpha and the Omega of an evolving world. Other Christian explorers of the human spirit found their identity by reconciling in themselves the worlds of science or of Eastern mysticisms. All were conscious, in some way, of the paradox of human identity—supremely and unsurpassably manifested in the God-Man— that the genuinely human is disclosed only through surrender to God and that the search for God cannot bypass the genuinely human.

As pioneers of a transformed and fully authentic humanity, the mystics give dramatic testimony to God's grace and to heroic human achievement. Called in a special way to listen to the whispers of God in every human heart, they become the loudspeakers of what is deepest in the human spirit. The Christian mystics also amplify what it means to be baptized into the life, death, and resurrection of Jesus Christ—and to have the Trinity living in them.

Revealing original and often paradoxical modes of expressing and imaging the divine-human relationship, the mystics teach innovative ways of knowing (often a "learned ignorance") and loving God, neighbor, self, and the world. Unusual forms of consciousness—such as visions, locutions, ecstasies—sometimes fill their lives. Others, however, reject such phenomena as distractions and temptations against life's real purpose: total surrender to God's love. They are God's fools, troubadours—the great explorers, thinkers, artists, and poets of the interior life who explain the art of loving God, neighbor, self, and the world.

It is customary for Jesuit provincials on their annual meeting with their men to ask, "And how is your spiritual life?" My recent answer—half-jokingly—was, "I have been reading and writing about the Christian mystics for the past fifty years." A half century of intense conversation with these remarkable figures has led to this book.

In 1959, I read my first mystical text, St. John of the Cross's *Dark Night of the Soul*. I was at the time an electrical engineer, who had read almost nothing religious since my grammar school catechisms. His text, however, has marked me to this day. My interest in the mystics deepened when I was exposed, on entering the Society of Jesus in 1960, to the profound spirituality and mysticism of St. Ignatius of Loyola.

During my final year of formal philosophical studies in 1965, I read Elmer O'Brien's *The Varieties of Mystic Experience*,[1] an anthology—the right book at the right time—that opened up a wider world of the Christian mystical tradition. In 1969, I began doctoral studies in theology as one of Karl Rahner's students because he was one of the few theologians with an unabashed interest in the writings of mystics as theological sources.

My doctoral dissertation, *The Spiritual Exercises and the Ignatian Mystical Horizon*,[2] attempted to translate the mystical wisdom of St. Ignatius of Loyola into a contemporary framework by using Rahner's theological method. The fascination with Ignatius Loyola as mystic culminated in a 1987 book, *Ignatius Loyola the Mystic*,[3] in which I argued that Ignatius's pragmatic successes in asceticism, spirituality, and humanism obscured appreciating him as one of the tradition's most profound trinitarian, Christocentric, and apostolic mystics.

At Santa Clara University in 1973, I began teaching courses in Eastern and Western mysticisms. During this period, I gave a series of talks on Christian spirituality and mysticism to an American Buddhist community—only to discover, to my astonishment, that most of the members were former Christians who knew little about their own Christian mystical heritage. Retreat work, liturgies, and conferences with the impressive community of Carmelite nuns in Santa Clara furthered my desire to study the Christian mystics more extensively.

Since 1975, when I began teaching at Boston College, I have written *What Are They Saying About Mysticism?*,[4] *Christian Mysticism: The Future of a Tradition*,[5] *An Anthology of Christian Mysticism*[6] (small parts of which have found their way into this volume), and *Karl Rahner: Mystic of Daily Life*.[7] I count as one of the great blessings of my life to have at my disposal the excellent Paulist Press series The Classics of Western Spirituality, and the standard-setting scholarship of Bernard McGinn of the University of Chicago and of Kurt Ruh (d. 2002) of the University of Würzburg.

The classics of the Christian mystical tradition are never fully understood, no matter how often they are read and reread. Over and above broadening the horizon of the readers, they also demand an intellectual, moral, religious conversion. The texts are never fully comprehended because interpreters can never fully comprehend either the cultural horizon of the writers or their own cultural horizon of understanding. Another problem arises because the writers of mystical texts—analogous to biblical authors—wrote primarily for mystagogical reasons. Writing this book has been for me a spiritual exercise more than an academic one. I hope that I have undergone to some degree the "conversions" required to do justice to mystical texts.

The psalmist wrote of "the deep calling to the deep." I have titled this book *Soundings in the Christian Mystical Tradition* because "soundings" can mean both the action of measuring depth and the acoustical vibrations emanating from an object. My experience has been that one cannot take "soundings" of mystical texts without being "sounded" in return. These texts have a paradoxical way of taking the measure of those who measure them. The German philosopher Martin Heidegger (d. 1976) emphasized that the human person is "the shepherd of Being," but the German Jesuit theologian Karl Rahner (d. 1984) said it best: "Being shepherds us."

The mystics treated in this volume were selected for three major reasons. First, any book that presents an overview of the tradition and a broad cross-section of mystical themes must include the titans of the tradition. Second, I wished also to introduce writers whom I consider to have been undeservedly neglected. Third, fifty years of reading mystical texts should allow me some leeway in either over-estimating or underestimating some figures in the tradition. A volume of this size can offer the reader only a partial taste of the richness of the Christian mystical tradition.

I am grateful to Michael A. Fahey, S.J., and Francis A. Sullivan, S.J., both of Boston College; to Robert Doran, S.J., of Marquette University; to Herr Dr. Wilhelm Hoye, Münster, Germany; to James A. Wiseman, O.S.B., of the Catholic University of America; to Sister Mary Augustine, Little Sisters of the Poor of Somerville, MA; and to Sister Ann Laforest, O.C.D., Beacon, NY, Carmel, for reading many of the chapters.

Harvey D. Egan, S.J.
Boston College
January 3, 2010
Solemnity of the Epiphany

# Introduction

The word "mysticism" rarely evokes a neutral response. Mass media often employ it to depict the "spooky," the irrational, the paranormal, and superstition at its worst. The Oxford English Dictionary incorrectly defines it as "religious belief that is characterized by vague, obscure, or confused spirituality; a belief system based on the assumption of occult forces, mysterious supernatural agencies, etc."

When I mentioned recently that I was writing a book on Christian mysticism, the person said immediately, "Oh, then you'll have something to say about *The Da Vinci Code*." Christian mysticism, however, has absolutely nothing to do with this or with the increasingly popularized "sightings" of the Virgin Mary.

The contemporary scene is replete with seekers of "experience," of "transcendence without dogma," that is, with spiritualities free from traditional religions. New Age spirituality—redolent with skewed Eastern pantheistic beliefs—further clouds the issue. What Harvey Cox has called a "spiritual consumerism" has sidetracked many a true seeker from a genuine spiritual quest.

Psychological studies on mysticism often attempt to explain it away as madness, hysteria, self-hypnosis, repressed eroticism, and escape from the duties and pressures of daily life. More recent studies frequently reduce it to regression, for example, to an experience of the earliest sensations of childhood. Mysticism is also mistakenly understood as an "altered state of consciousness" engendered, for example, by high-altitude flying or long kayak journeys. Aldous Huxley and Timothy Leary—to name only two—have popularized the notion that mystical experiences can be had by ingesting psychedelic drugs.[1] Of *what* or of *whom* the mystic is conscious is rarely asked by these researchers. Moreover, the radical spiritual annihilation and personal transformation witnessed in genuine Christian mysticism far transcends what results from the "bad trips" and "good trips" of a user of psychedelic drugs.

Some Jewish scholars share the erroneous opinion of Gershom Scholem that "it would be absurd to call Moses, the man of God, a mystic, or to apply this term to the prophets, on the strength of their immediate religious experience."[2] This is paradigmatic of the false assumption that the experience of undifferentiated unity (atman is Brahman), or the fusion experience of monism, is the hallmark of all mysticism.

In her book *The Protestant Mystics*,[3] Anne Fremantle contradicts the thesis of twentieth-century Protestant dialectical theologians that there are no Protestant mystics. She asserts, however, that all Catholic mystics—unlike their Protestant counterparts—travel a well-worn, well-known, well-marked, easily identifiable three-stage journey of purgation, illumination, and union. The following chapters of this book will disabuse the reader of Fremantle's view.

The Catholic Church's attitude toward mysticism has also been somewhat ambivalent. On the one hand, the Church fosters the contemplative life, which often leads to mystical consciousness. Many of the saints formally recognized as such by the Church were mystics. On the other hand, Church officials have tended to stress the mystical path as suitable only for an elite and counseled the path of approved devotions and liturgical life for the general faithful.

The famous psychologist Carl Jung and many other commentators hold the view that the mystic is necessarily a heretic. Exploring the deepest realms of the psyche, mystics discovered shocking and explosive truths, which they then rendered safe to reveal by using the protective covering of Church teachings.

Better scholarship has disclosed, however, that mysticism arises out of a lived tradition that fosters and nourishes the seeking and finding of God-consciousness. As this volume will disclose, the genuine Christian mystics upheld and enriched their tradition. To be sure, their tasting of and plunging into the depths of the incomprehensible, ineffable God sometimes prompted them to stretch and to transform both language and the ways to speak the ineffable. This on occasion led to tensions with Church authorities.

The word "mysticism" is not found in the Bible. Historically, the word is associated with the Hellenistic mystery religions and cults of the pre- and early Christian era. The "mystical ones" (Greek, *hoi mystai*; occasionally *hoi mystikoi*) were those who had been initiated into the secret rites (*ta mystika*) of the mystery religions. The mystics were required to keep secret the *rituals* into which they had been initiated. The word "mystical," therefore, originally referred to the cultic or ritual secrets revealed only to the initiated ones, the mystics. Note, however, that the mystical secret was only a secret about the purely material aspects of the rites and rituals of the Greek mystery religions.

The great Jewish religious thinker Philo of Alexandria (20 B.C.–50 A.D.) welded Jewish beliefs and spirituality with Greek thought. He focused sharply on the "mystical," or allegorical, interpretation of scripture. To him, "mystical" did not refer to the secret details of a ritual but to the secret and hidden meaning of God's word. Thus, he was probably the bridge between the Jewish and Greek worlds for the transposed meaning of the word "mystical" as it was used by the early Church Fathers to refer to the inner reality of scripture and the liturgy.

Late Second Temple Judaism, however, provided the matrix for Christian mysticism through its protomystical ascents to the vision of God found in the apocalypses, the movement to a canon of sacred texts, and the tools and techniques requisite to keep this movement alive. Neglecting the Jewish roots of Christian mysticism and viewing it as a purely Greek phenomenon seriously misconstrues the most important part of its history.

To many early Church Fathers, "mystical" signified the allegorical interpretation of scripture, especially the disclosing of Christ as the key to unlocking the secrets of the Old Testament. Scripture, Christologically interpreted, was the ground of all Christian thought, including mysticism, especially in the first centuries. Jesus was sometimes called the "mystical angel" whose entire life, death, resurrection, and glorification were understood as *the truly mystical*.

Eventually, Christians used the word "mystical" with respect to the sacraments, especially the Eucharist. The Fathers of the Church spoke of Christ's "mystical Pasch," the "mystical sacrifice of his Body and Blood," and the "mystical bread and wine." "Mystical waters," of course, referred to baptism. The profoundest mysteries of the faith—such as the Trinity and Christ's divinity—were likewise deemed supremely "ineffable and mystical." Especially in its formative stages, Christian mysticism was always both ecclesial, that is, realized only in and through the community, and scriptural, that is, tied to the spiritual, hidden, or mystical meaning of the sacred text.

By the time of the Roman emperor Constantine, the word "mystical" had biblical, liturgical, and sacramental connotations. It denoted the hidden presence of Christ in the scriptures, the liturgy, and the sacraments—his "spiritual" presence. Thus, Christologically interpreted and liturgically lived scripture provided the exegetical context of early Christian mysticism. The Christian mystical tradition finds its real origin here and nowhere else.

The word "mystical" definitively entered Christian vocabulary through the influential writings of Pseudo-Dionysius, a sixth-century Syrian monk. Although he too used the word "mystical" in discussing problems of the interpretation of scripture, his treatise, the *Mystica Theologia*, taught a "mystical theology" that permitted a person to know God as the "Divine Darkness" by way of unknowing. Commentators frequently overlook, however, that this "mystical theology" cannot be dissociated from the mystical exegesis and liturgy that suffused this monk's life.

The phrase "mystical theology" gradually came to mean the knowledge of God attained by direct, immediate, and ineffable contemplation. It was distinguished from both "natural theology" (knowledge of God obtained from creatures) and "dogmatic theology" (knowledge of God received from revelation). Saint John of the Cross (1542–91), for example, spoke of mystical theology as a secret wisdom infused by God into the soul through love. Therefore, the term "mystical theology" in this context refers to mystical *experience*. Contemporary usage, on the other hand, equates mystical theology with the doctrines and theories of mystical experience.

Thus, the terms "mystical" and "mystical theology" antedate by centuries the noun "mysticism." The latter term came into common parlance in the seventeenth-century dispute about the place of human effort in contemplative prayer. Mysticism denoted "infused contemplation" in contrast to "acquired contemplation." One attains the latter through "ordinary" grace, asceticism, and psychological concentration. In the former, God makes himself known to the individual through a special grace beyond all human effort.

One of the most influential, contemporary scholars of mysticism, Bernard McGinn, defines "the mystical element in Christianity [as] that part of its beliefs and practices that concerns the preparation for, the consciousness of, and the reaction to what can be described as the immediate or direct presence of God."[4] Because Christian mysticism springs from a living, dynamic, historical religion, McGinn views the contemporary quest for "transcendence without dogma," for an "unchurched mysticism," as misguided. Christian mysticism, in his view, is best understood in the light of its interaction with the other aspects of the whole of Christianity in which it came to fruition. One is always a Christian (or Hindu, Buddhist, or Muslim) before one is a mystic. McGinn rejects the opinion that mysticism can be understood as the inner common denominator of all religion—as a religion in itself.

Christian mysticism, in McGinn's view, is a way of life, a process, and not a series of transient experiences. Transformation is another of Christian mysticism's salient features: God-consciousness transforms one's heart, mind, and life. The encounter with the God of love changes the sinful, broken person into someone healed, enlightened, and transformed.

"Union with God" has long been considered to be the goal of the mystical life. McGinn points out, however, that many Christian mystics avoided unitive language and wrote instead of "contemplation," "vision," "ecstasy," the "birth of God in the soul," "endless desire," "fusion," the "abyss flowing into the Abyss," and so on. For synthesizing the various terms used to express the ultimate relationship of the mystic with God, he prefers what he considers to be a "more inclusive and flexible term": the "presence of God," the way lovers are "present" to each other. Moreover, in his opinion, the attempt to explain the mystical life according to the threefold schema of purgation, illumination, and union does not do justice to the richness of the tradition.

Many in the Christian tradition wrote of their "mystical experiences." The term "experience," in McGinn's view, lends itself to misunderstanding mysticism as unusual sensations, particular forms of feelings, or sensible perceptions easily deracinated from the spiritual activities of human consciousness that form the full range of human conscious life: understanding, judging, willing, and loving. He favors explaining Christian mysticism in terms of the "consciousness of God" because the mystic is one who becomes aware—"conscious"—of new and transformative ways of knowing and loving through states of awareness in which God becomes present in inner spiritual acts, not as an object to be grasped, but as the direct and transforming center of one's life. For this reason, McGinn finds the distinction between mystical experience and mystical theology "simplistic" and "unhelpful" because it tends to reduce mysticism to what can be found in autobiographical accounts of experiences of God, which are actually rare in the first thousand years of Christian history.

One of the paradoxes of Christian mysticism is the mystic's consciousness of God's "presence" and God's "absence." Consciousness of God's "presence" can result in a wide variety of awareness: from a painful awareness of the mystic's disorder, sinfulness, "nothingness," and great distance from God to ecstatic experiences and states of illumination and love.

The excruciating "absence" of the Beloved is a salient feature of mystical consciousness: God is sometimes most present to the mystic by his absence and most absent by his presence. Few mystics have not complained about a dark night of the spirit in which God has seemingly abandoned the lover, an immense longing that nothing finite can satisfy, and a brutal hell that is somehow heaven.

McGinn writes of another paradox of the Christian mystical life: mystical consciousness involves a complex form of "mediated immediacy." The sacraments, the liturgy, nature, various types of prayer, and ascetical practices "mediate" an awareness of God's mystical presence. However, numerous mystics have insisted on the absence of mediation at a point where the soul and God become identically one, at least on some level. Yet, even these mystics who claim to have reached identity with God—the fusion of the Beloved and the lover—usually also say that on another level some distinction between God and the creature remains. In different terms, it can be said that the mystic claims to be aware of something great enough to be God, yet intimate enough to be the mystic's own self.

Although McGinn's approach has already proven fruitful and I agree with much in his approach, I prefer to speak of "the preparation for" a mystical God-consciousness that is often not given as the ascetical dimension of Christian life. I would also distinguish more sharply than McGinn what it is that constitutes a mystic, a mystical theologian, and a mystagogue—granting that in practice the dividing line may be quite blurred. The mystic leads a mystical life, replete with the immediate consciousness of God. The mystical theologian provides the theory and understanding of such a life. The mystagogue leads others in the pursuit of this life. One and the same person may possess all three gifts, but frequently that is not the case.

The twentieth century witnessed a dramatic interest in and study of mysticism. It needs to be stressed at the start of this book, however, that love—not mysticism—is the zenith of Christian life. After a lecture I once gave, I was asked about *married* mystics. The audience became visibly upset when I said that we possess no mystical texts written by married (in the true sense) Christians. So, if there were married mystics, we simply do not know.

McGinn has convincingly argued that Western mysticism began in the fourth-century monasticism, which was fostered in large part by bishops who emphasized asceticism and virginity. Monasticism—almost alone—provided the context for the knowledge of scripture and the life of prayer and penance requisite for direct contact with God. In fact, the power of Western mysticism comes from its deliberate eroticizing of the relation between the human virgin and the divine Bridegroom, as if absorption of the erotic element into the spiritual dimension becomes more forceful the more it negates all deliberate external expression. This may explain somewhat why in the later tradition married people who obtained mystical graces chose to live as brothers and sisters, or even to abandon their spouses.

The hostility to my reply concerning no texts from married Christians also underscores a false assumption about Christian life and perfection. Saint Paul does not counsel Christians to seek the mystical path, but instructs them to follow a yet "more excellent way" (1 Cor 12:31)—the way of love. Love is patient, kind, not arrogant, not rude, never returns evil for evil, but bears, believes, hopes, and endures all things. Only faith, hope, and love will abide, these three; "but the greatest of these is love" (1 Cor 13:13).

Furthermore, as much as the Desert Fathers valued the higher states of prayer, they focused not on special states of mystical consciousness but on humility, kindness, patience, gentleness, and self-control. These are the fruits of the Holy Spirit (Gal 5:22). The Church canonizes saints for their *heroic virtue*, not for their direct consciousness of God—which the canonized may or may not have had. To my way of thinking, mysticism is only one of many ways to deepen the life of Christian faith, hope, and love. Christ was no yogi teaching higher forms of consciousness. Make love your aim, as St. Paul says. "Love one another, as I have loved you." Love—not mysticism—is the essence of Christian perfection.

# Mysticism in the Hebrew Scriptures

*"Thus the Lord used to speak to Moses face to face, as a man speaks to his friend." (Ex 33:11)*

The Church Fathers and the mystics of the Christian tradition drank from the fountain of the biblical word because they knew that God's revelation is the cornerstone of orthodoxy and authentic Christian living. They sought out the spiritual or mystical sense of the Bible because of their conviction—so aptly expressed by Thomas Aquinas—that the scriptures are the heart of Christ as they reveal it.

Not a few in the Christian tradition also found in God's revealed word paradigms of mystical consciousness. It was widely held, for example, that before the sin of Adam and Eve, our "first parents" enjoyed God's intimate presence without interruption and loved all creatures in God and God in all creatures. Their graced condition endowed them with a mystical knowledge and love of God far beyond "ordinary" faith—but still short of the beatific vision.

Abraham, Jacob, Moses, Samuel, and other patriarchs of the Old Testament were understood to have experienced God's intimate call, had their faith tested, wrestled with and were blessed by God, and spoke to God as to a personal friend. Often they were afraid and speechless in his presence, but visibly transformed by their encounters, drawn to him as their greatest good, and convinced that he was with his people in all they did and underwent.

The scriptures attest that Moses and Jacob met God face-to-face—with some qualifications as to how directly they gazed into his face (Gen 32:30; Ex 33:11, 23; Num 12:7; Deut 34:10). Hagar, Sarai's Egyptian maid, was perplexed after God spoke to her and asked, "Have I really seen God and remained alive after seeing him?" (Gen 16:13). Jacob boasted that he had wrestled with God and survived—an experience that left him with an overwhelming sense of God's awesome holiness (Gen 32:24ff.). When Job saw God ("now my eye sees thee" [Job 42:5]), his agonizing questions ceased and he repented "in dust and ashes."

The great Old Testament prophets—Elijah, Isaiah, Jeremiah, Ezekiel, Hosea, and Amos—were called intimately and personally to be God's spokesmen. They experienced God as overwhelmingly holy and as "living water," the source of all authentic life—the one they could always count upon because of his "everlasting love" (Jer 31:3). God's presence, they believed, rendered the people of God invincible in Holy War, if they obeyed his commands.

The prophets often experienced God's word burning in their hearts. It rendered them both incapable of holding it in and powerful in speaking it forth. Having "stood in the council of the LORD" (Jer 23:18), they were authenticated to speak God's word and received an invincible trust in God's steadfast love.

Having received God's Spirit into their hearts, some prophesied a time when all God's people would definitely receive the Holy Spirit. Other prophets called their people to conversion and insisted upon a mystical Sabbath rest (Is 30:15), that is, resting in the presence of God. Others prophesied about a coming "son of man" (Dan 7), and laid the foundations for a messianic mysticism, which engendered an intense desire for the "one who is to come" who would establish God's dominion and power over everything.

It is not anachronistic to view the prophets as essentially mystics in action. Their profound experience of God in the present sensitized them to what God had done both for his people in the past and to the contemporary social, political, and economic scene. By virtue of their mystical God-consciousness, they comprehended the incongruence of their times with God's will for his people. In this way they addressed the burning questions of their day. In view of how God had acted in the past when his people obeyed or disobeyed, the prophets did not hesitate to say what God would do for or to them in the future.

The patriarchs and prophets are Jewish examples of those who experienced God as the Holy, the tremendous and fascinating mystery. Although absolutely transcendent, wholly other, and darkness itself, he was intimately near and the very light of their lives. His awesome presence evoked feelings of fear, dread, powerlessness, openness to annihilation, creaturely nothingness, and sinfulness. More than one mystic found in the book of Job language apposite for describing the dark night of the soul in which the mystic feels justifiably rejected by God.

Nevertheless, this totally good God also attracted, charmed, intoxicated, ravished, and fascinated those exposed to his presence. The holy one awakened radical and transformative feelings of gratitude, dedication, praise, trust, submission, and love. He was experienced as the object of the deepest human desires and yearnings. To be united with this living, vital God was the end and goal of all living. It was life itself. This is authentic mysticism.

The patriarchs and the prophets taught the Israelites to expect the same gift of faith as they themselves had received. Israel's faithful certainly experienced communion with God, his saving presence, his protecting hand, and his steadfast love—and some in such a radically purifying, illuminating, and unitive way that it radically transformed their lives.

The Jewish scriptures indicate a difference of intensity between the mystical experience of the patriarchs and prophets and the living faith of the average Israelite, but they say nothing about a qualitative difference. The whole context of salvation history and the general laws of God's self-communication—grace—point in fact to faith as the theological locus of mystical experience.

The psalms attest in a special way to Israel's mystical faith. One finds there the mystic's emotions vis-à-vis the sense of God's transcendence, immanence, absence, and nearness. The hunger and thirst for the God who is light, love, living water, and life itself permeate the psalms. "Be still, and know that I am God" (Ps 46:10) is a profound call to mystical faith. The frequency of the words "love" (*ahabah*) and "loving kindness" (*hesed*) underscores the intense intimacy that existed between God and his people. The psalms attest that because we live, move, and have our being in God, no one can escape his loving presence (Ps 139:7-18).

The felt presence and absence of God that permeated Israel's life completed itself in the blessings, praise, and complaints found throughout the psalms. They confess that the believer is unconquerable because of God's steadfast love, which can be trusted and must be praised in all circumstances. Yahweh is praised not only for what he does but especially for what he is. His beauty, goodness, holiness, and love fill both the created universe and the depths of the human heart. So unselfish is the praise expressed in the psalms that the psalmist wishes to escape death only because in Sheol praise of God is no longer possible. To praise God, according to the psalmist, is life itself.

Augustine considered the psalms to be the prayer of the "total Christ," the Church. It was and still is the prayer of the "Body of Christ," again, the Church. For Aquinas, the psalms expressed Christ's very own emotions.

The Song of Songs probably originated from erotic poetry used to instruct young couples in the joys of connubial love. In time this book was understood to dramatize the love relationship between Yahweh and his people. Very early on, Christians saw in it the parable of the love relationship God has to the new people of God, the Christian Church. By the third century, the Song dramatized not only the loving bond between God and his people but also the erotic intercourse between God and the individual soul. The impact this book has had on the Christian mystical tradition cannot be overemphasized.

The Hebrew scriptures cry out with intense longings and contain a promise directed toward the future. As Jesus said, "many prophets and righteous men longed to see what you see, and did not see it, and to hear what you hear, and did not hear it" (Mt 13:17). Although God partially satisfied the desires of his people, Israel experienced that it "did not receive what was promised, since God had foreseen something better for us" (Heb 11:39b-40). That "something better" is, of course, Jesus Christ, who proclaimed to the Jews: "Your father Abraham rejoiced that he was to see my day" (Jn 8:56).

The mysticism found in the scriptures of the Israelites remains a preliminary stage to God's new covenant, which would "give the light of the knowledge of the glory of God in the face of Christ" (2 Cor 4:6). Humanity would be able to gaze upon the human face of God and live. The crucified and risen Christ highlights that God is definitively and irreversibly united with his people. "The mediator of a new covenant" (Heb 9:15) established, revealed, and made mysticism accessible in its purest and unsurpassable forms.

# Mysticism in the New Testament

*"For it is the God who said, 'Let light shine out of darkness,' who has shone in our hearts to give the light of the knowledge of the glory of God in the face of Christ."* (2 Cor 4:6)

Jesus Christ is the foundation of all Christian mysticism. Because of the permanent union of a human nature with the Divine Person of the Word, Jesus Christ possessed not only a divine knowledge but also an immediate, direct, and unique human knowledge of the Father, of himself as the Son, and of the Holy Spirit. Jesus' trinitarian consciousness can be called a mystical consciousness in at least an analogous sense. Moreover, the hypostatic union of Jesus' human and divine natures is the ground and goal of the mystical life: the ability for perfect, total surrender in love to the God who wishes us to be fully united with him.

The New Testament claims that "no one knows the Son except the Father, and no one knows the Father except the Son and any one to whom the Son chooses to reveal him" (Mt 11:27). This Testament witnesses to Jesus as having spoken of his intimate, full, personal, filial loving knowledge of his Father (Jn 7:29; 8:55). He knew that he had come from the Father (Jn 5:23) and would return to him (Jn 8:14). The oneness he enjoyed with his Father dominated his consciousness. He heard his Father's word (Jn 8:26), knew his will (Jn 5:30), and saw him working (Jn 5:19). So intimate was Jesus' relationship with his Father that the Father showed him everything he did (Jn 5:20).

In short, Jesus "knew" the Father in the fully biblical sense of the word: experiential loving knowledge. Not only did he lovingly know the Father at a level never known before but he could also enable others to share in his experience of the Father (Mt 11:27; Jn 1:18). Because he is God's Word, light, and life in the absolute sense, he could instill wisdom, light, and life in the heart of those who loved him (Eph 3:17).

To see and hear Christ, moreover, is to see and hear the Father (Jn 14:19; Lk 10:16). To know Christ is to know the Father, and this mystical knowledge of the Father and the Son is eternal life itself (Jn 17:3). To love Christ is to be loved by the Father, a God revealed by Jesus as Love itself (Jn 14:21; 1 Jn 4:8). Jesus promised that those who believed would become one with him and the Father and that they would be one, just as he and the Father are one (Jn 17:20).

As the visibility and tangibility of the Father's unconditional love for humanity, Christ is the visible sign that contains what it signifies, or the sacrament of what mysticism is all about: total union and oneness with the God of love. The union and oneness proclaimed by Jesus are described in terms of "abiding" and "dwelling in," not in the language of fusing with or dissolving in God. This is the mystery of mystical love: two or more become one, but never lose their individual identities.

Biblical scholars have underscored Jesus' use of the word "Abba" ("beloved Father") when he spoke to God. Because of the intimacy of this word, no Jew of Jesus' day (or before him) would ever address God in this way. To pray to God with such filial affection shocked Jewish religious sensibilities.

Jesus' use of "Abba" when he turned to God was unique. Confidently, reverently, obediently, but with full intimacy and familiarity, Jesus called God his "Beloved Father." This word captures the mystery of Jesus' identity and mission: a full, filial relationship with God. Because of the depths at which he and the Father were one, Jesus experienced himself as *the* Son, as the authenticated revelation of the Father and his will. Jesus' filial consciousness is the exemplar of the perfect mystic's intimate relationship with the Father, God above us, loving transcendence.

During Jesus' time, the Jews were convinced that with the death of the last writing prophets, the Spirit had been quenched because of Israel's sins. Only in the last days would the Spirit come to satisfy definitively Israel's great longings for God's presence.

In this context, it is significant that Jesus made the unusual and explicit claim that he himself possessed the Holy Spirit. The gospels portray Jesus both as driven and empowered by the Spirit. As its definitive bearer, he would give this Spirit at his death. The gospels depict Jesus as the eschatological prophet who brought final revelation and demanded absolute obedience, because in him the eschato-logical age had dawned.

John's gospel describes the Holy Spirit less as the impetus behind Jesus' ministry than as the "Counselor" to continue and complete it. To John, the Holy Spirit is another Jesus (Jn 14:16), or simply Jesus' Spirit, the Spirit of truth (Jn 14:17). Jesus proclaimed that only in and through his redemptive death would the Holy Spirit be definitively given (Jn 7:39). Moreover, the Holy Spirit is the "living water" flow-ing from Jesus' pierced heart (Jn 7:38; 19:34) and was then given by the risen Christ to the disciples who could now forgive sins (Jn 20:19-23).

This Spirit would lead Christians into all truth (Jn 16:13) and en-able Jesus always to be present to his people (Mt 28:20). Because the Spirit, as "another Counselor" (Jn 14:16), is also Jesus' permanent presence to his followers after the Easter appearances ceased, the Spirit would have the same relationship to Christians throughout the ages that Jesus had to the disciples during his ministry.

Jesus was intimately aware of the presence of the Holy Spirit, God in us, loving immanence. Therefore, Jesus' mystical consciousness is essentially trinitarian. He knew himself to be uniquely Son because of his relationship to his Father and to the Spirit of their love. Jesus experienced the Father ecstatically as God-above-us, the Holy Spirit *en*statically as God-within-us, and himself as the Son, or God-with-us. Because of Jesus' essentially trinitarian consciousness, all authentic Christian mysticism is at least implicitly trinitarian.

Even though there is an essential continuity in Jesus from the Old to the New Testaments, there is also discontinuity. The New Testa-ment depicts him, his consciousness, as transcending his Jewish mi-lieu, the wise men, religious founders, and philosophers of all ages. Jesus' certainty about his relationship to his Father and to the Holy Spirit did not come from philosophical argumentation or a retelling of the ancient traditions of his people or by meditation. A unique experience of the Father and the Holy Spirit permeated everything he did and was. What other religious founder has been raised from the dead as God's confirmation of his identity and mission, or given his followers a *new* commandment, to love others as he had loved them (Jn 15:12ff.)? It is no wonder that Jesus' disciples came to realize that they were in the presence of much more than another prophet or rabbi and adored him as "my Lord and my God" (Jn 20:28).

The phrase "in Christ" can be read as a summary of the mysticism of St. Paul, initiated by his encounter with the risen Christ on the road to Damascus (Acts 9:1-19; 22:3-16; 26:12-18; Gal 1:12). This event transformed the Jesus and Christian-hating Saul into Paul. This Paul denounced his prestigious past as so much "rubbish," willingly sacrificed everything, and would do anything so as to "gain Christ" (Phil 3:2-11).

Not only did Paul claim that this encounter was the last of the risen Christ's appearances (1 Cor 15:8) but he also maintained that it established his claim to be a full apostle of Christ Jesus. "Have I not seen Jesus our Lord?" (1 Cor 9:1), Paul said in defense of his "apostleship in the Lord," an apostleship to the Gentiles (Rom 11:13).

Moreover, Paul preached "not man's gospel," but a gospel that "came through a revelation of Jesus Christ" (Gal 1:12). Precisely as a "man *in Christ*" Paul was ecstatically taken up into the "third heaven," uncertain of being in or out of the body, and "heard things that cannot be told" (2 Cor 12:2).

Paul clearly experienced a God-given purgation that left him "utterly, unbearably crushed" and feeling that he "had received the sentence of death" (2 Cor 1:8-9). The God-given thorn in Paul's flesh and the "messenger" of Satan's harassment caused him such acute suffering that he implored God to remove them. But only through suffering did he learn that only Christ Jesus could and had rescued him "from this body of death" (Rom 7:24).

Indeed, Paul's experience led him to boast about the insults, hardships, persecutions, and calamities he suffered in Christ's service (2 Cor 11:21ff.). Although "always carrying in the body the death of Jesus" (2 Cor 4:10), he experienced Christ's power working through his weakness (2 Cor 12:9-10). Thus, he wished to glory only "in the cross of our Lord Jesus Christ" (Gal 6:14), "to know nothing among you except Jesus Christ and him crucified" (1 Cor 2:2), and to "complete what is lacking in Christ's afflictions for the sake of his body, that is, the church" (Col 1:24). Paul's sole desire was to know Christ "and the power of his resurrection," and to "share his sufferings, becoming like him in his death, that if possible I may attain the resurrection from the dead" (Phil 3:11). In a text that was to have a profound influence in the mystical tradition, Paul writes, "But he who is united to the Lord becomes one spirit with him" (1 Cor 6:17). Paul speaks of his union with Christ; the tradition will apply this to the union of the person with either God or Christ.

God mystically illuminated Paul and filled him with "all the riches of assured understanding and the knowledge of God's mystery, of Christ, in whom are hid all the treasures of wisdom and knowledge" (Col 2:2-3). For Paul, *the* mystery that was made known to him "by revelation," "the mystery hidden for ages," was nothing less than "the mystery of Christ" (Eph 3:1ff.), "in whom are hid all the treasures of wisdom and knowledge" (Col 2:3), "Christ the power of God and the wisdom of God" (1 Cor 1:24). In a beautiful statement on mystical illumination, Paul wrote, "For it is the God who said, 'Let light shine out of darkness,' who has shone in our hearts to give the light of the knowledge of the glory of God in the face of Christ" (2 Cor 4:6).

God also mystically transformed Paul "into [Christ's] likeness from one degree of glory to another" (2 Cor 3:18). "Predestined to be conformed to the image of his Son" (Rom 8:29), Paul experienced that for him "to live is Christ, and to die is gain" (Phil 1:21). Because Paul found himself "in Christ" as the mystical ambience in which he lived, moved, and had his being, he experienced that to be "in Christ . . . is [to be] a new creation" (2 Cor 5:17; Gal 5:15).

Paul was so profoundly transformed into Christ that he confessed that it was no longer he who lived, but Christ living in him (Gal 2:20). Paul was therefore convinced that nothing "will be able to separate us from the love of God in Christ Jesus our Lord" (Rom 8:38-39). Because the Lord is the Spirit (2 Cor 3:17), "God's love has been poured into our hearts" (Rom 5:5). Jesus' Spirit taught Paul the same loving confidence and intimacy that Jesus himself enjoyed with his Father.

Paul's trinitarian mysticism prompted him to pray, "For this reason I bow my knees before the *Father*, from whom every family in heaven and on earth is named, that according to the riches of his glory he may grant you to be strengthened with might through his *Spirit* in the inner man, and that *Christ* may dwell in your hearts through faith; that you, being rooted and grounded in love, may have power to comprehend with all the saints what is the breadth and length and height and depth, and to know the love of Christ which surpasses knowledge, that you may be filled with all the fulness of God" (Eph 3:14-19, my emphasis). The Pauline texts are replete with the triad of "one God and Father of us all," the "Lord Jesus Christ," and the "Spirit."

If the phrase "in Christ" summarizes Paul's trinitarian mysticism, the words "abide in me" encapsulates Johannine mysticism. John teaches, "If what you heard from the beginning abides in you, then you will abide in the Son and in the Father" (1 Jn 2:24). Of course, this is the "word of life" (1 Jn 1:1-3), the Word made flesh, "the eternal life which was with the Father and was made manifest to us." For John, not only the Father and the Son abide in the Christian but also "the anointing which you received from him abides in you" (1 Jn 2:27), that is, Jesus' own Spirit, "the Spirit of truth" (Jn 14:14-17). We know that Christ abides in us "by the Spirit which he has given us" (1 Jn 3:24).

Because Jesus and the Father are one (Jn 10:30), Johannine mysticism stresses that all Christians should be one. This is the reason Jesus prayed that "they may all be one; even as thou, Father, art in me, and I in thee, that they also may be in us, so that the world may believe that thou hast sent me" (Jn 17:21).

If the love with which the Father loved Jesus is in Jesus' disciples, then Jesus himself is in them (Jn 17:26). In John's view, God is love; therefore, "he who abides in love abides in God, and God abides in him" (1 Jn 4:16). Only on condition that we love one another will God abide in us and bring his love to perfection in us (1 Jn 4:12).

To John, Christ will draw everything to him once he is lifted up (Jn 12:32). The Spirit could be given only when Jesus was crucified, for out of his pierced heart would flow both blood and living water (Jn 7:38-39; 19:34). Hence, only Jesus, as the living bread and the giver of living water, can quench mystical hunger and thirst. Christians abide mystically in Christ especially through baptism and the Eucharist. Only someone "born of water and the Spirit" (Jn 3:5) can enter the kingdom of God. And only someone who eats Christ's flesh and drinks his blood can abide in Christ and Christ in him (Jn 6:56).

Authentic Christian mysticism sees in Jesus' death and resurrection its very cause and exemplar. Jesus' saving death on the cross underscores the self-abnegation requisite for one's total surrender to the mystery of the Father's unconditional love. By contemplating the cross one comprehends Jesus' new commandment: not only are we to love God with our whole being, not only are we to love our neighbor as ourselves, but we are also called to love as Christ himself loved us (Jn 13:34; 15:12).

Jesus' bodily resurrection is the ultimate revelation of the Father's acceptance and confirmation of this act of loving surrender to unconditional love. Moreover, it is the seed of the new creation, the sacramental visibility of God's definitive mystical marriage with all creation.

Jesus' risen, glorified body is what mysticism is all about: the loving union and transformation of all creation with and into the God of love, that in Christ one can truly be a "new creation" (2 Cor 5:17). Karl Rahner wrote, "Because Jesus Christ redeemed all creation in his love, along with mankind, Christian mysticism is neither a denial of the world nor a meeting with the infinite All, but a taking of the world with one to a loving encounter with the personal God."[1]

# Origen

## (ca. 185–254)

*"Let us enter the contest to win perfectly not only outward martyrdom, but also the martyrdom that is in secret, so that we too may utter the apostolic cry: 'For it is our boast, the martyrdom of our conscience that we have behaved in the world . . . with holiness and godly sincerity.'"*[1]

The oldest of seven children of fervent Christian parents, Origen, "man of steel," was probably born in Alexandria, Egypt, at the height of the Roman persecutions. Leonides, his father, educated him and was martyred for the faith by the Roman emperor Severus in 202, when Origen was in his teens. Only his mother's ingenuity in hiding his clothing prevented Origen from impulsively following his father to martyrdom. Origen expressed his constant desire for martyrdom in a letter to his father, which became the first draft of one of his treatises, *An Exhortation to Martyrdom*. As he writes, "I pray that when you are at the gates of death, or rather, freedom, especially if tortures are brought (for it is impossible to hope that you will not suffer this from the will of the opposing powers), you will use such words as these, 'It is clear to the Lord in His holy knowledge that though I might have been saved from death, I am enduring sufferings in my body, but in my soul I am glad to suffer these things because I fear Him' (2 Macc. 6:30)."[2]

Spared his father's fate, he proceeded to satisfy his own unquenchable thirst for martyrdom by a life of extreme penances. For example, he took literally the biblical text concerning "eunuchs for the sake of the kingdom of heaven" (Mt 19:12), and castrated himself, thus providing much fodder for his future enemies.

After their possessions were confiscated, Origen supported himself and his family by starting a school for grammar. Soon thereafter, the persecutions ended temporarily, and peace between church and state was restored for a time. Undoubtedly, his exceptional brilliance and heroic witness, as well as the scarcity of skilled catechists, prompted Bishop Demetrius of Alexandria to place the eighteen-year-old Origen in charge of a large school for catechumens.

His reputation for learning and holiness attracted the attention of Church leaders in many countries, though not always favorably. Thus, while in Palestine in 230, Origen was ordained. However, an Alexandrian synod under Bishop Demetrius, who obviously had second thoughts about his onetime protégé, declared his ordination illicit, proclaimed him unfit for catechetical work, and banished him. Hence, he went to Caesarea to continue his life of Christian intellectualism. Under Emperor Decius, in 249–50, he was imprisoned, tortured, and cruelly kept alive in an attempt to make him apostatize. But he never succumbed. Released from prison when the emperor died, Origen lived only a few more years in broken health.

Within two centuries of his death, many Church officials and theologians denounced him—both for the daring of some of his ideas and because of the excesses of some of his disciples. The Second Council of Constantinople in 553 formally condemned several of his views—two of which are the preexistence of the human soul and *apocatastasis*, that in the end, everyone will be saved. For many Eastern Christians, this condemnation earned him the epithet "heretic of the heretics."

Origen's Christian genius was recognized during the Renaissance, and interest in his theological genius revived in the twentieth century. He is widely recognized now as the first Christian exegetical giant, the first "systematic" theologian, and the first ascetical-mystical theologian.

Too much emphasis has been placed upon the intellectual achievements of this deeply spiritual man. Origen was a Christian humanist who blended great intellectual ability and a universal openness to all currents of thought with a passionate search for total truth that, for him, was to be found only in Christ crucified, the heart and key to scripture. For Christ, Origen was ready to "despoil the Egyptians," that is, to bring all the resources of his secular culture to bear on unlocking the mysteries of the Sacred Page.

Origen directed his ravenous intellectualism and passionate temperament to answering the objections of learned pagans to Christianity.

To do so, he mastered the secular sciences of his day, especially philology and philosophy. He excelled as a Master of the Sacred Page, that is, one who focused his universal intellectual interests upon the scholarly contemplation of scripture. He bequeathed critical texts, scientific commentaries, learned homilies, and scholia (short, exegetical notes) as his patrimony to the Christian tradition.

Origen is known as the father of "allegorical" interpretation. But his allegorical exegesis is mystical because he sought out—with all the tools at his disposal—the deepest meaning of scripture. He considered biblical exegesis as "mystical and ineffable contemplation" that must combine both scholarly erudition and experiential knowledge of God. Always a Church teacher, Origen understood and experienced exegesis as a process in which religious experience—especially mystical experience—is realized in the act of making the biblical language at its deepest and incommunicable level into the soul's language. For him, ecstasy meant sudden and new insights into scriptural revelation, not ravishment.

Origen viewed the divine-human drama—salvation history—not as the Platonic shadows of unchanging spiritual realities but as real history. Because the incarnate Word had been sought in the Old Testament, was given in the New, and is fully assimilated only in the Church's total experience, Origen contended that scripture's literal sense must flower into its mystical one.

The early Christians understood martyrdom as the apex of the Christian life and as perfect imitation of Christ. Through martyrdom, one also attained the full flowering of one's baptism into Christ crucified, total union with God, and the face-to-face vision of God. In addition to understanding martyrdom in this way, Origen emphasized it as the perfection of Christian wisdom, the loving-knowledge of the Unoriginated God revealed through his incarnate Word—a knowledge developed in contemplation that transforms one's entire life at the price of a crucifying asceticism. Only when one is freed from everything corporeal, follows Christ into the depths, ascends with him to the heavens, and attains God through Christ does the Christian know the greatest mysteries.

These mysteries are attainable only by "friends of the Father and Teacher in heaven" and in "face-to-face" vision of God. He speaks of his patron Ambrose in these terms. "Therefore, one of those already martyred and who possessed something more than many of the martyrs in their Christian love of learning will ascend quite swiftly to those heights."[3] Thus, for Origen, martyrdom is a form of mysticism through which one is definitively purged by, illuminated by, and united to God in Christ. Later mystics would speak of contemplative ecstasy as an imitation of martyrdom.

Origen spoke not only of an "outward martyrdom" but also of a "martyrdom that is in secret." Christian faith itself is a martyrdom because of the combat one must do against the world, the flesh, and the devil. This theme runs through the entire corpus of his writings and provides the proper context for understanding his moral-ascetical doctrine that would play an important role in the monastic tradition.

Origen conceived the mystical life as the full flowering of and the explicit realization of Christ's union with the soul effected through baptism. It is the full flowering of Christian life, the life of one baptized in the Church and nourished by the Church's sacramental Word and bread. But he understood martyrdom in this way, too. Both martyrdom and contemplation transform the soul into something "better than a soul," that is, into what it originally was, a mind (*nous*) made in God's image and likeness.

Without neglecting the traditional interpretation of the Song of Songs as the intimate relationship between Christ and the Church, Origen was nevertheless the first in the Christian tradition to interpret it as the intimate relationship between the Word and the soul. For him, this was *the* book for understanding the union of the bridal soul with the bridegroom Word, the ultimate book about the soul's intimate intercourse with God in Christ at the summit of the mystical life. He stresses the theme of Song of Songs as "love or loving affection" and calls God "loving Affection." Another first—he spoke of the soul as the "virgin-mother," a theme that was to have a long history in the Christian mystical tradition.

One sees in Origen's commentary on the Song of Songs his greatest contribution to the Christian mystical tradition: the view of the mystical life as successive stages of purgation, illumination, and unification. He compares these stages to the contents of three books of scripture. The book of Proverbs teaches morals, or virtue, and prepares the way for the assimilation of Ecclesiastes. That book teaches natural contemplation by which the correct attitude toward this world—a world both transient and yet holding together in

Christ—is attained. Only then can one deal with the "enoptics," or contemplation, found in the Song of Songs.

Contemplation, to Origen, is both knowing God and being known by God; it is union with God, a union that is never ending—even in the beatific vision. It is also the vision by which the image of God, that we are, is reformed. By contemplation, one becomes divinized—a favorite theme of the Greek fathers. Origen understands contemplation as the process by which the soul's highest point, the mind (*nous*), rediscovers its true nature by way of its noetic-erotic dynamism energized by God. Hence, in his view, ecstasy plays no role in contemplation, for it is the nature of *nous* to be united with God.

Origen also understood contemplation as the discovery of the deepest meaning of scripture. Only by sudden awakenings, inspirations, and illuminations received from the Word—thus, ecstasy in some sense—does the Sacred Page reveal its secrets to the Christian exegete. Origen's Christ-mysticism and Word-mysticism are inextricably bound to his scripture-mysticism, and vice versa.

He depicts the purgative, illuminative, and unitive stages as the seven songs sung by the soul that correspond to seven books of scripture. The soul sings of its escape from Egypt (conversion), its crossing the Red Sea (baptism), its desert wanderings (asceticism, aridity), its wars against its enemies (moral struggle), the quenching of its thirst at the wells of living water (consolations), and the like. Origen, the optimist, emphasizes that the soul sings and rejoices at every stage of its journey until, graced by divine love and mercy, it is ready to sing the most sublime song of all, the Song of Songs.

Origen also greatly influenced the Christian mystical tradition through his teaching on the "mystical senses." Because of the Fall, not all Christians have the mystical senses. Some have only one or two. Still, they can be regained as a person passes through the purgative, illuminative, and unitive stages of mystical ascent. Under grace, the soul becomes spiritually sensitive and discerning. The mystical senses also represent, to Origen, the richness and variety of the soul's experiences in contemplation of the Spirit, the incarnate Word, and the Father. Christ and the triune God can be spiritually seen, heard, tasted, touched, and smelled, as attested to in scripture. When the mystical senses become Christ, the scriptures reveal their hidden meaning.

Origen was also the first in the Christian mystical tradition to use the gospel Mary and Martha (Lk 10:38-42) as prototypes of the contemplative and active life. His book *On Prayer* blended both piety and speculation and gave the Christian tradition its first "systematic" treatment of private prayer. To him, the entire life of a saint is prayer.

He championed a "light mysticism," that darkness is only one stage of the mystical journey that ends in light through seeing and knowing God who is "loving Affection." This light mysticism stands in sharp contrast to the views of some other mystics in this Christian tradition, for example, Gregory of Nyssa and St. John of the Cross, who stressed God's unceasing darkness and total incomprehensibility.

Origen's Christian Platonism teaches that before one ascends with Christ, one must first descend by imitating and participating in his entire history. One is never more alive than when one hears the words, "what does it profit a man to gain the whole world and to lose his soul?" Like Christ, the soul must progressively uproot itself from the world by detachment and stripping. Like Christ, it must also do battle against the demons. In this way the soul participates in Christ's "double-cross," that is, both the royal throne from which Christ exercised his universal kingship and the instrument by which the principalities and powers of this world were crucified and defeated. And as Christ ascended to the Father, so also must the Christian. Paradoxically, to take up one's cross to follow Christ is to be already in heaven.

Origen held the theological view that there is one God because there is one Father, the Unoriginated God. The Word is the Father's image who unceasingly contemplates the Father. The Word contains the intelligible world that was created through and for the Word. One ascends to the Father through the Son in the Spirit.

Mystical exegete, mystical theologian, and mystagogue—Origen combines all three in himself. It is little wonder that his pupils spoke of his words as sparks that fell on their souls, enkindling in them the fire of trinitarian love.

# Gregory of Nyssa

(ca. 335–95)

*"Never to reach satiety of desiring is truly to see God."*[1]

One of the four great fathers of the Eastern Church, St. Gregory of Nyssa—"the first systematic theologian of negative theology" (what God is not)—was born into an illustrious Christian family in Caesarea, Cappadocia, around 335 during the Diocletian persecution. His father was St. Basil, the elder; his sister, St. Macrina; his brothers, St. Basil the Great and St. Peter of Sebaste. Ordained as lector and destined for the priesthood, Gregory soon left this course to embrace the ideals of pagan humanism revived by Roman Emperor Julian the Apostate. He married and pursued his father's career as a rhetorician.

Around 358, Basil the Great tried but failed to persuade his brother to go to Pontus, where Gregory of Nazianzus had settled at the Annesis monastery, but pressure from other family members seemingly caused him to change his mind. In 372, two years after he became bishop of Caesarea, Gregory was appointed bishop of Nyssa to help him in his disputes with the anti-Nicene emperor Valens. He continued to live with his wife, Theosebeia, as with a sister, even after he became bishop. In 374, the emperor banished Gregory from Nyssa. During this period of exile, Gregory underwent a powerful religious conversion, helped Basil with his monastic foundations in Cappadocia, and wrote the *Treatise on Virginity*.

Western mysticism began in the fourth-century monasticism fostered in large part by bishops who emphasized asceticism and virginity. It almost alone provided the context for the knowledge of scripture and the life of prayer and penance requisite for direct contact with God. In fact, the power of Western mysticism comes from its deliberate eroticizing of the relation between the human virgin and the divine Bridegroom, as if absorption of the erotic element into the

18

spiritual dimension becomes more forceful the more it negates all deliberate external expression.

After the death of Emperor Valens around 377, Gregory returned as bishop of Nyssa. After his brother's death in 379, Gregory assumed and completed Basil's far-ranging theological, monastic, and ecclesiastical activities.

Our saint from Nyssa became prominent at the Council of Constantinople (381), where he received the acceptance of his brother's and his own theological and ecclesiastical views and became a leader in the Eastern Church. For the next five years, he played an important role in the ecclesiastical affairs of Asia Minor through his theological publications and his resolving of many Christological, trinitarian, and ecclesiastical controversies.

Toward the end of his life, free of administrative obligations and theological controversies, Gregory turned to the spiritual life and wrote his well-known classics, *Commentary on the Song of Songs* and *The Life of Moses*. These works demonstrate Gregory's awesome mastery of the scriptures, his penetrating originality, and his desire to give a more mystical orientation to the monastic movement initiated by Basil.

Gregory remains indebted to Philo, the Jewish mystical philosopher; Plotinus, the Greek mystic; and the controversial Christian titan, Origen. One of Gregory's accomplishments was to transpose their thinking for later ages, while maintaining his full commitment to the Church, to scripture, and to the Hellenistic tradition—without compromise. Indeed, many commentators see Gregory as the founder of Christian mystical theology.

Greek philosophy in the Hellenistic age was first religious, then ascetical and contemplative, so that Christianity assimilated certain Greek ideas and values for its own. Moreover, the atmosphere that influenced Origen—the prospect of martyrdom—vanished with the Edict of Milan (313). The "white," bloodless martyrdom proffered by the monastic movement was fully underway and functioned as a cooperative laboratory for the ascetical and mystical life.

Gregory read the Bible as an Alexandrian, not as one interested in salvation history as such, but as one who valued it for its ability to lift the human spirit to God. Origen, too, had read scripture this "anagogical" way. In so doing, he sought the mystical sense (*theoria*) in scriptures' literal sense (*historia*), and his writings refer frequently to the mystical senses, which are distinct from the bodily senses.

His *Commentary on the Song of Songs* shows that Gregory's mysticism of darkness emphasizes that God is limitless, therefore incomprehensible. Through the Incarnation, God made it possible to experience his immediacy in love and in ever-deeper levels of darkness that transcend all knowledge.

In Moses' life, Gregory saw a paradigm of the spiritual journey to God. Moses' threefold experience in light, in the cloud, and in darkness represents human growth from spiritual infancy to youth to full maturity. Unlike Origen, Gregory sees this journey as three overlapping stages, or three aspects of the person's approach to God.

The way of light purifies the person, restores the divine image to the soul, and bestows psychosomatic wholeness (*apatheia*) and boldness in the quest for God. Origen viewed the purgative stage as preparation for contemplation, while Gregory stresses that the way of light contains a contemplative aspect through which the person learns that God alone truly exists.

For Gregory, contemplation in the strict sense belongs to the way of the cloud wherein one discovers the emptiness of all created things and God's glory manifested throughout creation. He writes, "For the wonderful harmony of the heavens proclaims the wisdom which shines forth in the creation and sets forth the great glory of God through the things which are seen, in keeping with the statement, *the heavens declare the glory of God.*"[2] Yet, the proper object for contemplation is not only the world created in, through, and for the Word but it is also the incarnate Word himself.

However, contemplation must be abandoned in the way of darkness. The deeper the darkness, the more is one aware of God's incomprehensibility. In "sober intoxication," "watchful sleep," "passionless passion," and "dazzling darkness," one sees God by not seeing and knows God by not knowing. These oxymora reveal Gregory as a proponent of the negative way, of apophatic (Greek: *apophatikos* = negative) mysticism, which transcends all images, concepts, and ideas of God because the divine nature "transcends all cognitive thought and representation and cannot be likened to anything which is known."[3] The true vision of God, says Gregory, is "never to be satisfied in the desire to see him" and "the unending journey accomplished by following directly behind the Word."[4] Thus did he view Moses in his dark encounter with God in the cloud as the ideal mystic. Free from all seeing, Moses plunged into the mysterious darkness of the cloud of unknowing. In part, Gregory's dark apophaticism stands as a critical corrective to the light imagery of late antique pagan theology.

His view of *epektasis*, a graced straining toward God (Phil 3:13), may be Gregory's most significant contribution. The goal of Christian life is the endless pursuit of the inexhaustible divine nature. The "wound of love" bestows a heightened sense of self-possession in the possession of God in the interior of one's spirit and the sense of transcending self into God's luminous darkness. This mystical movement results in an ongoing discovery of the divine essence, a movement from "glory to glory" (2 Cor 3:18). Gregory describes this process as a "satisfied dissatisfaction" of the experience of God. Like the bride in the Song of Songs, the soul is on a never-ending quest for the bridegroom whom she possesses only briefly.

The soul's experience of God is inexhaustible because the incomprehensible God is present. Because we are created in God's image—the soul mirroring the triune divine nature when purified—self-knowledge is a way of knowing God. But unlike Origen, Gregory emphasizes both the similarity and the greater dissimilarity reflected.

The Word awakens the mystical senses so that the soul's core can smell, taste, touch, and feel God's presence in darkness beyond bodily senses and intellect. A "passionless passion" is enkindled and draws the soul out of itself, forcing it to center on God in an act of total detachment. In contrast to the more intellectual approach of some of the Greek fathers, Gregory stresses that the soul learns that the true satisfaction of her desire consists in constantly going on with her quest and never ceasing in her ascent, seeing that every fulfillment of her desire continually generates a further desire for the God of Mystery. To Gregory, knowledge then becomes love.

Because of Gregory's emphasis on *epektasis*, one finds great erotic tension in his writings. This accounts, too, for the theme from the Song of Songs of the Beloved's presence-absence. Finally, his unmitigated apophaticism penetrates and permeates his profound teaching on the mystical senses, the stages of the soul's journey, the perception of divine presence, ecstasy, the nature of contemplation, and divinization.

# Evagrius Ponticus

## (345–99)

*"If you are a theologian, one who has experiential knowledge of God, you truly pray. If you truly pray, you are a theologian."*[1]

Evagrius was born in Ibora, Pontus, or modern-day Iverönü, Turkey. His father was a "chorbishop"—a country bishop of somewhat restricted powers who traveled about to minister to the various churches under his jurisdiction. Evagrius came to enjoy the company and the esteem of the great Cappadocian fathers. Saint Basil the Great ordained him lector; St. Gregory of Nazianzus ordained him deacon.

Constantinople naturally attracted the brilliant, urbane Evagrius. There he attained great social prominence, especially as the "destroyer of the twaddle of the [anti-Nicene] heretics." But he gradually lost his religious fervor and fell in love with the wife of a prominent member of society. Warned in a dream about the danger to his soul, he left promptly for Jerusalem, where he became the disciple of Melania the Elder. She was an ascetic Roman woman, well-read in Origen, who ran a hospice for Christian pilgrims on the Mount of Olives. After an illness, he went to live with a community of Origenist monks in Nitria, Egypt.

Because Constantine the Great (d. 337) bestowed imperial favors upon the Christian faith, he unwittingly eliminated the opportunity for the ideal following of Christ, namely, martyrdom. Thus, many Christians now sought the "white," or bloodless, martyrdom of the monastic life. The monks replaced the martyrs as the warriors of the Christian life.

At Nitria, Evagrius became a severe ascetic, though his intellectual life continued, resulting in a body of writings. In addition to this work, he became widely known for his prudent and loving spiritual direction. Occasionally, he went to Alexandria, where he used his

penetrating mind and oratorical skills against the heretics. His reputation for holiness, learning, and eloquence attracted the attention of
Theophilus of Alexandria, the patriarch of Egypt, who wished to
make Evagrius a bishop. Following the maxim of the Desert Fathers,
"avoid women and bishops," Evagrius refused this honor and continued to live as a Desert Father.

Evagrius was the first to organize in a concise, nuanced way the
writings of the Desert Fathers. His lapidary, gnomic, highly polished
sentences were easily memorized capsule meditations. Only a mature
monk—after years of prolonged asceticism and meditation—could
penetrate to the depths of these seemingly simple teachings.

Evagrius may well have been the first to give an almost complete
and coherent monastic, ascetical, and mystical theology to the Christian world. As Origen's intellectual heir and disciple of the Desert
Fathers, he synthesized in his person and writings Hellenistic intellectualism and the Desert Fathers' spirituality and mysticism of the
heart that is solidly anchored in the Trinity and in Jesus Christ.

With Evagrius, the history of Christian spirituality and mysticism
reached a decisive turning point, for through his *Praktikos* and *Chapters
on Prayer* he influenced the entire Christian monastic tradition after
him—despite the Church's condemnation of some of his infelicitous
speculative views contained in his "Origenist" *Kephalaia Gnostica*.

His writings illustrate Evagrius's love of the monastic life, especially
in its eremitical form. As he says, "the demons fight openly against the
solitaries, but they arm the more careless of the brethren against the
cenobites, or those who practice virtue in the company of others. Now
this second form of combat is much lighter than the first, for there is
not to be found on earth any men more fierce than the demons."[2] Thus,
the demons, in his view, fight the hermit directly; in coenobitic monasticism, indirectly, through the less fervent in the community.

Evagrius's last years were spent in contemplation and peace. So
great was his spiritual reputation that he was considered a Church
Father in his own time. On the feast of the Epiphany in 399, he asked
to be taken to church, where he received Holy Communion and died
shortly thereafter. It is astonishing that someone as remarkable and
influential in the history of Christian spirituality and mysticism has
remained almost unknown to all but specialists.

Evagrius's writings indicate that he distinguished, but never separated, three stages of spiritual progress in the monk's ascent to God. In

the ascetical stage (*praktike*), the monk seeks the right ordering of the emotions and liberating the soul from inordinate passions. By observing the commandments and practicing virtue, the desert warrior must also rid the intellect of sense reactions and remove obstacles to contemplation. Before ascending to God, he must follow the way of the incarnation: descent into the sinful world to do battle with demons.

Following Origen, Evagrius writes of a "natural" contemplation (*theoria physike*), which involves meditating upon the scriptures and the universe in the light of the incarnate Logos in order to attain knowledge of God's universe and attributes. Comprehending the *logoi*—the "reasons" for all things as they exist in the eternal Logos—results in a knowledge that resembles divine reason and replaces knowledge distorted by passion and desire.

Evagrius then writes of "first contemplation" (*theologia*) in which "the contemplative soul resembles the heavens where the light of the Holy Trinity shines."[3] The intellect (*nous*) becomes a place of ineffable peace, receiving a simple, intuitive, loving knowledge of the Trinity. "When the spirit has put off the old man to replace him with the new man, created by charity," Evagrius writes, "then he will see that his own state at the time of prayer resembles that of a sapphire. . . . The scriptures refer to this experience as the place of God which was seen by our ancestors, the elders, on Mount Sinai."[4]

Because of his distinction between asceticism, natural contemplation, and *theologia*, Evagrius has been criticized for dividing the path of mystical ascent into three distinct stages. However, in his view, these three stages—roughly parallel to the later classical purgative, illuminative, and unitive ways—are inextricably connected. Each stage contains aspects of the other two stages. Thus, Evagrius stressed the ascetical foundation of mysticism and the mystical basis of asceticism.

Evagrius is best known for his meticulous, experiential, concise description and analysis of the eight passions and the accompanying passionate thoughts (*logismoi*), which the demons use in their war against us: acedia, anger, avarice, gluttony, impurity, pride, sadness, and vainglory. His perceptive observation of the connection between the demons and the passions, and between moods and thoughts, played a significant role in the Christian mystical tradition's teaching on the discernment of spirits.

Evagrius was not immediately concerned with sinful acts. The demons attack the monk by stirring up the passions and the imagination that induce passionate thoughts and lines of thought incongruous with the Christian life. So, for Evagrius, the monk's chief battle is against sins of the heart. The number of times his texts mention *thoughts* and the need for continual recollection exemplifies the Desert Fathers' conviction that thoughts were sometimes the monk's chief opponents.

Evagrius judged acedia, or monastic boredom, as the "fiercest demon of all." This enemy of the monk makes a day seem fifty hours long and instills in him a hatred of his brethren—and life itself. "No other demon," Evagrius writes, "follows close upon the heels of this one (when he is defeated) but only a state of deep peace and inexpressible joy arise out of this struggle."[5]

Again, Evagrius urges the monk to pay attention to the thoughts and the line of thinking suggested by the devil. Fasting, vigils, the singing of psalms, confessing of one's sins, tears, works of mercy, and other monastic disciplines often rout the demons. Angels aid in the warfare against the demons by bestowing peace upon the monk. Defeating acedia also means the monk's easy victory over the other demons.

Evagrius frequently mentions *apatheia*, often rendered in English as "passionlessness," "impassibility," "serenity," "indifference," or "abnegation." "Psychosomatic wholeness" is perhaps a more appropriate term for the relatively permanent state of deep calm that results from the purification, integration, and transformation of all levels of the emotional and psychic life. Not even the stirring of passionate memories, or vivid dreams, or external events can ruffle this integrative calm. As *apatheia* deepens, the human spirit (*nous*) sees its own light and enables the monk to pray without distractions. It seems to be the most profound form of psychosomatic wholeness and integration humanly possible. However, only through effort, grace, and a total love of Christ and the Trinity does the monk obtain it.

Evagrius considers *apatheia* to be the very health of the soul, the flowering of asceticism, and as the way discreet charity is attained. Thus, the monk labors to remove all passionate disorders in order to attain the integration of emotional love and the deeper passions, but for the sake of increased charity. As he says, "Happy is the monk who views the welfare and progress of all men with as much joy as if it were his own."[6]

Even though Evagrius emphasizes that *agape* is *apatheia*'s daughter, he also sees it as the mother of *apatheia*. The paradox: the monk flees from the world to the desert to battle the demons and to attain an angelic state, which in fact brings about a deeper compassion for all humanity. Evagrius wrote, "By true prayer a monk becomes another angel, for he ardently longs to see the face of the Father in heaven"—and, "a monk is a man who considers himself one with all men because he seems constantly to see himself in every man."[7]

Evagrius's light mysticism is apophatic. Unlike Gregory of Nyssa, he contends that contemplation without distraction results in deeper knowledge of God. He inherited the view from Origen that God is knowable, though beyond images, thoughts, concepts, and forms. To Evagrius, knowledge of God is a wholly luminous "infinite ignorance" and a perfect forgetfulness. One attains to a "complete loss of self-consciousness" during prayer when one is not even aware of praying. The Trinity is best known in simple, unself-conscious, loving knowledge beyond all clearly defined images, thoughts, and knowledge.

The monastic life, in Evagrius's estimation, is prayer. He is convinced that it is the soul's very essence to pray and that one must "renounce all things" to pray without distractions. Prayer without distraction, "pure prayer," results in the final routing of the demons and restores the human spirit (*nous*) to its true nature. In this way the monk is divinized and attains a "formless unity" with the Trinity. Thus, the monk is the theologian par excellence because "if you are a theologian [one who has experiential knowledge of God] you truly pray. If you truly pray you are a theologian."[8] Evagrius was also one of the first mystics in the Christian mystical tradition to speak of prayer becoming a permanent state.

Evagrius distinguishes between "the kingdom of Christ" and the "kingdom of God, the Father." The former involves natural contemplation, the latter, *theologia*. Although he writes that perfection is "hidden in the breast of Christ," this mystic is the first in the Christian tradition to suggest explicitly that contemplation of the divinity requires going beyond Christ's humanity. Thus, he is sometimes called a "pure mystic" who at some stage seems to bypass salvation history and Christ's humanity.

Although his writings give the impression that he never accepted the Greek notion that *nous*, or pure intellect, is naturally divine and had originally existed without matter, he does write, "happy is the spirit that becomes free of all matter and is stripped of all at the time of prayer."[9] This illustrates his unease with matter. Finally, he definitely teaches the universality of Christianity—unlike the Gnostics of his day who maintained that it was for only an elite. On the other hand, he stresses that the contemplative goal of pure prayer is reserved only to advanced monks. This tension has perdured right down to the present day.

# Augustine of Hippo

## (354–430)

*"You stir us to take pleasure in praising you, because you made us for yourself, and our heart is restless until it rests in you."*[1]

Augustine is the most significant formative personality in the history of the Western Christian tradition. His 113 books, 800 sermons, and 250 letters left an indelible mark on the shape, scope, direction, range, and development of that tradition. Excelling as a doctrinal and speculative theologian, a Church leader, a monastic founder, a preacher, and a polemicist, he has been called the "prince of mystics" because of his profound understanding of the mystical element in Christianity.

Describing both his exterior and interior journey, Augustine's *Confessions* gave the West its first autobiography. The highly sophisticated way in which he described the interaction between God's action at the depths of the human soul and a person's psychological makeup may explain why his text has been one of the most widely read books in the Christian West. The account in book VIII of his conversion remains one of the most stirring in Christian history.

Augustine was born in Thagaste, a small town in the Souk-Ahras region of Algeria near the Tunisian border, of a pagan father (baptized on his deathbed) and a zealous Christian mother. Educated in the classics at Madaura and trained as a professional rhetorician at Carthage, he eventually went to Rome and then to Milan to further his career as a rhetorician.

Even as a teenager and as a young man, Augustine had been attracted to wisdom and the search for truth. But he also experienced that his self-love and his strong sensuality conflicted with his ardent desire to seek eternal Beauty and to live accordingly. The Manicheans' uncompromising dualism, their claim to possess hidden truths of universal validity and to be able to prove Christian truths from reason, and their praise of Christ claimed Augustine's allegiance for about nine years. Augustine also gave his loyalty to his mistress, "Una" (One Bed), of fifteen years and their son, Adeodatus.

Although Neo-Platonic philosophy freed Augustine from his material notions of God and his heretical Manicheanism, he realized instinctively that Neo-Platonism knew only the goal, not the way, to true wisdom. Augustine was to learn from the erudite, urbane, and politically astute St. Ambrose, then bishop of Milan, that the true wisdom of the scriptures is none other than Christ crucified, that genuine ascent to God comes by imitating the humble Christ.

Shortly after the Easter of 387 when Ambrose baptized him, Augustine left for his native Africa. While at the Roman port of Ostia, Augustine and his mother had the conversation that led to a mystical experience of the divine "Wisdom" that transcends all things, even the soul itself. This "touching" of God in the garden (read: Church) transcends almost everything in Augustine's Neo-Platonic background not only because it was a *shared* experience but also because it was granted to someone untrained in philosophy and a woman at that. After Monica's death at Ostia, Augustine returned to Thagaste for a few happy years of monastic living. The desire to live a monastic life inspired by the gospels went back to his youth when he undoubtedly came into contact with Athanasius's *Life of Antony*.

However, in 391, Bishop Valerius of Hippo convinced Augustine to accept ordination, and to become his assistant. After Valerius's death, Augustine became bishop of Hippo for thirty-five years. He died at the age of seventy-six when the invading Vandals besieged his city.

Augustine's *Homily on Psalm 41* has been called a "masterpiece" and his best exposition of the process and nature of the mystic experience. This text—as well as many of his other treatises—indicates clearly that, for Augustine, mysticism is the desire and immense longing of the entire Church because Augustinian mysticism is essentially the longing to assimilate and to interiorize everything given in baptism. This homily also underscores his love for the psalms, through which he had experienced the emotions they express. The psalms, in his view, are expressions of the immensely rich deposit of the emotions of Christ and of his members.

Moreover, for Augustine, contemplation of the holiness of the saints both destroys vice and provides the impetus for experiencing—

even ecstatically—the ineffable, sweet, heavenly music that brings such joy and refreshment. He stressed that one cannot recognize grace in oneself unless one can recognize it in others. The person's social nature, love of neighbor, and the Church as Body of Christ are definitely important factors in Augustinian mysticism. He explored with precision and depth the way the God-Man actually brings about our redemption by uniting us to his Body, the Church.

Augustine speaks of a vague, yet ardent, yearning for something only obscurely known. Light and desire provide the motivation for the mystical ascent. However, Augustine insists upon the ascetical foundation requisite for this ascent. Only the clean of heart will see God with their inner eyes. Cleansing the heart demands waging war against the demons, controlling passions, striving for virtue, and also rooting out sins, vices, and imperfections. Although Augustine is known for saying, "Love, and do what you will," he also said, "Love, and be careful what you love" because a person becomes what he loves.

Perhaps because of the sins of his youth, Augustine avoids erotic imagery and wrote nothing about the Song of Songs. However, he remains one of the few in the Christian tradition to view the soul as male in the presence of a female Wisdom who strips herself so that all her lovers can feast on her beauty without jealousy.

Although "faith," not vision, is the "normal" Christian state, Augustine maintains what all Christian mystics have averred: God can be seen in some way in this life. By a process of recollection that unifies the person's scattered powers and by plunging into the soul's depths through introversion, Augustine discovers that unchangeable Truth is found only when one transcends both creation and the soul itself. Withdrawing from both the external and the internal sense world, one goes to the soul's depths to go above the soul for the experience of God. For Augustine, to go within is also to go beyond—the enstatic for the ecstatic.

Various Augustinian scholars underscore the "intellectualism" of Augustine's mysticism, because he does say on occasion: "And then in a flash of a trembling glance, my mind arrived at That Which is."[2] But the Augustinian corpus shows definitely that he experienced God not only through the intellect's dynamism for truth but also through the will's insatiable desire for love. Augustine's views on the mystical senses bring out dramatically that he heard, saw, felt, smelled, clung, and cleaved to God not only as unchanging Truth but also as Love,

Beauty, Wisdom, Food, Perfume, Light, Song, and Embracement that nourish the inner person.

His writings also show that Augustine experienced mystical ecstasy, raptures that suddenly and violently draw the soul away from the senses and itself to bestow a foretaste of the joys of heaven. Without claiming the same for himself, he contended that both Moses and St. Paul had a foretaste of the beatific vision in this life. In mystical ecstasy they saw—without intermediary—God, and lived. In answer to the question, how can one see God and live? Augustine explained that mystical ecstasy is a temporary death, because a person is removed from the senses.

However, in contrast to the Neo-Platonic chimera that eternal Beauty can be contemplated without interruption, Augustine underscores the transient nature of his experience. The deep realization of human frailty, the acute experience of always being "beaten back," and the profound sense of the pure gift and grace-quality of this experience are all features of his and all genuine Christian mysticism.

Augustine likewise emphasizes the need for contemplation of God's creation, then for entering the soul's deepest depths through introversion, and finally for the soul's eye to look to the Light above and beyond all created things, even beyond the soul itself. With love and dread, Augustine experienced the paradox of the awesome difference between God and all created things—even the infinitely mysterious depths of the self. In the act of transcending all creatures, he heard the call to be transformed into God. God's very Word had pierced his heart, taught him that nothing created is God—not even the soul. But all creation, especially the soul, calls him to love God and to be one with God. Because God is the Life of the soul's life, Augustine experienced God as more interior to himself than he was to himself.

Augustine is well known for his emphasis on finding God in the soul, on Christ as the "inner teacher," a "psychocentrism," and introspection. A dimension of inwardness and psychological self-probing penetrates all his works, so that his "voice" is more personal than the "objective" mystical exegesis of the Eastern fathers. One does not find in their writings an account of their personal experiences. Their mystical exegesis of scripture never swerved from knowing the mystery of God in Christ and from examining the soul's quest for God in that light. However, Augustine uses scripture primarily to discover the true nature of the human person. Thus, his emphasis is anthropocentric, but in the sense that he viewed the soul as the image of the trinitarian God.

Augustine's *On the Trinity* underscores his image-mysticism. For some of the fathers, the human soul is the image of the eternal Logos; for Augustine, the soul is made in God's trinitarian image. The mind's ability to know and to love itself parallels God's inner-trinitarian life. The soul's ability to cleave to the Trinity by remembering, knowing, and loving the Trinity reforms it as God's image.

In his *Literal Meaning of Genesis*, Augustine distinguishes between corporeal, spiritual ("imaginative"), and intellectual visions—a distinction that has lasted to the present day. Corporeal visions are seen with the physical eyes; spiritual visions, with the inner eyes; intellectual visions, with the eyes of the spirit. "These three kinds of vision, therefore, namely, corporeal, spiritual, and intellectual," he writes, "must be considered separately, so that reason may ascend from the lower to the higher. . . . For when we read, *You shall love your neighbor as yourself*, the letters are seen corporeally, the neighbor is thought of spiritually, and love is beheld intellectually. But the letters when absent can also be thought of spiritually, and the neighbor when present can be seen corporeally. But love can neither be seen in its own essence with the eyes of the body nor be thought of in the spirit by means of an image like a body; but only in the mind, that is, in the intellect, can it be known and perceived."[3]

There is a long-standing scholarly debate about whether Augustine was a mystic or someone who only used the language of Neo-Platonic philosophy to describe his very deep piety. There is no evidence that he passed through the radically purgative dark nights of sense and spirit. Nor did he reach the summit of transforming union with God. However, his acute sense of sin, of human frailty, and of the infinite distance between the Creator and creatures—the painful way he experienced being beaten back after he had "touched" God, his stirring delight in God's wonderful condescension in the Incarnation, his haunting restlessness for God, his painful awareness of being unable to love as much as he was loved by God, and his grasp of God's Wisdom, Light, and Beauty contain a mystical maturity that few attain. These are some of the salient features of a genuine mystical consciousness. Mystic, mystical theologian, and mystagogue—this is Augustine.

# John Cassian

## (ca. 365–ca. 435)

*"The Our Father lifts up to that prayer of fire known to so few. It lifts up to that ineffable prayer which rises above all human consciousness, with no voice sounding, no tongue moving, no words uttered."*[1]

At a time when the Mediterranean area was experiencing the breakdown of Roman rule, civil unrest, theological controversies, and varied—sometimes fanatical—monastic movements, there arose a man who was to write the most interesting documents of fifth-century monasticism, give the West its first summa of Christian spirituality, state the problems of this spirituality in a way that has remained largely unchanged to the present day, and become the guide of Western monasticism. John Cassian's *Institutes* and *Conferences* became the links between Eastern and Western monasticism for over one thousand years. Such was his stature that even the great St. Benedict stated in his famous Rule for monks that these two works should be read regularly.

John Cassian was born in Scythia Minor (present-day Romania), traveled in his youth to a monastery in Bethlehem to live an ascetic life, went to Egypt around 386 with his friend Germanus to sit at the feet of the great Egyptian monastic masters for seven years, then lived the monastic life in Palestine, the Nile region, and Constantinople, where he was ordained deacon by St. John Chrysostom. In 404, he went to Rome for ten years, was ordained priest, went to Marseilles, where he founded two monasteries, and died with a reputation for great sanctity.

If Augustine had a strong penchant for the monastic life, Cassian was thoroughly a monk. He believed that the early Christians lived in Jerusalem as a coenobitic monastic community, that the Church was founded to be a monastic institution, and that Christian perfection could be attained only by monks. Monasticism existed as the Christian alternative to society itself.

The Egyptian Desert Fathers who favored the eremitic, anchoritic, hermit way of life as the best means to complete solitude with God were Cassian's great heroes. Nonetheless, his austere ascetic ideal remains always firmly anchored to an attractive, realistic humaneness and moderation. For example, Cassian forbade anchoritic living, or solitary living, before having passed through a lengthy and fruitful coenobitic life, that is, monastic life in a community. On the other hand, "pure prayer" might be given to a coenobitic monk, but the desert hermit remained the privileged candidate. Cassian seemed to have grasped the mutual and inseparable link between "pure prayer" and active love in community. With him, monasticism never lost sight of its graced, mystical, agapic, eschatological orientation.

Cassian understood the goal of the monastic life as entrance into the kingdom of God, into eternal life, which could be experienced here in some form. The monk must have the "passion for the unseen," and tend to union with God through loving attention to him alone. His third conference on the three renunciations states his agenda: "The first renunciation has to do with the body. We come to despise all the riches and all goods of the world. With the second renunciation we repel our past, our vices, the passions governing spirit and flesh. And in the third renunciation we draw our spirit away from the here and the visible and we do so in order solely to contemplate the things of the future. Our passion is for the unseen."[2]

As with the best of the Desert Fathers, Cassian saw contemplation as the fruit of, or at least as made possible by, asceticism but condemned asceticism for its own sake. Christian asceticism must uproot the seven deadly vices and aspire to contemplative union with God. The monk renounces comfort, sin, and everything but God alone for the sake of Christian love of God and neighbor. The monk undertakes the spiritual combat against the self and the demons in order to attain "purity of heart," the loving, detached, tranquil purity that borders on contemplative union with God. "Purity of heart" is the equivalent of Evagrian *apatheia*, a term Cassian avoided because of the controversies of his day.

Cassian appreciated deeply both the ascetical foundation of mysticism and the mystical basis of asceticism. Asceticism prepares the soul for contemplative union with God. Contemplative union with God not only nourishes and animates the spiritual ascent but it also completes the first two stages of renunciation. He understands—like Evagrius—the threefold aspects of the ascent to God as concomitant, not consecutive. However, he—like Origen—compares these aspects to the books of Proverbs, Ecclesiastes, and Song of Songs. Almost absent from his writings, however, is the eroticism found in the Song.

The goal of monastic life is unceasing prayer—which the monk must become. Keeping one's eyes on Christ, one prays as Christ himself, who is prayer incarnate. One sees Christ according to one's level of purification. For Cassian, the soul "loses sight of earthly and material things in proportion to its purity, so that it sees Jesus either in his lowly creaturehood or else, with the inner gaze of the soul, it sees the glorified Jesus coming in the splendor of His majesty. . . . Only those of purest eyes can look upon His divinity, those who have risen up beyond lowly works and earthly thoughts and have gone off with Him to the high mountain of solitude."[3]

Cassian was perhaps the first in the Christian tradition to write of the four levels of scripture. First, one must assimilate the past historical facts. Second, one contemplates this history for the allegorical way in which it prefigures an event in the New Testament. For example, the sacrifice of Abraham's son Isaac foreshadows Christ's sacrifice. Third, the anagogic level raises the person to the heavenly mysteries. Finally, the tropological level discloses the moral implications of the text at hand.

In line with the Church Fathers, Cassian teaches that one must contemplate the scriptures in order to become connatural with them. However, one also studies, meditates on, and contemplates the scriptures so that in one sense one becomes their author. As he says, "Then indeed the scriptures lie ever more clearly open to us. . . . Our experience not only brings us to know them but actually anticipates what they convey. The meaning of the words comes through to us not just by way of commentaries but by what we ourselves have gone through. Seized of the identical feelings in which the psalm was composed or sung we become, as it were, its author."[4]

"Pure prayer," to Cassian's way of thinking, remains the aim of the monastic life and is the essence of perfection and a foretaste of heaven. "This prayer," Cassian writes, "centers on no contemplation of some image or other. It is masked by no attendant sounds or words. It is a fiery outbreak, an indescribable exaltation, an insatiable thrust of the soul. Free of what is sensed and seen, ineffable in its groans and sighs, the soul pours itself out to God."[5] As a proponent of an apophatic light mysticism, Cassian understands pure prayer as full of limitless, unbounded light totally beyond concepts, visions, and forms.

Cassian's writings reveal that he had experienced the seamless bond between the "simple" scriptural knowledge of God and the heights of mysticism. For him, through the perfect assimilation of psalmody and worship, the "prayer of fire" is born. Even the most mystical of prayer begins its ascent from psalmody and worship. But only mystical prayer is capable of revealing the whole meaning of the Scriptures. And because the human mind can come to authentic truth only if it is transformed through virtue, meditation, and mystical contemplation, even illiterate monks may attain to the deepest truths of the scriptures. Moreover, Cassian's emphasis upon the monk's entire communal, liturgical, and scriptural life as the context of "pure prayer" is less likely to be misunderstood as the angelism of some Desert Fathers.

Cassian is also a proponent of the Eastern monastic practice of *monologistos* prayer, that is, prayer in one formula. Although the Jesus Prayer is perhaps the most famous, Cassian may well be the first to give full articulation to the continuous repetition of an evocative verse, in this case, Psalm 69:2: "O God, come to my assistance, Lord make haste to help me" (Douay-Rheims Version). For him, this psalm verse "carries within it all the feelings of which human nature is capable."[6] Moreover, perseverance in this prayer "will lead you on to the contemplation of the unseen and heavenly and to that fiery urgency of prayer which is indescribable and which is experienced by very few."[7] Guarded by angels, one is ecstatically lifted up to silent prayer and becomes absorbed in the loving union that binds the three trinitarian Persons.

# Pseudo-Macarius

(late fourth to early fifth centuries)

*"For the soul that is privileged to be in communion with the Spirit of [Christ's] light becomes all light, all face, all eye."*[1]

Because of their penetrating ascetical and mystical insights, the so-called *Fifty Homilies* of Macarius had a tremendous influence in furthering the monastic movements initiated by Gregory of Nyssa and Basil the Great. By making the ideas of Basil, but especially of Gregory, more available to a "popular" audience, these homilies played a significant role in integrating the burgeoning monastic movements into the Church's broader life. So far-ranging was their influence that these homilies eventually found their way into Jesuit spirituality, Lutheran pietism, John Wesley's spirituality, and the beginnings of the Catholic Pentecostal movement in the United States.

These homilies are actually monastic conferences and spiritual conversations, laced with biblical quotations and allusions. They express the immense longing for God found in the soul's mysterious depths. Highly dependent upon Gregory of Nyssa, but devoid of Gregory's darkness imagery, their central theme is the soul's transformation into light when the divine light enters.

Recent scholarship has shown that the true author of these homilies is a Macarius from Mesopotamia and not Macarius the Egyptian (also known as "the Elder" and "the Great"), who had enjoyed a great reputation as a miracle-worker and a genius of spiritual direction. These homilies were written when sects of heretical Messalians, also called "Euchites," or "Bogomils" ("Cathars" in the West), with their dualistic conceptions rooted in Manicheanism were becoming widespread in Asia Minor. These so-called "praying people" believed that because of Adam's sin, a demon united itself substantially to every human soul and is not expelled even through baptism. Bodily secretions indicate when a demon has been properly exorcised.

The Messalians maintained that severe ascetical practices—especially concentrated, ceaseless prayer—eradicate all passion and desire, and exorcise the demon. The perfect can receive the beatifying immediate vision of the Trinity in this life, even to the point of seeing God with their physical eyes. They emphasized also that one should abstain from all forms of work and the Church's sacraments because these were of no use to obtain this highly desired vision. Their "idleness" foreshadows what was to become the so-called "Quietism controversy" later in the Christian tradition.

These homilies are free of Messalianism's misguided emphasis upon angelic prayer, as well as its grosser errors. In fact, Macarius considered the heart, not the Greek mind (*nous*), to be the center of human consciousness. "And when grace pastures the heart," Macarius writes, "it rules over all the members and the thoughts. For there, in the heart, the mind abides as well as all the thoughts of the soul and all its hopes. This is how grace penetrates throughout all parts of the body."[2] This aptly summarizes Macarius's teaching.

Christ descended into the unfathomable depths of the "hell-heart" so all could ascend with him to the Father. Thus, Macarius sought not a disembodied person but the transfiguration of the entire body-person through union with God. His Christocentric and sacramental emphases also stand as a strong counterpoint to Messalianism. His emphases were also to give a new orientation to Evagrian-type prayer in later monastic movements. For Macarius, if baptism and the Eucharist sanctify the whole person, then pure prayer must likewise involve not only the mind but also the entire body-person.

Macarius taught a coenobitic form of monasticism. Urging a radical separation from the world and from oneself by practicing strict poverty and obedience in a desert community, he exhorted his monks to live in harmony and to serve each other for the love of God. If his first commandment is to love God totally, he considered zealous, unceasing prayer to be the primary monastic virtue. One of the chief fruits of unceasing prayer: charity. From this prayer arises a state that "calms all the members of the heart, so that the soul, for much joy, appears like an innocent child, and the man no longer condemns Greek or Jew, sinner or worldling. The inner man regards all men with a pure eye . . . and desires that all should worship and love."[3]

He viewed the fallen human person as free, but pulled by two powers: the Holy Spirit and the devil. Christian life on earth is a never-ending spiritual combat between the forces of good and evil, with the human soul as the battlefield and the booty. The monk must do battle against himself, his passions, the various demons that stir up these passions, and his own propensity toward presumption and pride.

To win this battle, the monk must expect nothing from himself, but constantly cry out and beg for God's grace. Through prayer the monk cooperates actively with grace and opens himself to the Holy Spirit's further work in the soul. For those not proficient in this combat, he taught an ascetical, "natural" prayer. By declaring war on oneself, by practicing the virtues, by the ruthless elimination of all distracting thoughts, one constrains and forces oneself to pray by concentrating one's thoughts heavenward. Thus, one should compel oneself to do what God will eventually grant.

Macarius views thoughts as the devil's chief weapon in spiritual combat. "For our thoughts," he writes, "are not external to us, but from within, out of the heart."[4] Because the devil proposes evil thoughts or even seemingly good thoughts—but distracting ones— the monk must learn the source of his thoughts: God, the good angels, the devil, or the self.

One is baptized in the Holy Spirit when one attains deep compunction for sins and a vivid awareness of Jesus Christ as Lord and Savior. The Holy Spirit burns out evil thoughts, teaches discernment, instills calm in the soul, and may lead the monk eventually to "true" or "pure" prayer. This experiential prayer is a genuine consciousness of the Holy Spirit working in the soul; it bestows interior tasting, various joys, and even different kinds of ecstasies. It may even produce a type of spiritual stigmata: "To some, however, the sign of the cross has appeared in light and fastened itself upon the inward man."[5] Because ineffable light often accompanied pure prayer, Macarius is judged to be an early proponent of "Tabor," or "light" mysticism.

Paradoxically, the monk of true prayer experiences total dependence and total liberty. He is like a poor man befriended by a rich man who has given the poor man total access to his house and wealth. Pure prayer gives true repose and freedom from all evil thoughts that assail the soul. However, the monk should not presume that this state of ineffable peace and perfect joy in which he is a "body-bearing spirit" (*pneuma sarkophoron*) will last. He must invoke continually the Holy Spirit and Jesus, for the spiritual combat never ends in this life.

Macarius's texts highlight themes especially salient in Eastern Christian mysticism. They emphasize the human person as a psychosomatic whole and offer a penetrating analysis of the ongoing battle between good and evil in the human heart. His homilies also depict the person as a redeemed sinner always threatened by sin but always empowered by grace to make continual progress in the spiritual life, the *epektasis* theme he inherited from Gregory of Nyssa. They emphasize continual custody of the heart by unceasing concentration upon Christ, the divine artist, who implants his own image upon the soul, and enables the life of pure prayer leading to union with the Trinity.

Macarius's writings also bring out his fire, light and heart mysticism. They describe acutely and with captivating language how the soul's longing for God is often rewarded by an awakening of the spiritual senses, raptures, miracles, freedom from sin, profound peace, charity toward all, and becoming one spirit with God, deification. As he writes in his "Great Letter," "For such a soul, wounded by love for Christ, dies to any other desire in order . . . to possess the most beautiful intellectual and mystical communion with Christ according to the immortal quality of divinizing fellowship. Truly, such a soul is blessed and happy, when conquered by spiritual passion, it has worthily become espoused to God the Word."[6]

# Pseudo-Dionysius

## (fifth or sixth century)

*"O Trinity, beyond essence and beyond divinity and goodness direct us towards mysticism's heights beyond knowing, beyond lights, beyond limits, there where the mysteries of theology in the dazzling dark of the welcoming silence lie hidden, in the intensity of their darkness, all brilliance outshining. In the earnest exercise of mystical contemplation, abandon all sensation, all intellection, and all being, all non-being—and in unknowing, be one with the beyond being and knowing, of the divine dark."*[1]

The most influential person in the Eastern and Western Christian mystical tradition is in many ways the most enigmatic. Scholars have discovered neither his identity nor the exact dates in which he lived and wrote. Furthermore, his relatively brief corpus of writings seems impenetrable, mystifying, and open to diverse—and sometimes contradictory—interpretations.

By claiming to be the Dionysius the Areopagite mentioned in Acts 17:34, this fascinating figure demands apostolic sanction for his writings: four Greek treatises on liturgy and mystical theology and ten letters. This benign impostor avers to have been converted by St. Paul, to have been his disciple, to have witnessed the eclipse when Christ was crucified, to have been with the apostles Peter and James when the Virgin died, and to have corresponded with John the Evangelist. The later tradition also identified Pseudo-Dionysius with the first bishop of Athens (second century) and the martyred first bishop of Paris (third century).

Because of his alleged apostolic connections, his profoundly mystical and cosmic vision, and his creation of an almost perfect system, his writings attained almost canonical status—at least in the Western medieval world. His credentials were never seriously questioned until the nineteenth century, when scholars unmasked him incorrectly as Dionysius of Alexandria, a third-century saint; as an unknown disciple of St. Basil the Great who lived in the second half of the fourth century; and also as Severus of Antioch, a sixth-century heretic. Contemporary scholarship conjectures that he was a sixth-century Syrian monk.

For hundreds of years scholars asked, was "Dionysius" a Neo-Platonist masquerading as a Christian or a misguided Christian overpowered by Neo-Platonism who thereby compromised basic biblical beliefs? Some experts point out that the Areopagite depended heavily upon Proclus, a fifth-century Neo-Platonic philosopher who systematized the third-century Neo-Platonic philosopher Plotinus. Therefore, the Dionysian mystical vision and system can be reduced to a Christian-veneered paganism. For such scholars, Pseudo-Dionysius allegedly transposed the asceticism of the Desert Fathers (the purification of the passions and the achievement of virtue) to the intellectual order. Thus, instead of self-denial and self-emptying in imitation of Christ, one empties the *mind* of all concepts and ideas of God. Even God-language is emptied, for nothing can ever be affirmed of God because he is always "not this, not that"—above and beyond all that is.

More important, these scholars argue that for "Dionysius" the purifying and unifying factor in the mystical ascent to God is not love. Rather, it is only the stripping away of all thoughts in the mind that creates a state of nescience as the prelude to *intellectual* ecstasy into God. In other words, voiding the mind, nescience, and intellectual fainting are the mystical steps in the ascent to God—not moral purification and personal transformation initiated by and culminating in unitive love.

While admitting Dionysius's clear dependence on Proclus, other experts—correctly, to my mind—point out that he profoundly transposed Proclus to suit his own *Christian* interests. Finally, these commentators emphasize that if the four treatises are read in the order in which Dionysius wrote them, it is beyond a doubt that he must be interpreted and appreciated as a fully *Christian*, patristic theologian and spiritual writer with solid roots in the Greek Christian mystical tradition.

Thus, the Areopagite—like many before him—used Greek categories and thought but transformed them through the scriptures, the Church's authoritative teachers, and the liturgy. Not only did he judge all things in the light of Christ but his mysticism also remains inextricably linked to the fullness of Church life. He found God not in philosophical speculation and magical practices as the Greeks did but in the plenitude of Christian life. For him, the hidden depths of the scriptures, the sacraments, and the liturgy are the truly mystical; and, the mystical reality can be none other than Christ in the Church. With love at the center of his vision—portraying God as a drunken lover—and understanding mystical love as a love of the Trinity, Christ, and his Body, "Dionysius" moved far beyond Neo-Platonism.

Dionysian mysticism flows from a cosmic and ecclesiastical perspective drawn from scripture and the liturgy. In his view, to be a genuine theologian is to pray liturgically. His treatise, *The Celestial Hierarchy*, depicts a God of love who creates so that creation may share in the trinitarian life. Creation results from a divine love-ecstasy that implants in every creature the desire for the ecstatic movement back to God. The love that moves all creatures is *agape*, pure gift and generosity, the love that is proper to the Christian God. Moreover, the heavenly hierarchy of nine choirs of angels grouped in three triads is modeled after the trinitarian thearchy. By contemplating them, one is lifted up ("anagogy") into the trinitarian life.

In the text *The Ecclesiastical Hierarchy*, the Areopagite indicates how the heavenly hierarchy is manifested on earth. Love's self-communication takes place in the Logos' incarnation and its consequences: Church, scripture, liturgy, and sacraments. In the process of the creatures' reascent to the source of love, "Dionysius" depicts the deacons as purifying, the priests as enlightening, the bishops as consummating; the catechumens, energumens (those thought possessed), and penitents as being purified, the faithful as being illuminated, and the monks as surrendering to consummating love and knowledge. Thus, the Dionysian steps of purification, illumination, and union correspond to Evagrian asceticism (*praktike*), natural contemplation of God in creation (*theoria physike*), and loving knowledge (*gnosis*) of the Trinity—not to Plotinian mystical intellectualism.

Dionysius's writings are redolent with his love of Jesus Christ, whom he calls "my Christ," and the one who guides his writings. Our benign impostor views him as the source and perfection of every hierarchy. The revelation of Jesus' love for humanity was first revealed to angels, who then revealed it to us. Christ—"the most exalted revelation" in the Bible and in the Church's preaching and liturgy—is called by Dionysius "the angel of great counsel" because he announced what he knew of the Father. His wordplay on "angel" and "announce" cannot be missed in Greek.

In his description of Jesus Christ, this benign impostor employs a baffling array of redoubling negation: "For, . . . [Jesus] was neither human nor nonhuman; although humanly born he was far superior to man, and being above men he yet truly did become man. Furthermore, it was not by virtue of being God that he did divine things, not by virtue of being a man that he did what was human, but rather, by the fact of being God-made-man he accomplished something new in our midst—the activity of the God-man."[2]

As one rung in the triad in the ecclesiastical hierarchy, the Church's liturgy and sacraments are especially efficacious in effecting that "sacred uplifting to the divine," known as Dionysian "anagogy." He explains them as part of his "symbolic theology" that likewise purify, illuminate, and perfect the Christian. In fact, everything culminates in the Eucharist as "'Communion' and 'gathering' [*synaxis*]. Every sacredly initiating operation draws our fragmented lives together in one-like divinization. It forges a divine unity with the One."[3] Through the Eucharist, all is reunited in God, through Christ.

Therefore, Dionysius's last and most well-known treatise, *The Mystical Theology*, must be read in the fully Christian, scriptural, sacramental, and liturgical context of the above two treatises. Like the Church Fathers before him, the Areopagite uses the word "mystical" to denote the experience of God's loving self-communication through Christ. This is precisely what scripture reveals, what gives the Bible its full meaning, and what the liturgy and the sacraments—especially the Eucharist—contain.

"Mystical theology," a term coined by Dionysius, focuses on a transrational knowledge that deals with God in himself and how one attains union with God—the "Ineffable Itself"—in darkness and silence, where "one is supremely united by a completely unknowing inactivity of all knowledge, and knows beyond the mind by knowing nothing."[4] This unknowing state of mind is the subjective correlation to God as absolute Mystery. God is not only unknowable but also more than unknowable—and lies beyond both affirmation and negation. For the Areopagite, learned ignorance is the only true knowledge of God. His distinctive biblical apophaticism indirectly criticized the pagan light mysticism of his day.

The radically "negative" (apophatic) mysticism of his work *The Mystical Theology* demands that those called "pass beyond the summit of every holy ascent, . . . leave behind them every divine light, every voice, every word from heaven, and . . . plunge into the darkness where . . . there dwells the One who is beyond all things."[5] Although the experience of the divine darkness is beyond both knowing and unknowing, it is inextricably linked to the experience of the divine self-communication in the ecclesiastical hierarchy as the reflection and earthly extension of the heavenly hierarchy.

One must therefore read his treatise *The Divine Names* as an introduction to *The Mystical Theology*. The former treatise on "affirmative" (kataphatic) theology is imbued with a stirring conviction that God really is manifested in the world. Because of God's immanence, Christian life should be the breaking open and rendering transparent of the theophany that is God's creation. This text puts forward that the utterly incomprehensible God is cosmic Eros who manifests himself in creation so that all things may attain union with him. Therefore, all creation yearns for and loves the Beautiful and the Good. The divine Eros refracts itself in the universe of theophanies it has created. Hence, all things—even material reality—manifest the ecstatic divine Eros and gradually unveil what remains ever mysterious. God stands outside all good things as the super-fullness of all these things. In this way, Dionysius expresses God's paradoxical transcendence and immanence.

*The Divine Names* explains the truths of the faith as proclaimed by the Church, and emphasizes that the concepts and images used by scripture to describe God are at most anagogical. Thus, everything positive in these expressions can and must be applied to God. Nevertheless, they must always be united with a negative theology that proclaims the inadequacy of all God-language. For example, God can be called "spirit" and this is true metaphorically. God must also be called "not spirit" and this is true anagogically. That God is neither spirit nor not spirit is true for the Areopagite on the unitive level. In other words, when one truly perceives God's manifestations in the world, one also realizes that the Trinity thus manifested transcends any and all manifestations. As the Areopagite says, "God is therefore known in all things and as distinct from all things."[6]

Because apophatic theology affirms God's incomprehensibility, the Areopagite maintains that it is more fitting God-language than kataphatic theology. Nevertheless, to sever the link between apophatic and kataphatic theology is to render the former empty. Pseudo-Dionysius teaches implicitly that a purely apophatic theology is a contradiction, for if nothing can be affirmed about God, then theology should be absolutely silent. As he says, "every attribute may be predicated of him and yet he is not any one thing."[7]

The emptiness found in apophatic theology, however, prepares a person for "mystical theology," wherein God's loving self-communication and presence are experienced in an ecstasy of pure love through which one goes beyond all things and out of oneself—in a way beyond analogies, beyond supereminent negations, beyond knowing, *and* beyond unknowing. But his sharp distinction between apophatic and kataphatic theology seemingly paved the way for the later split between mystical experience of God and faith seeking understanding.

The key to the Dionysian cosmic vision is "hierarchy," which he defines as "a sacred order, a state of understanding and an activity approximating as closely as possible to the divine. . . . *The goal of a hierarchy, then, is to enable beings to be as like as possible to God and to be at one with him.*"[8] Thus, hierarchy is the principle of the radiation of the trinitarian life throughout creation and the principle of divinization.

Therefore, Pseudo-Dionysius stands in the tradition of the great Church Fathers who emphasized life's goal as ascending to full union with God, that is, divinization. Unlike Plotinus, who emphasized the withdrawal from all multiplicity to unify oneself and to discover the soul's own divinity, "the flight of the alone to the Alone," Dionysius teaches a unification with God through a God-given loving and ecstatic self-transcendence. For Plotinus, the self must be extinguished to regain itself as the One of undifferentiated unity. For Dionysius, the self is united to God who transcends the soul and all else, and becomes God while remaining itself. Thus, Dionysian divinization is one of differentiated unity—of two becoming one, while remaining two—of genuinely becoming the other, while remaining oneself, of becoming God by participation, "of being as much as possible like and in union with God."[9]

To summarize, the Areopagite describes three theologies: affirmative (kataphatic), symbolic, and negative (apophatic). The first two focus on what we can affirm about God; the last is about the radical failure of all speech and thought in God's presence. "What is to be said of it remains unsayable; what is to be understood of it remains unknowable."[10] The first two also focus upon God's manifestation in creation; the last is about the secret God-soul relationship discovered only through the soul's inward movement. The deepest knowledge of God occurs when one "suffers" God in total passivity through loving union with the unknowable God in the unknowable way of deep darkness.

But his three theologies all center on mystical, loving knowledge of God attained through contemplation and communion. All three theologies underscore that the creature's response to God's love must be praise and worship, that mystical loving knowledge is liturgy, and that the soul in ecstasy meets God's ecstatic love for it and becomes one with the Good and the Beautiful in a dazzling darkness.

# Gregory the Great

(ca. 540–604)

*"However much it strives, the soul is not able fully to fathom itself; how much less the greatness of Him who was able to make the soul. But when, striving and straining, we desire to see something of the invisible Nature, we are fatigued and beaten back and driven off."*[1]

The monastic pope Gregory the Great was born of a Roman senator and a pious mother, and received an excellent education—especially in law—to prepare him for a political and governmental career. He became prefect of Rome and presided over the senate at the young age of thirty. However, soon after his father's death, he "escaped naked from the shipwreck of this life," and entered a monastery to follow the "grace of conversion," which he said he had ignored for too long. As a monk, he became a profound contemplative, undermining his health somewhat by rigorous asceticism, and devoting much time to the study of scripture and the Latin fathers. He never lost his conviction that the monastic life aims at partially restoring Adam's contemplative oneness with God before his fall.

Pope Pelagius II interrupted Gregory's monastic life by ordaining him deacon, then making him the papal representative at the Byzantine court in Constantinople. About 585, Gregory returned to Rome and became abbot of his former monastery, St. Andrew's, and also became the pope's own personal counselor.

Although his past life underscored his skills as a politician, statesman, and administrator capable of accepting responsibility and using authority well, it was only after an intense interior struggle that Gregory, the joyful *monk*, agreed to become pope. He spoke achingly of how "earthly activities" had defiled the monastic quiet in his soul. "I loved the beauty of the contemplative life," he wrote, "just as if it were the sterile Rachel—beautiful and keen of sight, though of fewer children because of her repose, but seeing the light with a keener vision. Because of some decision or other, however, I was married to Leah in the night, she of the active life, fertile but poor-sighted, the one who sees less but is more fruitful."[2] His background, however, may explain why Gregory labored to integrate Roman and Christian values.

Because of floods, famine, disease, the invasion of the Lombards, and the Church's precarious position vis-à-vis the Imperial power at Constantinople, Italy was in a dreadful state. However, Gregory's firmness, strength, gentleness, and charity overcame many of these obstacles. With almost no help from the emperor, he personally saved Rome from the Lombards by establishing a separate peace with them. Thus, he earned the great respect of the Roman people.

In addition, he eliminated much of the corruption in the Church's administration of wealth and used its vast resources to help the poor, the destitute, the sick, and to ransom captives. In his frequently strained relations with the churches of the East, Gregory reasserted Rome's universal jurisdiction, but defended the legitimate rights of individual churches. He meant it sincerely when he called himself "servant of the servants of God." Moreover, under his skillful direction, England was converted and the Church was strengthened in Gaul, Northern Italy, and Spain. Thus, his person, life, and accomplishments contradict the view that contemplation and mysticism have no or little effect on the so-called real world of power and politics.

Gregory was a prolific writer with a practical, not a speculative, bent. His *Liber Regulae Pastoralis* (*Book of Pastoral Rule*) set forth directives for a bishop's pastoral life, underscored the bishop as the "shepherd of souls," and served as the textbook of the medieval episcopate. His *Dialogues* recount for popular piety the life and miracles of St. Benedict and other Latin saints. It became the model for medieval hagiographers. His forty homilies on the gospel, twenty-two homilies on Ezekiel, fourteen volumes of letters, and the twenty-five-volume *Expositio in Librum Iob* (also called *Moralium Libri XXV*) are a summa of dogma, theology, moral teaching, and ascetical and mystical theology that became a storehouse of theology for later centuries. By setting forth a profound view of the Christian life that could reach the heights of contemplation and mysticism, Gregory earned the title "Doctor of the Desire for God."

He also put an indelible stamp on the Church's liturgy, and was an ardent promoter of monasticism. By giving the monks privileges that exempted them partially from the authority of their local bishop, he laid the foundation for the future exemption of religious orders that were to come directly under papal control. Moreover, whereas Benedict may have given the Western monks a Rule, Gregory definitely gave them a mysticism.

Hence, in a period of decline, he served as a bridge over which the wisdom and culture of the patristic age would be passed on to the medieval world. In fact, the writers in the Middle Ages saw him as the equal of Ambrose, Jerome, and Augustine, and considered him one of the four doctors of the Latin Church. Contemporary commentators view him both as the first medieval spiritual and mystical author and as a great stabilizer of the Western world in a period of tremendous political, religious, and ecclesiastical turmoil.

Because of his ecclesiastical and theological accomplishments, scholars have tended to overlook Gregory the *mystic* and the teacher of the mystical life. He devoted himself to show how Christians in this life can see God. We were created to contemplate God's beauty and to dwell in his love. Adam—the contemplative prototype—enjoyed this intimacy with his Lord until he sinned. To Gregory, the Word became flesh not only to restore partially our ability to see God but also to give us experiential knowledge of what we believe. Only through Christ and his Spirit is the crown of all human knowing and loving—contemplation—possible.

Gregory understood contemplation as attentive regard for God alone. Only by a wholehearted seeking of its Maker and a reverential listening to its sole Lord does the human spirit obtain its true food. Because graced love alone enables the person to see God, one must ask how much one loves and desires even before attempting contemplation. Gregory spoke often of desire, panting, yearning, fire, and burning—earning him the title "Doctor of Desire."

Moreover, devout Christian living, humility, fear of God, and a sense of one's unworthiness and sinfulness lay the requisite groundwork. Because the self is fragmented, "recollection"—or gathering oneself together—is also required. Then, by "introversion," the soul contemplates itself, strives to discover its true nature, and grasps itself as a "ladder of ascent." As he writes, "And so the first step is that it collect itself within itself (recollection); the second, that it con-

sider what its nature is so collected (introversion); the third, that it
rise above itself and yield itself to the intent contemplation of its
invisible Maker (contemplation)."[3] Because God is the "Unlimited
Spirit," mystical ascent also requires an apophatic process of voiding
the mind of all images, and then using the soul's naked knowledge
of itself as a springboard to contemplate what is beyond itself, namely,
God. Paradoxically, in Gregory's view, both the soul and God are
ultimately incomprehensible.

Only the meditative study of the scriptures makes contemplation
possible. Gregory distinguished between the Bible's letter-spirit,
exterior-interior, and history-allegory. As the fathers before him,
Gregory understood the mystical as the hidden, deeper sense of
scripture whose unity and meaning are to be found in Christ and
Christ alone. Gregory's major mystical texts can be found in the context of his commentaries on scripture—and with a more experiential
valence than his predecessors. The perfect Christian knows how to
plumb the scriptures both in a liturgical and a private setting. Impossible is the contemplation of God without the ecclesial setting of the
Bible. Gregory also viewed the saints as incarnations of biblical truth
and contemplated their lives to attain the "saving knowledge" contained in the scriptures. In fact, the Church's nature and the progress
of Christian life within it underpin Gregory's entire thought on contemplation and mysticism.

Gregory maintained that both Moses and St. Paul enjoyed something of the direct consciousness of God in this life. In describing a
vision by St. Benedict, Gregory was to give to the medieval world
the most famous nonbiblical vision. According to him, the ecstatic-
giving divine Light given to Benedict enlarged his soul so that all
creation appeared small and petty. For most contemplatives, however,
the divine Light can be beheld only through a "chink," a "sprayed
window," or through "fog." This light purifies, illuminates, transforms, and unites the person to God; moreover, it reveals that only
God can fully satisfy the person.

The Light produces a paradox: the closer one moves to God, the
more one experiences his absence. Gregory stated the paradox of the
contemplative soul well: "The closer it approaches the Truth the more
it knows it is far from it, because had it not beheld it at least in some
form it would never have realized that it could not behold it."[4] One
may experience God briefly—the truth of the half-hour silence in

Revelation 8:1—but one is soon "beaten back." The theme of being "beaten back" and "relapse" is a Gregorian favorite not only because of the strong sense of one's creaturehood and sinfulness it conveys but also because of its worth in keeping the person humble. Gregory underscored, too, that those most carried away in contemplation also suffer great temptations later to keep them from being puffed up.

Our monk pope spoke of constant struggle and a continuing conversion. For him, *apatheia* cannot be attained in this life. Instead of distinguishing between the flesh and the spirit as many had done before him, Gregory differentiates this fallen world of sin from the world to come. One must follow the "Job-Christ" in patient suffering and imitating the eucharistic victim who sacrificed himself for us.

The experience of this distinction produces compunction in that it pierces a person to the heart. In a sense it commits the person to the whole of Christian life. Sorrow for sins, awe before the Almighty who will judge, longing for heaven, awareness of one's creaturehood and sinfulness, sorrow after the descent from the heights—all this is the result of compunction. Because Gregory has written so powerfully and eloquently about this, he is called the "Doctor of Compunction."

The locust image from Job 39:20 illustrates well Gregory's view of the human ability to contemplate God: much hopping about to attain very brief flights. Jacob, who wrestled with the angel and enjoyed some sort of imperfect facial vision of God, is another contemplative archetype. The contemplative wrestler does not stay on top for long but his "lameness" afterwards indicates a lessening of early desires. Attaining the top of the ladder, Jacob was "beaten back," and could only lament. Job's night visions produced an awe and fear of God's holiness. Job 42:6 reveals that when he saw God, he despised himself and repented in dust and ashes.

Gregory highly valued the monastic life but he was no Cassian. He explicitly taught that contemplation was open to all Christians, even to the married, if less frequently. The Desert Fathers viewed the active life as the ascetical dimension of their calling, but Gregory saw it as the exercise of love. He focused on the mixed life, understanding the gospel Mary as having the better part but Martha as doing necessary and fruitful work. The Rachel and Leah of Genesis 29–30 Gregory employed as archetypes of the contemplative and active life: the beautiful, clear-sighted Rachel as contemplative and the poor-sighted but fertile Leah as the active person effecting good works. These complement each other, as we see in the lives of contemplatives in action: Moses, Isaiah, Jeremiah, and Jesus himself. The "Doctor of the Mixed Life" knew that after the Fall, life here is not the garden of paradise. The truest mystic is the contemplative in action with one eye on the world to come and the other on suffering humanity.

# John Climacus

(ca. 579–649)

*"Hesychia [stillness] is worshipping God unceasingly and waiting on Him. Let the remembrance of Jesus be present with your every breath."*[1]

We know almost nothing about the life of St. John Climacus (also known as Scholasticus), except that he spent forty years in solitude at Tholas in the Sinai desert before becoming abbot of the monastery on Mount Sinai. He wrote the ascetical-mystical classic *Klimax* (*Ladder*), from which his name is derived. Its thirty chapters symbolize the thirty years of Christ's hidden life.

This volume evinces John's intimate and passionate experiences of God. It speaks often of "fire dwelling in the heart," fire descending into the "upper chambers of the soul," and raptures that carry a person into Christ's light. Although a hatred of the body and the world might seem to set the tone for the book, John saw the monk's real war as that against self-love and the demons, whom he described as "countless, hidden, and powerful enemies." So, as Christ's "real servant," the monk promises to master his mysterious and "dangerous" nature and to conquer the demons for a life of unceasing communion with God in Christ. This is nothing short of a "resurrection of the soul before the body," as John contends. He speaks warmly of the bond of love in the monastic community and how monks edify each other. "There is no one among them," John writes, "who is foolish. . . . They are openly gentle, kindly, radiant, genuine, without hypocrisy, affectation, or falsity of either speech or disposition because their bodies are made holy, their tongues purified, and their minds enlightened."[2] Thus, John offers an exceptional exposition of the ascetical foundations of mysticism and the mystical foundations of radical asceticism that sanctify, transform, and unite the entire person with God.

John was a master at disclosing human motivation. He possessed a deeply analytical mind, acute powers of observation, and deep insights into human nature—especially its uncanny ability to deceive itself. He is one of the most humane of ascetical teachers who spoke little about physical, but much about inner, asceticism, and the need for the Holy Spirit's help. Even a casual reading of his text reveals John's eloquence in describing the vices, their "sons and daughters," and human impotence. Both the thought of death and the "sweet" experience of the Holy Spirit's aid brought about by fervent prayer are perhaps the most powerful weapons to use against the vices.

John's description of the monastic life illustrates a paradox: severe, but graced, self-discipline can be viewed as a kind of personal "tough love" that integrates and transforms a person in what contemporary people understand as a "self-actualized" way. The extravagant penances, eccentricities, and "holy follies" of those who were punished for their faults in the isolation monastery (the "Prison") must be seen in the context of the deep desire for God that motivated these men. They denied nature "for what is above." Although they "were no different from corpses," John considers them more blessed than those who have never fallen "because through having fallen, they have pulled themselves up by a sure resurrection."[3]

Severity transformed their nature. The monk's ego-strength, wisdom, humanity, integrated personality, penetrating discernment, conviction of being a light to the world, and passionate love for God are the fruits of such a life—fruits that can come only from God's Spirit. Moreover, have not twentieth-century persons, such as Alexander Solzhenitsyn, Jacobo Timerman, Viktor Frankl, Nelson Mandela, and a host of others attested to experiencing some connection between extreme hardship and the discovery of hitherto inner and unsuspected resources?

The monks withdrew to the desert, not to escape the world, but to serve it through their battle against self-love and the demons. They knew that in their passionate love of God and neighbor, they resembled God, because "love, by its nature, is a resemblance of God."[4] John speaks powerfully of love being greater than prayer and the monk being a light for the world. Although the monk may seem like a figure best left in the past, it can be argued that all persons discover authentic human and Christian living only if they discover the "monk" in themselves. Who is not called to withdraw deliberately at times from "normal" life, to face one's own desert, and to wage war against self-love, one's demons, and the demons ripping apart the social fabric? Furthermore, are not the monks always with us, even if in bogus form? For example, are not many of the often bizarre, contemporary lifestyles and techniques touted to promote self-actualization and self-realization illustrations of the hunger for a new monasticism?

John Climacus is part of the hesychastic tradition, which taught starting prayer by expelling distractions, then employing the unceasing repetition of the Jesus Prayer ("Lord Jesus Christ, Son of God, have mercy on me [a sinner]"), in conjunction with a certain bodily posture, outer and "mystical" eyes fixed on the heart, controlled breathing, a voiding of the mind of all images, and a concentration that allows no idle thought to enter the heart. The true hesychast fastens his mind to his heart as to the wood of the cross. This effects not only rapture in the Lord but also unceasing union with him.

Hesychasm results in a prayer that "holds the world together," as well as direct experience of God, raptures in the Lord, humility, serenity (*apatheia*), and stillness of soul (*hesychia*). The fire of the Holy Spirit awakens in the heart. One is transported and transformed into Christ's light, the divine light—"the non-material light which shines beyond all fire"[5]—that surrounded Jesus on Mt. Tabor. Therefore, John is a proponent of an apophatic, light mysticism, not the apophatic mysticism of darkness we have already seen.

The genuine hesychast, in John's view, possesses uncanny discernment. He not only knows which of his thoughts come from God, which from the self, and which from the devils but he can also discern another's state of soul by observing that person's body language.

Like many of the Desert Fathers before him, John emphasized the importance of genuine repentance and tears. Authentic repentance and "tears of the soul" result in the soul "mingling with God." Tears wash away postbaptismal sins; without them, fewer people would be saved. Moreover, they are both the mother and the daughter of prayer.

He also wrote that "the man who believes in dreams is like someone running to catch up with his own shadows. . . . The man who distrusts every dream is very sensible."[6] Here stands one Church Father who cannot be called on to support the extravagant contemporary claims sometimes made for the spiritual and mystical significance of dreams.

Although written mainly for monks, John of the Ladder's ascetical and mystical classic influenced far wider circles throughout history. After reading John's work, it is easy to appreciate why there is no work in Eastern Christendom—except the Bible and liturgical books—that has been studied, copied, and translated more often. Its popularity in the East can be compared with the popularity of *The Imitation of Christ* in the West.

# Maximus Confessor

(ca. 580–662)

*"In the active person the Word grows fat by the practice of virtue and becomes flesh. In the contemplative it grows lean by spiritual understanding and becomes as it was in the beginning, God the Word."*[1]

Maximus Confessor has been called one of the greatest theologians of the Greek fathers and the last independent theologian of the Byzantine church. In him, the Alexandrian and Cappadocian traditions came to full fruition. His highly speculative mind always remained tethered to and fed on the scriptures, the liturgy, and his fully Christian spirituality and mysticism. Therefore, although subtle, but never abstract, his mystical theology is redolent with experience derived from a rich liturgical life and deep personal prayer.

Maximus's person, thinking, and life contradict the common opinion that mysticism and dogma are incompatible. In his view, there is always a reciprocal relationship between the two. Not only did he possess the speculative genius of the Greek fathers but he also enjoyed the soteriological brilliance of the Western fathers. So great were his accomplishments and his influence—especially in perfecting the Christology of the fathers—that he belongs almost equally to both the Eastern and Western Christian churches.

A prominent aristocrat of Constantinople, Maximus's mastery of the Bible, the fathers, and the pre-Christian philosophers indicates that he received a broad Christian and humanistic education. As first-secretary to the emperor Heraclius, he clearly belonged to the upper levels of his society. However, after only three years of imperial service, Maximus changed his life radically by entering a monastery at Chrysopolis on the other side of the Bosphorus. A few years later, his love for monastic spirituality brought him to the monastery of St. George at Cyzicus, where he remained until the Persian invasion of 626 forced him into exile. From Crete and Cyprus, he eventually made his way to North Africa.

Maximus was a prolific, theological genius whose profoundly Christian sense kept his speculation solidly rooted in the Church's entire life. He became an opponent of Monothelitism—the view that denied that Christ had a human will. Convinced that Monothelitism's watering down of Christ's full humanity would have a devastating effect on Christian life, Maximus clashed with Pyrrhus, the ex-patriarch of Constantinople, over the latter's Monothelitism. In 649, at the invitation of Pope Martin I, Maximus attended the Lateran synod in Rome that formally condemned this doctrine.

Emperor Constans II had Maximus and Pope Martin I arrested and brought to Constantinople to be tried for treason. Exiled to Bizye in Thrace, Maximus's tongue and right hand were cut off because he refused to comply with the imperial interdict on Monothelitism. Banished with his disciples to Lazica, he died there within a few years.

He should be considered a martyr for both the Council of Chalcedon and that of the Lateran synod. Chalcedon taught that Jesus Christ is one Divine Person with two natures, divine and human. These natures exist in this one person without confusion, without change, without division, and without separation. The Lateran synod proclaimed—in line with Chalcedon and the scriptures—that Christ is like us in all things but sin. If like us, he must possess a human will. If what is not assumed is not saved, the incarnate Word must have had a human will.

Maximus valued deeply the "heritage of the Faith." In order to be catholic and orthodox, this faith must be in accord with the tradition handed down by one's predecessors. This critical reverence for the tradition, combined with his penetrating intelligence, enabled him to restore the balance between Christocentric orthodoxy, trinitarian-Christocentric spirituality, and Neo-Platonism. A brilliant interpreter of Pseudo-Dionysius, Maximus made the Areopagite acceptable to orthodox spirituality and theology by avoiding the speculative nihilism into which "Dionysius" had seemingly led so many contemplatives. In short, Maximus brought to the fore the somewhat latent trinitarian Christocentrism of "Dionysius."

Maximus's writings reveal his great love of the monastic life. Using the same lapidary, pithy writing style of the Desert Fathers, Maximus speaks passionately about light mysticism, and the pure, undistracted, ceaseless, rapturous prayer that illuminates and transforms the monk into the divine Light. For him, the "active," or ascetical, life often rewards its adherents with undistracted prayer; the contemplative life, with instantaneous rapture as soon as the mind turns to God. At this stage one is conscious only of God. Pure prayer draws even one's concupiscence into divine desire. Completely undistracted prayer discloses that one truly loves God and neighbor and self for the sake of God.

Requisite for prayer is self-mastery abnegation because self-love is the mother of all vices. Because sinning in thought is easier than in deeds, the Confessor viewed distractions—especially memories—as great enemies. Because Jesus died for all, nothing is greater than love. The monk is not only called to love everyone but also to prefer the mystical experience of God, which illuminates the mind, ravishes, and reveals one's own lowliness. Prayer is both the mother and daughter of love of God and neighbor.

The Confessor focused on the negative way, an apophaticism that underscores God's utter transcendence, otherness, and complete incomprehensibility totally beyond all images and concepts. The supreme state of prayer, prayer without ceasing, employs neither form nor matter. "The perfect mind," he wrote, "is the one that through genuine faith supremely knows in supreme ignorance the supremely unknowable."[2] However, this apophaticism is mitigated because he stresses God's oneness with the Word incarnate so what is completely inexpressible and incomprehensible to all created intellects became what can to some extent be grasped by human understanding.

In Maximus's view, inasmuch as Jesus is the WORD-man, mysticism must be apophatic. Inasmuch as Jesus is the Word-INCARNATE, mysticism must be kataphatic. Inasmuch as the human spirit is open to the ever greater God, mysticism must be apophatic. Inasmuch as the person is always spirit-in-WORLD, mysticism must be kataphatic. With respect to scripture, Maximus also held that kataphatic theology makes the Word FLESH; apophatic theology, spirit. By teaching the morality of the scriptures, one makes the Word flesh. Through the sublime contemplation of experiential mystical theology, one makes the Word spirit and the utterly Unknowable better known. Thus, Christian mysticism can never be either purely apophatic or kataphatic.

The Confessor focused on the Incarnation as the Father's great plan. God's Son became man so that we may become gods and sons of God. We are summoned to "become partakers of the divine nature" (2 Pet 1:4). Before this mystery that can be grasped only in faith, Maximus calls for silent adoration. Because of the salient features of Maximus's views on the Incarnation, he is called the doctor of *theosis* (deification).

The cosmic dimension of this mystery merits emphasis. Maximus viewed the human person as an integral part of God's creation. He saw creation in the person and the person in creation. To paraphrase St. Paul, all creation groans so that Christ may be all in all (Rom 8:22; Col 3:11). In line with the Greek fathers, Maximus understood Jesus' resurrection as the firstfruits of the entire, new creation.

As much as the Confessor reverenced dogma, he was acutely aware of the limitations of the human mind vis-à-vis the trinitarian mystery in Christ. He thoroughly appreciated worship as an appropriate vehicle for comprehending the incomprehensible and for expressing the ineffable. Maximus viewed mystagogy as an initiation into the Church's liturgy and the liturgy as the springboard into the experience of mystery itself. The goal of the Church's liturgy is to bestow, through asceticism and contemplation, mystical loving knowledge of the Trinity, that is, supreme gnosis.

In what may be a good concluding summary of his life and teaching, he writes:

> The profession "One is Holy, [one is Lord, Jesus Christ, to the glory of God the Father]" and what follows, which is voiced by all the people at the end of the mystical service, represents the gathering and union beyond reason and understanding which will take place between those who have been mystically and wisely initiated by God and the mysterious oneness of the divine simplicity in the incorruptible age of the spiritual world. There they behold the light of the invisible and ineffable glory and become themselves together with the angels on high open to the blessed purity. After this, as the climax of everything, comes the distribution of the sacrament, which transforms into itself and renders similar to the causal good by grace and participation those who worthily share in it. To them is there lacking nothing of this good that is possible and attainable for men, so that they also can be and be called gods by adoption through grace because all of God entirely fills them and leaves no part of them empty of his presence.[3]

# Isaac the Syrian

## (d. ca. 700)

*"One must not call this gift and grace spiritual prayer, but the offspring of pure prayer which is engulfed by the Holy Spirit. At that moment the intellect is yonder, above prayer, and by discovery of something better, prayer is abandoned. Then the intellect does not pray with prayer, but it gazes into ecstasy at incomprehensible things which surpass this mortal world, and is silenced by its ignorance of all that is found there."*[1]

Relatively little is known about Isaac the Syrian (also known as Isaac of Nineveh) except that he withdrew to desert solitude only five months after his episcopal consecration. There he devoted himself to the study of scripture, went blind because of his austere life, and then dictated the rest of his five treatises on the monastic life to his disciples. These treatises made a tremendous impact on monastic movements, especially in the Syrian and Eastern churches because of the wealth of his personal experience and psychological insight. Reading him is like venturing into the life and mind of a rather astonishing person gifted with the power of vast ascetical and mystical experience.

This seventh-century Persian ascetic was a brilliant writer in a remarkable but largely neglected tradition of East Syriac writers. Isaac stands at the head of an intellectual flowering of Syriac culture in the seventh and eighth centuries of what is now Iraq, Iran, Kuwait, and Qatar. His writings had such irresistible force that within about one hundred years after his death many of them in Greek translation had crossed the nearly impenetrable political and theological barrier between Eastern Byzantine and Western Roman Christianity.

Undoubtedly a mystic and a thinker of unusual clarity and richness, Isaac wrote to guide his monks in reaching ecstatic contemplation of God that foreshadows the glories of heaven. He clarified, deepened, and made a unique contribution to the influential Evagrian tradition. Like Evagrius, Isaac taught a three-stage ascent to God. In the first stage, the monk engages in *praktike*, that is, the asceticism required to battle the demons and the body's bondage to the passions. He maintained with Evagrius that the monk must labor to recapture the soul's (*nous*) original serenity (*apatheia*) lost because of its union with an unruly body. The proper battlefield for *praktike* is the solitude of the desert, the weapons, fasting, vigils, psalmody, and the study of scripture. Without this ascetical phase, any attempts by the monk at a contemplative life are as fruitless as a young, wingless bird's attempt to fly.

During the second stage, the monk grows in self-control and reverential fear of the Lord. God graces his mind with thoughts that enter the heart and guide his life. The insight derived by "natural contemplation" into the world's transitoriness and death penetrates his being, resulting in a "contempt for the world" because of its delusions. This realization destroys the devil's sway over the monk, and voids the heart of its passionate thoughts. If all people were granted this true contemplation (*theoria*), which he speaks of as "profound, divine visions," future generations would not come into being.

Isaac emphasizes that the desert warrior also becomes certain of God's providence for every person. The Creator's love for his creation, especially rational creatures, leaves him awestruck with wonder. Forgetful of self, he becomes like someone drunk on wine. This vision of a wholly loving Creator begins the monk's journey into the most hidden things of God. No longer moved by "things corruptible," the monk experiences mystical tears, *apatheia*, psychosomatic integration, and "revelations of intelligible things," often insights into the soul's and creation's mysterious nature.

Isaac distinguishes between the sweetness of prayer and prayer itself, which consists of petition, adoration, thanksgiving, desire, love. These are the manifold ways in which a person employs his graced freedom to pierce the "heart's veil" and to lift it up to God. Every manner of prayer culminates in pure prayer but our monk teaches paradoxically that only one person in a thousand attains pure prayer.

Isaac further distinguishes between the sweetness of prayer, prayer, and "the divine vision of prayer." "But sometimes a certain divine vision is born of prayer," he writes, "and the prayer of the man's lips is cut short, and stricken with awe by this vision he becomes as it were a body bereft of breath. This (and the like) we call the divine vision of prayer, and not, as fools affirm it to be, some image and form, or a representation of the imagination."[2]

In contrast to Evagrius, Isaac speaks of a "prayer of no prayer," which is attained only by a single person in generations. Because what is genuinely spiritual for Isaac is free of all movement, in the "prayer of no prayer," every motion of the tongue, intellect, will, imagination, and heart ceases. Only through the "prayer of no prayer" does a person gain entrance into the heart's secret chamber where stillness and silence reign. There is no prayer, no weeping, no desire, no exterior or interior movement at all, and even no free will—only the "prayer of no prayer."

Awe, wonder, ravishing, self-forgetfulness, divine vision, and, paradoxically, no vision follow in the wake of the "prayer of no prayer." One is conscious only of the light of the Holy Spirit, which seizes the inner and outer man, producing a profound spiritual inebriation. Engulfed by the Holy Spirit, this daughter of pure prayer forces the spirit above itself to gaze ecstatically into the incomprehensible silence and bestows an unknowing more sublime than knowledge, a learned ignorance. This paradise-like prayer may be transitory but it is indeed an actual foretaste of the resurrected life after death. Isaac's homilies underscore, too, that all prayer—even the highest state of "no prayer"—is inextricably connected with psalmody and liturgy, especially the Eucharist.

# Symeon the New Theologian

## (942–1022)

*"You, O Christ, O God of the universe, appeared as light, illuminating me completely from Your total light. And I became light in the night, I who was found in the midst of darkness."*[1]

"And how is it," Symeon the New Theologian writes, "that one made god by grace and by adoption will not be god in awareness and contemplation, he who has put on the Son of God?"[2] This quotation summarizes the person and teachings of this great Byzantine monk. Symeon had discovered mystically that in him "was the Kingdom of Heaven which is the Father, the Son, and Spirit, the Divinity inseparable in three Persons."[3] He also underscores a theme found in most of the great Christian mystics: God's attractive beauty is also terrifying. Moreover, he is the first Byzantine mystic to speak so openly and freely about his own mystical life.

The Eastern Christian tradition underscores that the true theologian is one who has been taught by God through mystical experience of the mystery of the Trinity's indwelling in the soul. Thus, the Orthodox Church canonized Symeon and bestowed upon him the title "New Theologian." Just as it had surnamed both St. John the Evangelist and St. Gregory of Nazianzus "the Theologian," the Orthodox Church honored Symeon because he was so deeply rooted in the tradition of the great mystical theologians of the East.

The "Enthusiastic Zealot" was born in Galatia in Paphogoria (Asia Minor) of a Byzantine provincial noble family. His uncle, who had an important position at the imperial court, brought Symeon to Constantinople at an early age for his secondary education. After meeting Symeon the Studite, a monk of the Stoudion Monastery in Constantinople, who introduced him to the importance of mystical experience of the indwelling Trinity, the younger Symeon refused to go on for higher studies. From then on Symeon understood that consciousness of the indwelling of Christ and the Trinity was nothing less than the goal of Christian life.

Although Symeon was in charge of a patrician's household and later entered imperial service, he began to give himself to long nightly prayer. He was wounded by God's love, was drawn to the "terrifying and attractive beauty of God," and received visions of Christ and the Trinity as light. He came to comprehend that "illumination is the end of all those who love; and repose of all contemplation is the Divine Light."[4]

He also became acutely conscious of his brokenness and sinfulness. God's light laid bare his debauches, the sins of his youth, and his disorder. Saying that he had descended into hell thousands of times, he wished that the earth would open up and swallow him. Crazed by pleasures, he had become sin itself. He desired, then, to enter a monastery.

Through the Spirit-filled assistance of the Studite, his spiritual director, Symeon was able to end his backsliding, laxity, and immorality. When he was twenty-seven years old, Symeon finally entered the monastery at Stoudion, where he experienced a conflict between the common life at the monastery and total obedience to his charismatic spiritual father. Thus, he followed the Studite's advice and transferred to the monastery of St. Mamas, where he gave himself to great penances, long hours of contemplation, and the copying of the scriptures.

Within three years, he was tonsured monk, ordained priest, and elected abbot. His writings are redolent with love of the priesthood, psalmody, the liturgy, and especially the eucharistic sacrifice, which open one to the divine Light. Symeon insisted that all Christians— especially his monks—must progress in the explicit experience of the triune indwelling in their souls. On the other hand, he soon realized that "there is one out of a thousand or better out of 10,000 who has arrived at mystical contemplation."[5] Those not attaining contemplation he deemed "babies born dead." Finding his monastery a "refuge for worldly monks" and a "cemetery for the living dead," he urged his monks back to their prophetic and charismatic vocation through a life of austere asceticism, purity of heart, and constant prayer. He encountered great resistance from "the enraged dogs" in his monastery—almost to the point of incurring physical harm.

In the Byzantine Christian world of Symeon's day, the monasteries were too often social vehicles for the maintenance of order and unity throughout the empire. They possessed wealth and indulged in complicated liturgical celebrations that did little to engender genuine piety. The ninth-century monastic reforms initiated by St. Theodore the Studite contributed partially to the imposition even on parish life of the monastic Office and the more formalized practices of prayer and worship. In addition, by divorcing theology from living Christian experience—especially from mystical experience—Byzantine scholastic theology threatened the Church's vital patristic heritage. Thus, Symeon directed his fiery zeal against the somewhat formalized Byzantine spirituality of his day.

His archenemy was Archbishop Stephen of Nicomedia, the chief adviser to and the official theologian of the patriarch of Constantinople. This formidable scholastic theologian eschewed Symeon's view that theology was a mystical wisdom given by the Holy Spirit only after total purification through rigorous asceticism. Furthermore, Symeon claimed to be a "theodidact," that is, one taught directly by God. Appealing to his own mystical experiences as normative, he maintained that his writings were somehow inspired by the Holy Spirit. Stephen branded these claims as ignorant and obscurant enthusiasm that denied, in essence, legitimate ecclesiastical authority and jurisdiction. Symeon added fuel to the fire by contending that a charismatic, nonordained spiritual father could forgive sins and that a sinful priest could not. However, it would seem that Symeon had in mind a spiritual father's charismatic ability to free sinners from their enslavement to sin.

Both the continued harassment from Stephen and the burdens of office prompted Symeon to resign as abbot in 1005. In 1009, after an ecclesiastical trial, he was banished to the small town of Paloukiton across the Bosporus. Eventually exonerated by both the emperor and the patriarch, he was offered an archbishopric. He declined, and continued his life of asceticism, contemplation, and writing for the thirteen remaining years of his life at the monastery of St. Marina that he had reconstructed.

By blending the best of the intellectual tradition of the Alexandrian fathers, the monastic affective school of the heart, and his own mystical experiences, Symeon produced a new genre of spiritual and mystical writing. Highly unusual in his tradition, Symeon's writings are a mirror of the man whom some consider the most personal of all Byzantine writers. Written and given as conferences when he was abbot, the *Catecheses*, or *Discourses*, is his central work. *The Hymns of Divine Love* is essentially the discourses in poetic form. In his numerous theological and ethical treatises, Symeon shows himself as the guardian of the patristic teaching on mystical theology that emphasized authentic theology as an apophatic wisdom given by the Holy Spirit and transcending human reasoning. His *Practical and Theological Chapters* instructs monks and others in Christian asceticism and contemplation.

In most of his works, Symeon gives a traditional presentation of themes dear to the Eastern fathers: spiritual combat versus the passions and the demons, constant vigilance (*nepsis*), spiritual sobriety, abiding sorrow for sins, the gift of tears, purity of heart, fasting, discernment, *apatheia*, sensitive love of God's will, fasting, charity, and divinization (*theosis*).

When the monk has performed all the asceticism in his power, "the stripping, the indifference, the separation from one's family, the pruning of his will, the renunciation of the world, the endurance of trials, prayer, compunction, poverty, humility, with all the fortitude he can, then dimly, like a delicate ray, minute, having enveloped his mind suddenly, it enraptures him in ecstasy, rapidly forsaking him so that he may not die."[6] In this context, Symeon asks rhetorically why we are so ashamed to become God since God was not ashamed to become man.

Although all the Desert Fathers emphasized the importance of fasting, Symeon saw it as especially important for monks. Fasting disciplines unruly appetites and passions; it heals and brings about "sobriety," that is, attentiveness to the promptings of the Holy Spirit. A serious life of prayer cannot exist without it.

His works are redolent with the conviction that one must engage in unceasing spiritual combat and mystical prayer for the sake of the perfection of universal love. Detachment from the world and the self is the foundation of charity, which is the true measure both of one's holiness and of one's progress in contemplation. Because the poor monk has no material goods to share, he must share his presence with his brothers and sisters. Charity in this context is nothing less than edifying others by detachment, recollection, a prayerful spirit, and holiness.

At St. Mamas, Symeon had experienced the descent of the Holy Spirit upon him as fire and light. He understood this experience as one that transformed him into light and fire and deified him—that is, it made him a god by grace and by adoption. This may account for his emphasis on the operations of the Holy Spirit in effecting mystical union with the Trinity. In his view, the Holy Spirit as sanctifier brings about Christian asceticism and holiness and is the one through whom Christ speaks directly to the human heart. For Symeon, Christ is conceived spiritually and substantially in the mystic by way of the Holy Spirit. Mystical union with the Trinity experienced as a triple light in unity is also caused by the Holy Spirit. The "great blasphemy against the Holy Spirit" for him is the heresy of the Pneumatomachoi, who denied the full divinity of the Holy Spirit and the Spirit's role in divinizing and making Christians gods by adoption and sons and daughters of God.

The chief work of the Holy Spirit is stirring the Christian to genuine repentance and bestowing the fairly common gift of mystical tears that soften the heart and promote spiritual humility. For Symeon, "baptism in the Holy Spirit" is the deepened awareness of sins committed after baptism with water. Spirit baptism also bestows a deeper consciousness of Jesus as Lord and Savior. Through the Spirit, Symeon experienced the habitual presence of Christ in his heart—often ecstatically. This "formless form" of light transformed Symeon into the light and fire of Christ. His descriptions of the apophatic experience of the Trinity and of Jesus Christ as a deifying light and fire in a soul surrendering all for God are unsurpassed in the Christian mystical tradition.

Symeon's life and treatises illustrate his bold, paradoxical apophatic language and his trinitarian and light mysticism, which are essentially teachings about *theosis*, deification. "For this Holy Spirit," he wrote, "descends on you, becomes like a pool of light to you, which encompasses completely in an unutterable manner. As it regenerates you, it changes you from corruptible to incorruptible, from mortal to immortal, from sons of men into sons of God and gods by adoption and grace."[7]

# William of St. Thierry

## (ca. 1085–1148)

*"Why do you not believe, O infidel? Surely because you do not love!
You do not believe because you do not love; you do not love because
you do not believe."*[1]

Psychologist, moralist, theologian, experienced mystic, spiritual guide,
and reformer of the monastic life, William has been called a witness
to and a paradigm of the Golden Age of monasticism and mysticism.
Because of his theological and mystical profundity, urbanity, and attractive personality, William was immensely popular with his contemporaries. His deeply mystical approach to theology, however,
placed him at odds with the theologians Peter Abelard and William
of Conches, who formed part of the intellectual environment of that
period. Although theologically different from his good friend Bernard
of Clairvaux, numerous scribes ascribed Bernard's name to William's
works. Only in the twentieth century has "Pseudo-Bernard," or "Bernard's alter ego," been appreciated on his own.

Known as the "reasonable mystic," the "learned lover," the "mystic of the Holy Spirit," and as one of the most original minds of the
twelfth century, William's writings disclose a cultivated mind of
unrivaled speculative power, united to a heart burning with the love
of God. One finds in his works a penetrating, yet impeccably orthodox, intelligence united with a deeply contemplative and passionate
religious spirit inclined to solitude for the sake of knowing the triune
God. Here is a contemplative who pushes reason to its limits and
knows that eventually reason must kneel before the Trinity's ineffable
mystery to find its fulfillment in love.

Born in Liège of noble parentage, William received an excellent
education at the Laon (or Rheims) Cathedral school. However, before
completing his studies, William's contemplative spirit led him to

enter the Benedictine abbey of St. Nicasius of Rheims. Within three years, he befriended Bernard of Clairvaux, the man who soon became his ideal. After only six years of monastic life, he was elected abbot of the abbey of St. Thierry. Zealous in both his religious and secular responsibilities, William nonetheless felt hemmed in by the burdens of office. On numerous occasions he requested Bernard that he be allowed to enter the monastery of Clairvaux to satisfy his desire for solitude and to be close to his friend. Bernard resolutely refused.

While in office, William found time to write numerous treatises on the Church Fathers as well as his works *The Nature and Dignity of Love*, *On Contemplating God*, *Grace and Free Will*, *On the Sacrament of the Altar*, *Prayers* and *Meditations*—which reflect his ardent soul in a way reminiscent of Augustine's *Confessions*—and his greatest work, a commentary on the Song of Songs.

After fifteen years as abbot, William resigned to take the white habit of the Cistercian monks at Signy, an abbey established by his friend Bernard. In his thirst for ever deeper solitude, William often visited the austere and strictly contemplative eremitical Carthusians of Mount Dieu. During this period, William wrote *The Mirror of Faith* and *The Enigma of Faith*, works aimed at strengthening the faith of and consoling the monks at Signy and Mount Dieu.

His most popular work, *The Golden Epistle* (originally called the *Treatise on the Solitary Life*), was written toward the end of William's life. A brilliant blending of his creative theology and of his profound contemplative experience, this work, dedicated to the Mount Dieu Carthusians, eulogizes the Cistercian way of life and breathes forth the hunger for God that animated the monastic movements of his century. In this work, William discusses the "animal," the "rational," and the "spiritual" man, or the beginner, the progressive, and the perfect in the spiritual life. The spiritual person is the perfect person who wills only what God wills and becomes so closely united to God that only this mortal life itself prevents perfect union.

This learned monk emphasizes that the Trinity created us through "creative grace" in its own image (*imago*) and likeness (*similitudo*) so that we may be like God. The triune unity of the human spirit's memory, understanding, and will is its image of and likeness to God. Human perfection, therefore, consists in deification, that is, sharing God's very own life, and becoming sons and daughters of the Trinity. One becomes by grace what God is by nature. Although sin has adversely affected this likeness, God's "illuminating grace" enables the likeness to be restored through the acquisition of virtue. This grace also accompanies and brings about mystical experience, and the eventual loving knowledge or knowing love that is union with God. How the soul as the image of the Trinity wins back its lost likeness to the Trinity through the life of prayer and contemplation is undoubtedly William's main concern.

In the tradition of the Greek fathers, William emphasizes that everything comes from, subsists in, and must return to the Trinity. However, William applied this Greek emanation-return schema only to the individual soul. The return to God demands the "active life," that is, the asceticism required to eradicate sin, vice, and disorder in the soul and to establish it in virtue. Asceticism makes the flesh obey reason, submits reason to the spirit, engenders virtue, and restores the spirit's original dynamism for the trinitarian life. Most important, asceticism exists only for the sake of the mystical contemplation that guides and crowns it. Contemplation—which only the Holy Spirit can teach—effects true spiritual union with God, or deification, in which the person actually becomes God, "but not in every way." This life is open to all genuinely disciplined persons.

William is a proponent of "learned ignorance," of apophatic mysticism. Because the Trinity is absolutely incomprehensible, "this ineffable reality can be seen only in an ineffable way." As with many of the Greek fathers, William taught "that knowledge [of God] is best known in this life by unknowing; the highest knowledge that a man can here and now attain consists in knowing in what way he does not know."[2] Even brief glimpses of God's countenance, "O face, face of my soul," purify the person, often render the person ecstatic, and transform the person into God. Like many others in the Christian mystical tradition, William taught the purifying, illuminating, and transforming effects of mystical contemplation.

Because he begins from the positive experience of our encounter with the Word incarnate, his apophaticism does not dominate his theology. Focusing more on the positive aspects of our pursuit of God, gradual illumination, and the increasing power of love, William maintains that through contemplative experience a person does come to know God. "And yet, O Majesty transcending understanding," he prayed, "to the soul that loves you, you do seem understandable. For though no faculty of soul or spirit can ever comprehend you, nevertheless, the man who loves you in his loving understands you totally."[3] The soul may know best how it does not know, but for William genuine love of God is knowledge and understanding.

Our Cistercian's warm "carnal love" for the human Jesus determines his starting point. In William's work *On Contemplating God*, he compares himself to Moses who hid in the cleft of the rock and saw God's back. However, for William, the rock is Christ, the "rock of the Christian faith." Moreover, he says, "And sometimes, when I gaze with longing, I do see the 'back' of him who sees me; I see your Son Christ 'passing by' in the abasement of his incarnation."[4]

Christ's humility as manifested in his self-emptying love to the point of death on the cross is the pattern for our transformative love. Christ's cross reveals the reality of God's face and his tender kiss to us. Although William calls "sacraments" all the mysteries that connect us to Christ's saving work, the "sacrament" par excellence is Jesus' passion. It is the tree of life in paradise. Embracing it restores life to a dead soul. Moreover, through the Eucharist we are transformed into what we eat.

The Trinity, especially the Holy Spirit, dominates William's theological and mystical vision. The originality of his mystical theology resides in the way he inserts the human spirit's knowledge and love of God into the inner-trinitarian life. The Holy Spirit, for him, is the reciprocal love of the Father and the Son, their mutual knowledge, and the unity of the Trinity itself.

The Holy Spirit not only brings about our unity with the Trinity but also is this unity itself. "It is called unity of spirit," he writes, "not only because the Holy Spirit brings it about or inclines a man's spirit to it, but because it is the Holy Spirit himself, the God who is Charity. He who is the Love of the Father and Son, their Unity, Sweetness, Good, Kiss, Embrace and whatever else they can have in common in that supreme unity of truth and truth of unity, becomes for man in regard to God in the manner appropriate to him what he is for the Son in regard to the Son through unity of substance."[5]

The unity of spirit espoused by William unites a person not only to God but also to one's neighbor. Unity of spirit, deification, is spiritually fecund and demonstrates its power in self-emptying love for others. The Cistercian ideal was to be poor with the poor of Christ. The contemplation of trinitarian "Beauty" transforms the spiritual person into a person of self-emptying love.

Although William's mysticism goes beyond the simplicity, direct-ness, and trust of love that a young child has for its mother—and is at times erotic—it is never bridal. And because he believed, he wanted to understand. Because he believed, he desired to love experientially. In wrestling with the problem of how love could be knowledge, he came to understand that only the "perception of enlightened love" can grasp the ineffable. He says, "When the soul reaches out in love to anything, a certain change takes place in it by which it is trans-muted into the object loved."[6]

Love, to William's way of thinking, is the spirit's power of percep-tion, transforming it into what is perceived. Moreover, one does not perceive unless one has already been transformed. The ability to see God is one and the same as advancing in God's love. That God could not be sought unless he had already been found remains a mystical paradox. By becoming connatural with God, the person attains a loving knowledge or a knowing love of God, "an understanding that comes from love." This supra-rational and supra-discursive loving knowledge absorbs but does not destroy reason. "The understanding of the one thinking," he writes, "becomes the contemplation of one loving and it shapes it into certain experiences of spiritual or divine sweetness which it brings before the gaze of the spirit so that the spirit rejoices in them."[7] Few have written so profoundly and con-vincingly about the human desire to know God in perfect love as this monk.

# Bernard of Clairvaux

## (1090–1153)

*"I want to tell you of my own experience, as I promised."*[1]

No less a person than Dante judged Bernard of Clairvaux to be the supreme guide to the contemplative life. Of him, Dante said, "What a contemplative!" He also considered Bernard to be the human mirror in which one could see God. To this day, many consider Bernard to be the apotheosis of the monastic tradition in the medieval period.

During his life of prodigious and ceaseless activity, Bernard had tremendous influence over popes, bishops, and councils; undertook sensitive missions for both church and state; and was the eloquent preacher of the Second Crusade. He also gave himself wholeheartedly to the theological controversies and ecclesiastical politics of his times. He was called "the conscience of all Europe." Passionately in love with God, Christ, and Mary, he maintained a vigorous contemplative life to the end of his days.

Due to his exceptional penetration of scripture, the fathers, the liturgy, and psalmody—and his awesome artistic power to describe and communicate this to others—he has been aptly described as "the last of the Fathers, and not inferior to the earliest." The structure of his sentences causes his works to sound like a soul sighing or singing hymns to God. His erudition—an unrivaled mastery of and skill with Latin—was such that many in the Christian tradition contend that everything *Doctor mellifluous* wrote is a masterpiece. Many scholars maintain that his *Sermons on the Song of Songs* is the supreme masterpiece of Christian mysticism. The sacramental humaneness of his spirituality and mysticism has shaped Catholic piety, spirituality, and mysticism to the present day.

Born of an especially holy mother at Fontaines-les-Dijon in Burgundy, Bernard received an education commensurate with his noble lineage and lively intellect. However, when he was twenty-one years old, he decided to become a monk at the Cistercian proto-monastery in Cîteaux, famous for its fervor and discipline. He convinced his brothers, his uncle, and several other noblemen to take the same step.

Within three years he was chosen abbot for a new foundation in the solitary valley of Clara Vallis, or Clairvaux. Clairvaux soon became a model of strict observance, and Bernard averred that—for all practical purposes—there was no salvation outside Clairvaux. Convinced of the superiority of the Cistercian life for the practice of Christian perfection, Bernard railed against the alleged disciplinary decadence of the Cluniacs who observed a modified version of the Rule of St. Benedict. (He also eschewed the incipient scholasticism of his day for its emphasis upon great subtlety in reasoning and its claims to be a "scientific" theology.) He attracted thousands to the cloistered, contemplative life, established 68 foundations, and had almost direct authority over 164 of the 350 houses that existed across the whole of Europe. Because of his charming and forceful personality, women hid their sons or their fiancées from Bernard for fear of losing them to the monastic life.

Autobiographical descriptions of mystical experiences of God's presence from the mystics looked at thus far remain few and far between. Yet Bernard considers scripture—especially the Song of Songs—to be a "book of experience" whose meaning he expounds through his own personal experience. Because our monk author is always Bernard the preacher, he informs his listeners that only those experienced in the things of God can understand what he is saying. "If you are holy," he writes, "you have understood and known. If not, be holy and you will know by experience."[2] On the other hand, all personal experience—because it can deceive—must be measured against the Church's objective faith. Bernard grounds his spirituality and mysticism solidly in Church truths.

Sermon 74 can be read as one of the most stunning attempts in the entire Christian mystical tradition to describe mystical experience. Bernard confesses that the Word came to him "many times." Although the Word cannot be perceived by the senses, he invades the heart, suddenly animating the person's deepest center. What was cold is warmed; what was hard, now softened; what was parched, now slaked. When the Word leaves, it is like a boiling pot removed from the stove. The Life of the soul's life seems to have disappeared, but it leaves behind both burning desire and awareness of the soul's most secret faults.

Bernard is perhaps the first in the Christian tradition to emphasize carnal love of Jesus Christ who is lovable on the basic level of human attraction. Carnal love of Christ remains the starting point of Bernard's spiritual and mystical life. Loving him carnally leads to spiritual love of his divinity. "He became incarnate," writes Bernard, "for the sake of carnal men, that he might induce them to relish the life of the Spirit. In the body and through the body he performed works of which not man but God was the author."[3] Through Jesus Christ, anthropomorphic God language becomes literally true.

Christ is the Father's perfect image. We were made in this image but damaged it through sin. Because God has no body and because through sin we are a slave to the body, salvation can occur only through the body of the God-man. Bernard taught that in creating us, Christ gave us ourselves; when he gave himself in his passion and death, he gave us back to ourselves. And, salvation, for our monk, is nothing less than union with God, partially and imperfectly here, more nearly full after death, and full and perfect after the resurrection.

Thus, Bernard's spirituality and mysticism are profoundly Christocentric. As he says, "Write what you will, I shall not relish it unless it tells of Jesus. Talk or argue about what you will, I shall not relish it if you exclude the name of Jesus. Jesus is to me honey in the mouth, music in the ear, a song in the heart."[4] For Bernard, it is essential to "remember" Christ in order to "imitate" him. By praying the mysteries of the life, death, and resurrection, Bernard desires that the "affections for our Lord Jesus should be both tender and intimate, to oppose the sweet enticements of sensual life."[5]

For Bernard, the invisible God assumed flesh because God desired to recapture the affections of "carnal men" who were unable to love in any other way, by first drawing them to the salutary love of his own humanity, and then gradually to raise them to a spiritual love. Thus, he urged praying with a "sacred-image of the God-man." Bernard writes even more emphatically: "I have said that wisdom is to be found in meditating on these truths [Christ's life, death, and resurrection]. . . . This is my philosophy, one more refined and interior, to know Jesus and him crucified."[6]

Our monk's spirituality and mysticism are also ecclesial because one enters into "these truths" primarily through participation in the

Church and its yearly liturgy. Still, as profitable as meditations on Christ's humanity may be, Bernard viewed them as "imperfect," because they are tinged with "carnal love." The proficient in the spiritual life loves Christ with "rational" and "spiritual love."

Central to Bernard's theology is the notion that God is love. This is both all we need to know and only what we do know. Love created us out of love to share Love itself, and then redeemed us after we had sinned. God's gift of both the Incarnation and the Mother of God are proof of this. Moreover, the ultimate and culminating end of all theology, the summit of all God's works, is mystical experience.

Bernard's treatises indicate that *epektasis*, a graced straining toward God (Phil 3:13), is one of the most salient features of the Christian mystical tradition. One can never get enough of God or exhaust God's presence. Pure Love satisfies without surfeiting, even in the beatific vision. The role of unending yearning in different forms of satiating union reveals the deepest mystery of both theology and anthropology.

Bernard's eighty-six sermons allegorically interpret the Song of Songs and they summarize his mystical theology. Like Origen and Augustine, Bernard views the relationship between the divine Word and the individual soul as a spiritual marriage between the heavenly Bridegroom and the human bride. But unlike them, he grounds this marriage in the relationship between the divine Bridegroom and the Church. He fully developed the notion of spiritual marriage and introduced a new element in the Christian mystical tradition: preoccupation with understanding mystical union.

Commenting on the biblical words "Let him kiss me with the kiss of his mouth," Bernard draws an analogy between kissing Christ's feet, hand, and mouth and the purgative, illuminative, and unitive way. As he says, "these kisses were given to the feet, the hand and the mouth, in that order. The first is the sign of genuine conversion of life, the second is accorded to those making progress, the third is the experience of only a few of the more perfect."[7]

Thus, the remote preparation for the mystical kiss of the mouth is the asceticism required to obtain solid virtue. The proximate preparation—recollection and introversion—is profoundly affective. For Bernard, the soul's Bridegroom will reveal himself "only to the one who is proved to be a worthy bride by intense devotion, vehement desire and the sweetest affection. And the Word who comes to visit will be clothed in beauty, in every aspect a Bridegroom."[8] What the bride really desires and asks for is "to be filled with the grace of this threefold knowledge [of the Father, Son, and Holy Spirit], filled to the utmost capacity of mortal flesh. . . . Furthermore, this revelation, which is made through the Holy Spirit, not only conveys the light of knowledge but also lights the fire of love."[9]

In Sermon 41, Bernard gives the earliest account in the Christian tradition of the distinction between apophatic contemplation (in which both reason and the imagination play no part) and revelatory contemplation. In the latter, the purely spiritual experiences of God are translated into communicable images and language. With an eloquence unusual even for Bernard, he describes the role the angels play to produce in the imagination and mind the images, concepts, and language through which God's pure light can be comprehended and communicated to others. In this way the angels blended intellectual with "imaginative" visions.

Sermon 52 illustrates Bernard's conviction that contemplation is a foretaste of heaven and a mystical (bridal) sleep that vivifies the mystical senses. But he also views it as a type of ecstatic dying to the world and as an apophatic, imageless—therefore, "angelic"—contemplation of God. The supreme Godhead consummates its marriage to the errant soul. Richly sensuous, it is also intellectual because God is both love and truth. The illuminated intellect becomes rational, prudent, and wise. The will becomes forceful, powerful, and even violent because God is a violent lover loved violently by the bride. And in a statement that was to have great resonance in the later mystical tradition, Bernard writes, "If the soul knows this—or because it knows this—is it any wonder that this soul, this bride, boasts that that great majesty cares for her alone as though he had no others to care for."[10]

Bernard describes the dynamism of the soul's progress as a step-by-step process, yet one often punctuated by the soul's impatient, vehement love. In relation to the Word, the soul may have the attitude of a slave, then a mercenary, then a disciple, then a son, and finally a bride. To be sure, the bride is best for even a son may have his eye on an inheritance. The bride exemplifies pure, total, disinterested, even spiritually drunken (satiated with wine but never satisfied) love and may even love herself unselfishly because the Bridegroom loves her.

Sermons 83 and 85 describe spiritual marriage and spiritual fecundity. The Word actually takes the soul as his bride, and two become one in spirit, yet remain two. Spousal mysticism emphasizes a differentiated unity. In other words, love actually makes two one, but also enhances personal identity. Love makes the soul equal to God, God by participation, but not simply God. The soul is bound to the Word by "spiritual glue." Or, the soul in God may resemble a drop of water in a glass of wine or a red hot iron in a blazing fire wherein the substance remains but is transformed.

Because the Word fecundates the bride, she is both bride and mother. As mother she may bring souls to birth by preaching or may give birth to "spiritual insights" by meditation. In this latter kind of birth, the sweetness of the Word's truth enraptures her in ineffable ecstasies. The mother is happy with her children but the bride even happier in the Bridegroom's embrace. A mother finds her children dear but the bride finds more pleasure in the Bridegroom's kisses. To be sure, it is good to save souls, but intercourse with the Word brings far more pleasure—although it is brief intoxication and rarely experienced. "We learn from this," Bernard writes, "that only too often we must interrupt the sweet kisses to feed the needy with the milk of doctrine."[11] Although as bride the soul desires the Bridegroom's embrace, as mother she loves her children, that is, her neighbor.

# Hildegard of Bingen

## (1098–1179)

*"When I was 42 years and seven months old, Heaven was opened and
a fiery light of exceeding brilliance came and permeated my whole
brain, and inflamed my whole heart and my whole breast like a
warming flame, as the sun warms anything its rays touch. And
immediately I knew the meaning of the exposition of the Scriptures."*[1]

Hildegard of Bingen has been called the first great woman theologian
in Christian history. Not only was she the most significant woman
author and musical composer of the Middle Ages but she was also
an abbess, the founder of a monastery, a religious reformer, a natural
scientist, a seer, and a great mystic. Her prophetic and visionary
mysticism profoundly marked her age and earned her the epithets
Teutonic Prophetess and Sibyl of the Rhine.

Born in 1098 of a noble family in Bermersheim, near Alzey in
Rhein-Hessen, Hildegard began to have visions when she was only
five years old. When she reached the age of eight, her parents entrusted her to the care of Jutta of Spanheim, the Benedictine abbess
at the Disibodenberg monastery, where Hildegard eventually took
the habit. Upon Jutta's death, Hildegard became the abbess. Ten years
later, because of a revelation, she founded a monastery at Ruperts-
berg, near Bingen, as well as other daughter houses.

Hildegard composed seventy-seven songs, *Symphonia armonie ce-
lestium revelationum* (*Harmonious Symphonies of Heavenly Revelations*),
which were gathered for a liturgical cycle. Although these subtle, unusual songs show a dependence upon Gregorian chant, they are musi-
cally unique. Only someone of powerful voice and a God-filled heart
can do them justice. Hildegard was convinced that heavenly music
embraces the human spirit and causes in it a resounding symphony.

81

To her, therefore, the source, meaning, sense, and task of liturgical music is to restore the heavenly voice with which Adam praised God before he fell into sin.

Hildegard wrote a mystical treatise with a Jeremianic tone, the *Liber vitae meritorum* (*The Book of the Meritorious Life*). It contains apocalyptic denunciations of the evil in the temporal and spiritual realms, as well as chiliastic and prophetic themes. Another mystical treatise, the *Liber divinorum operum simplicis hominis* or *De operatione dei* (*On God's Work*), is a penetrating cosmology with theodicy that emphasizes the eventual victory of good over evil. She also wrote an *Explication of the Rule of St. Benedict*; *Lives of St. Rupert and St. Disibode*; *Exposition on the Gospels*; books on pharmacology, medicine, and natural history; numerous allegorical homilies, a morality play, and two other esoteric works. For diversion, she authored the fascinating *Lingua ignota*, a book about a secret language of eight hundred words and a twenty-five-letter alphabet.

Her letters to popes, cardinals, bishops, abbots, kings, emperors, nuns, monks, and people from all walks of life illustrate how deeply she was involved in the great political, ecclesiastical, intellectual, and religious currents of her times. This was a period of great spiritual awakening, of heightened sensitivity to the corruption in both church and state, and of immense longing for a richer spiritual life.

Because of Emperor Frederick I's ("Barbarossa") "obstinacy" in promoting schism by setting up the three "emperor popes," Hildegard actually threatened him with a (spiritual?) sword. When an episcopal interdict endangered the well-being of her monastery, she held fast because of a divine revelation, and the matter was eventually resolved in her favor. Seriously ill and incapacitated during her last years of life, Hildegard still insisted on being carried from place to place to continue exhorting, preaching to, encouraging, warning, and urging people to heed the divine word imparted to her.

Hildegard is an exceptional example of the "bridal mystics" and "visionary-prophetic mystics" who graced the German Benedictine and Cistercian convents during the twelfth and thirteenth centuries. These women of exceptional wisdom and practical charity experienced themselves as the spouses of either divine Wisdom and/or Jesus Christ, but also spoke of the "embrace of God's maternal love." Their writings often raise the issue of the role of visions in the mystical life. Visionaries need not be mystics nor mystics visionaries, but this Bingen nun was both. On the other hand, unlike other mystical authors, she spent no time explaining how believers may attain or are affected by the direct consciousness of God.

Hildegard received mystical ecstasies, captivating visions, and prophecies. The basic element of her visions is the symbol, that is, a *reality* that actually contains what is symbolized and is different from it. She also used primordial words, or words that defy definition because they express reality itself, contain reality's mysteries within them, and must be experienced before they can be used and explained. Her spousal union with God occurred not only at the core of her soul but also in and through dramatic visions and inner words (locutions) that commanded her in God's name to encourage and admonish others. For this reason, Hildegard's bridal, visionary, and prophetic mysticism flowered into intense apostolic service that actively fought the moral and religious laxity, the many social injustices, and the numerous heretical movements of her day.

Her masterpiece is the *Scivias* ("Know the ways [of the Lord]"), a book read by Pope Eugene III and several bishops. This work is a collection of twenty-six visions treating of the relationship between God, the cosmos, the human person, and major theological themes. During the inaugural vision, a fiery light embraced her brain, heart, and breast—empowering her to apply her visionary experiences to the task of interpreting scripture.

In fact, Hildegard experienced a double light: God's light as it shines in the human heart ("the living light") and the "shadow of the living light" that bathes all creation. This light enabled her to grasp the sacramental transparency not only of the scriptures but also of all creation—and how Christianity's central truths are inextricably linked to the inner trinitarian life. She saw all things in God and God in all things. Through genuine symbols—not fabricated images—she beheld and perceived the architectonic unity-in-difference that exists between the triune Unity and all creatures.

Hildegard maintained that she saw visions not "in dreams, or sleep, or delirium, or by the eyes of the body, or by the ears of the outer self, or in hidden places; but I received them while awake and seeing with a pure mind and the eyes and ears of the inner self, in open places, as God willed it."[2] The purity of the divine light and the crystal clarity of these God-given visions so vivified her spiritual senses that she was able to express her experiences and visions of

God in melody, tone, word, and symbol with biblical soundness, theological profundity, and artistic mastery.

One example of this is presented in her striking second vision: "Then I saw a bright light, and in this light the figure of a man the color of a sapphire, which was all blazing with a gentle glowing fire. And that bright light bathed the whole of the glowing fire, and the glowing fire bathed the bright light; and the bright light and the glowing fire poured over the whole human figure, so that the three were one light in one power of potential."[3] The light symbolizes the Father; "the figure of a man," the Son; and the fire, the Holy Spirit.

Hildegard lived and practiced what she had heard from the triune Unity: "But let the one who sees with watchful eyes and hears with attentive ears welcome with a kiss My mystical words, which proceed from Me Who am life."[4]

# Aelred of Rievaulx

## (ca. 1110–67)

*"But still what is true of charity, I surely do not hesitate to grant to friendship, since 'he who abides in friendship, abides in God and God in him.'"*[1]

One of three sons, Aelred was born around 1110 shortly after his father Eliaf, the last of the hereditary priests of the Northumbria region, moved from Durham to Hexham. As recipient of the tradition of learning in his noble family, he spent much of his youth in the court of the half-English king Daniel I. Because of his intelligence and winning personality, he became popular and successful in court. But worldly success was not enough for him. While on an official journey, Aelred experienced a traumatic crisis of conscience, and decided to become a Cistercian monk.

This was the Golden Age of Cistercian monasticism. In less than a century, more than five hundred Cistercian monasteries had sprung up in Europe. These great monks were "pioneers," clearers of forests, drainers of swamps, reclaimers of land, and excellent farmers. But they were also great intellectuals whose unprecedented spirituality shifted the emphasis away from the stern Lord to a warm, personal love of the person of Jesus Christ.

Because of Aelred's personal charm, shrewd intellect, oratorical eloquence, and literary gifts, this contemporary of the great Bernard of Clairvaux was soon to be known as the "Bernard of the North." From a relatively early age, he had also attained a reputation for holiness and wisdom and was highly praised for his "fatherly love." As abbot of the monastery at Rievaulx, he led a life of tireless activity, even during his last years when he was chronically ill. In the period of anarchy following the death of Henry I, Aelred was entrusted with important matters of state.

His Cistercian training added the love of Scripture to his love of the secular classics. The Rule of Saint Benedict and the patristic tradition—especially Augustine's *Confessions*—also became his patrimony. As one of the greatest writers of medieval England, he wrote numerous influential sermons, a meditation on Jesus' boyhood ("the wonderful sweetness of holy history"), a letter on Christian asceticism, and his two classics, *The Mirror of Charity* and *On Spiritual Friendship*.

Typical Cistercian emphases are found in Aelred's writings: 1) the human person is made in the image of the Trinity, an image damaged by sin, but restored through Christ; 2) Christians must live the mysteries of Christ's life, death, and resurrection; 3) affectivity and Christ's humanity must play a dominant role in Christian spirituality; 4) Christ communicates himself to the person by way of his Church; 5) Mary's mediation in the salvific process is necessary; 6) asceticism is a preparation for the "Lord's visitations" in the heart; 7) the crown of charity is contemplation through which the soul enjoys "Sabbath" rest, which is the mutual delight of the Father and the Son.

Aelred viewed original sin as a powerful interior force for self-seeking that causes the person to lose both one's true self and God. By "fainting away from self in charity," the person is lifted up to God, for whom he was created. Through contemplation, in his view, one attains a goal rarely achieved elsewhere: the Sabbath rest of God in the soul. God's stillness silences the soul's faculties, puts an end to preoccupation with self and others, and teaches the heart and intellect the mysteries of the inner-trinitarian life. In Sabbath rest one experiences the tranquility of order that God as love and friendship ordained for the universe.

Our monk differed from his Cistercian brethren, however, on two key points. First, Aelred emphasized the cosmic role of love suffused throughout the universe that unites all things. Second, he underscored affection and friendship as central to the person's return to God. To this monk, if God is love, then he is certainly friendship and he who abides in friendship abides in God and God in him. Moreover, he considered the friendless person to be a "beast."

Affection, as the spontaneous and sweet inclination of the person toward someone, roots all love. Reason—the spirit's ability to discern good from evil and to decide what should be accepted or rejected—forms love's second root. Reason must often compel choice when affection is lacking, especially in the case of loving one's enemies. In line with the Cistercian tradition, Aelred teaches an "ordered love" that is not only attracted to the good but also discerns and decides for it with fortitude.

From an early age, Aelred intensely desired affection, love, and friendship—but confessed that in his youthful search for true friendship he was "often deceived by its mere semblance." Christ's light illuminated his eyes—"once dimmed by carnal darkness"—to comprehend that only God could grace a person through Christ with the highest form of love: genuine friendship. Friendship seeks only friendship, which is its own reward, "a reward friendship will certainly be for those cultivating it, when, wholly translated to God, it immerses in the divine contemplation those whom it has united."[2] Not only is friendship filled with wisdom but our monk also avers that one "might almost say friendship is nothing else but wisdom."[3]

Aelred spoke from his own personal experience of deep friendships. For example, when his most beloved friend Simon died, Aelred wrote, "My soul wishes to be together with his, a part of his own, in enjoying Christ's embraces, but my infirmity resists . . . ."[4] Another incident occasioned one of the most unusual mystical experiences in the tradition: "The day before yesterday, as I was walking the round of the cloister of the monastery, the brethren were sitting around forming as it were a most loving crown. . . . In that multitude of brethren I found no one whom I did not love, and no one by whom, I felt sure, I was not loved. I was filled with such joy that it surpassed all the delights of this world. I felt, indeed, my spirit transfused into all and the affection of all to have passed into me, so that I could say with the Prophet: 'Behold, how good and how pleasant it is for brethren to dwell together in unity.'"[5] Striking, too, is Aelred's view of Adam and Eve as "friends."

Aelred's deep friendship with Jesus Christ grounds his view of Christian friendship. "Nothing which had not been sweetened by the honey of the most sweet name of Jesus," he writes, "drew my affection so entirely to itself."[6] Genuine friendship begins from, progresses through, and is perfected in Christ. True friendship always involves not only an affectionate I-Thou relationship but also and always Christ as the one binding the two together. The eyes of our hearts must be used to extend our affections to the sweetness of Jesus' flesh because carnal love of Christ is always needed in this life. By loving the fleshy Christ one already loves God. We must embrace

Christ's cross, drink his blood, and allow ourselves to be fed in the Eucharist by Jesus our mother. Aelred combined contemplation of the mysteries of Christ's life, death, and resurrection with access to the so-called higher states of mystical consciousness.

Aelred understood friendship, therefore, as both the model of and the way to the direct experience of God and allowed his monks to use signs of affection that sometimes raised the eyebrows of his fellow abbots. His unique contribution consists in employing friendship's chaste erotic energy as a source of mystical experience of God. To some extent, he grafted the erotic language of the Song of Songs onto the vine of spiritual friendship. Unlike his forebears, Aelred does not emphasize the necessity of passing from carnal to spiritual friendship. Because God reveals himself in and through human forms of mutual attraction, spiritual love may at times transcend all human love but it still always subsumes it. Flesh, especially Christ's, is always needed on the way to God.

# Richard of St. Victor

## (d. 1173)

*"But if nothing is more present than the most absent One, if nothing is more absent than the most present One, is anything more marvelous, anything more incomprehensible?"*[1]

The twelfth-century spiritual giant Richard of St. Victor was a gifted preacher, spiritual director, theologian, and contemplative whose writings have had immense influence throughout the ages. Dante praised him for his superhuman contemplative ability. Saint Bonaventure considered him to be not only *the* "modern" master of contemplation but also the equal of the early Fathers of the Church. To this day, this Victorine is appreciated for both his mystical genius and theological sophistication, especially in regard to explaining the nature of contemplation and love.

Little is known of Richard's early life except that he may have been born in Scotland. At a young age, he entered the abbey of St. Victor, located on the Seine's left bank at the outskirts of the university city of Paris. The abbey followed the rule of St. Augustine and enjoyed great esteem for its disciplined community life, which was dedicated to contemplation and to rigorous study of the Bible and the Fathers of the Church. The monks of the abbey were also known for their exceptionally beautiful liturgies. Because of St. Victor's proximity and openness to the theological schools of Paris, it participated in and contributed to that age's "new" theology, that is, scholasticism, a form of philosophical and theological inquiry based upon formal and exceptionally rigorous methods of reasoning. Thus, the monks were well known for their theological sophistication.

Richard was a faithful disciple of Hugh of St. Victor, whom he judged to be "the best theologian of our time." Hugh imparted to Richard an exceptional skill in the theological methods of the day.

However, differing somewhat from Hugh's more "scientific" approach, Richard emphasizes that truth is reached by meditation and contemplation, not by rational induction. Only contemplation can ultimately penetrate God's material and spiritual creation, as well as the mystery of the divine essence and Trinity. With love as its driving force, contemplation is satisfied by nothing less than the vision of God.

Richard blends the monastic desire to "believe in order to experience" with the more scholastic goal to "believe in order to understand." Despite his emphasis on contemplative wisdom as the highest form of learning, he still seeks through an interior questioning of faith's intelligibility the "necessary reasons" for the truths of the faith. Embracing all forms of human disciplines, Richard insists on learning everything because he contends that there is nothing superfluous in the quest for God. The integration of all knowledge in the service of divine wisdom leading to mystical experience defines his goal. One finds with Richard a new emphasis on the Bible's literal sense and he chides those who allegedly discover a hidden, mystical sense—when, in fact, there is none.

Richard's deeply contemplative attitude toward theology contrasts sharply with the rationalistic emphases of both Abelard and Peter the Lombard. But as the disciple of Hugh of St. Victor, he gives rational dialectics a greater role in the theological enterprise than either William of St. Thierry or St. Bernard. Both William and Bernard seemingly confused knowledge and love. Richard's subtle, original mind grasps that love is born of knowledge and that speculation must come before contemplation.

For example, although Richard considers the Trinity to be the supreme object of contemplation and a reality "above and beyond" reason, he does not hesitate to wrestle with the "necessary reasons" for the Trinity's existence. His penetrating theological treatise on the Trinity cogently argues that God, as perfect love, cannot remain in himself but must go out to another person of equal dignity and worth. In Richard's view, the second Divine Person "proceeds" from love. Furthermore, perfect love demands a third person to whom the first two can communicate the delights of their love, or who can be the object of their common love. Since perfect love must be given, received, and shared in community—God, as perfectly one in essence—must give, receive, and share this love in a trinity of persons. And because the Trinity is the divine community of love and contemplation's supreme object, love must be the contemplative's all and truth.

Richard specializes and excels in mystical theology, and as such he created an almost complete, systematic assimilation of the entire monastic tradition. His two masterpieces, *The Twelve Patriarchs* (also known as *Benjamin Minor*) and *The Mystical Ark* (also known as *Benjamin Major*), evince a subtle mind, a psychological perception, and a skillful analysis of the soul's faculties. To his way of thinking, the human spirit is the foremost and principle mirror in which one sees God. Moreover, Richard directs his psychological and theological profundity toward a thoroughly practical goal: the instruction of others in the ascetical-mystical ascent to God.

The Sacred Page nourishes Richard's thought. For him, the scriptures contain the patterns of the interior life. Symbolically, they embody the journey from ascetical purification to self-knowledge and culminate in the contemplative awareness of God's deepest mysteries. The scriptures reveal their spiritual sense to Richard not only in and through their words but also, and especially, in biblical persons and events, which he uses to express and relate various spiritual states.

For example, when a person attains a particular state, he or she becomes a particular biblical person. Moses symbolizes the effortless contemplative empowered by grace alone; Bezaleel, the one who combines grace and effort; Aaron, who is instructed by others. Richard focuses primarily on the patriarch Jacob and his children but also upon the Song of Songs and Jesus' transfiguration. He prefers the mystical and tropological (figurative) interpretations of scripture, but bases these solidly upon the scriptures' literal meaning. He also takes great care that his allegories are consistent with the analogy of faith, that is, the Church's overall faith.

His *Twelve Patriarchs*, subtitled *On the Soul's Preparation for Contemplation*, begins with the line "Benjamin a young man in ecstasy of mind" (Ps 67:28, Vulgate) and tropologically interprets the patriarch, Jacob, and his children as representing successive stages of awareness. Reason, symbolized by Rachel, must give birth to discretion, symbolized by Joseph. When Benjamin—who symbolizes ecstatic contemplation—is born, Rachel dies, for contemplation transcends reason. Mystical ascent, in Richard's view, demands an exacting interior asceticism, the acquisition of virtue and moderation, and a redirection of one's affections, mind, and will toward God in order to attain peace and quiet in mind and body. Discipline of the imagination and mind is even more important than bodily penance.

*The Mystical Ark* is aptly subtitled *On the Grace of Contemplation*, and it tropologically interprets the ark of the covenant. This work brilliantly analyzes the different kinds of contemplation, the objects of contemplation, and the human-divine means required for attaining contemplative states—especially those of grace, liturgy, and psalmody. To Richard, contemplation "is the free, more penetrating gaze of the mind, suspended with wonder concerning the manifestations of wisdom."[2] It is also "a penetrating and free gaze of the soul extended everywhere in perceiving things."[3] Contemplatives must focus on material creatures, discover the divine reason for their existence, ponder both the spiritual soul and the angelic realm, and transcend to the divine nature and the Trinity. Contemplation, in Richard's view, enlarges the mind, raises it up, and finally "alienates" it in ecstatic love.

Although Richard is a link between the great mystical awakening in medieval Europe and renewed interest in Pseudo-Dionysius, his mysticism is decidedly affirmative (kataphatic). Mystical ascent proceeds by way of a love that desires to know ever more deeply. Richard writes in the *Twelve Patriarchs* that "where there is love, there is seeing"[4] and that love drives the person to know. Yet, unlike those in the mystical tradition who assign a priority either to love or to knowledge, Richard deftly shows their reciprocal relationship.

Although Richard teaches that reason dies in mystical ecstasy, he underscores that one must always return to reason after the experience. Nonetheless, a Dionysian, negative (apophatic) redolence does permeate his works. As he says, "although we may retain in memory something from that [ecstatic] experience and see it through a veil, as it were, and as though in the middle of a cloud, we lack the ability to comprehend or call to mind either the manner of seeing or the quality of the vision. And marvelously, in a way remembering, we do not remember; and not remembering, we remember; while seeing we do not discern; looking at, we do not examine; and as we direct our attention to something, we do not penetrate it."[5]

To our Victorine, love not only wounds and chains a person but also reduces that person to a singular and insatiable desire for the beloved. Richard then transposes his analysis to a love that thirsts for God, then thirsts to go to God, then thirsts to be in God, and finally thirsts in the way God thirsts. This *epektasis* thirst cannot be quenched by anything. It enkindles the affections, attracts the contemplative into himself or herself, purges all disorder, and unifies the person. God's love calls the soul into, above, and beyond itself into ecstatic dissolution through which it melts into God's own life, forgets everything—including itself—for God's sake, and submits to its divine remolding into the image of the humble Christ.

Richard also stresses liberating, divine visitations in which God is felt as a burning fire but is not seen. Eventually, the contemplative sees the inaccessible, divine light but cannot reach it. However, the divine light binds the soul and empties the imagination, memory, and mind of everything except God. The divine light causes the contemplative to swoon in delight and to melt into God's life to become God by participation. Yet, by dying in God, the contemplative is raised in Christ and rendered spiritually fertile in a perfect charity willing to lay down his or her life for others. Thus, for Richard, contemplation results not only in an ever-deepening penetration of the mysteries of creation and the Trinity, not only in divine revelations and transforming union with God, but also in Christ's perfect charity that transforms human community through the humble service of others.

# Guigo II

## (d. 1188)

*"One day when I was busy working with my hands I began to think about our spiritual work, and all at once four stages in spiritual exercises came into my mind: reading, meditation, prayer, and contemplation. These make a ladder for monks by which they are lifted up from earth to heaven. It has few rungs, yet its length is immense and wonderful, for its lower end rests upon the earth, but its top pierces the clouds and touches heavenly secrets."*[1]

Guigo II, surnamed "the angelic," deserves to be praised as one of the many remarkable monks of the twelfth century. The writings of this ninth prior of La Grande-Chartreuse and superior general of the Carthusian Order faithfully reflect the medieval Western monastic mystical tradition, as found in Augustine, Anselm, Bernard, and Bonaventure. Attracted to the biblical imagery found in the books of Exodus and the Song of Songs, Guigo often depicted the soul as a chaste virgin who will know no husband save Christ.

His most famous work, *Ladder of Monks*, aptly subtitled *A Letter on the Contemplative Life*, may very well be the first sketch of methodical prayer given in the Western mystical tradition. It enjoyed immense popularity, perhaps because of the manner in which it gives reasons for and system to traditional spiritual practices. It speaks of prayer in terms of Jacob's dream (Gen 28:12) of a ladder, which is set on earth but reaches into the heavens. In describing prayer in terms of this ladder with discrete rungs, this work contrasts somewhat with the earlier monastic tradition that viewed prayer more in terms of the soul's disposition. Guigo views the soul as moving up and down the ladder, with the top rung providing brief access to the supreme degree of the immediate experience of God.

Guigo's treatise speaks of a four-rung ladder in the ascent to God. His method underscores his love of scripture and his approach to *lectio divina*. One must first read scripture, actively apply one's understanding (meditation) to the readings, and then lift up one's heart to God in fervent prayer. God may then reward the person with contemplation by awakening the mystical senses so that the soul can taste, smell, and perhaps even hear, touch, and see something of "God's glory." It is instructive that Guigo understands mystical consciousness as the climax of an entire program that he calls "a person's spiritual exercises." In contrast to what "human learning" brings, "the Spirit of wisdom alone grants true wisdom, that sweet tasting knowledge that rejoices and refreshes the soul in which it dwells with the sweetness beyond telling."[2]

Our monk speaks of the first rung as suitable for beginners; the second, for proficients; the third, for devotees; the fourth, for the blessed. The four rungs are all linked. The first degrees are of little or no use without the last and the last is hardly, if ever, given without the first three. If the movement from reading, meditation, and prayer culminates in the "sweetness of contemplation" and spiritual inebriation, this is wholly God's gift. During this process, Guigo hopes that the person will also experience the gift of tears, a gift valued right from the beginnings of the Christian mystical tradition.

Guigo compares these four stages to the eating of a grape. One plops the grape in one's mouth, mouths and enjoys its texture, then slowly chews, delighted by both the resulting taste and smell. He also speaks of this process as breaking the bread of scripture, for Jesus revealed himself to the Emmaus disciples in the breaking of the bread.

The "desire for greater sweetness of knowledge and experience" prompts the monk to prayer. However, the Lord does not wait for him to finish but breaks into the middle of prayer. Spiritually drunk, the monk forgets all worldly things. If conjugal relations climax in making a person almost wholly flesh, contemplation makes the monk almost wholly spiritual. "And the more the monk sees and loves God," Guigo writes, "the more he sees and loves himself."[3]

Contemplative wisdom is strictly God's gift, and a gift that transforms a person from being "carnal" to being "spiritual." This reforms the soul as it once was, the image of God. All affectivity is reordered into a loving desire for face-to-face vision of God. But this gift is given only to the pure of heart who have prepared themselves in solitude, silence, and humility in order to experience God's presence in the heart. Because such exalted experiences of God may puff the person up, the Beloved withdraws to teach humility, that such gifts are totally beyond the reach of human nature.

Although not as popular as the *Ladder*, his *Twelve Meditations* reflects the same Carthusian spirit: a humane asceticism tinged with anti-intellectualism, deep love of Jesus Christ, an appeal to the book of experience, and an ardent desire for mystical union with God. These meditations also emphasize the necessity of a silent, solitary life for hearing God's whispers.

This work exhorts the monk to pray to Jesus as a friend and to embrace three crosses. By mortifying the flesh, the monk accepts the first cross. Fear and awe of God constitute the second cross. One experiences the third cross, the cross of the spirit, through the love that nailed Jesus to the cross, a love that "gives us a heart of flesh, a soft and tender heart."[4] Only if one sacramentally and spiritually eats Christ's body and drinks his blood can one love Christ. And only those who love Christ imitate and follow him. In so doing, the monk passes through the cloud between himself and God and prays in God's presence as Moses passed through the cloud and encountered the burning bush. "Sabbath rest" is attained here.

Legend has it that after Guigo's death, the new prior went to his grave and commanded him to stop performing so many miracles. This attests to the reverence and esteem in which he must have been held.

# Francis of Assisi

## (1182–1226)

*"My Lord, Jesus Christ, I pray you to grant me two graces before I die: the first is that during my life I may feel in my soul and in my body, as much as possible, that pain which you, dear Jesus, sustained in the hour of your most bitter Passion. The second is that I may feel in my heart, as much as possible, that excessive love with which you, O Son of God, were inflamed in willingly enduring such suffering for us sinners."*[1]

The great disparity between Francis of Assisi's own writings and that of later hagiography makes it extremely difficult to present an accurate portrait of the saint. For example, although Francis considered himself neither a mystic nor a theologian, hagiography has focused on him as the ecstatic contemplative, as the mystic par excellence, and the stigmatic—his reward for his unflinching embrace of the crucified Christ. Dante spoke of his stigmata as the "final seal" of his following of Christ. His spiritual and physical likeness to Christ is the reason why all later Franciscan spirituality and mysticism finds Christ in and through Francis.

Hagiography also underscores the numerous daytime and dream visions of Christ that punctuated his life. Drunk with divine love and filled with Christ's prophetic Spirit, he strove without compromise to imitate Christ literally. His focus on every event of Christ's life brought forth what has been designated as "the mysticism of the historical event" (Ewert Cousins). The *Poverello* ("Little Poor Man") has been called "another Christ," and may very well be the most popular saint in history—revered by Christians and non-Christians alike.

Francesco Bernadone was born in Assisi in central Italy of a wealthy middle-class merchant family. He received the normal education of his times, but also learned Latin and French. The ideals of medieval chivalry, as expressed in the songs of troubadours, appealed to him because he wished to find glory in being a knight selflessly devoted to high ideals, loyal to his lord, courteous to all, and compassionate with the poor and the weak. Undoubtedly his fun-loving, gentle, generous, and somewhat playboy nature accounted for his popularity with his peers.

After spending a year as a prisoner of war after the battle between Assisi and Perugia and undergoing a serious illness, he headed for Rome to fight for the pope. However, because of a revelation received at Spoleto, he returned to Assisi, where Christ spoke and urged him to seek out the company of lepers. He withdrew from society and devoted himself to penance and to the service of outcasts. While praying before the crucified Christ in the half-ruined church of San Damiano, he heard the words "Francis, don't you see that my house is in ruins? Go then and repair it for me," to which he replied, "I'll gladly do it."

Francis's father dragged him before the town officials of Assisi because his son had lavishly spent his money on the poor. Before a large crowd, his father, and Bishop Guido, Francis handed over what money he had to his father and stripped himself naked. Bishop Guido covered him with his own mantle to express the Church's protection and approval of his new life.

After a period of eremitical living, Francis abandoned the hermit's garb for a wretched tunic and cord to fulfill his call to apostolic poverty, to preaching, and to service to the Church. Because of his great devotion to the Eucharist—he claimed he saw nothing corporeal of the God-Man in the world except Christ's most sacred Body and Blood—he greatly reverenced the clergy and served them.

He quickly attracted followers and journeyed to Rome with twelve of his disciples, where Pope Innocent III verbally approved Francis's proto-rule based on Matthew 10:5-14 for a new religious order. Wishing to reactivate the Church's missionary spirit, he undertook several unsuccessful journeys to preach to the Muslims in Spain and North Africa. Francis also risked his life to preach to the sultan in the Holy Land.

Ridden with malaria and suffering from glaucoma, he returned to Italy in 1220, only to undergo great spiritual trials. Interiorly, he experienced a sword-like pain that often stabbed his heart throughout the day. Exteriorly, as his order grew, he experienced the tensions between those attracted to the literal and deliberate imitation of Christ poor and suffering and those attracted to a more conventual life for the sake of an intellectual and missionary apostolate. His strong personality kept the legally unstable order together during his lifetime, but the Franciscan "Spiritual" and "Conventual" controversy was soon to erupt.

Francis's powerful evangelical life also attracted women. Clare of Assisi—whom Francis called "the Christian"—was the first female convert to his understanding of the evangelical way of life. Despite his appreciation for Clare and her companions, he did not want women as part of the structure of his "fraternity." He is supposed to have said, "God has taken away our wives, and now the devil gives us sisters."[2] So Clare founded her own order, the Poor Clares. She was the first woman in Christian history to write her own rules for religious life and to have them approved.

In September 1224 on Mount Alvernia during a long period of fasting, Francis prayed to experience both the pain of Christ's passion and Christ's "excessive love" of sinners. Through a vision of a seraph angel with six magnificent wings who bore the likeness of a crucified man, Francis received the wounds of the crucified Christ not only in spirit but also on his body.

This "martyrdom of love" substituted for actual martyrdom. During this period, Francis received revelations that he never disclosed to anyone. He also experienced himself as married to Christ, a brother of Christ, and a mother of Christ by giving birth to Christ in his soul and in the souls of others. And just as Christ had descended into limbo to lead souls to paradise, Francis was promised that he, too, on his yearly feast day would so descend.

During two more years of increasingly painful illness, Francis composed his classic hymn *Canticle of Brother Sun*, in which he counsels praising the "Most High Almighty Good Lord" with and through all creatures—especially "Sir Brother Sun," "Sister Moon and the Stars," "Brother Wind and for the air," "Sister Water," "Brother Fire," "Sister Mother Earth," and even "Sister Bodily Death."

Through his persistent meditation of the nature of things (analogous to the "natural contemplation" of the Desert Fathers), Francis experienced the mutual interconnection of all creation, the world as a single theophany of God. His Christian nature mysticism appreciated that God can be experienced in all things. On the other hand, his famous paean recognizes that only God can render true praise to

God. One should also note the apophatic redolence in the hymn, "no man is worthy to mention You" and Francis's praise for "Sister Bodily Death"—which is often forgotten by those who overly romanticize this hymn.

While dying, Francis asked that he be stripped naked and placed on the naked earth. Thus were Job's famous words relived: "Naked I came from my mother's womb, and naked shall I return." The *Poverello* was canonized by Pope Gregory IX on July 16, 1228.

# Giles of Assisi

## (ca. 1190–1262)

*"I know a man who saw God so clearly that he lost all faith."*[1]


One of the prominent figures among the large number of early Franciscan ecstatic contemplatives, Giles (also called Aegidius) was born of a peasant family in Assisi, became one of Francis's early companions, and accompanied him to Rome for Pope Innocent III's approval of the new religious order's proto-rule. After an aborted missionary journey to Tunis, he spent most of his life at remote hermitages in manual labor and in contemplation. Appreciated as a preacher, missionary, pilgrim, and contemplative, he acquired such a reputation for sanctity that he is the only one among Francis's companions to have his own sayings and hagiographical tradition—with three different lives and four surviving collections of *Sayings* attributed to him.

Famous for frequent and prolonged mystical ecstasies, Giles was praised by Francis for his contemplative spirit. Hagiography has it that whenever he was recognized by town children, they would send him into ecstasy by shouting, "Paradise, Paradise." This man of mystical prayer also became well known for his discerning spiritual advice, with even Bonaventure and Pope Gregory visiting him for the benefit of their interior lives. That an unlearned, simple person received such adulation is a testimony to his great holiness.

Giles claimed that St. Francis appeared to him in a dream and commanded him to examine himself carefully. During his many mystical ecstasies—some lasting for weeks—he felt as if his body were dying and the soul was being wrenched. These God-given states empowered him to contemplate the beauty of his own soul, to learn "divine secrets," and inspired him "to labor still more in the service of God." Mystically married to God, Giles became a parent of transcendental life for others. When asked if he desired martyrdom, he claimed that mystical death—that is, contemplation—was the better death.

Giles spoke of a seven-stage progression in the mystical ascent to God, a pattern employed by many after him. At first, God's fire and light bring enlightenment to the soul. The "unction of ointments" then permeates and raptures the soul. The contemplation of God heightens the sensitivity of the spiritual senses and draws the soul away from the bodily ones. The spirit now tastes the sweetness of the Lord, rests in it, and rejoices in the peace and joy of God's glory. Because of his experiences, Giles claimed that even the scriptures cannot speak adequately about God because God's works are one thing, but God himself something else entirely.

When King Louis of France visited Giles, neither of them said a word. In the "light of divine wisdom" and in the "eternal mirror," the king and he revealed their hearts to each other in mystical friendship. This mystical encounter is analogous to the famous mystical experience that Augustine and Monica had during their conversation at Ostia. It has parallels with Aelred of Rievaulx's experience of mystical friendship. Teresa of Avila and John of the Cross, Francis de Sales and Jane Frances de Chantal, and numerous others in the tradition also experienced the mystical power of friendship rooted in Christ.

Giles spoke of his four births: physical, baptismal, entrance into his religious order, and seeing God in some way—the latter being a pledge of eternal life. In a striking testament to the power of ecstatic consciousness, "Once [Giles] said, 'I know a man who saw God so clearly that he lost all faith.' Another time Brother Andreas said to him, 'You say that in a vision God took away your faith; tell me, if it pleases you, whether you have hope.' He answered, 'He who has no faith, how should he have hope?' . . . Then Brother Aegidius answered with a very joyous countenance and sang in a loud voice, 'I *know* one God, the Almighty Father.'"[2] However, most mystics and mystical theologians stress that even ecstatic mystical experiences cannot transcend faith and hope, which vanish only in the face-to-face vision of God after death.

Toward the end of his life, Giles became an outspoken critic of relaxation and intellectual pride among the Franciscans, a pride he blamed on their studies at the university of Paris. He not only opposed the building of the basilica in Assisi dedicated to Francis but he also disproved of what he judged to be the "excessive" cult rendered him. Beatified by Pope Pius VI in 1777, Giles is the only companion of Francis to have attained this honor.

# A Few Women of the New Mysticism

*"Daughter, from these wounds [of Christ] you absorb what preachers seek to express."*[1]

The thirteenth century ushered in what the renowned scholar Bernard McGinn calls the "new mysticism." Although in line with the earlier monastic mysticism, the new mysticism arose in part because of the dialogue between Latin and the vernacular, the "conversation" between men and women, and a new attitude toward cloister and the world.

This new mysticism often found expression in hagiographies and autohagiographies, in texts that frequently contain candid accounts of deep mystical friendships between a God-enlightened female and her clerical director, of "embodied" (a merging of corporeal, spiritual, and intellectual visions) accounts of both visionary and nonvisionary experiences, of prolonged and sometimes violent ecstasies, of excessive ascetical practices, of a passionate—and often highly erotic—love of God and Christ.

One also finds dizzying new forms of both kataphatic and apophatic language that speak about the madness of love, spiritual annihilation, and the mutual yearning of both the soul and God in a union of indistinct identity. Although orthodox in belief and practice, these mystics manifest a striking spiritual liberty. Because of the intensity of their experience of God, they often appear to be a law unto themselves. Although McGinn finds no themes restricted only to women, the suddenness and intensity of women's contribution to the new mysticism both surprises and mystifies him.

## Christina of St. Trond (1150–1224)

The many extant manuscripts concerning Christina of St. Trond—based on the learned Thomas of Cantimpré's book of her life—attest to her medieval popularity. Thomas wrote of her: "What else did Christina proclaim throughout her life, save to do penance and be prepared [for death] at every hour? With many words and tears and laments, with infinite cries, she taught this by the example of her life, she proclaimed it, more than anyone before or since that we have read or heard about."[2] Greatly devoted to the Eucharist, this exemplary "holy woman" (as such women were called in her day) enjoyed the spirit of prophecy. Manifold ecstasies, raptures, visions, and severe penance—such as radical fasting—filled her life. This "fool for Christ" manifested in her own life the sufferings that are experienced by the souls in purgatory.

Thomas also saw her as an ecstatic visionary possessing miraculous powers. Paradoxically, he presents her as already enjoying the risen life here. Early in life, she showed the same aversion to bodily existence as one finds in some mystics. Later, however, she spoke of the "miserable soul" and the "most beloved body." It was said that she discovered that she was able to enter blazing ovens, to jump into vats of boiling water, to fly like a bird, to scrunch up her body like a ball and roll around, to immerse herself for days in the wintry water of the river Meuse—all without suffering any bodily harm. Her breasts exuded purifying and healing oils. Is it any wonder that Thomas called her "Christina the Astonishing"?

## Clare of Assisi (1193–1253)

Clare of Assisi presents a far less dramatic form of the new mysticism. As the first female follower of Francis of Assisi, her interaction with him underscores one aspect of the new mysticism—a mysticism nourished by the spiritual friendship between a woman and her male spiritual director. "The Christian," as Francis called her, had a vision of Francis nourishing her from his own breast. The heavenly milk of "Mother Francis" was to fortify her in her determination to found a new religious order based on absolute poverty, manual work, and common life. She is perhaps the first to speak of finding Christ in and through Francis.

Our founder of the Poor Clares experienced herself as a mother, sister, and bride of Christ. Her spousal love of the poor and crucified Christ, however, was not expressed in the highly erotic tones characteristic of many mystics of her age. The image of Christ as mirror played a significant role in her spirituality and mysticism. One finds on the mirror's surface the virtues manifest in Christ's last few years, especially the ineffable love that flows from the cross. Visual meditation of this mirror should be followed by contemplation of it, which leads to transformative imitation of Christ. Then one becomes a mirror of Christ, which shines forth with public responsibility for the entire Church.

The bull of her canonization highlights the salient features of the new apostolic form of mysticism. Clare withdrew to deepen her humility, poverty, and charity, but she was not confined, as women were both before and after her. We read: "She [Clare] was kept inside, and remained outside. Clare was hidden, yet her way of life was open. Clare kept silent, but her fame cried out. She was concealed in a cell, but she was taught in the cities. It is no wonder that so bright and gleaming a light could not be hidden, but must shine forth and give clear light in the Lord's house."[3]

## Mary of Oignies (1176–1213)

Mary of Oignies is more representative of the unusual women of the new mysticism than Clare of Assisi. Born in Nivelles, France, of well-to-do parents, she received some education, and married at age fourteen. After a few years, she convinced her husband that they should live as brother and sister for the sake of a life of an evangelical apostolate to the lepers. She quickly attracted like-minded women.

This "little poor woman" (as she was called) lived her entire life for others. Such was her holiness that Mary taught and preached through her bearing. The divine authority she manifested attracted the gifted James of Vitry, who put himself under her direction and was later ordained priest. Crediting her for his reputation as a preacher, he maintained that he gave official voice to her living sermons.

One finds in his *Life of Mary of Oignies* the archetype of the Beguine way of life and the "new mysticism," which consisted of the ecstatic mystic given to urban and vernacular forms of apostolic labors. The Beguines were pious women who rejected both a woman's constricted life at court and the stricter obligations of the cloistered life. Like the primitive monastic tradition in which a spiritual father gathered disciples around him without ecclesiastical sanction, the early stages of the Beguine movement saw laywomen uniting in much the same way. Embracing a loose form of community life, apostolic poverty, contemplation, and recitation of the Hours, they also gave spiritual direction, and cared for the sick and the needy.

The crusades had some influence on the spirituality of the Beguines. Sharply focused on the mysteries of the humanity of Christ's life, especially his childhood and passion, this spirituality was also strongly eucharistic and Marian.

The name "Beguine" may be derived either from the name of Lambert le Bègue (d. 1177), a revivalist preacher at Liège, or from the gray cloth of their distinctive garb. Perhaps because of their threatening independence, holiness of life, good works—and, occasionally, eccentricities and unorthodox beliefs—the Beguines were frequently the object of clerical and lay criticism. Nonetheless, Pope Honorius III gave them full ecclesiastical authorization in 1216.

Because of Mary's reputation for holiness, working miracles, prophecies, and exorcisms, she purposely stayed away from crowds. When praying before the crucified Christ, she often experienced ecstatic states, which in some cases could last for weeks. When she went to confession, she would shout and cry like a woman in labor— thus she is a patron saint of women in labor.

That Mary cut off large pieces of her flesh says much about the excessive asceticism found in the new mysticism. Her ecstatic states were accompanied by the gift of tears. She was gifted not only with powerful visions of Jesus Christ—as depicted in the mysteries of his life, with visions of angels, devils, and saints—but also with an uncanny ability to discern God-given from diabolically induced visions. James attests that she lived for long periods of time solely on the eucharistic bread and manifested an intense and insatiable spiritual hunger and inebriation. Weeks before Mary's death, she expressed her joy through charismatic jubilation, that is, singing mystical doctrine concerning the psalms and gospels for days on end. It is claimed that only by doing violence to her body could she break free of ecstatic contemplation to serve others.

### Douceline of Digne (1214–74)

The Franciscan Felipa de Porcelet wrote an important hagiography of Douceline of Digne. As the work of a woman and in the vernacular, it speaks loudly of what one finds in the new mysticism. It was said of Douceline that she was a saint from birth who lived more like an angel than a woman. Her contemplation of Christ's sacred blood engendered long periods of rapture, accompanied by physical levitations. Felipa said that Douceline's severe asceticism went as far as plunging parts of her body into molten lead, often with no somatic consequences. Her charismatic jubilation took the form of singing songs of unknown words for hours. Deeply devoted to St. Francis and her love of poverty, Douceline also spent much time caring for the sick and involved herself in secular politics on their behalf. Christ once appeared and instructed her to found a Beguine convent because his mother Mary had been the first Beguine. In what may be her best-known vision, Christ appeared to her as a sick man and asked her to touch his breast. When she recoiled from this because of modesty, Christ told her not to be ashamed of him—the one who had not been ashamed to show her to his Father.

### Margaret the Cripple (1225–ca. 1265)

Whatever is known about Margaret the Cripple comes from the *Life* written by her friend and confessor, the Dominican John of Magdeburg. Born in that city of prosperous parents, Margaret was stricken with a crippling disease when just an infant. She suffered terribly not only from the crippling and the concomitant headaches but also from the contempt heaped upon her by relatives and friends. In her early teens she desired to devote herself to the service of the Lord in some lonely place but paradoxically feared losing the "scorn" of others. In fact, "scorn" seems to be the key to her mysticism. God had graced her with pain and contempt. She thus spoke of herself and her physical debility as a treasure God hid in a loathsome sack to keep it safe. Eventually Margaret became an anchorite in some unknown church in Magdeburg.

Margaret exemplifies the urban anchoress, that is, a woman who lived in a small, sealed room inside a church. She had visual access to the sanctuary and to Holy Communion. Usually there was also a small side window at which she could converse with visitors and receive foods and other provisions.

She is also a powerful example of what I have called suffering-servant, or "victim-soul" mysticism. It is the profound mystery of suffering with Christ crucified. Such mystics are not those who experience the cross as the setbacks encountered in great apostolic undertakings, but rather the ones who manifest God's hand even in life's apparent absurdities: natural failings, physical defects, sickness, suffering, old age, and death. More important, they have also grasped the redemptive value of suffering, that is, how even hidden, sacrificial love is apostolic. The victim-soul mystic is the prime example of the person who allows God alone to determine who and what one is.

To Margaret, suffering is the instrument by which one can measure the love in a soul. The more she and others despised her, the closer she felt to God. Plunged into the abyss of humility and poverty, she came to realize the depths of her sinful nature and also her inability to love God as much as she was loved. However, she had also grasped the mystery of the cross, that suffering is redemptive, that Christ redeemed the world through his loneliness, isolation, and sufferings on the cross. By focusing on suffering, and not sweetness, as the way to God she indirectly criticized the fascination of her age with rapturous consolations. Anchoritic life, in Margaret's view, was nothing less than hanging on the cross with Christ.

Margaret was graced with brief periods of union with God. She worked no miracles, had no visions, and experienced no erotic union with Christ. However, God spoke powerfully to her heart and awakened her spiritual eyes to the meaning of the divine mysteries. She claimed that she would love God and strive for a perfect union of wills, even if God had willed her damnation. She experienced that God's and her heart were one, that the eye by which God saw her and the eye by which she saw God was one and the same.

The most fascinating aspect of Margaret's mysticism is her claim that Christ told her that she was specially chosen, just as the Virgin Mary was. "At the time when I willed to become man," Christ said, "I elected you beforehand in a special way in your mother's womb, [just as] the greatest thing that I have ever done for a person was that I chose a virgin mother. In the last time you are the now the greatest thing that has happened to a person in your time—this happens in you. . . . Except for me alone, no one has ever atoned for the world in his heart as you have."[4] She accepted her role as co-redeemer with Christ and averred that God so graces only those who have been annihilated, reduced to nothing.

## Christina Bruso of Stommeln (1242–1312)

Christina Bruso of Stommeln is the first woman stigmatic in recorded Christian history. She spent a good part of her life as a Beguine. The learned Dominican priest Peter of Dacia was her confessor, spiritual director, and close friend. He called her "his dearest" and his love letters—replete with effusive language—underscore the spiritual friendship that can exist between a talented priest and an uneducated woman. Peter claimed that if carnal love can make a man and a woman one, then spiritual love in Christ can make them even more deeply one.

Christ appeared to Christina when she was only ten years old. As with the many female ecstatics of her period, she experienced frequent ecstasies and periods of jubilation, that is, spontaneous spiritual song, throughout her life. Quite striking, however, are the diabolical torments from which she suffered. Peter testified that "from the ages it has never been heard that a person was so horribly and openly tortured by demons."[5] He claimed that he witnessed the devil inflicting cruel nail wounds upon her. The devil often pelted her and others with her with excrement. Ripped apart piece by piece by the devil during the night, the angels put her back together in the morning, it is claimed.

Many view Christina more as a martyr than as a mystic. This victim of diabolical torture manifested the reality of the punishments of hell, the sufferings of the damned, the necessity to repent of one's sins and to do penance. It is obvious why she is both venerated and vilified—and viewed with astonishment, amusement, and sometimes disgust. She provides perhaps the earliest example of the ambivalence that was to continue to plague such women—saint or witch? However, she was beatified in 1908.

## Agnes Blannbekin (ca. 1244–1315)

Agnes Blannbekin, of Viennese peasant stock, became a Beguine at an early age because of her desire to receive Holy Communion frequently, a devotion uncommon in her age. That her many visions and locutions (words from God and/or Christ) took place in a eucharistic setting, therefore, is not surprising. This farmer's daughter might be viewed as representative of medieval women's "street mysticism" in contrast with the better-known female mystics of the courtly tradition we shall see later on.

Little is known about Agnes except what is found in the account of her life by an anonymous Franciscan friar. She exemplifies the visionary mysticism dominant in her age. Her visions of the devil were only a nuisance and hardly terrifying. Her ecstatic visions brought in their wake feelings of extreme unworthiness. After being told in a vision not to fear, she experienced a delectable sweet heat rising from the depths of her being, which penetrated the very extremities of her body. Agnes's life gradually became one of almost constant visionary experience of heaven, angels, saints, Mary, Christ, the wounds of Christ, and God. She once enjoyed a "chaste melting" with Christ, but in a way devoid of all eroticism.

Agnes was briefly notorious because of one revelation that she was reluctant to disclose. On the feast commemorating Christ's circumcision—that is, the shedding of the first drop of blood for our salvation—Agnes felt the Lord's foreskin on her tongue, thin as the membrane of an egg, and swallowed it with great sweetness (as many as a hundred times). Christ then revealed to her that his foreskin had been resurrected with him on Easter—although several churches claimed to possess the relic. Thus, her theological—not sexual—confusion: how could the risen Christ have his foreskin if some churches had the relic? (The devotion to the Holy Prepuce in various forms existed both before and after Agnes's times.) When the first edition of Agnes's *Revelations* was published in 1731, it was attacked as blasphemous and promptly disappeared from view.

Despite this scandalous history, Agnes's text (which does contain a vision of the nude Christ) is considerably less erotic than the mystical writings of other Beguines. The variety of her visions is typical of high medieval devotion. She uses familiar teaching techniques, such as vivid color symbolism and animal imagery to explain the twelve glories of the Virgin, the five types of confessors, and the four ways of receiving the Eucharist.

In one of Agnes's visions, Christ dispensed different kinds of grace from three venues: a kitchen, a pharmacy, and a shop with general merchandise. Her revelations took the form of a spiritual diary organized around the liturgical year. Agnes's comments on the calendar can be most revealing when they are most disconcerting. For instance, she experienced Eastertide as the saddest time of year because Christ's followers no longer enjoy his bodily presence, but have not yet received the consolation of the Holy Spirit. The Beguine's Lenten devotions entailed five thousand "Our Fathers" and the same number of "Hail Marys," with a genuflection to accompany each, and on Good Friday she flagellated herself a thousand times with a juniper branch.

### Margaret of Cortona (1247–97)

At age sixteen, Margaret of Cortona fled her family to become the mistress of a nobleman. Upon his death, she went to Cortona, where she gave up her son to charity (an act not uncommon among women penitents). There she was permitted to enter the Order of Penance of St. Francis, which meant a public role. In fact, Friar Giunta of Bevegnati's *Life* of Margaret depicts her as a model for members of the Third Order of St. Francis, a role Christ had told her she would assume. Margaret is also presented here as the teacher of a vernacular theology directed to the lay penitents distinct from the scholastic and monastic models.

However, Margaret implored Christ to make it possible for her to stay in her cell to enjoy contemplative prayer. But Christ ordered her to go to Assisi so that she could attend Mass, adore him, see him in the priest's hands. There she was to wait for Christ's permission to enclose herself. For thirteen years or so, Margaret practiced extreme penances in Assisi because she considered herself to be the worst of sinners. Striking mystical graces filled her life. Contemplating Christ's passion and the life of St. Francis propelled her into states of rapture. In her public role as the principal penitent of Cortona, Margaret—as a new Magdalene—became the town's patron, which shows that in her time, a penitential mystic had an appreciated public function. She also founded a hospital for the poor and participated in the political life of the town to try to bring peace to local factions.

During this time, Christ appeared and promised her that she would participate both in his own passion and in the sufferings of Mary at the cross. The next day, from nine in the morning until three in the afternoon, she ecstatically relived each aspect of Christ's passion and death—as a public event—that the people of Cortona assembled to witness. "There they saw Margaret," wrote Friar Giunta, "not alongside the cross, but as if she were on the cross, tortured by severe sufferings. . . . In the terrible excess of suffering she ground her teeth, writhed like a worm or a twisted wreath, grew as pale as ash, lost her pulse and speech, grew totally cold. Her throat grew so hoarse that she could hardly be understood when she came to her senses."[6] This living passion play had the purpose of both edifying and entertaining the citizens of Cortona.

A passion mysticism dominated Margaret's life from then on. She considered herself Christ's "martyr" and "plant," "daughter, sister, and accomplice who waters the dry plants of other Christians."[7] During a vision, the crucified Christ's wounded side opened, allowing Margaret to gaze upon his sacred heart. Ecstatically raising up into heaven, Christ spoke to her: "Daughter, from these wounds you absorb what preachers seek to express."[8]

Why some scholars admire or scorn or ridicule these women seems obvious. The pejorative term "women's mysticism" arose because of some of the above figures. I suggest that these lives should serve as a reminder that the heights of mysticism are sometimes found with concomitant paranormal phenomena that hagiography exaggerates for a variety of reasons. Stupendous feats—entering fiery furnaces without bodily harm, for example—should be categorized as hagiographical spiritual fiction designed to hold the reader's attention, to entertain, and to engender admiration for—not imitation of—the holiness of these unusual women. Moreover, such imaginary feats have nothing to do with genuine mysticism, an immediate God-consciousness that transforms a person into a parent of transcendental life.

# Hadewijch of Antwerp

(thirteenth century)

*"Hell is the seventh name of this Love wherein I suffer. For there is nothing Love does not engulf and damn, and no one who falls into her and whom she seizes comes out again, because no grace exists there."*[1]

Little is known about Hadewijch, one of the greatest women of the "new mysticism." Her intensely personal writings reveal that she was of noble birth, highly educated, an ecstatic, a profound mystic, and a subtle and daring mystical theologian—but little of the particulars of her life. Although hardly known by her contemporaries, she was highly esteemed one century later by the great mystic and theologian John Ruusbroec, who spoke of texts written by a "Hadewijch." His contemporary, Jan Van Leeuwen—also a not insignificant theologian and mystic—deemed her the equal of any of the evangelists! Yet only in the twentieth century have her mystical riches come to be appreciated on a broad scale.

Hadewijch, a Beguine, stands out as one of the most sublime exponents of love mysticism in the Western mystical tradition. To her, Love (*Minne*) is everything and, therefore, the very meaning of existence. Love is both the trinitarian life permeating all reality and the experience of being subject to this life. "I will tell you without beating about the bush," she wrote. "Be satisfied with nothing less than Love."[2] She also confessed that she had nothing else to live on, except Love, and urged her readers to live not for self-satisfaction but solely for holy Love, out of pure love, and only to "content Love."

In Hadewijch's sixteenth poem in couplets, she writes of Love's seven names. Love is a "chain" that binds, driving the one bound with madness to devour the Beloved and to be devoured and experience way beyond one's dreams "the Godhead and the Manhood."[3] Love is a "light" that enlightens reason as to how to love the "God-Man."

"Live coal" is yet another name because Love burns to death and consumes "man's desire and God's refusal."[4] "Fire" is a name for Love because it burns to death everything it ever touches so that both blessings and damnation no longer matter. "Dew" is the name under which Love works to impart the kisses that pertain to love, that same kiss that unites the Three Persons in the one God. "Living Spring" is Love's sixth name, because Love is nothing less than Life, which gives life to our life, a spring that flows forth but also returns to itself.

"Hell," however, is Love's highest name. No grace exists there because this Love engulfs and damns everything. Hadewijch claimed that she was burned to ashes by the fire of this impenetrable, "insurmountable darkness of Love" that surpassed even hell's torment. A more poignant statement of mystical dereliction cannot be found in the mystical tradition.

Thus, the joys and sufferings encountered by the soul in its longing for God fill Hadewijch's works. Love is an abyss not only of joy, bliss, peace, and "unheard of songs" but also of violent storms and of hellishly dark whirlpools. A seraph in a vision raised her to heaven and said, "Behold, this is Love, whom you see in the midst of the Countenance of God's nature; she has never yet been shown here to a created being"[5]—a "Countenance" she was to see numerous times.

Because our Beguine had looked upon the face of God, she claimed to have had the beatific vision. Christ himself had granted her personally a glimpse of his eternal glory: "And he took me out of the spirit in that highest fruition of wonder beyond reason; there I had fruition of him as I shall eternally."[6] She therefore considered herself the most favored of all creatures who surpassed in this respect even the Virgin Mary prior to her assumption.

Hadewijch wrestled with Love so violently at times that she spoke of bouts of "holy madness," during which limb and life were endangered. For example, on one Pentecost Sunday, "desirous love" seized her so powerfully that her heart, limbs, and veins quivered. Physical pain swamped her body, as if her bones were being broken; madness and fear overtook her mind, instilling a feeling that she would die of love.

Hadewijch confessed that Love had been more cruel to her than the devil ever was because the evil one could never stop her from loving God, but Love had taken this away from her. Paradoxically, she valued the hellish cruelty of divine Love more than her youthful raptures and joys. As an "old and wise lover" (a salient feature of her mysticism), she understood that one must forsake love for Love. Love's "highest voice" in her view was to deny Love with humility. In line with an older tradition, Hadewijch experienced and taught an *epektasis* view of Love, that "inseparable satiety and hunger are the apanage of lavish Love, as is ever well known by those whom Love has touched."[7]

Hadewijch's distinction between the precreational (exemplary) self and the created self is one of the most fascinating aspects of her mystical theology. Using the analogy of a builder's mental image of what she is about to construct, she held that all creation is one with and in God's mind prior to creation. Mystical union should be therefore understood as the soul's return to its precreational existence, to its eternal standing in God. This Beguine actually held that her mystical consciousness attained the same state and status it had in God's mind before she was created. Convinced that she was expressing herself in terms of her precreational consciousness in God, she wrote, "The old age I had was in the perfect nature of eternal being, even though I was youthful in created nature."[8]

Hadewijch taught that one must live the trinitarian life. One "lives the Son of God,"[9] if one desires Love and does Love's will; one "lives the Holy Spirit,"[10] if one wills only what Love wills; however, one "is the Father,"[11] when one is in the unity of Love.

Hadewijch was told in a vision, however, that no one had lived the God-Man life as well as she had. In fact, she had given birth to Christ in her soul: "Then I perceived an infant being born in the souls who love in secret, the souls hidden from their own eyes in the deep abyss of which I speak, and to whom nothing is lacking but that they should lose themselves in it."[12] Christ often revealed himself to her— first as a "Child," then as a "Man," even giving her the sacrament of the altar, causing her to dissolve into him: "Then it was to me," Hadewijch wrote, "that as if we were one without a difference."[13]

These mystical graces enabled Hadewijch to suffer much in imitation of Christ—to forsake love for Love—and to live as a perfect human being. Deploring the Brethren of the Free Spirit who advocated becoming God without remaining human, she insisted that one must "live God and man." The Brethren may wish to "be God with God," but this is impossible—unless one "lives man" by hanging on the cross with Christ. Hadewijch had grasped the human paradox: to attain divine life, one must become fully human, as Christ is.

The whole human being, in Hadewijch's view, is the "old and wise lover." Such a person no longer has joy or sorrow in anything, "except in this, that I was a human being, and that I experienced Love with a loving heart."[14] What is the perfect earthly life for Hadewijch: "To be favorable and zealous for every virtue, and not to fail with regard to a multitude of things, and to have compassionate good will for every need. This seems indeed to be the most perfect life one can attain on earth."[15]

# Bonaventure

## (ca. 1217–74)

*"This was shown also to blessed Francis, when in ecstatic contemplation there appeared to him a six-winged Seraph fastened to a cross. There he passed over into God in ecstatic contemplation and became an example of perfect contemplation as he had previously been of action."*[1]

Bonaventure was born John di Fidanza into a well-to-do family in the small town of Bagnoregio, near Viterbo, some sixty miles north of Rome. He left for studies at the University of Paris when he was seventeen years old. Nine years later he entered the Franciscan Order, received the name Bonaventure, and continued his studies under Alexander of Hales, the illustrious Franciscan theologian at the University of Paris.

Within a few years, Bonaventure began to lecture at the University of Paris and wrote numerous scholastic treatises, eventually becoming the head of the Franciscan theological school there. During this period, he joined with Thomas Aquinas to defend the new mendicant orders—especially in their emphasis upon poverty—against the attacks of the secular masters at the university.

In 1257, he was elected general of the Franciscan Order, a position he held for seventeen years. As general, Bonaventure wrote a number of spiritual works, sermons, and two biographies of St. Francis. Because he prudently maintained a moderate course in the conflict between the Franciscan Spirituals (who desired a strict imitation of St. Francis) and the Conventuals (who saw the need for more adaptation), he managed to shape those ideals into institutional forms that have existed to the present day. He is rightly called the second founder of the Franciscans and the chief architect of their enduring spirituality.

Pope Clement IV wanted to make Bonaventure archbishop of York, an honor he promptly declined. However, Pope Gregory X gave him the red hat in 1273 by making him cardinal archbishop of Albano. Before dying on July 15, 1274, Bonaventure had spent a year aiding the pope to prepare for the Second Council of Lyons. He stood out in his day as the major instrument for Church reform, for reconciling the mendicant orders and the secular clergy, and for the tentative reconciliation between the Roman and Greek Churches.

Because of the theological acumen and the religious fervor of his spirituality, the Christian world bestowed upon Bonaventure soon after his death the title "Devout Teacher." Six years after his canonization in 1482, Pope Sixtus V designated him "Doctor Seraphicus" of the Church. Late in the nineteenth century, Pope Leo XIII called Bonaventure "the Prince of Mystics."

In his person, Bonaventure combined Franciscan simplicity and intellectualism. All his writings focus upon how a person may attain union with God. By effecting a profound melding of philosophical speculation and mystical affectivity, he eschewed both pure intellectualism and naive emotionalism. Theoretical reflection enriched his spirituality and mysticism; but mystical experience remained at the heart of his speculative reflections. Bonaventure's writings evince a brilliant and creative transposition of the major mystical currents before him. Major commentators aver that what Bonaventure achieved in his century for spirituality and mysticism may be compared to what Thomas Aquinas achieved for theology: the apotheosis of the Christian tradition.

Like Francis, Bonaventure found God in all things and all things in God. Like Augustine, he focused upon God in the soul's depths; finally, like the great Dionysius, Bonaventure saw all creatures flowing out of God and finding their way back to the "superessential, superdivine, supereminent, super-unknown" Trinity. It was Bonaventure's genius to integrate the Franciscan love of Christ's humanity with the Dionysian joy of finding God ultimately beyond all things in an apophatic mystical ecstasy of "superluminous darkness." As Bonaventure wrote, "in this passing over, if it is to be perfect, all intellectual activities ought to be relinquished and the loftiest affection transported to God and transformed into Him. This, however, is mystical and most secret."[2] Thus, Bonaventure interlaced the sensible, the psychological, and the metaphysical with the mystical.

Bonaventure's *The Soul's Journey into God* may well be the most concise, comprehensive, architectonic mystical treatise ever written. Herein he contemplates God, as he is reflected in creation, in sensation, in the soul's memory, understanding, and will, and in the soul's graced faculties. He also contemplates God as Being and as the Good. Moreover, with Pseudo-Dionysius, Bonaventure focuses upon the Trinity as the self-diffusive Good. Like the Greek fathers, he views the Father as the womb, or the "fontal fullness" of divine fecundity, the Word as the Father's perfect expression of this fecundity, and the Holy Spirit as the mutual love of Father and Son—Gift, in and through whom all gifts are given.

The world is the overflow and expression of divine fecundity. In generating the Son, the Father likewise effects the eternal reasons for everything that exists. Thus, the Son as eternal exemplar is the link between the Father and all creation. Bonaventure can contemplate all creatures as reflecting God's power, wisdom, and goodness because of his exemplarism: all creatures have their archetypes in the divine mind and flow out of the divine fecundity.

Hence, all creatures are shadows, echoes, pictures, vestiges, representations, or footprints of the Trinity. Bonaventure, therefore, eloquently rejoices in creation's intelligible structure as a reflection of the Son's wisdom. Of course, contemplation on the soul's faculties and their elevation by grace discloses an even more intimate reflection of the Trinity, because memory, understanding, and will are created and graced in the Trinity's image and likeness.

The *Journey* also illustrates that St. Francis of Assisi's deep love for the crucified Christ prompted both Bonaventure's journey into God and the writing of this classic. Bonaventure, long attracted to St. Francis, described him as "the outstanding follower of Jesus Christ." He considered Francis to be the mirror of sanctity, the paradigm of all evangelical perfection, the way to Christ, and the exemplar of our way back to the Trinity. In the prologue to the longer of the two biographies of St. Francis (considered a hagiographical and theological masterpiece), he wrote, "I recognized that God saved my life through him, and I realize that I have experienced his power in my very person."[3] When meditating upon Francis's vision of the winged seraph angel in the form of Christ crucified, Bonaventure understood that "this vision might suggest the rising of Saint Francis into contemplation and point out the way by which that state of contemplation may be reached."[4] Because of Francis's profound identification with Christ, he received the stigmata, became the sixth angel found in the book of Revelation (7:2), and ushered in a new age of contemplatives.

Bonaventure places Christ at the beginning, in the middle, and at the end of the *Journey* to underscore, like Francis before him, Jesus' major role in the soul's mystical ascent *into* God. In this treatise, however, our Franciscan focuses upon the mystical Christ, the soul's Bridegroom, the God-Man who is the gateway and door to ecstatic mystical contemplation, to "ecstatic anointings" that produce the "learned ignorance" so dear to many mystics. Thus, the mystical Christ, the very life of the soul's life, the Christ who heals and transforms the soul's mystical senses, and then plunges it into its deepest depths, dominates the *Journey*. Bonaventure urges, "Let us, then, die and enter into this darkness. Let us silence all our cares, our desires, and our imaginings."[5] With Christ crucified, one "passes over" in mystical death to the Father.

However, Bonaventure comprehends the mystical Christ in the context of the *Tree of Life*, his meditations on Christ's life, death, and resurrection that evoke a simple and direct devotion to Christ's humanity. Because of the God-Man, the highest is always linked to the lowest. Christ's person, the historical events of his life, and the Church's life, to Bonaventure, are not only redemptive but also the necessary foundation for all mystical contact. Only someone who can say with Bonaventure while pondering Christ crucified, "O human heart, you are harder than any hardness of rocks, if at the recollection of such great expiation you are not struck with terror, nor moved with compassion, nor shattered with compunction nor softened with devoted love,"[6] is prepared to follow the mystical Christ into the divine darkness of mystical ecstasy. "There is no other path," he says, "but through the burning love of the Crucified."[7]

Bonaventure was a strong proponent of the triple way of the soul's journey into God. Purgation, illumination, and union, in his view, should not be considered as three successive ways because the activity proper to each way is always concomitant with the other ways. The purgative way focuses upon the outer man, disciplines the senses and the passions, and leads to inner peace. Only frequent confession, the examination of one's conscience, and meditation can assuage "the sting of conscience" that animates the purgative way. In the illuminative way, the "beam of intelligence" disciplines reason, enlightens the spirit, and teaches the person to know Christ and to follow him ever more closely. "The living flame of wisdom" initiates the unitive way by engendering loving-knowledge of God. It concentrates the spirit by turning it away from all creatures, feeds it by turning the heart toward its spouse, and raises it above all things to the incomprehensible God who is "all delight." In summary, the purgative way expels sins, the illuminative way leads to the imitation of Christ, and the unitive way brings about union with the spouse. The threefold way causes the repose of peace, the splendor of truth, and the sweetness of love.

Bonaventure's Christian architectonic, cosmic vision centers on the Trinity, Christ, St. Francis, and creation. It is a masterpiece of the Franciscan journey from St. Francis, to the crucified Christ, to the mystical Christ, to a sacramental grasp of all creation, to God as Being and Good, to the triune God—all ultimately grasped in the darkness of ecstatic love.

# Thomas Aquinas

## (1224/25–1274)

*"I cannot do any more. Everything I have written seems to me as straw in comparison with what I have seen."*[1]

Born at Roccasecco in southern Italy, Thomas was the youngest son of Count Landulf of Aquino (hence, Thomas Aquinas), who was related to the emperor and to the king of France. At age five, he was sent to the nearby Benedictine school at Monte Cassino, where his parents destined Thomas to become its future abbot. In 1240 he went to Naples to complete his coursework but decided to seek admission to the recently founded Order of Preachers, the Dominicans.

Strongly opposed to this decision, Thomas's family had him kidnapped and brought to a family castle at Montesangiovanni. Hagiography has it that when a prostitute was sent into his bedroom, the temptress was quickly driven out with a brand Thomas had snatched from the fireplace. After kneeling and imploring God to grant him integrity of mind and body, Thomas fell into a gentle sleep. As he slept, two angels appeared to assure him that his prayer had been heard. They then girded him about with a white cord, saying, "We gird thee with the girdle of perpetual virginity." From that day forward, Thomas never experienced the slightest hint of sexual disorder.

After a brief stay at the castle, his captors took him to Roccasecco, where he spent approximately a year in benign house arrest. However, knowing that Thomas had not changed his mind, his family finally gave in to his wishes and brought him to the Dominican priory in Naples. Despite this episode, he maintained a lifelong strong bond with his family.

From the autumn of 1245 to 1248, Thomas came under the influence of Albert the Great at the University of Paris and eventually accompanied him to the Dominican house of studies in Cologne—but he returned to Paris in 1252 to become a Master of Theology. He also taught at several Dominican houses in Italy, returned to Paris in 1269, and moved once again to Naples in 1272 to set up a Dominican house of studies. On his way to the Second Council of Lyons, he died on March 7, 1274, at the Cistercian monastery of Fossanuova.

According to hagiography, Thomas's body—even after several months in the grave—did not corrupt; it even emitted a very pleasant and healing odor. He was canonized in 1323 because of his great reputation for holiness. (The canonization process mentions three hundred miracles performed through his intercession.) Called *doctor communis* (teacher for everyone) and *doctor angelicus* (the angelic teacher) because of his brilliance, he was proclaimed an official Doctor of the Church by Pius V in 1567. Only four others before him had been so honored. Thomas, however, would have preferred to be called "Friar Thomas."

Thomas's exceptional reputation as perhaps the greatest theologian in Christian history has obscured that he was not only a mystic but also an ecstatic. Only in recent years have scholars underscored Aquinas as a mystic, as one intensely consumed by the love of God. His own brethren had attested, however, that he was frequently lost in spirit during contemplation—sometimes for very long periods. Prolonged ecstasies, sometimes accompanied by tears, often occurred when he celebrated Mass, especially in the last months of his life. During a public Mass on Passion Sunday, 1273, his ecstasy lasted so long that some congregants intervened so that Mass could continue.

Thomas's most famous mystical experience occurred toward the end of his life. On December 6, 1273, he confided to his friend Reginald of Piperno, "I cannot do any more. Everything I have written seems to me as straw in comparison *with what I have seen.*"[2] Commentators have interpreted this statement in a variety of ways: for example, as only the result of mystical experience; as caused by increasing doubts about the value of his work; as an insight into supposedly deep contradictions in his theology; as a result of having been poisoned; and, finally, as stemming from a physical and psychological breakdown brought on by overworking and illness. The better Aquinas scholars, to my mind, suggest that extreme physical and nervous exhaustion—coupled with the mystical experiences especially of his last year of life—may be the most plausible causes for his well-known utterance.

Thomas never used the word "mystic" and never produced a commentary on Pseudo-Dionysius's major work, *The Mystical Theology*. A person blessed with an intense God-consciousness he called a "spiritual," a "holy one," a "perfect one," or a "contemplative." Central to Thomas's mysticism is the absolute simplicity of the divine nature that is absolutely unknowable to the finite mind. "Because we do not know what God is," Thomas wrote, "the proposition [God exists] is not self evident to us."[3] Because God is above everything we can know, naming God through negation is appropriate. The ever greater God is known as unknown and is the name above every name. Although the human mind can never comprehend *what* God is, it does know that God exists and is *ipsum esse subsistens*, that is, IS-ING ITSELF. This echoes, of course, the name God disclosed to Moses on Mount Sinai, "I AM WHO I AM" (Ex 3:14) and Jesus' own confession, "before Abraham was, I am" (Jn 8:58).

As with many before him, Aquinas emphasized that human happiness consists in the vision of God. The blessed see God; we do not. As intimate as "Adam" was with God before the Fall, in Thomas's view, not even he saw God. To the classical question, "Why did God become man?" Thomas replied that the Word became flesh so that we could *see* God.

Thomas taught that although no one in this earthly life can return to the condition that Adam enjoyed before his sin, he viewed contemplation as a state not only close to that of unfallen humanity but also as ordered to the beatifying vision of God in heaven: "In contemplation," he wrote, "God is seen through the medium of the light of wisdom that elevates the mind to behold divine things. It is not that the divine essence itself is seen in an immediate way, but this is the way God is seen through grace by a contemplative after the state of sin, though it was realized more perfectly before the Fall."[4]

Aquinas understood that contemplation bestows an experiential, sapiential knowledge of God. Because grace as God's self-communication makes the person in some sense one with God, contemplation is a form of immediate knowledge, analogous to the connatural knowledge that husband and wife have of each other—as two in one flesh. Thomas often spoke of a "connatural knowledge" of God in which one attains a graced affective knowledge of God and delights in seeing—however vaguely—what is loved, namely, God. In Thomas's view, mystical loving-knowledge is a form of experiential and connatural knowing, based on union with God through charity and leading to the reception of the divine gift of wisdom that deepens love of God. In this way, one is deified and becomes by grace what God is by nature. Illuminated by the very depths of divine wisdom, the contemplative knows that the highest form of knowing God is knowing him in ignorance.

Thomas's understanding of the contemplative life contains a certain tension. Just as Mary—in contrast to Martha—had chosen the better part (Lk 10:42), Thomas taught that the contemplative life is superior to the active life. Yet, the fullness of contemplation, in his view, should flow into an active life of preaching and teaching: the famous phrase *contemplata aliis tradere*, passing on to others what one has contemplated.

Although Aquinas insisted that the human mind cannot behold God in this life, he did maintain that, by miraculous exceptions, both Moses and Paul saw the divine essence through the transient reception of the light of glory. God-given raptures can impel the soul with such violence *from above* that it is drawn away from what belongs to it by nature and given a brief vision of the divine essence. During this spiritual death, the person's spirit lives in God but not on earth because no one can see God and live (Gen 33:20).

Thomas saw God in all things and all things in God. The whole world, in his view, was nothing other than a vast representation of the divine Wisdom in the mind of the Father. Although he emphasized that God is "in all things in the most intimate way," he seemingly held the panentheistic view that "things are in God much more than God is in things."[5]

Thomas also distinguished the violence of rapture from "normal" ecstasy that he had undoubtedly experienced. Ecstasy, in his view, is a nonviolent going out of self by being placed beyond one's natural self. Divine love causes the spirit to stretch forward to and taste God as its supreme good in an ecstasy of love.

Thomas consistently linked prayer and contemplation to study and teaching. Withdrawing into silent prayer, he strove to understand the divine mysteries about which he wrote, taught, and discussed in disputes with others. With his notebooks in front of him, Thomas frequently prayed with outstretched arms before the crucifix to verify in prayer the soundness of his theology. His brethren said of him: "Every time that he wishes to study, to undertake a dispute, to teach, to write or dictate, he first withdraws into secret prayer and prays, pouring out tears, in order to obtain understanding of the divine mysteries."[6]

Thomas's spirituality and mysticism are Christ-centered. As with St. Francis of Assisi, Thomas loved the poor and naked Christ; he found in his humanity the true way to his divinity—a divinity that he adored as "hidden God," as stated in his famous hymn, "Adoro te devote." In contemplating and writing about Christ's life, death, and resurrection, Thomas sometimes levitated. A voice from the crucifix once addressed him: "You have spoken well of me, Thomas, what should be your reward?" Aquinas's reply: "Nothing other than Thee, Lord."[7]

The person and actions of Jesus Christ, in Thomas's view, are instructions for our lives. Two daily Masses (one of which he celebrated) and daily confession before Mass were an intrinsic part of this friar's life. Some of the most stunning eucharistic hymns in Christian history were penned by Aquinas. He also understood Christ's humanity as the instrument though which all grace is given; therefore, all grace is the grace of Jesus Christ.

As a contemplative of "sacred teachings," Aquinas was not a theologian in the modern, academic sense of the term. Bringing his profound Christian love and enormous intellectual prowess to bear on the Christian faith, he strove to understand what both the natural and the graced intellect could affirm about God and God's creation. Because he insisted that God is theology's subject matter, theology is necessarily orientated to contemplation and is a kind of participation in God. "Speculative theology," in his view, meant contemplative theology, not philosophical abstraction and "speculation," in the contemporary, pejorative sense. This Master of the Sacred Page developed and focused his entire philosophical-theological enterprise to understand God's revealed word. Throughout his commentaries on biblical books, he often spoke of the text's "mystical meaning" that could only be grasped "by experience." This mystical theologian sought out the Bible's deepest meaning, and thus followed in the footsteps of the Fathers of the Church.

Thomas's mental abstraction—for which he was renowned—is illustrated by one amusing incident. When dining with King Louis IX of France, Thomas was so caught up in pondering a theological issue that he forgot his surroundings, pounded on the table, and cried out: "That takes care of the Manicheans." The king, a saint himself, was not offended and asked that a scribe be called to take down Thomas's line of argument. When a young monk wrote him and asked how to become a theologian, Thomas wrote back with the instructions: live a holy life. On other occasions, when colleagues and students vilified Job for his alleged blasphemies, Thomas retorted that Job spoke the truth and that God is Truth itself. The first word in both his monumental *Summa Theologiae* and his *Summa Contra Gentiles* is *veritas* (truth).

Despite the caricature of Thomas as a fat friar, many people who met him commented both on his imposing stature and his physical attractiveness. Moreover, he led an austere, retired life of piety and study—eating and sleeping little. All ecclesiastical honors offered him—sometimes with great pressure—he refused.

Spiritual friendship also marked his life. He called his Dominican companion Reginald of Piperno his "very dear son" and said that without friends, who would want to live? Friendship also played a key role in his treatise on charity. Thomas considered the human person to be the most noble creature in the world because "it is the Holy Spirit who makes us friends of God and makes us dwell in him and him in us."[8] Thomas Aquinas has correctly been called the mystic of deification, or divinization.

# Jacopone da Todi

## (ca. 1230–1306)

*"Christ, You have pierced my heart. And now You speak of orderly love! How can I experience love of that sort once united with You?"*[1]

The scion of an aristocratic Umbrian family in Todi, Jacopone married and worked as a *notatio*, a profession that mixed accounting and law. When he was forty-seven years old, his wife died. For unknown reasons, Jacopone became a "holy fool" (*bizoconne*), a ragged public penitent. Ten years later he entered the Franciscan Order and took part in the raging conflict within the order between the latitudinarian group of Conventuals and the stricter one of Spirituals.

Jacopone had spent much time meditating on the life of Francis of Assisi, who inspired his ardent desire to emulate Christ crucified and his passionate love for Dame Poverty—who has the only heart large enough in which God can dwell. Like Francis, he was wounded by the madness and drunkenness of the love Christ has for us. He writes, "Where did it lead You, O Christ, this drunken love? They hung You from the tree."[2] Thus, Jacopone may have become a Spiritual intentionally in order to suffer the severe persecutions they were then enduring.

Shocked by the mediocrity and corruption he saw in society, in the Franciscan Order (he called some of his brothers "miter-cuckolded" friars and "bastard sons"), and in the Church (about which Christ "laments"), he found hope in the election to the papacy of Pier da Morrone, a seventy-year-old abbot of an order of hermits and a friend of many Spirituals. But Jacopone's hopes were quickly dashed. Within a few months, the "angel-pope" Celestine V made what Dante bitterly called "the great refusal": he resigned. The venal, greedy, politically ambitious, and ruthless Cardinal Benedetto Gaetani became the new pope, Boniface VIII. Filled with fury, Jacopone, other Spirituals, and rebellious cardinals signed the Longhezza Manifesto in 1297, which denounced the conclave that elected Boniface VIII and demanded a new election.

The rebellion failed. Jacopone was excommunicated, stripped of his Franciscan habit, and imprisoned in an underground cell at the monastery of San Fortunato in Todi. Because of his great longing to suffer with Christ crucified, he wrote of this imprisonment as "the handsome benefice I have won at the Court of Rome."[3] However, his great love of the Church prompted him to write to the pope to beg for the lifting of the excommunication. Against the onslaughts of his fierce enemy, Boniface VIII, Jacopone employed the "two shields" of "self hatred" and "ardent love of neighbor." "Do what you will," he wrote to the pope, "this love will overcome you."[4] In the final analysis, he realized that "I am the only enemy that stands between me and salvation."[5] In 1303, our friar was released from prison by the new Pope Benedict XI. That Jacopone returned to the Franciscans and spent his last years at the Monastery of San Lorenzo in Collazzone in great peace underscores our friar's spiritual depths.

His masterpiece, *The Lauds*, undoubtedly the most powerful Italian religious poetry before Dante, should be read against this background. Jacopone's God-intoxication from his experiences of the overwhelming power of Christ's love permeates these writings. Unparalleled as prison literature, his text contains some of the fiercest love poetry in the Christian mystical tradition. Like his counterparts in the Muslim tradition, the Sufis, Jacopone used invocation and incantation to stir up the heart, then to maintain its swelling and ascent, and finally to send the ecstatic heart diving into Love itself.

Jacopone experienced through his contemplation of Christ's Incarnation and crucifixion a form of divine madness. "For love of man You seem to have gone mad!" he wrote. "Jesus cannot cure Himself of love; He seems to be out of His senses."[6] Jacopone responded accordingly: "Love, you are driving me to madness; I can do no more."[7] Madness for the love of Christ, in his view, was the highest wisdom. "Love, Love-Jesus" became his frequent refrain; the cross, his "bed." This might explain his ferocious prayers that called down various ills and evils upon himself, his strident paeans to self-hatred, to spiritual annihilation, and to uncompromising poverty. "For You created me as Your beloved," he wrote, "and I, ungrateful wretch, put You to death."[8] I have taught students who judged Jacopone to be insane, but these timid souls understand neither the passionate Umbrian temperament nor the excessive, ecstatic, annihilating love lived by many mystics.

Jacopone sang of a soul drowning in ecstatic love. The soul, like a "drop of wine" that is poured into the sea, loses "all sense of self and self-consciousness" and "becomes one with God"—even "fused with God."[9] United with Christ, it becomes "almost Christ."[10] As the soul drinks in this love, it is imbibed by Love. And so, in "lofty self-annihilation," "two are made one" in a "true union that admits no divisions."[11] Even faith, hope, and desire seem to cease because the soul sees, clings to, and has even more now than it knew how to yearn for before. This Franciscan "fool of Love" heard all creation shout this Love.

Through Jacopone's experiences of the madness of divine love, this crotchety Old Testament-like prophet of Love simultaneously grasped the awesomeness of his sins, his radical creaturehood, and his inability to love as profoundly as he was loved. Jacopone could be churlish, coarse, boorish, shrill, wrathful, and excessive toward whoever tried to diminish the vision Love revealed through the incarnate and crucified Christ. This is perhaps the proper context for understanding his savage attacks on his weaknesses, the body, "the dangerous charms of women," the "filthy world" that stripped him of everything, the wretchedness of man, "conceived by human seed—how repugnant,"[12] and his views on the bitterness of life. His jeremiad remembrance of old age and death are striking—one "stumbles" into old age, "ugly, slovenly, repulsive, condemned to die,"[13] with death delivering him to a "tomb littered with [his] peacock feathers."[14]

God's love had also assaulted his senses: "From five sides, You move against me: hearing, sight, taste, touch, and scent. To come out is to be caught; I cannot hide from you."[15] His vehement denunciations of world and self are redolent with the comprehension of having been redeemed and loved by God. This Franciscan, willing to give away all creation for the sake of Love, discovers that as a "new creature born in Christ," all things are his; all creation shouts "Love, Love"—a summary of Jacopone's Franciscan mysticism of joy in the world.

Jacopone may have been an ecstatic mystic, but he preferred to experience God's absence. "I have always held, and still do," he wrote, "that it is a great thing to be filled with God. But I have also always thought, and still do, that to know how to suffer His absence, how to endure that fast when He imposes it, is even greater."[16]

# Ramon Llull

## (1232–1316)

*"And he thought to himself: the strength of love knows no bounds when the Lover loves the Beloved with a very fervent love. As a result, it came to Blanquerna that he should make a Book of the Lover and the Beloved in which the Lover should be a faithful and fervent Christian, and the Beloved should be God."*[1]

Ramon Llull exemplifies the fecundity, sublimity, and variety of early Franciscan mysticism. Considered to be the first great Christian Spanish mystic and the forerunner to Teresa of Avila and John of the Cross, scholars are still puzzled why his almost 250 published works (out of approximately 500) that contain mystical material played almost no role in the development of late medieval mysticism.

Born an aristocrat in Palma, Majorca, shortly after the end of three centuries of Muslim domination, Ramon Llull spent several years as a courtier at the Majorcan royal court. There he composed troubadour-style love songs for his mistresses, a passion he indulged even after his marriage to Blanca Picany.

The apocryphal story of Llull's conversion has gripped the imagination of numerous historical figures. The German philosopher Arthur Schopenhauer (d. 1860), for example, made much of the legend that Llull had finally succeeded in having his way with a beautiful woman he had long wooed. When he entered her room, she opened her dress—which revealed her cancer-ridden bosom. As if he had looked into hell, he was converted, left the court of the King of Majorca, and went into the wilderness to do penance.

The real story is quite different. When Llull was approximately thirty years old, Christ crucified appeared to him five times and transformed the worldly troubadour into Christ's troubadour. Now he desired only to sing of God's love and to be a "Fool of Love," a name he often called himself. Inspired later by a sermon on St. Francis of Assisi, Llull provided for his wife and family, gave away the rest of his money, and devoted himself to writing a book against Jewish and Muslim errors. Encouraged in his efforts by the learned Dominican Raymond of Penafort, he spent the next decade or so learning Arabic and Christian thought.

In 1274, on Mount Randa, near Palma, Ramon received an illumination of the trinitarian structure of all reality that gave him the form and method for his writings. Retiring to a monastery, he completed there his famous *Ars Magna*, the first of about forty treatises. Regarded as the earliest attempt in the history of formal logic to employ geometrical diagrams for the purpose of discovering nonmathematical truths, the "Great Art" is also the first attempt to use a mechanical device—a kind of primitive logic machine—to facilitate the operations of a logic system. Llull's work applied the analogy of being to God's attributes as a way of integrating and relating all forms of knowledge to theology and was aimed primarily as demonstrating the truths of Christianity to Muslims and Jews. The conviction that the inquiring mind could acquire all truths in such a way is what probably prompted his contemporaries to ridicule him as the "Fantastic One."

This Majorcan polymath also wrote what is perhaps the first European novel—a somewhat extravagant religious romance—the *Blanquerna.* He also published numerous volumes on theology, alchemy, poetry, medicine, and even seminal ideas that are now found in contemporary relational databases and statistics.

Llull underwent a great spiritual crisis in Genoa. Long attracted to Franciscan ideals and ways of life, his request to be clothed as a Franciscan was denied. Like Jacopone da Todi, he then became a *bizoconne*, a wondering penitent. Poverty, missionary preaching, and extensive travel for the sake of his apostolate became his way of life. Success was his in founding language schools for missionaries. His numerous "Llullist"-philosophy disciples became quite influential in Spain. Despite his frequent contact with the Franciscan wing of Spirituals, there is no proof that he became one or even a formal member of its Third Order. On the other hand, Franciscan spirituality dominated his way of life and outlook until his death. The pious legend that he died a martyr's death from stoning by North African Muslims has been firmly laid to rest. He probably died in Palma in 1316. Revered as *Doctor Illuminatus* by the Franciscans, he is praised to this day for his pioneering understanding of Arabic, his religious tolerance, and his emphasis on graced dialogue as the means of conversion.

The *Blanquerna* contains Llull's most famous mystical work, *The Book of the Lover and Beloved*. In our Majorcan's words, "While Blanquerna wept and adored, and God caused his soul to rise to the supreme height of its strength in contemplation of Him, Blanquerna felt himself carried away in spirit through the great fervor and devotion which he had, and he considered that the strength of love knows no bounds when the Lover has very fervent love of his Beloved. Wherefore it came to the will of Blanquerna that he should make a book of the Lover and the Beloved. The Lover should be a faithful and devout Christian, and the Beloved should be God."[2] This guide to contemplation has one short passage for each day of the year. This work of Franciscan tenderness toward Christ's Incarnation, passion, and love of God speaks of the folly of all human knowledge (for which he had the utmost respect)—when compared with divine illumination. Filled with grace and charm, this new genre in Christian mystical literature rivals the love language of the Sufis. Llull himself writes, "The Muslims have various holy men called Sufis. They offer words of love and brief *exempla* that inspire a person to great devotion. Their words require exposition, and thanks to the exposition the intellect rises higher, which develops it, and spurs the will to devotion."[3]

At first glance, this strangely nonscriptural work appears to be a collection of love aphorisms. The three main characters—the Lover, the Beloved, and Love—give the book its unity. The Lover denotes the seeking Christian and, at times, Christ himself. The Beloved is God, whom the Lover seeks on a long and dangerous journey. Love is a mysterious transcendent person that represents both the love of the Lover and the Beloved. Although largely forgotten in our age, Llull's book attained such popularity that it has been called the second greatest devotional book in the Western world, second only to the *Imitation of Christ*.

In what may be a good summary of his Love mysticism and one of the loveliest paeans to Love in the Christian mystical tradition, Llull wrote, "They asked the Lover, 'Whence art thou?' He answered, 'From Love.' 'To whom dost thou belong?' 'I belong to Love.' 'Who gave thee birth?' 'Love.' 'Where were thou born?' 'In Love.' 'Who brought thee up?' 'Love.' 'How dost thou live?' 'By Love.' 'What is thy name?' 'Love.' 'Whence comest thou?' 'From Love.' 'Whither goest thou?' 'To Love.' 'Where dwellest thou?' 'In Love.'"[4]

The salient feature of Llull's text is the perfect union of the Beloved and the Lover. Although the Lover and the Beloved are distinct beings, in his view, they are "one reality in essence." The Lover and the Beloved become one—analogous to the way that water mingles with wine and "heat is with light." In fact, the relationship among Lover, Beloved, and Love offers a "demonstration of the Trinity."[5]

In one intriguing and cryptic aphorism, Llull enunciated a theme we shall see later with the German mystics, that is, a mysticism of the ground that claims that the radical union of God and the soul seems to dissolve the distinction between them. "The Lover," Llull wrote, "gazed upon himself that he might be a mirror wherein to behold his Beloved; and he gazed upon his Beloved, as in a mirror wherein he might have knowledge of himself. Which of these two mirrors, think you, was the nearer to his understanding?"[6]

Llull's Christ-centered mysticism permeates his aphorisms. Because of Christ's divine and human natures, the Beloved descends to empower the Lover to ascend. Although the Lover's heart may soar, the Beloved must still be loved in the world's abyss and contemplated in trials and adversities. With even more emphasis on kenosis, Llull wrote, "The Beloved is far above Love. The Lover is far beneath it. And Love, which lies between these two, makes the Beloved descend on the Lover, and makes the Lover rise toward the Beloved. This ascending and descending are the beginning and the life of that love by which the Lover suffers and the Beloved is served."[7]

Following an Augustinian pattern, Llull underscored that will, understanding, and memory must ascend in contemplation of the Beloved. "The will of the Lover," he wrote, "desired to soar on high, that he might greatly love his Beloved; so he commanded the understanding to soar as high as it might; and even so the understanding commanded the memory, so that all three mounted to the contemplation of the Beloved in His honors."[8] In his view, the understanding, memory, and will both unite the Lover and the Beloved in love and bind them so that they can never be parted.

It seems apposite to conclude with one of Llull's most baffling aphorisms: "Theology and Philosophy, Medicine and Law met the Lover. He asked them if they had seen his Beloved. Theology wept, Philosophy doubted, Medicine and Law were glad. So the question arises: what do each of these four mean to the Lover who goes looking for his Beloved?"[9]

# Angela of Foligno

## (ca. 1248–1309)

*"In Him, therefore, do I understand and possess all truth that is in heaven and earth and hell and in all creatures; and so great is the truth and the certainty that were the whole world to declare the contrary, I would not believe it, yea, I should mock at it."*[1]

Angela of Foligno has been called the apotheosis of the Christian mystical tradition—as significant for mysticism as Dante is for poetry. These exaggerated claims notwithstanding, she may well be the most remarkable and significant Franciscan woman in this tradition. The profundity of her mystical life, her penetrating intelligence, the unusual phenomena she experienced, the skill with which she described them, the interaction of her visionary and apostolic mysticism, and the far-reaching influence she exerted during her lifetime right down to the present day account for her well-deserved praise.

Her widely read *Liber* ("Book")—consisting of two parts, the *Memorial* and the *Instructions*—stands out as one of the great treasures of medieval mysticism. Claiming that her message came directly from God, Angela believed in the quasi-scriptural authority of her book—one of the earliest, longest, and most complex of autohagiographies. Although strangely devoid of the language of courtly love, it nevertheless stands as one of the representative texts of the new mysticism. Some of the strikingly erotic descriptions of her mystical experiences have prompted some commentators to call her a "swooning, bedded mystic." Written in her vernacular Umbrian Italian, a certain "Brother A," a learned cleric, emended and translated her tome into Latin.

Little is known about her early life except that she was born of a wealthy family in Foligno, Umbria, and that she eventually married and had children. Her less than perfect Christian life troubled her and she admitted to having often received Communion in a state of sin because shame undermined her courage to reveal all her sins during sacramental confession.

When approximately forty years old, she underwent a mysterious conversion in which a dream of St. Francis of Assisi played a role. Wishing now to go "naked" to the cross, she prayed for the deaths of her husband, her sons, and her mother (whom she considered a "great obstacle" to her new spiritual life)—a highly questionable Christian request. When her prayers were answered, she experienced this both as a "great consolation" and as a deep "pain and sorrow."

Angela became a member of the Third Order of St. Francis. The First and Second Orders consist of Franciscan friars and nuns bound by ecclesiastical vows to an austere life of poverty, chastity, and obedience. The Third Order comprises people from all walks of life who possess the Franciscan spirit and who wish to associate with kindred souls in formal or informal groups. Although they do not take religious vows, they live under mitigated Franciscan rules, are spiritually directed by the friars, and promise solemnly to strive for perfection.

Because of her many years of intense purification, scholars have called Angela a "bit-by-bit" mystic. Her twenty (ten were later added) stage schema of ascent to God that begins with sacramental confession and ends with the beatific vision is penetrating, but highly unusual (confusing even Brother A).

This Umbrian Franciscan also taught seven ways by which God reveals his presence in the soul. In the first way, one experiences the fire and love of the sweet presence of his grace; in the second, mysterious divine words make the soul secure in the knowledge that God is present. The third way begins when the soul wants God perfectly; in the fourth way, the soul sees itself replete with God's fullness; in the fifth, God's presence renews the soul with divine unctions. The sixth way commences when even the body participates in the soul's embrace by God. Finally, the greatest and most ineffable experience of God occurs when it bestows hospitality upon him as "the Pilgrim." This state, Angela underscores, is devoid of ecstasies and raptures—one remains in total self-possession. However, this condition renders one powerless to speak about God, the "Unknown Nothingness."[2] "If you had attained this state," she wrote, "you would then say to the people with total self assurance: 'Go with God, because about God I can say nothing.'"[3]

Angela likewise spoke of three transformations. The first occurs when the person makes every effort to imitate Christ crucified; the second, when the soul experiences consoling union with God and can express it in concepts and words. The third takes place when the soul—by a "most perfect union"—is transformed within God and God within the soul. "Then," she wrote, "[the soul] feels and tastes God's presence in such a sublime way that it is beyond words and conception."[4]

Angela—as the many Franciscans before and after her who saw in St. Francis of Assisi the ultimate manifestation of Christ crucified and the surest way to God—reinterpreted the traditional Western mystical tradition in the light of St. Francis. Numerous mystical experiences occurred during her pilgrimages to Assisi and visits to his church there. The Holy Spirit, for example, told her that he was in her deepest self and would never part, if she maintained her love for him. While pondering a stained glass window that pictured Christ firmly holding Francis, Christ told her that he, too, will hold her even more closely than bodily eyes can observe. So powerful and consoling was this experience that when withdrawn, she wanted to die and screamed, "Love still unknown, why? why? why?"[5]

When returning home, Christ again assured her that she would receive both the cross and God's love within her: "This sign will be with you for eternity."[6] Immediately she experienced the cross and the love of God deep within her soul, along with psychosomatic repercussions. The God-Man appeared yet again and stressed that he came to serve *her*. (Angela often hummed her replies when Christ addressed her, another form of "jubilation.") After bestowing great peace and joy in her soul, Jesus revealed St. Francis to her and said, "I want him to serve you."[7] She then experienced not only Francis's deeply consoling friendship but also heard his "secret, lofty words": "You are the only one born of me."[8]

Devotion to St. Francis of Assisi and her contemplation of Christ's life, death, and resurrection enkindled Angela's remarkable Christocentric mysticism. Sacramental confession and Mass often sparked visions—even in dreams—and profound experiences of Jesus, whom she called the "Book of Life." Christ revealed to her that he suffered and died especially for her and then explained in detail what transpired during his "entire passion." This resulted in a painful, yet purifying, remembrance of her sins.

On the road home from Assisi, Christ informed Angela that although the apostles often saw him with their bodily eyes, they did not feel him the way it was granted to her: "You do not see me but you feel me."[9] After Christ gave her a ring of mystical betrothal (which only she could see), he invoked the blessings of the Trinity upon her and her companions. Delightful fragrances often accompanied these experiences of Christ.

As Angela gazed upon the crucifix during Vespers, her soul burst forth with love and joy because she saw and felt Christ within her, who embraced her soul with the very arm with which he was crucified. Numerous times she felt her soul entering into Christ's pierced side and transformed into Christ's passion. The greater the clarity of the soul's vision, the more painfully it was transformed into the sufferings of the God-Man, who became her only source of joy.

One Holy Saturday, she found herself in ecstasy and in Christ's tomb. Fascinated by the beauty of his neck and throat, she kissed him on the breast and mouth. As she placed her cheek against Christ's, he placed his hand on her other cheek, embraced her, and said, "Before I was laid in the sepulcher, I held you this tightly to me."[10] During one Sunday Mass, Angela ecstatically felt herself absorbed "into the fathomless depths of God,"[11] had a vision of Christ just as he was being taken down from the cross, and felt herself "pierced."

Angela's crucifixion with Christ crucified deified and christified her: "the elevations into the Uncreated and the transformation into the Crucified placed her in a continual state of being plunged into the fathomless depths of God and of being transformed into the Crucified, a state which she believes will be hers forever."[12] Although varying in intensity, this experience became a "continuous and uninterrupted" state. Such excessive states of rapture and new forms of ecstasy are a salient feature of the new mysticism and contrast with the monastic understanding of rapture and ecstasy as both brief and rare.

Angela found herself in a most exalted and ineffable way "standing or lying in the Trinity"[13] on three separate occasions and saw the "All Good" in darkness. She comprehended that the thicker the darkness was, the more profound the experience. In this darkness, her soul saw "everything and nothing at once."[14] When the Trinity plunged her into this "extremely deep abyss," all fear was removed from the soul and God secured it firmly in faith and hope. Incapable of describing this experience, she cried out: "whatever I say about it is blasphemy."[15]

This darkness drew her out of *everything*, including her devotion to the God-Man. However, when this experience ceased, she saw

Christ, who sometimes said to her: "You are I and I am You."[16] Whenever Christ embraced her, she gazed upon his face, stared into his eyes, and beheld the "fertile darkness of the Father." Despite the power of her prior visions in darkness, Angela maintained that "I am in the God-Man much more than in the other vision of seeing God with darkness. I am in the God-Man almost continually."[17] From that point on she experienced continual joy in Christ's humanity and felt assured that no intermediary existed between her and God.

The triune God so penetrated Angela's soul on another occasion that she understood not only how God dwells in the soul but also how God is present in all creatures. Her view of creation as "pregnant with God"[18] enabled her to see the triune reality in everything that has being—be it in a good angel or a devil, in heaven or in hell, in both good or evil deeds—and in everything, whether beautiful or ugly. Experiencing the triune immanence as a permanent state, Angela discovered that when she tried to speak with her friends or to think of anything, she could think only of God. This state empowered her body to obey her spirit perfectly (*apatheia*, or psychosomatic wholeness); it also rendered her psychologically incapable of sin.

God then transcended all the previous ways he had entered into Angela's soul by enlarging it, drawing her totally into the trinitarian "abyss" (a frequent word with this mystic), and giving her "that good which the saints enjoy in eternal life."[19] This gift lasted not only for long periods of time but was also given to her "thousands of times." It banished all darkness from her soul and filled it with clarity, certitude, and "abysmal profundity." She even claimed to know how the scriptures came to be written.

Angela contended that all the delights enjoyed by the great saints and all the world's pleasures, both good and evil, could never entice her to give up this grace for even a moment. In her view, however, the least saint in heaven has more of what can be given to any soul before death. Few mystics have claimed as boldly as Angela to have been granted a glimpse of the beatific vision in this life—which most theologians deny is possible.

Concomitant with this experience, she discovered in her soul "a chamber into which there enters no sort of grief or joy of any virtue whatsoever, nor anything else that can be named or expressed. But unto it there enters that greatest Good, and in that manifestation of God (which I do blaspheme in thus naming it, seeing that I have no word wherewith to speak of it perfectly) is the whole truth."[20] Because nothing can explain God, "nothing at all can be said or babbled"[21] about the ineffable wonders the Trinity produced in her soul. "My secret is mine," she contended—and spoke of her efforts to speak of God as so much "blasphemy."

Several years of mystical purgation preceded Angela's transformation into God. She spoke of experiencing the seeming destruction of her virtues and the resurrection of past vices—some that she never knew existed. The "shameful parts" of her body burned and "an overwhelming vice" entered her soul—one so great that she was ashamed to speak of it. Paradoxically, countervailing virtues were also given that were "so liberating that it seems to me I could not sin for all the good or evil that is in this world."[22] Bouts of angry rage, demonic assault, self flagellation, horrifying darkness, and temptations to despair tormented her. Feelings of pride, sadness, bitterness, and conceit also washed over her. Most bitter of all, however, was the pain of God's absence and the trenchant remembrance of past sins. She felt like a "man hanged by the neck who, with his hands tied behind him, and his eyes blindfolded, remains dangling on the gallows and yet lives, with no help, no support, no remedy, swinging in the empty air."[23] These experiences, however, both humbled her, and, in time, transformed her. Her rich and nuanced descriptions of the dark night of the spirit have resonated right down to the present day.

Angela enjoyed a wide reputation as a spiritual director and teacher, especially during the decade before her death. The Trinity had promised her spiritual fecundity—that she would have sons, "for all my sons are yours, and yours, mine." [24] As the guiding light for a large group of people in Italy and elsewhere, she wrote many letters of spiritual counsel, spoke out against the heresies of her day, and was designated "Teacher of Theologians" by the many theologians and priests who sought her advice. Her wisdom and ardent virtue converted the brilliant Umberto da Casale from a self-indulgent friar into a person who eventually became a luminary of the Franciscan Spirituals. Although Angela's spirituality and mysticism are distinctively Franciscan, her emphasis on the Trinity, her powerful apophaticism, and her view of both God and the soul as abysses depart from this tradition. She is rightly remembered as the "nightingale of the ineffable." God had been correct when he told her: "My love for you has not been a hoax."[25]

# Gertrude the Great

## (1256–1302)

*"I perceived in spirit that Thou had imprinted in the depths of my heart the adorable marks of Thy sacred Wounds, even as they are on Thy Body; that Thou had cured my soul in imprinting these Wounds on it."*[1]

The German Cistercian-Benedictine convent at Helfta in Saxony, Germany, has been called the crown of German convents. Combining a love of learning and a desire for God, many of these nuns enjoyed a mysticism that flowed from the sacramental-liturgical life of the entire Church. They understood union with the triune God and Christ as rooted in their daily liturgical life. Combined with the visionary aspects of the new mysticism, the spirituality of the Helfta nuns produced visionary commentaries on the mystical significance of the liturgical year.

Although these nuns expressed their union with Christ and the Trinity in nuptial terms, their serene mysticism was devoid of the frenzy and overt sexuality seen in some of the women mystics of this period. These regal queens in the King's presence testified to the most intimate union of the total human being with the "abyss" of the triune God in wholly unselfish love. Their significant contribution to the mystical tradition offers little ammunition to those commentators who speak derisively of "the mysticism of nuns and of women."

We know nothing about the birthplace, the family, or the circumstances under which Gertrude the Great was entrusted to the care of the Helfta nuns when she was only four years old. But we do know that she received a good education, showed intellectual promise, became a skilled Latinist, worked as a copyist in the monastery scriptorium, and was called "Great" because of her theological sophistication and mystical acumen. Her most important book is the *Revelationes* or *Legatus divinae pietatis* (*Herald of God's Loving Kindness*), which consists of five books, the second of which certainly comes from Gertrude's hand; the others, from her notes. Her other work, the *Exercitia Spiritualia* (*Spiritual Exercises*), contains seven contemplations on the awareness of grace that permeates Christian life.

Gertrude confessed in her writings that she spent her youth in intellectual pursuits and "girlish vanities"—to the neglect of her spiritual well-being. A profound conversion, when she was about twenty-five years old, detached her from everything except God alone. The triune God began to visit her, at various times and ways, as a "friend and spouse" and gradually made her soul his permanent abode. "For whenever I entered into my interior," Gertrude wrote, "you were always there."[2] These powerful experiences convinced her that the triune God had chosen her as a special instrument to manifest the secrets of his love.

The Holy Spirit, in Gertrude's view, prompted her with "the most violent impulses" to write (in Latin, not the vernacular) about her mystical life "for the salvation of many." The "clarity and sweetness" with which the Spirit moved her enabled her "to write it without difficulty and without reflection, even as if I had learned it by heart."[3] During a vision of Christ, he informed her "by the same effectiveness with which in this Mass I have transubstantiated bread and wine for the salvation of all, I have now sanctified everything written in this book for all with my heavenly blessings."[4] Her text, Christ disclosed, was stamped on his own heart to indicate that it participated in his divine-human nature.

Gertrude's mystical life began, deepened, and reached full maturity through the study of scripture, spiritual reading, communal prayer, the chanting of the Divine Office, and eucharistic celebrations. Two examples must suffice. First, when she was reciting the canonical Hours with less attention than usual, the devil appeared and ridiculed her for being able to speak so eloquently on any subject she wanted but was so "hasty and careless" in reciting the psalms. "The divine face" often appeared to her during the chanting of the Office. "When you showed me your most longed-for face, full of blessedness, so close to mine," she wrote, "I felt as though an ineffable light from your divine eyes was entering through my eyes, softly penetrating, passing through all my interior being, in a way beyond measure wonderful, working with marvelous power in every limb."[5] Most of her ecstasies, illuminations, revelations, wounds of love, and trinitarian embraces took place during Mass.

Ecstatic visions disclosed to Gertrude that Christ's heart and wounds are the supreme symbol of God's self-giving love. "I knew in my spirit," she wrote, "that I had received the stigmata of your adorable and venerable wounds interiorly in my heart, just as though they had been made on the natural places of the body. By these wounds you not only healed my soul, but you gave me to drink of the inebriating cup of love's nectar."[6] She gloried in his heart not only as a pledge of Christ's love but also as a place of refuge and rest. The Christ Child was also born in ecstatic love in her heart. When Gertrude's soul was imprinted by the trinitarian Christ like wax by a hot seal, her soul melted into Christ with the realization that his love "could not be hindered from communicating itself."[7] These experiences deified her and transformed her into an icon of Christ's presence. "As I am the figure of the substance of God, my Father, in His Divinity," Christ instructed her, "so also you shall be the figure of My substance in My Humanity, receiving in your deified soul the infusions of My Divinity . . . to prepare you for the closest union with Me."[8] Like her Helfta sisters, Gertrude expressed this romantic nuptial mysticism in the literary language of her day: the language of courtly love and of the minnesingers.

The purging, illuminating, and transforming significance of Christ's heart and wounds dominated Gertrude's mysticism. Later devotion to the Sacred Heart—sometimes called the "doloristic" view—would emphasize being sad with and consoling Christ because of the ingratitude of many toward his sufferings. Gertrude also focused much more on comprehending Christ's heart as the font of the Trinity's love of the world. By reflecting upon the philosophical and theological significance of mystical union with the Trinity in the depths of one's soul, Gertrude contributed to the increasingly popular speculative mysticism of the Low Countries and the Rhineland.

It had been revealed to Gertrude that God was like a mighty emperor who had not only ladies-in-waiting (contemplatives) but also men-at-arms (those in the active apostolate). Using imagery perhaps unpleasant to our contemporary sensibilities, Gertrude wrote of leaving the wine cellar of contemplation with "belches of drunkenness" so that others may benefit from the scent of wine. In her view, both contemplation and activity that afforded the opportunity to exercise patience, humility, and practical charity pleased the Lord.

Christ himself had revealed to Gertrude that because of her union with him, her entire life—even her illness—would not only transform her but also have an apostolic effect upon the entire mystical body. About one vision, she wrote that Christ "turned His right Side toward me, and there came forth from His blessed and inmost Heart a pure and solid stream, like crystal. Then our Lord said to me: 'This sickness that you suffer will sanctify your soul; so that each time you go forth from Me, like the stream which I have shown you, for the good of your neighbor, either in thought, word, or act, even then, as the purity of the crystal renders the color of the gold and the rose more brilliant, so the cooperation of the precious gold of My Divinity, and the rose of the perfect patience of My Humanity, will render your works always agreeable to Me by the purity of your intention.'"[9] Gertrude was indeed "Great."

# Mechthild of Magdeburg

(ca. 1208–ca. 1282/94)

*"The writing in this book flowed out of the living Godhead into the heart of Sister Mechthild."*[1]

Mechthild of Magdeburg—often called the Lord's nightingale—was born of a noble family in Saxony. When she was only twelve years old, she received such a powerful experience of the Holy Spirit (a "divine greeting") that from that moment on she saw God in everything and everything in God. This mystical event also protected her from serious sin throughout her life. When she was about twenty-three, Mechthild became a Beguine in Magdeburg. Years later, she had much contact with Dominican friars and intensified her life of asceticism, contemplation, and practical charity.

After a serious illness in 1281, Mechthild felt moved by God to write about her experiences, writings that she claimed resulted from what she saw and heard with her soul and what she felt throughout her body because of the power of the Holy Spirit. "I cannot write nor do I wish to write," she confessed, "but I see this book with the eyes of my soul and hear it with the ears of my eternal spirit and feel in every part of my body the power of the Holy Spirit."[2] God had instructed her that he was a "flowing spring, toiling without toil," that only a distracted human heart can block. Thus, her mystical classic is called *The Flowing Light of the Godhead*, which "flowed out of the living Godhead" into Mechthild's heart.

The text of this "flowing" mystic is one of the first vernacular (Middle Low German) texts to be translated into Latin, the official language of theology and spirituality. Although she knew that God had instructed her to write, she feared the book might be burned by the authorities. However, God comforted her with these words: "For someone to take this book out of my hand, he must be mightier than l."[3] God also informed Mechthild that the book portrayed him alone. Its parchment symbolized Christ's humanity; the words, his "marvelous Godhead"; and the sound of the words, the Holy Spirit. Her writings—Christ later informed her—had captured his "heart's blood."

Considered as one of the major mystical poets of the thirteenth century, Mechthild also wrote prose, songs of divine love, allegories, moral reflections, admonitions, and practical advice on daily conduct. Her descriptions of visions, revelations, and mystical experiences of the highest order exemplify the love, bridal, visionary, and prophetic dimensions of the "new mysticism." Her text, however, was originally a series of disconnected compositions of varying length, written on loose sheets of paper that her Dominican spiritual director, Heinrich of Halle, collected and put into its present form.

It had been revealed to Mechthild that the least soul was the daughter of the Father, the sister of the Son, and a friend of the Holy Spirit. Delighting in the flowing Love within the Trinity that gushes outward to create and to beckon the soul back to its source, she highlighted the mutual craving between God and the soul and the supreme value of interiorly experiencing it. She exclaimed that "when God could no longer contain himself, he created the soul and, in his immense love, gave himself to her as his own."[4] She ecstatically cried out that God cannot get enough of "caressing souls." Love penetrated her to such an extent that she confessed: "Nothing tastes good to me but God alone; I am wondrously dead."[5] Perhaps her experiences of her profound union with God explain one of the text's mysteries: God speaks directly to Mechthild but she is addressed as superior to Love. In fact, Mechthild maintained that the game of love God played with her was hidden even from the Blessed Virgin.

Part 1 of Mechthild's book presents an exceptional example of her skillful use of images and poetry, as well as her fondness for dialogue as a literary device, to express the rhythm of divine-human intercourse. It is perhaps the most striking text in the entire Christian tradition on the mystical dance that leads to deification. "Then the beloved goes in to the Lover," she wrote, "into the secret hiding place of the sinless Godhead. And there, the soul being fashioned in the very nature of God, no hindrance can come between it and God."[6]

Within a trinitarian framework, Mechthild taught the necessity of being clothed with the virtues before the soul can meet her lover.

The Old Testament, the longing of the prophets, our Lady, the saints—
the entire Church—prepare and lead the soul to the "noble Dance of
Praise" with Christ, the beautiful youth. But she stressed the necessity
of grace, for the soul cannot dance "unless thou [Christ] lead me."
When her senses complained that no one can endure the presence of
God's burning and blinding glory, Mechthild cried out that gold does
not perish in the refiner's fire, nor can fish drown in water, nor are
birds out of place in the air.

The use of explicitly sexual language to describe the love between
the triune God and the soul is one of the salient features of Mechthild's text. Surpassing even the eroticism of the Song of Songs, she
asserted that she would take the "noblest angel, Jesus Christ," into
her arms, "eat him and drink him, and have my way with him."[7]
Boasting that this surpassed even what angels are capable of, she
made light of their experience because "no matter how high he dwells
above me, his Godhead shall never be so distant that I cannot constantly entwine my limbs with him."[8] "Lord, your blood and mine
are one, untainted," she wrote. "Your love and mine are one, inseparable. . . . Your mouth and mine are one, unkissed. Your breast and
mine are one, not caressed by any man but you alone."[9]

When Mechthild asked the triune God what was expected of her,
she was commanded "to lay herself in utter nakedness" so that when
God "flows," she "shall become wet. . . . But when you love, we
two become one being."[10] Complying, Mechthild became a "naked
soul," and experienced the quiescence of the mutual surrender of
God and the soul. Employing poetic hyperbole to express her over-
powering experience of Love, she made light of even the Virgin
Mary's love of God, the blood of martyrs, the counsel of confessors,
the wisdom of the apostles, the austerity of John the Baptist, the
dandling of and giving suck to the divine infant. Mechthild proclaimed herself a "full-gown bride" who belonged at her Lover's
side. But she realizes this intimacy cannot "last long. When two lovers
meet secretly, they must often part from one another inseparably."[11]

Freudians' eyebrows rise at this point, but this Beguine was as
aware of using erotic language to express her bridal mysticism as,
say, Michelangelo was in using marble. Furthermore, many mystics
before and after Mechthild used the eroticism of the Song of Songs
to express mystical divine-human intercourse—albeit not as daringly
as Mechthild.

The way of true love, however, in Mechthild's view, consisted not only in ecstasies but also in hanging on "the cross of love in the pure air of the Holy Spirit, turned towards the Son of the living Godhead, oblivious of all earthly things."[12] She was taught to love "nothingness" and to flee "somethingness." The paradox: if one truly desires to love, then one must leave it.

"Sinking humility" led her to embrace not only "Lady Pain" but also the "most blessed Estrangement from God," which plunged her first into purgatory and then even "under Lucifer's tail," into hell itself. "Thy SELF must go,"[13] she is instructed, if she wished to drink the "unmingled wine." As with others in the new mysticism, she experienced that "the deeper I sink, the sweeter I drink."[14]

God instructed Mechthild that her mystical life comprised three stages: "your childhood was a playmate of my Holy Spirit. Your youth was a bride of my humanity. Your old age is now a housewife of my Godhead."[15] Tenderness first marked her mystical journey, then sublime intimacy, and finally intense affliction. Strikingly enough, Mechthild much preferred the state of "blessed Estrangement from God" to the states of tenderness and intimacy.

Because of her unusual experiences and outspoken denunciations of corruption in the clergy and religious life, Mechthild was severely criticized, denounced as a heretic, and forced to flee to the Cistercian convent of Helfta, a center widely known for its mystical and literary talent. There she was warmly received by Mechthild of Hackeborn and Gertrude the Great, two other outstanding mystics of Mechthild's caliber. Her mystical and literary skills fully matured at Helfta, where she remained for the rest of her life—regarded by her contemporaries as a saint.

# Marguerite Porete

## (d. 1310)

*"God's farness is greater nearness . . . All things are one for her, without a why, and she is nothing in a One of this sort . . . She retains nothing more of herself in nothingness, because He is sufficient of Himself, that is, because He is and she is not. Thus she is stripped of all things because she is without existence, where she was before she was. Thus she has from God what He has."*[1]

Around the year 1296, Bishop Guy II of Cambrai ordered a mendicant Beguine to cease her itinerant preaching and to watch the public burning of her book, *The Mirror of Simple Annihilated Souls and Those Who Remain Only in Will and Desire of Love*, in Valenciennes, France. Despite the threats, she continued to promulgate her message and attained approbation for her book from the Cistercian Dom Franco of the Villers Abbey, the Franciscan John of Quaregnon (who admitted that he did not understand such a profound book), and the renowned Paris university master Godfrey of Fontaines, who said of it: "this alone is divine practice and nothing other than this."[2]

Because Marguerite Porete continued to promote her book and its teaching, she was rearrested and imprisoned for eighteen months. Refusing to cooperate with authorities, she was tried and condemned as a relapsed heretic, a "pseudo-woman," whose book was "filled with errors and heresies." Porete was burned at the stake on June 1, 1310, at the Place de Grèves in Paris—the first documented case of an execution for mystical heresy in Western Christianity.

Although historians disagree on precisely why Marguerite was executed, one point is clear: she was a victim of the political-ecclesiastical maelstrom of her day, especially of the tensions between the French king Philip IV and the papacy. Both the crown and the French ecclesiastical leadership (more pro-crown than anti-papal) perceived her as a threat to the established order and held the view that a genuine Beguine lived in a moderate enclosure. That Marguerite wrote in the vernacular (she is considered to be one of the greatest vernacular authors of the Middle Ages), and thus used translated biblical texts in her work, also made her suspect. Only a few years after her death, the Council of Vienne (1311–12) promulgated the document *Ad nostrum*, which lists eight articles that seem to be related to the errors for which she was executed. From then on, the term "Beguine" was synonymous with "heretic."

Unlike the "holy women" of the medieval period, Porete placed little emphasis upon prayers, fasting, and the sacraments. The new gospel that Love wrote on the "precious parchment" of her soul, in her view, could not possibly be understood by priests, clerics, members of religious orders, and enclosed Beguines. "Love's teaching" about attaining the will's "annihilation" in divinity surpassed reason, scripture, the Church's teachings, the ability to work miracles daily, continual martyrdom, and St. Paul's ecstatic journey into paradise.

Other than the details of her trial and execution, history knows very little about Porete except that she came from Hainaut in Northern France and was highly educated. Despite the condemnation of her text, it enjoyed wide dissemination—Eckhart made use of it—and exists in six versions, four languages, and thirteen manuscripts. However, its authorship was misattributed for almost six hundred years and only in 1946 was it definitely established that Porete wrote *The Mirror* and a critical edition published.

Despite scholarly disagreement about Porete's orthodoxy, her work nevertheless stands out as one of the most profound and captivating texts on apophatic mysticism in the Christian tradition. Its central theme is the will's annihilation through which the soul grasps its own nothingness and God's goodness—which she views as salvation. The allegorical figures of Soul, Reason, Love, Holy Church the Great and Holy Church the Little—in addition to a complexity of other voices—speak through poetry and prose. Although the text lacks the direct sexual imagery used by some mystics, it is redolent with the eroticism of the courtly love tradition.

The created human will, according to Porete's thinking, is the central problem of human existence. The very possibility of sin—not only its actuality—caused this Beguine great suffering. She sought much more than having her will in harmony with God's will and accomplishing it; she desired that God replace her annihilated will with his own will.

Porete employed a number of dialectical terms to describe the process by which the created will is annihilated and replaced with the divine will: all/nothing, generosity/meanness, ravishing/gentleness, distance/nearness, worthiness/unworthiness, and yearning/fulfillment. Both God and the soul, in her view, were the authors of this text that strives to negate itself through vertiginous inner contradictions. Its language borders between opposition to both orthodoxy and heterodoxy—and, what possibly can the mystical "I," that is, "an 'I' without a Me" (Paul Moemmars), mirror?

Porete considered everything that she said about God to be "slander" and a "great villainy" because not even those in paradise can comprehend the unfathomable God. Yet, this "mendicant creature" set out to write a book—a task as "futile" as "enclosing the sea in the eye"[3]—so that others could become the "perfect one." Love, in her view, produced *The Mirror*, which only the annihilated soul can comprehend, that is, the soul that has lost its being in God. Porete stated paradoxically that whatever she or anyone else said about her "miraculous work" was a lie. As the book progresses, therefore, both she and it disappear into the Trinity, in whom both have their precreational existence.

The human soul is created in the image of the Trinity. This image grounds its spiritual progress. The soul's goal is to become the "unencumbered," "annihilated," "intoxicated," "drunken forsaken soul" that drinks "the supreme beverage, which none drinks except the Trinity."[4] Its destiny is to be totally dissolved, melted, drawn, joined and united to the most high Trinity—which she described not only according to the traditional triads of Power-Wisdom-Goodness, Lover-Loved-Love but also according to her novel terms: "eternal substance" (Father), "pleasing fruition" (Son), and "loving conjunction" (Holy Spirit). The Father, in Porete's view, is the source of the Trinity; the Holy Spirit, the soul's Beloved. The Holy Spirit—who possesses everything the Father and Son have—leads her into annihilation. Through this annihilation, the image of the Trinity is transformed into the Trinity itself. The soul as nothing is all.

Porete described three types of souls, three sorts of deaths, three kinds of life, and seven "stages" or "states" of the journey of mystical annihilation. In the first stage, the soul dies the "death of sin"[5] and lives the life of grace. By stripping the soul of its power to sin mortally, God enables it to keep the commandments. The soul, however, remains "in sloth," is "cowardly," yet will be saved.

In the second stage, with Jesus Christ as the "exemplar," the "special lover" dies "the death of nature" and lives the "life of the spirit" by embracing the evangelical counsels. Although these souls are virtuous, love God and neighbor, and even desire martyrdom, Porete deemed them to be "lost in their works," "one-eyed," and unable to "grasp anything about the being of Noble Love."[6]

The "sad" soul of the third stage experiences a "boiling desire of love in multiplying"[7] the works of perfection. It also embraces a "martyrdom of the will" because the will wills its own death by fulfilling the will of another. The self must be pulverized in order to enlarge the place where love desires to be. These "sad souls" act more like "servants and merchants" than "nobility" by clinging to their virtues and works. However, they are "wise," if compared to "lost souls" because they know that they are sad, realize that there is something better, and seek a way out of their predicament. "Lady Understanding" has pity on them and will show them "the right royal road, which runs through the land of willing nothing."[8]

The soul in the fourth stage has reached what is normally considered to be the summit of the contemplative life: loving union with God. The soul has become "impenetrable" to all except "the touch of the pure delight of love."[9] Her inebriation, however, seduces her into believing that there is no higher life and she does not realize that there are two more stages beyond this.

God acts in a special way to annihilate the soul in the fifth state. The now "unencumbered" soul experiences divine life through the death of the spirit. Recognizing the coincidence of her "total wretchedness" and the "Divine Goodness," she experiences herself as a "flood of sin" sinking into a "bottomless abyss." Her will vanishes as a created something. "Now she is All," Porete wrote, "and so she is nothing, for her Beloved makes her One. Now this Soul has fallen from love into nothingness, and without such nothingness she cannot be All."[10]

The unencumbered, annihilated soul "swims, bobs, and floats"[11] in a sea of nothingness; nothing concerns her: not herself, not her neighbor, not even God Himself. Having "fallen into the certainty of knowing nothing and into certainty of willing nothing,"[12] the divine peace of the Trinity, the "FarNearness," reigns. Just as a river loses its name as it flows into the sea, just as iron is transformed into fire because of the "strength" of the flame, the unencumbered soul loses her name to become "no-thing"—"Love and such souls are one thing."[13] Although Marguerite understands the difference between becoming God by grace and being God by nature, she places little emphasis on this distinction. Her mysticism of the abyss is one of undifferentiated union wherein two become one—period.

Chapter 31 of Porete's text stands out as one of the most evocative texts on pure love in the history of Christian mysticism. The courtly love tradition of her day delighted in tests of love that measure the quality of one's love for the beloved. In Marguerite's schema, these tests are also transformative of the soul. She states that she wills only what God wills—even if God had never willed her into existence to prevent her from doing evil. Even if God willed to use his full power to torment her for her sins or for nothing at all, she confesses that she would prefer whatever came from God to anything else, even to eternal glory coming from herself.

Rather than receive something that did not come from God, Porete would gladly will the annihilation of all things. If she could avoid displeasing God in any way, she would will that Jesus suffer again and again as much as he had for her. If she did not "have this gift from the pure love which He has for me of Himself, from His pure goodness, from His will alone, as a lover has for his beloved,"[14] then she would refuse even the gifts she received through Christ's humanity, the Virgin Mary, and the saints—and accept eternal torment.

"FarNearness" then asked her three questions. First, what would happen to her if she knew that God would be better pleased, if she loved another more than him; second, if God loved someone else more than her; third, if someone else loved her more than God. "*And there I fainted,*" she wrote, "for I could respond nothing to these three things, nor refuse, nor deny."[15] The annihilated, perfect soul at this stage also comprehends that she can never slip back to any of the previous stages because God has replaced her will with his own.

In the sixth stage, the soul has become such an "abyss of humility" that she no longer sees either herself or God. "But God," Porete wrote, "sees Himself in her by His divine majesty, who clarifies this Soul with Himself, so that she sees only that there is nothing except God Himself Who is, and from whom all things are."[16] In this state,

"Ravishing FarNearness" acts like an "aperture," a "spark," and "is nothing other than the showing of the glory of the soul."[17] This experience of beatifying "glory" is transient because the aperture closes quickly, but for as long as it is open, the soul experiences heavenly bliss. The "glory" of the sixth stage actually comes from the seventh stage, the beatific afterlife, the ineffable stage of which we have no understanding until the soul leaves the body.

The lightning of glory that flashes into the sixth from the seventh stage comes so suddenly that the soul has no awareness of it and is lifted up to its precreational existence in the Father, the source of the Trinity and of all things. As often as the Trinity moves within the soul—which now knows nothing and All, is nothing and All—the soul rises from the fifth to the sixth stage, only to fall back quickly to the fifth stage. Porete understood the manifestations of the Trinity, the "FarNearness," as "movement," not because the soul moves herself in the Trinity but because "the Trinity works the showing of her glory in this soul."[18] These moments of *epektasis* are analogous to the systole and diastole of the heart.

Porete did not emphasize—unlike other women of the new mysticism—the role of the eternal Son or of Christ's physicality in mystical annihilation. On the other hand, the pure wine that inebriates the annihilated soul, in her view, is known to Christ's humanity, which "drinks at the most noble tap after the Trinity."[19] The kenosis of the eternal Son into his "sweet humanity" is also the exemplar of the soul's descent into wretchedness—a theophany of true kenosis, the emptying of the will by annihilation—and what empowers the soul's ascent. Marguerite also views the Blessed Virgin Mary as a model of the annihilated soul.

Love had taught Marguerite that the annihilated soul "is *scorched* through mortification and *burned* through the ardor of the *fire* of charity, and her *ashes* are thrown into the open sea through the nothingness of will."[20] The cruel incineration of her bodily life at the stake in Paris mirrored the mystical annihilation she had lived. The woman who had said that she "lived not by the life of grace, or by the life of spirit only, but by the divine life, unencumbered—but not gloriously, for she is not glorified—but lives divinely, for God has sanctified her of Himself,"[21] can now say that she lives the glorious life.

# Meister Eckhart

## (ca. 1260–1328)

*"The eye by which I see God is the same as the eye by which God sees me. My eye and God's eye are one and the same—one in seeing, one in knowing, and one in loving."*[1]

Born in a Thuringian village called Hochheim, Meister Eckhart entered the Order of Preachers (Dominicans) at Erfurt when he was approximately fifteen years old. Because of his prodigious intellectual promise, Eckhart was sent to study at the center of the Western intellectual world, Paris, and later, at Cologne. He received his master's degree from Paris—hence his nickname "Meister." So enormous was his popularity and success that he taught there on three different occasions. Later, our friar spent ten years teaching theology at Strasbourg, where he, in addition, attained fame as a preacher and spiritual director. Well respected among his Dominican confreres, the Meister also interlaced his academic career with various positions of high authority in his order.

In 1326, the Franciscan archbishop of Cologne charged Eckhart with heresy. The two lists of questionable propositions drawn up from his writings prompted the Meister to write his trenchant text *The Defense*, which, among other things, stated: "For I am able to err, but I cannot be a heretic, since one has to do with the intellect and the other with the will."[2] However, he renounced the twenty-six questionable articles *insofar as* they could generate in the minds of the faithful a heretical opinion, or one erroneous and hostile to the faith.

Appealing to the Holy See, Eckhart left for Avignon to defend himself but died before the case was concluded. On March 27, 1329, Pope John XXII condemned the two lists of propositions according to their "obvious meaning," a relatively benign denunciation prompted by the Meister's undoubtedly orthodox intent and sincere submission to Church authority. But the pope's language made it clear that he wished to put an end to Eckhart's influence.

Even scholars sympathetic to Eckhart admit that his modes of expression—despite their profundity—are at times infelicitous. He seemed to have given insufficient attention to the intellectual ability of his audience and to how easily some of his expressions could be misunderstood. The Meister occasionally succumbed to intellectual abstraction founded on little more than wordplay. Even his greatest supporters admit that not all his statements can be defended.

Meister Eckhart still looms as one of the most controversial, most difficult, and most fascinating figures in the Christian mystical tradition. This medieval enigma has been called a monist, a pantheist, a Quietist, a mystic of pure inwardness, a mystic of joy in the world, and a reformer before the Reformation. He has also been called the father of German idealism, a medieval Zen master, a source for Nazi thinking, the first Marxist, a forerunner of deconstructionist philosophy, and the champion of those who mistakenly assume that a mystic must necessarily be an iconoclast.

Past studies on Eckhart usually overlooked the dynamic relationship that existed between his role as preacher, spiritual director, philosopher, theologian, and mystic. Contemporary studies have corrected this by underscoring what he actually was: a highly educated, non-conventional, *medieval Dominican friar* whose vocation was *preaching* God's word—be it in the pulpit, in the classroom as a Master of the Sacred Page, or in private conversation with others as a master of life. The Meister sought to awaken mystical consciousness in the liturgical act of interpreting, preaching, and hearing the biblical word—not to create a theological system.

As the hinge between the "old" Latin and the new vernacular mysticisms—which he appropriated and transposed—Eckhart stressed a mysticism of the *grunt*. Not only is the *grunt* an uncreated something in (not of) the soul but it is also the groundless ground of both God and the soul. It transcends the soul and even the Father, the Son, the Holy Spirit, and the divine essence.

Eckhart's "metaphysics of flow" (Bernard McGinn) comprehended the dynamic reciprocity of the "flowing forth" of all things from God's hidden *grunt* and the "flowing-back" or "breaking-through" of the universe into essential identity with this divine source. The Godhead "becomes" God in the flowing forth of creation and God "unbecomes" in the silent, unmoving Godhead. God's inner "boiling" results in the Divine Persons; the "boiling over" results in creation. The precreational existence and oneness of all things in God may very well be the hermeneutical key to understanding the Meister. More controversial is Eckhart's assertion that creation is a "fall" from Oneness, the ground for evil in the world, and ultimately an illusion.

The Meister's creative mystagogy centered on aiding Christians to "break through" to the *grunt*—that he also called the "spark," the "tiny village," the "tiny castle," and the "virgin-wife." "God's ground is my ground," he preached, "and my ground is God's ground. Here I live from what is my own, as God lives from what is his own."[3] One experiences in the *grunt* the fused identity, that is, the distinct-indistinct union of God and the soul. "The eye in which I see God," the preacher said, "is the same eye in which God sees me. My eye and God's eye are one eye and one seeing, one knowing and one loving."[4] One might also say that when the soul sinks into God's abyss that God sinks into the soul's abyss, one sinking and one abyss. In Eckhart's view, however, not even the Father, the Son, or the Holy Spirit can "peek into" this mysterious ground—"it is only as he is One and onefold that he may enter into that One which I have called the Little Castle of the soul."[5]

Eckhart taught that there are three paths to God. The first path seeks God in all creatures. The second path is, paradoxically, "a pathless path, free yet bound, raised aloft and wafted off almost beyond self and all things, beyond will and images."[6] The third path is a "being at home," upon which one sees God as he is. This path focuses on Christ as the way, the truth, and the life: "One Christ, one Person; one Christ, one Father; one Christ, one Spirit; three, one; three: way, truth, and life; one beloved Christ in whom all this is."[7]

Eckhart's writings and sermons—unlike that of his contemporaries—show little interest in Jesus' outward passion, the minute details of his physical sufferings and death, and the historical realities of his life, death, and resurrection. The Word became flesh, in the preacher's view, so that we might become divine. The Meister's pan-Christic ontology links the Incarnation to creation, that is, the Word assumed not *a* human nature but the human nature common to all, a nature "without image or particularity." Eckhart makes the astonishing claim that the Father begets Christ in the soul in the very same way the Father begets the Son eternally: "When the Father begets his Son in me, I am that one and no other."[8]

The true follower of Christ, in Eckhart's view, possesses true inner poverty and "wants nothing, knows nothing, and has nothing,"[9]—not even "god" (the false god created by the human mind). True poverty demands having no will of one's own, not even the will to fulfill God's will! One is indifferent to all creatures, to one's past sins, to one's salvation, and even to God. One is simply empty.

True poverty is attained by a "breaking through" to one's precreational existence in the *grunt*. "In this breakthrough," Eckhart says that "I receive that God and I are one. Then I am what I was."[10] However, human means can neither reach nor comprehend this *grunt*. Only by abandoning all human ingenuity can one descend into the "virgin-wife" that is "bare" and "free of all names," as empty and free of all names as is God. Paradoxically, inner poverty forces God to love the person because God must pour himself into a perfectly empty soul.

The Meister is supposed to have preached: "When God laughs at the soul and the soul laughs back at God, the persons of the Trinity are begotten. When the Father laughs at the Son and the Son laughs back at the Father, that laughter gives pleasure, that pleasure gives joy, that joy gives love, and that love is the Holy Spirit."[11] But he preferred to speak of the Trinity as the indistinct One. The differentiation between Father, Son, and Holy Spirit came, in his view, from the oneness. "The oneness is the difference," he preached, "and the difference is the oneness. The greater the difference, the greater the unity, because this is difference beyond difference."[12] Eckhart seemed to have located God's oneness in the "silent darkness of the hidden Fatherhood."[13]

In the view of some scholars, the Meister's god is a "quaternity," that is, a foursome god, comprised of a trinity and a distinct godhead. Others understand his god as the Gnostic god, the absolutely hidden god—the God above and distinct from the God of revelation. Still others deem Eckhart's God beyond God, "in which distinction never gazed," to be both trinitarian and supertrinitarian.

Was "the man from whom God hid nothing"[14] a mystic? Let it be said in closing that some scholars say no and others—the better scholars, to my mind—say yes. Despite Eckhart's silence about his own mystical life, he seems to have spoken from the *grunt*. There is no doubt, however, that the Meister was and still is an influential mystical theologian and mystagogue.

# John Ruusbroec

## (1293–1381)

*"In this tempest of love two spirits contend, the Spirit of God and our spirit. From these two there arises the strife of love."*[1]

John Ruusbroec, "the Admirable," has been called the "second Dionysius the Areopagite," the West's most articulate trinitarian mystic, and even the greatest mystical writer in the Christian tradition. This spiritual titan not only reached the summit of mystical contemplation but also possessed the theological profundity and the limpid prose to express it—especially that of the unitive life. Where other mystics have stammered, faltered, resorted to dizzying paradoxes, and complained of their inability to express the heights of the mystical life, "the ecstatic doctor" stands out as mellifluous, straightforward, lucid, and nuanced. Paradoxically, his works remain relatively unknown outside of learned circles.

John was born in Ruusbroec, South Brabant, about five miles from Brussels. When he was eleven years old, he went to live with an uncle, a canon of the Brussels cathedral, the collegiate church of St. Gudula. Ordained there at the age of twenty-four, he spent the following twenty-six years in priestly ministry, and quickly acquired a reputation for holiness and penetrating discernment. In the early 1330s, he wrote his first work, *The Kingdom of Lovers*, which depicts the seven gifts of the Holy Spirit as seven streams by which the Spirit leads a person.

Dissatisfied with this text and receiving "brotherly" criticism for his view that one can become one with God "without a difference," John wrote his masterpiece, *The Spiritual Espousals*. At the request of a hermit, he then wrote the anti-Quietist treatise *The Sparkling Stone*, which describes the perfect Christian as one who is zealous, interiorly fervent and spiritual, lifted up to the contemplation of God, and generous in virtuous service to all. Two ascetical-catechetical texts,

*The Four Temptations* and *The Christian Faith*, soon followed. His highly allegorical and highly popular work, *The Spiritual Tabernacle*, contains excellent material on contemplation.

At fifty years of age, Ruusbroec, along with two companions, retired for a more contemplative life to the forest of Soignes, Groenendaal (green valley), just outside Brussels, where they eventually became Augustinians. Living the "God-seeing" life for thirty-eight years, he wrote the treatise, *The Seven Enclosures*, that gives instructions on how to live the cloistered life. The book *A Mirror of Eternal Blessedness* likewise sprang from this period. The treatise focuses on the soul as a "living mirror" upon which God has stamped his image to make our created life one, without intermediary, with this image and the life we have eternally in God.

Ruusbroec's treatise *The Seven Rungs in the Ladder of Spiritual Love* describes the Christian as continually ascending the "ladder" in contemplation and descending it in good works. The concise treatise of his mature thought, *The Little Book of Clarification*, emphasizes a salient feature of John's mystical theology: that our final participation in God's beatitude is a oneness in love, not simply a oneness in being or nature. Through *re*union with God in contemplative love, a person's precreational union with God—severed by Adam's alienating sin—is now restored. The last of Ruusbroec's eleven treatises, *The Twelve Beguines*, is a one-volume compilation of three or four separate works dealing with topics ranging from astrology to contemplation. His treatises—all written in Middle Dutch—stand out primarily as works adapting and clarifying the *Espousals* for different audiences. Despite living in an age of incessant war, famine, and plague, Ruusbroec's books radiate peace, tranquility, and love of neighbor.

The skewed beliefs and practices of the Brethren of the Free Spirit prompted Ruusbroec to write his treatises. He spoke at length of "diabolical persons" who considered themselves to be Christ, or "the Creator and Sustainer of the universe," and who cried out: "Rejoice with me, for I am God!" The "beastly practices of their evil wicked sect" led the Brethren to reject Christian practices and to indulge in licentious and antinomian behavior. On the Last Day, they claimed, everything will become a single, simple divine substance, "one essential beatitude," without any knowledge or love of God—a view Ruusbroec repudiated as "the most perverse and foolish heresy that has ever been heard."[2]

Bloemardinne (perhaps Ruusbroec's first opponent), known as the female apostle of "seraphic love," proclaimed that she was not only perfect in virtue and impeccable but also that her love was as pure as that of the seraphim—even of God himself. She counseled permitting the flesh to do whatever it wanted in order to avoid distracting one's so-called deified spirit.

Ruusbroec assessed some of his Free Spirit opponents as worthy, cunning, and rhetorically skilled. The deception of those who claimed that they were not perfect, still capable of advancing in virtue, and practiced great penances in order to acquire a reputation for holiness was the most difficult, in his view, to unmask. He literally wept over these "deceived persons" who fancied themselves to be great contemplatives but were not.

Ruusbroec distinguished a graced state of "emptiness and rest" from a purely natural one. He knew of a deep and satisfying state of "bare emptiness," which—although not sinful in itself—was simply an "empty idleness" devoid of God.[3] All too often, however, it led pseudo-contemplatives to assume that their experience of the "bare essence of their soul" was identical with genuine God-consciousness. Becoming prideful, self-satisfied practitioners of Quietism, they lived out their last days filled with anxiety and restlessness. Ruusbroec had undoubtedly known or even met those who had lost their state of "empty, restful introversion," despaired, and died like "rabid dogs."[4]

Trinitarian exemplarism is the key to Ruusbroec's mystical theology. This theological view emphasizes that creatures not only have their created being in time but also an eternal being in God—a precreational existence in which they are identical with God. Writing of the dynamic indwelling of the Father, Son, and Holy Spirit—the dynamic dance of the Three Persons in each other that is the source of all life and becoming—Ruusbroec contends that "here all creatures are therefore one being and one life with God—apart from themselves, in their eternal origin."[5] Contemplatives alone, to his way of thinking, are able to experience and to "behold" this precreational existence of everything in God.

Ruusbroec retrieved the view attributed to the Greek fathers that the "Father is the origin of the entire Godhead both essentially and personally."[6] The Father eternally begets and spirates from his "divine darkness," "divine silence," and "fertile desert" a glowing Word of Love. The ever Three Persons are ever One, ever at work and ever at rest. Like the heart's systole and diastole, the Trinity lives in the eternal contraction from the trinity of Persons to the triune Unity and expansion from the Unity to the trinity of Persons. The triune oneness of the human spirit as memory, intellect, and will can possess the Trinity's communication of its own life and participate in the divine movements within the triune Unity.

Ruusbroec's treatises—unlike texts of other mystics who describe mystical ascent in terms of discrete stages—delineate three interpenetrating and coexisting levels of union: the active, the interior, and the contemplative lives. The active life, in his view, contains a dynamism toward both the interior and the contemplative life; the interior life, a movement toward both the active and the contemplative life; the contemplative life, a threefold unity with the triune God. In order to discover and experience within oneself these three unions, the Christian must "go forth in virtue, and dying he must enter into God."[7] These two movements constitute the "perfect life" and must be joined together within a person as closely as soul and body.

The active life—the first level of union with God "through an intermediary"—requires asceticism, virtue, good works, and a full participation in the Church's sacramental life. Genuine union with God is impossible without God's grace, active striving for virtue, and a fully Christian life. Because our nature is "scattered," reunifying it demands directing everything we are to God; in this endeavor, we must also emulate the strength, industry, and social cohesiveness of both the "ant" and the "bee."

Ruusbroec's apophaticism focuses on God as the "nameless simple One" who dwells in "incomprehensible sublimity." "This," he writes, "is the highest knowledge of God that a person may have in the active life: that he recognize, in the light of faith, that God is incomprehensible and unknowable."[8] One must therefore direct one's spirit to him alone and rest in him who alone is above all creatures. "When [the soul] loves and rests above all gifts and above itself and above all creatures," Ruusbroec writes, "then it dwells in God and God in it. This is how we should meet Christ in the highest level of the active life."[9]

The interior life—the second level of union with God "without intermediary"—impels the contemplative to follow a "homeward-turning love" to the "topmost part of spirit" and, with a mind "bare and devoid of images," to adhere to God in "fathomless love."[10] The contemplative feels that his love, in its ground where it begins and ends, is blissful and—paradoxically—without any ground because "whenever the higher powers turn inward through active love, they are united with God without intermediary in a simple knowledge of all truth and in an essential experience and savoring of all goodness."[11] Although Ruusbroec says surprisingly little about what has come to be called the dark nights of the senses and spirit, he does call attention to the "hellish pain" that alternates with the "beatitude" of the interior life.

In one of the most beautiful passages in the Christian mystical tradition, Ruusbroec depicts the wrestling of love between God's Spirit and the contemplative's spirit when they unite. "God," he writes, "through the Holy Spirit, inclines Himself toward us, and thereby we are touched in love. And by God's operation and the faculty of loving, our spirit presses into and inclines itself towards God, and thereby God is touched. From these two, there arises the strife of love."[12] This encounter wounds both God and the human spirit with love and intensifies their mutual craving for each other. God's Spirit and the human spirit also mutually illuminate each other, sparkle, reveal their faces, and "flow" into each other. "This flowing out and flowing back," Ruusbroec writes, "cause the fountain of love to overflow. Thus God's touch and our loving craving and our giving in return, keep love steadfast. This flowing out and flowing back cause the fountain of love to overflow."[13]

The human soul's constant craving seeks to devour God but "God's touch" has already "swallowed up" the soul. Although the soul dwells in "simple, undifferentiated love," there remains a dynamism to go forward because of the essential distinction between the soul's and God's being—the highest distinction that a person can *experience*—and the most interior exercise a person can practice.

The contemplative life—the third level of union with God "without a difference"—moves the "enlightened spirit" into the Father's silence who speaks his eternal Word in a "maelstrom of essential love." This spirit rests no longer in its own "essential being" but in the Trinity's "superessential being"—the incomprehensible darkness of the Father, the radiance of the Word, and the burning love of the Holy Spirit. In the contemplative life, the enlightened spirit experiences undifferentiated unity with God: "we *feel* ourselves to be one with God, for by means of our transformation in God we feel ourselves to be swallowed up in the groundless abyss of our eternal blessedness, in which we can never discover any difference between ourselves and God. This is the *highest* of all experiences."[14] Resting in the Trinity's heart, the contemplative concomitantly experiences the preexisting oneness of all things in God.

The Bridegroom also comes to the "enlightened spirit" in such a way that it becomes the very Light it sees, through which it sees, the Breath which it breathes, and by which it breathes. In this simple act of spiritual seeing and breathing, the human spirit is one life and one spirit with the Trinity. The nondualistic experience of "beatitude"—this mystical *feeling* (one of his operative words)—does not imply in Ruusbroec's thinking a metaphysical identity with God. The datum of mystical consciousness diminishes in no way that God remains God and the creature remains creature.

In imitation of the Trinity and its "inflow" and "outflow" of love, the authentic contemplative lives the "common life" when he is equally ready for contemplation and action and is perfect in both. However, no one can possess this "common life" unless he is a contemplative, that is, a person who is grounded in true peace and interior silence and who cleaves to God in self-effacing love. The enlightened spirit rests in God whom it enjoys and there falls asleep. Falling into a transrational darkness, the contemplative feels that he has lost his way and died—"that he has become one with God without a difference."[15] However, the contemplative is resurrected in this "fathomless abyss" by "flowing forth to all who need him, for the living spring of the Holy Spirit is so rich that it can never be drained dry."[16] When Ruusbroec died at the ripe old age of eighty-eight, he had clearly lived what he so ardently taught.

# Gregory Palamas

## (1296–1359)

*"Thus the perfect contemplation of God and divine things is a participation in divine things, a gift and a possession rather than a process of negation. But these possessions and gifts are ineffable."*[1]

Gregory Palamas—the last great mystical theologian of medieval Mount Athos—is one of the leading spokesmen of the Greek patristic tradition. This fascinating Byzantine figure was born in Constantinople of a noble family with connections at the court of Emperor Andronicus II. While receiving a liberal education at the imperial university, he befriended the mystically inclined metropolitan of Philadelphia. When he was twenty-two years old, he not only entered one of the famous Mount Athos monasteries—the centers par excellence of Byzantine spirituality—but also convinced his mother, two brothers, and two sisters to enter monastic life.

Turkish raids in 1325 prompted him and some of his companions to go to Thessalonica, where they formed a semimonastic community. After ordination to the priesthood, Palamas and ten others retired to a hermitage near Beroea, where they lived the hesychastic (*hesychia* = quietude) life of one who rests in God. The hesychast monk spent five days a week in solitude and in the constant repetition of the Jesus Prayer, with weekends in community for Eucharist and spiritual conversation. The goal, content, and justification of this way of life were permanent prayer that transformed the entire person through the direct consciousness of the triune God.

Returning to Mount Athos in 1331, Palamas continued his hesychast way of life. However, he was soon to be embroiled in a bitter political, ecclesiastical, and theological strife that continued for most of his life. In 1347, he became archbishop of Thessalonica. Kidnapped and held for ransom by the Turks from 1354 to 1355, he died in 1359, and was canonized by the Orthodox Church in 1368.

One key source of Orthodox spirituality and mysticism is ecclesiastical and hierarchical: the Orthodox liturgy that witnesses regally to the ineffable, invisible, and incomprehensible God. The other significant source was hesychasm. With deep roots in the Desert Fathers, the hesychasts emphasize the unceasing repetition of the Jesus Prayer, "Lord Jesus Christ, Son of God, have mercy on me, a sinner," or a simplified version of it. By attaching Christ to one's breathing, according to the hesychasts, one thereby places Christ in one's heart, the human center of consciousness.

The Calabrian monk-philosopher Barlaam fiercely attacked the hesychast monks for their beliefs, way of life, and method of prayer—especially its physical aspects. He ridiculed hesychasts as omphalopsychites—those who have their souls in their navels—because of the body posture they assumed while praying. For this antimystical, Platonic humanist the human body could play no role in pure prayer. Moreover, knowledge of God, for him, must be founded on reasoning from the existence of creatures to the Creator. The claim that God can be directly experienced he rejected as the ravings of obscurantist fanatics. Because of the hesychasts' emphasis upon the divinizing and transforming Taboric light, he denounced them as heretical Messalians, that is, as the "praying people" who contended that they could see the Trinity with their physical eyes.

From 1338 to 1341, Gregory Palamas wrote nine treatises, *For the Defense of Those Who Practice Sacred Quietude*, three groups of three books also called *The Triads*, against Barlaam. These treatises offer a magnificent exposition of the Orthodox position on the deification of the human person in Christ and an invincible defense of the hesychasts' position.

The Byzantine Church, however, at four councils in Constantinople, affirmed the orthodoxy of hesychast spirituality and mysticism through the promulgation of "The Declaration of the Holy Mountain in Defense of Those who Devoutly Practice a Life of Stillness," otherwise known as the "Hagioritic Tome." This work sanctioned the view that mystical experience is some sort of immediate God-consciousness, a foretaste of eternal life, and the normal counterpart of a properly oriented ascetical life. Palamas had won the day over Barlaam.

Palamas defends the hesychasts' way of life and method of prayer for many reasons. First, the life of prayer requires ascetical combat because interior prayer is impossible without disciplining of the senses. Second, because the mind is so easily distracted, Gregory suggests a method—especially for beginners—to attain "unified recollection." Controlled breathing and concentrating one's eyes upon either the navel or the breast brings about both outer and inner quiet. This bodily exercise enables the hesychast to "recall into the interior of the heart a power which is ever flowing outward through the faculty of sight."[2]

Unlike the intellectualistic orientation of Origen, Evagrius, and Pseudo-Dionysius, the hesychasts seek to unite the mind (*nous*) and heart so that contemplation becomes the prayer of a heart totally dedicated to Christ. The monk attains divinization (*theosis*) by forcing the mind to descend into the heart, the "seat of thoughts." The spiritual combat of the hesychasts is directed more against inordinate desires and less against distracting thoughts.

By reorienting their prayer to the biblical heart, the hesychasts prevent what Gregory calls "the greatest of Hellenic errors" and "an invention of demons," that is, the attempt to make "the mind 'go out,' not only from fleshly thoughts but out of the body itself."[3] He knows of a contemplative technique that results in a type of intellectual fainting and death. This corpse-like method of prayer requires an ascetical life that produced "insensibility" (*analgesia*), which Palamas—in the tradition of the Desert Fathers—branded as "petrification," or becoming like stone. The true hesychast, on the other hand, seeks to "recollect the mind not only within the body and heart but also within itself."[4] This results in a healing, transforming, and divinizing "unified recollection," which flows out of itself in a genuine love of neighbor.

Palamas writes penetratingly of the Word becoming flesh and of our bodies as temples of the Holy Spirit. In his view, we carry in our bodies the Father's light seen in the face of Jesus Christ. Because we are body-persons, Palamas dismisses Barlaam's claim that physical pain and true prayer cannot coexist. Killing the passionate part of the soul renders true union with God an impossibility; the "insensible" person of "petrification" has simply done away with prayer. Contrary to Barlaam's assertion that the body can play no role in prayer, Gregory emphasizes that contemplative joy reverberates into the body to quell, reorder, and transform its evil appetites.

Taming and transforming the irascible and concupiscent human appetites is one of the goals of the true hesychast. Palamas applauds the monks whose passions obey reason—an obedience gained by asceticism and the constant remembrance of God. *Apatheia*, true psychosomatic wholeness, has nothing in common with insensibility, or petrification. As an intrinsic aspect of the process of deification, it gives a foretaste of the risen life.

The prayer of the heart, for those chosen by God, leads to the vision of the Holy Spirit as uncreated grace and divinization. The Holy Spirit reveals himself as a transforming divine light that can be seen in this life by those with graced mystical eyes. Identical with the light that filled Christ during his transfiguration on Mount Tabor, the "Taboric light" is, in Gregory's view, the "uncreated energy" of the Godhead. Although God's essence can never be known, the inexhaustible God can be known and experienced through his "uncreated energies." As he writes, "this light is thus divine, and the saints rightly call it 'divinity,' because it is the source of deification. It is not only 'divinity,' but also deification-in-itself, and thearchy. While it appears to produce a distinction and multiplication within the one God, yet it is nonetheless the Divine Principle, more-than-God, and more-than-Principle."[5] The distinction between God's essence and his uncreated energies is as controversial now as it is classical.

Because of his own experience in worship and contemplation, Palamas speaks with great authority on the hesychast view of the ineffable, incomprehensible God who is beyond both knowing and unknowing. Against those who understood the contemplative experience as some sort of nescience generated by transsensual and transintellectual abstraction and negation, this Athos monk views it as a "union and a divinization." The graced stripping away of everything—both earthly and spiritual—that imprints itself upon the mind attains the gift and possession of participating in "divine things" through the "ineffable vision" of God.

The visionless vision of God, in Palamas's view, transcends the entire body-person; nonetheless, the entire body-person participates in it. Gregory's incarnational perspective could not be clearer. Because the divinity of the incarnate Word is united to Christ's human nature (both body and soul), Christ's deified flesh, through the soul's mediation, enables it to accomplish God's work. "So similarly," Palamas writes, "in the spiritual man, the grace of the Spirit, transmitted to the body through the soul, grants to the body also the experience of things divine, and allows it the same blessed experiences as the soul undergoes."[6] Few, if any, authors in the Christian mystical tradition have written so lucidly on genuine Christian apophatic prayer and the body's participation in it.

When the movie version of Nikos Kazantzakis's novel, *The Last Temptation of Christ*, appeared in 1988, some commentators espoused the view that Jesus—because he is like us in all things but sin—experienced sexual disorder (for example, nocturnal emissions) and sexual temptations. They further asserted that to deny this opinion was tantamount to Docetism, that is, the heretical belief that Christ only seemed to be human.

Palamas would have rejected this as psilanthropy, that is, the heretical position that Christ was a "mere man." Gregory's high Christology stresses the hypostatic union of Christ's human nature with the divine Word. The God-Man—like us in all things, *sin excepted*—was not only free of original sin but also possessed total human wholeness. The passionate part of his humanity perfectly obeyed reason and will. The Taboritic light that emanated from his body was one sign of this. Palamas knew, as did many in the Christian mystical tradition, from deep personal experience that the monk who attains *apatheia*, perfect psychosomatic wholeness, has tamed the passionate part of his nature and is no longer plagued by sexual temptations and sexual disorder. (The same teaching can be found in other religions—Theravada Buddhism, for example.) What the monk gains only through years of graced asceticism and contemplation, Christ had by virtue of being the God-Man.

# Richard Rolle

## (ca. 1300–1349)

*"I was sitting in a certain chapel, delighting in the sweetness of prayer or meditation, when suddenly I felt within myself an unusually pleasant heat. At first I wondered where it came from, but it was not long before I realized that it was from none of his creatures but from the Creator himself."*[1]

Richard Rolle—a prolific author of Latin and English devotional treatises and poetry—was the most widely read spiritual writer up to the time of the Reformation. Scholars have called attention to both the verbal brilliance of his Latin and his audacity to write in English. Latin was the language of learning; French, the socially acceptable language. Acknowledged as a genuine pioneer of vernacular writing and even as "the father of English literature," he is believed to have had the gift of "automatic writing," that is, writing produced with little or no conscious effort.

Rolle's most significant work, *The Fire of Love*, is a passionate, sometimes impetuous, defense of the eremitical life that he considers superior to communal, religious life and to the busy life of the clergy. Unlike the lazy tramps of his time (the *girovagi*), the true hermit, in his view, lives loving God and neighbor. He may "flee from the face of man," but he also despises worldly approval and esteems all men and women as more worthy than himself. Eschewing idleness and firmly resisting the pleasures of the flesh, he finds his joy in devotion and in the "sweetness of prayer."

Born in the village of Thornton, near Pickering, in the diocese of York, Richard Rolle studied at Oxford but dropped out before obtaining his degree. Disenchanted by those who preferred "useless theological debates," fame, and dignities to the love of Christ, he donned a homemade traditional hermit's habit and ran away from home.

The Holy Spirit had instilled in Rolle a deep regret for the "worldly corruption" of his youth and a desire for the solitary life. Overcoming all obstacles—especially vilification from family and friends—he surrendered totally to Christ. From that point on, Rolle continually sought solitude and moved "from one place to another," often necessary because of hostile circumstances.

Although hermits were not required to stay in one location, this frequent change of venue disturbed Rolle's conscience. Because he had not received episcopal approval for his way of life, he was not a conventional hermit. Moreover, the eremitical life sanctioned by the Church required proof—which he lacked—that he could support himself, either by undertaking some public work (ferryboat operation, small farm, and the like) or by endowment. Neither did Rolle become a total recluse, that is, one totally confined to one house and "enclosed" by a formal episcopal ceremony. Later on, however, Richard's father recognized the authenticity of his son's vocation and provided some means of support for his new way of life.

Approximately three years after Rolle's initial conversion, "heaven's door" opened and the "Face" was uncovered so that "the eye of his heart might contemplate heavenly things."[2] One year later, the "heat of eternal love" seized his heart. While sitting in chapel, he experienced within himself "an unaccustomed and joyous burning ardor." Rolle judged that it came not from any creature but from God because of its agreeable, burning quality. Along with this "conscious and incredibly sweet warmth," came an "infusion and understanding of heavenly, spiritual sounds," melodies and sounds that can be heard only by those dead to earthly things.

This heavenly symphony gave rise to a corresponding inner harmony that transformed Rolle's thinking into song. Because of such internal, spiritual harmony, he rejected any and all exterior auditory experiences that conflicted with it. Puzzled why he had been the recipient of heavenly wonders, he realized they were pure gifts beyond human attainment and also bestowed upon those with a special love for Jesus' name. Claiming that God had given him the grace to scale the "heights of loving Christ," he also thought that he had been "confirmed in grace" and was at peace, as much as it is possible for "mortal man" to be.

Rolle confessed that his heart on many occasions was so enflamed that he almost died from an excess of love. He wrote, "Whence he is continually pierced, as it were, in the physical embraces of eternal love, because in contemplating incessantly, he tries to ascend to the seeing of that uncircumscribed light with his whole desire."[3] This hermit not only experienced God as fire, song, and sweetness but also as ineffable and incomprehensible. Speaking about God, for him, was comparable to attempting to "empty the sea drop by drop, and bit by bit to squeeze it all into a tiny hole in the earth."[4]

A deep love of Jesus' name is also a salient feature of Rolle's spirituality and mysticism. He urged his readers to fix the name of Jesus firmly in their hearts so that the name "Jesu" is honey in the mouth, melody in the heart, and joy to the ear. The name "Jesu" also cleanses from sin, bestows peace, and fills the heart with overflowing love. "It will chase off the devil," Rolle wrote, "and eliminate terror, open heaven, and create a mystic."[5]

Rolle used an incantatory language redolent of ecstatic transports. After years of solitary prayer, he had received intoxicating, ravishing, and annihilating experiences of the Beloved's embraces. His "seraphic" (the angels known for their burning love) mysticism of love focused upon God as inner fire, sweetness, heavenly melody, and song. Because of his experiences of heavenly music, Rolle also possessed a heightened sense of the angelic world; contemplatives, in his view, sit among the seraphim who are "completely absorbed in supreme love, an indescribable love blazes in their souls and makes them love God with such sweetness and devotion. Fundamentally they know nothing within themselves but spiritual heat, heavenly song, divine sweetness."[6]

Because of Rolle's *seeming* emphasis upon the psychosomatic effects of contemplation and his minimal statements on mystical purgation, two later influential English mystics, Walter Hilton and the anonymous author of *The Cloud of Unknowing*, distrusted Rolle as a spiritual guide. Labeled as a "sensory mystic" because of the sensuousness of his experiences, he has often been dismissed as overly emotional and superficial.

Rolle, however, described many of his mystical experiences in terms of the *spiritual* senses. He was much more interested in the *spiritual* fire, melody, and sweetness that *transformed* him than in the physical phenomena as such. "I judge it better," he wrote, "to be 'rapt' of the love in which a man may most greatly merit."[7] He praised those raptures in which a "vile sinner" is filled with spiritual joy, taken to God, and transformed into a child of God. Richard did enjoy sensuous spiritual experiences but he preferred to be "wholly and perfectly bound to the desires of [his] Savior."[8] He stressed, too, that Christ always had divine contemplation but never "the absence of control of the body."

Rolle wrote *The Fire of Love* with the conviction that those who love God will experience transformative warmth, music, and sweetness both in the depths of their soul and, on occasion, with their entire person. The most trustworthy mystics in the Christian tradition likewise expected this. The extremely sober and prudent St. Ignatius of Loyola, for example, not only experienced many somatic phenomena in conjunction with his deepest mystical graces but also expected those making his famous spiritual exercises to reorder and transform their psychosomatic life through intense Christian emotions.

Rolle demanded of himself a wholehearted and uncompromising love of God and Christ. The hermit, to his way of thinking, leaves parents, property, and the world for the sake of following Christ. Refraining from wanton and improper desires as much as possible, he was dead to the world for the sake of cleaving to God and Christ. The love of Christ and of the Creator burned so powerfully in him that he was able to "trample down" every temptation. The "calm of holy desires" permeated his being. The abnegated Rolle could write: "If he were thrown into the fire of hell he would not burn! For he has completely extinguished the seductions and delights of life which come to him from outside."[9]

Rolle considered the contemplative life—which for him is the eremitical life—as superior to the active life of preaching, administering the sacraments (there is some evidence that he became a priest in his later life), and practical charity. Some participants in the active life may be much holier, in his view, than some in the contemplative life, but he nevertheless maintained that "the best contemplatives are superior to the best actives."[10] Contemplative life properly lived demands more grace than the active life because contemplatives love God more ardently, have a more fervent love, and "enjoy continually the embrace of their Beloved."[11] In addition, because love is in the will and not in good works as such, the contemplative is still superior to the active because of his superior love—"the one who loves more is the superior and better."[12] Great indeed would be the person, in Rolle's view, who could live both the active and the contemplative lives—"he would maintain a ministry with his body, and at the same time experience within himself the song of heaven, absorbed in melody and the joy of everlasting love."[13] But he maintained that he never knew anyone who actually accomplished this; he deemed it to be impossible. The Christian mystical tradition contradicts him.

Rolle counseled avoiding the company of women, whom he called immoderate both in loving and in scorning. However, Rolle, with tongue in cheek, laughed at himself for being "properly rebuked" and "despised" by four women for examining the suggestive clothing of one, making comments about the large breasts of another, rudely touching another, and not being man enough toward the fourth. Protesting that he was "not after anything improper" and that he was looking only to further their salvation, the hermit confessed that his sole wish was to devote himself fully to Christ's grace and to be found irreproachable in his dealings with women. Critics forget that Rolle also counseled fleeing the company of men; he also spoke out boldly against men who seduced and despised women.

Richard stridently rejected the excesses of his culture that was often filled with the greed, lust, and the arrogance of those infatuated with the courtly love tradition. Thus, the decadence found in both genders was the target of his mordant criticisms. No enemy of women could say: "there is a certain natural love of a man towards woman, and of a woman towards a man, from which no one is free, not even the saint. It was instituted by God in the beginning according to nature, by which they dwell together, and in concord with one another, and make one another happy socially by natural instinct."[14]

Rolle has been seriously misjudged and called a "solitary solipsist." However, in addition to what he said about the genuine hermit, Richard wrote eloquently of "an evil solitude," the solitude of pride, and taught that the only person actually alone is the one without God. Christian solitude is neither isolation nor solipsism. No solipsist—which Rolle definitely was not—could speak so eloquently on friendship: "For friendship is true when one friend acts towards another as he would to himself; when his friend is his alter ego, loved for his own sake."[15] Thus did he love the sickly recluse Margaret Kirkby (legend has it that his death played a role in curing her seizures), and the nuns at Hampole convent, to whom he gave spiritual direction.

The criticisms notwithstanding, this charismatic hermit added much to the variety and richness found in the Christian mystical tradition. There are many ways of being a Christian mystic. Rolle enjoyed a deep consciousness of the incomprehensible God and of Jesus Christ. Moreover, because of his tender concern for the weak, the poor, and the outcasts (many of whom were women)—as well as the miracles performed on their behalf, both during and after his lifetime—he was called "Saint Richard Hermit."

# Johannes Tauler

## (ca. 1300–1361)

*"Who then could make a separation in the divine and supernatural union in which the spirit is pulled and drawn into the abyss of its origin? Know that if it were possible to see the spirit in the Spirit, one would without a doubt see it as God himself."*[1]

Johannes Tauler is considered to be one of the great "masters of life" of the medieval period and also the Rhineland's most influential preacher. Christina Ebner, his contemporary and a mystic in her own right, said that his fiery tongue had enkindled the entire world. Our preacher also enjoys the reputation of being the only medieval mystagogue whose work has been known and esteemed in both manuscript and print in an almost continuous sequence from his own lifetime to the present day.

Though born into a prosperous family of the newly ascendant merchant class in Strasbourg, Tauler entered the Order of Preachers when he was approximately fifteen years old. During his general studies in Cologne he indirectly became a disciple of Meister Eckhart, the most important mystical theologian of the fourteenth century. There he also met John Ruusbroec, the famous Flemish mystic, and befriended the other renowned Rhineland Dominican mystic, Henry Suso. Although Tauler possessed the formidable theological acumen consonant with the Dominicans of that period, he never went on—as Meister Eckhart had done—to become an academic theologian.

Tauler lived through one of the most troubled periods of the Middle Ages. The Black Death and devastating famines were ravaging Europe. The conflict between church and empire resulted in the pope's exile to Avignon, which also intensified the internal struggles within his religious order. Yet, Tauler's sermons hardly reflect these circumstances. For him, the "one thing necessary" of the Gospel—and his central message—is to know one's nothingness, "that is what is yours, what you are, and who you are from yourself."[2]

After his Cologne period, Tauler exercised his ministry in Strasbourg. Because of the tensions between Pope John XXII and Emperor Louis of Bavaria, our Dominican was then exiled to Basel for about five years but was able to return to Strasbourg shortly before the emperor's death. Both cities were vital centers of learning and commerce. As a mendicant preacher and spiritual director, Tauler came into close contact with the emerging burgher class, many Dominican nunneries, the Beguines, the Brethren of the Free Spirit, and the Friends of God.

The Friends of God was an informal association of people from many walks of life. Nourished by Eckhart's intellectualism and the older German visionary mysticism, the Friends sought a richer and deeper interior life. Tauler not only added clarity, balance, and nuance to Eckhart's system but also propagated, expanded, and transposed its intellectualism into a more affective and practical mystical theology. In this way, Tauler kept the powerful movement within mainstream Christianity.

The much more amorphous groups of the Brethren of the Free Spirit also consisted of Christians desiring to live a deeper spiritual life. However, the more extreme "wild ones"—as they were often called—claimed the continuous inspiration of the Holy Spirit, sinlessness, and even identity with God. Because nothing mattered to them except passive surrender to the Spirit, they eschewed asceticism, virtue, active prayer, and the sacraments—with immorality often filling their lives.

Tauler takes to task these "silly fools" who claim that in mystical union they are physically changed into God. Rejecting the "false illuminations" and "false passivity" of these so-called "free spirits," he emphasizes the intense inner and outer effort requisite for the practice of virtue. In contradistinction to the "false peace" of these so-called "free spirits," Tauler insists that "essential peace" flows only from genuine self-denial.

Because of the excessive passivity of the "free spirits" and Eckhart's heady intellectualism, Tauler often preaches in praise of the active life. His sermons illustrate his practical appreciation of farmers, artisans, and craftsmen—without denigrating the aristocracy and its values. However, much of his preaching was directed to holy women and reflects a convent situation. While redolent with Eckhart's apophatic mysticism, these sermons are more sensitive to the needs of a down-to-earth, active spirituality. On the other hand, Tauler also exhorts his listeners to be less concerned with external affairs, to appreciate the limits of external devotions, and to melt into the ground of the soul—where God and the soul seem to be one. To remain in one's ground even briefly has enormous practical effect both for oneself and for others. In this way Tauler teaches that true prayer is indeed apostolic.

Practical and crafted with less linguistic boldness than Eckhart's, Tauler's homilies nonetheless encourage a profound interior life by awakening his hearers to their own deepest mystery. As he says, "To experience the working of the Trinity is better than to talk about it."[3] (This statement also reflects the ambivalence our friar had toward the academic theology of his day, an ambivalence shared by many "spirituals" because of the growing divorce between theology and living spirituality.) Using a biblical quotation from the day's liturgical readings as a point of departure, his down-to-earth sermons blend popular images, practical spiritual advice, and mystical themes. Tauler's sermons illustrate, too, how he elevates the German vernacular language to a level beyond that of scholarly Latin.

The nuns he addressed copied many of his sermons and the Friends of God freely adopted them, which resulted in their remarkably wide social impact. In fact, for many centuries, Tauler had a far greater impact than Eckhart on European (not only Rhineland) spirituality and mysticism. Thus, Tauler is a spiritual master in his own right and deserves his title, *Doctor Illuminatus.*

The entire mystical life, to Tauler, consists of turning away from all created things, being freed from anything less than God, and then sinking into one's ground wherein dwells the Trinity. "True detachment" requires turning away and withdrawing from all that is not God. Renouncing everything is the condition of possibility for returning to one's source. In this "unfathomable abyss," the soul forgets itself in God's simplicity: "Now God grants the soul by grace that which He is by nature, uniting it with His nameless, unchartered, wayless Being."[4]

Tauler speaks of the soul as the image of the Trinity. Unlike the theologians who consider the memory, intellect, and will as the image of the Trinity, this Dominican preaches "something of greater significance," namely, that the image of the Blessed Trinity resides in the soul's innermost region. If we sink into the ground—where God is "more inherent" to the soul than the soul is to itself—then we allow the birth of the Trinity in the soul.

Entering the ground requires abandoning everything pertaining to sense perception, images, rational distinctions, and discursive reasoning. The senses, the imagination, and reason itself are utterly impotent to look into the ground. However, to reside in the ground for only a second is worth more than all exterior works; "it is in the depth of this ground that we should pray for our friends, living or dead."[5] In short, Tauler underscores the apostolic dimension of contemplation.

As with several mystics we have already seen, Tauler's mysticism of the ground holds that the soul's ground has a virtual existence in essential unity in and with God before its creation. Therefore, the mystic's goal is the return of the created spirit to God to be as it was before it was. When the soul goes back to its original and uncreated state, then it knows itself as God *in God*, and yet as created. Tauler also uses the language of the abyss to express his teaching about the soul's indistinct union with God. The created abyss in the soul attracts the uncreated abyss into itself, and "the two abysses become a Single One, a pure divine being, so that the spirit is lost in God's Spirit. It is drowned in the bottomless sea."[6]

"Ground" denotes what is deepest in both God and the soul. The ground is the soul's base, crown, spark, and "Jerusalem." Ineffable and unknowable, the ground is a "wilderness," an "empty desert," but especially an "abyss" of total incomprehension. God's ground and the soul's ground seem to merge into one ground. In the ground and abyss dwells the mystery of the union of indistinction between God and the soul. In Tauler's view, by recognizing its own nothingness, the created abyss charms the "uncreated open Abyss" into itself and "there the one abyss flows into the other abyss and there is a single One—one nothing in the other nothing."[7] The soul is truly nothing; God, a No-thing, fullness itself.

The term *Gemüte* also permeates Tauler's sermons. Translated as "root-will"—and more recently as "essential inclination"—*Gemüte* always pertains to the soul and never to God. Our Dominican understands it as the soul's eternal inclination and attentive gaze back into the ground of its origin, that is, the Trinity. The soul's imagination, reason, and will flow from this "root-will" that is more inward and more noble than they are. Always at work in a person—awake or asleep—the soul's *Gemüte* "has a divinely formed, ineffable, eternal inclination back to God."[8] Not only does *Gemüte* always and unceasingly see, love, and delight in God but it also "knows itself as God in God, and yet it is created."[9] As the person's essential inclination, the soul's *Gemüte* is the hinge between the soul's and God's grounds.

Tauler expects his hearers to experience "sweet love," "wise love," and "strong love" during the mystical journey. God awakens in them a disgust for the world so that they put aside worldly frivolities and fight against the seven deadly sins. But God also pours out "delectable drops" of living water to refresh them during spiritual warfare and to slake somewhat their thirst for the divine. These drops often give way to great floods from which they can drink until they are fully inebriated. In this state, they may cry, laugh aloud, and sing because of the ecstatic joy associated with "jubilation," a religious phenomenon also found in present-day charismatic groups.

In order to prevent the soul from drowning in its drunken ecstasies, God intervenes like a caring father to sober it up—and often so vehemently that the person seems not to be able to bear it. Tauler speaks of "dying with a broken heart" during this period of strong love. Falling into states of the loss of self-consciousness, the graced soul awakens to the agonizing awareness of its own nothingness. Losing all supports, the soul falls into the abyss and experiences a crucifying sense of annihilation. "If you want to become God," Tauler teaches, "you must unbecome yourself."[10]

Thus, God as "Bitter Affliction" takes everything away from the mystic of the ground and leads him or her down a path "dark, wild, and foreign." At this stage, one does not even know if one once had a God! During the "night-work" of mystical dereliction, God is torturously absent. The seemingly abandoned soul sinks in its own absolute neediness, nakedness, and poverty. The totally denuded soul, however, has completely surrendered to God and would remain in this state even if God willed it the eternal pains of hell.

This is a higher love through which the soul, in Tauler's view, becomes "God-hued" and divinized by sinking into God to possess everything by grace that God possesses by nature. Soaring far above itself into God's very ground, the soul becomes so God-hued "that, could it behold itself, it would take itself for God."[11]

Tauler's mysticism of the ground remains solidly anchored in the person of Jesus Christ, even at the higher stages. The ardent love of the man Jesus found in many other Christian mystics may be lacking in his sermons, but our Strasbourger does preach, "No one can ever go beyond the image of our Lord Jesus Christ."[12] Like the serpent shedding its skin by slithering between two rocks, so too must the Christian—to become a new creature—drag himself between the rock of Jesus the Word and the rock of "the adorable humanity of Christ" because these are the two stones from which the Christian must draw his or her entire life and being.

Christ's five wounds enable a person to escape the five prisons of love of creatures, self-love, self-will, inordinate attachment to reason, and dependence upon religious feelings and visionary experiences. Christ's passion points the way to the innermost part of the soul wherein the hidden darkness of the supreme, superabundant Unity unfolds into Trinity. Detachment, self-emptying, self-denial, abandonment—the "labor of the night"—are required for immersion into the hidden abyss of the Trinity whose "imageless Image" is in the soul. Because one cannot have a soul filled with God unless one has a body full of suffering, Tauler links the entire contemplative life, Christian life, to Christ's passion and death.

In Tauler's view, the imitation of Christ is the imitation of Christ's passion. The "adorable life and suffering of Our Lord Jesus Christ" is the road on which one must walk, the truth that illuminates this way, and the life for which one strives. Jesus Christ is also the exemplar of the contemplative in action, the one "in whom activity and joyful contemplation have become one."[13] Moreover, Tauler encourages his hearers to see the Church—which they are—as the mystical Body of Christ, to seek forgiveness often in the sacrament of penance, and to receive the Body and Blood of Christ daily, if possible.

In short, Tauler's mysticism of the ground focuses on the fused identity of God and the person, but a mystical journey inextricably linked to the Church's liturgical life and the daily lives of his audience. The salient feature of his mysticism of the *Gemüte* is Christological: forgetting everything and self in imitation of Christ's mystical dereliction on the cross to become nothing in the No-thing, to see the spirit in the Spirit as God itself.

# Henry Suso

## (ca. 1295–1366)

*"Now hear the sweet music of the lute of a God-suffering man.
Suffering makes men lovable to Me, for a suffering man is like unto
Me. Out of an earthly man it makes a heavenly man. Ah, how many a
man there is who was once a child of eternal death, and had fallen
asleep into a deep slumber, whom suffering death has revived and
roused to a good life!"*[1]

Born in the city of Constance, Henry Suso (German, Seuse) joined
the Order of Preachers at the canonically illegal age of thirteen, and
went through the Dominican standard course of studies at Constance,
Strasbourg, and Cologne. Returning to his home friary around 1327,
he taught theology but soon provoked criticism because of his connection with Meister Eckhart, his mentor and inspiration from his
student days in Cologne.

When he was approximately forty years old, Suso abandoned his
teaching career to become a wandering preacher and spiritual director. During a period of active ministry that focused mainly on the
Dominican nuns and the Friends of God in Switzerland and the
Upper Rhine, he was briefly exiled for his loyalty to the pope during
the papal disputes with Louis of Bavaria. In addition, because of his
defense of the now discredited Eckhart, and for his association with
women (many of whom he encouraged to enter monasteries), he
suffered severe physical hardship, hostility, calumny, and persecution. Once again forced into exile, he died in Ulm.

Suso had the misfortune to live during the waning of the Middle
Ages—a time of pestilence and hunger, the "Babylonian captivity"
of the papacy at Avignon, the decline of philosophy and theology,
and the need for reform both in the mendicant orders and in the wider

Church. He also suffered the shock of seeing his much beloved teacher, Meister Eckhart, condemned by the Church. Despite these misfortunes, Suso's message focused on inner transformation.

The over five hundred extant manuscripts of his works indicate that he was the most widely read and influential of the mystics of this period. Suso insisted that his works be read with a love-filled heart; otherwise, they would be mistaken for dead German words on parchment. He wrote with one purpose: to enable the reader to unite with "Eternal Wisdom." Scholars speculate that his Swabian background enabled him to become the greatest poet and lyricist of all the German mystics—their minnesinger in prose. But history has obscured his uniqueness as a mystical writer by treating him merely as one of Eckhart's disciples.

Suso's most popular text, *The Life of the Servant*, originated in conversations and correspondence between Suso and Elsbeth Stagel, his spiritual daughter. Although it has been called both an autobiography and a biography, contemporary scholars describe it as an "auto-hagiography," that is, a text in which Suso blended autobiographical material—while never explicitly naming himself in the work—with other material, to tell the life story of the "Friar Preacher in Germany, a Swabian by birth, whose desire was to become and to be called a servitor of eternal Wisdom."[2]

The servant relates in this work that when he was about eighteen years of age, Eternal Wisdom chided him because of his "undisciplined heart": "The person who wants to catch a slippery eel by the tail and enters upon a holy life with a lukewarm spirit is doubly deceived."[3] The Swabian soon experienced a conversion so sudden that it surprised both him and those around him. During an almost hour-long transforming rapture, he saw and heard ineffable things, bursts of divine delight, divine flashes, and "heavenly fragrances" that aroused in him a deep longing for God.

One morning, the "love crazed" servant heard words urging him to take "gentle Wisdom" as his dearly Beloved. During a gender-bending vision, Suso saw a mysterious figure who flowed from the "naked Godhead." This person first seemed to be a beautiful young woman (dressed "to please male inclination"), then was transformed into a "proud young man," and finally was changed back to a woman who acted sometimes like a "wise teacher" and other times like a "pert young thing."

The sweet sounds of heavenly music caused his heart to overflow and his eyes to gush forth tears. Visions transported him to unknown lands where he saw and heard angels singing and dancing. Hearing Jesus' name sung wiped out memories of past sufferings and present anguish. An angel told him to look into his heart to view God's game of love played in the Godhead. Wisdom sat in the middle of his heart and invited him to participate in the "dance of joy." Wisdom now demanded the servant's entire heart and reminded him that love requires enormous suffering, even martyrdom.

The servant took up Wisdom's challenge to do penance for his past sins and to suffer for love. Determined to reach the "pure Godhead" by means of Jesus' "suffering humanity," he inscribed with a stylus the name of Jesus in the skin above his heart and fastened a barbed cross between his shoulder blades. Donning a shirt and underwear, both made of hair and laced with pointed nails, he bound parts of his body with chains. Selecting vermin-rife places of rest, he hardly slept, and always in a penitential position. In addition to eating and drinking as little as possible, he avoided warming himself during the cold winter days and nights.

More than twenty years of this severe asceticism left him on the brink of death. However, God intervened and instructed him that such austerities were only a "good beginning"; now he was to be taught "the art of true detachment," the art of being a true "spiritual knight" of Eternal Wisdom. A feeling of abandonment by God and public persecution by friends and foes were to put the finishing touches to the testing of Wisdom's knight. Like the tattered doormat the servant saw tossed in the air and bitten repeatedly by a dog running around the cloister, so would the spiritual knight be treated by even his fellow friars.

The servant suffered from severe temptations against the faith and was plagued with the thought that he would be eternally damned. He was accused of fathering a child, poisoning wells, desecrating shrines, and teaching "heretical garbage." He saw his beloved sister leave religious life to lead a dissolute life. (He was able eventually to rescue her and to place her in a better religious community.) Wisdom taught him that the constant contemplation of Wisdom/Christ's sufferings would turn a person into a "highly learned master" and overcome suffering and depression. Eventually prayer to the "saintly Meister Eckhart" freed him from these years of the dark night.

It was revealed to the servant that those who die with Christ not only rise with Christ but are also blessed in three special ways. First, whatever they wish for comes true. Second, unshakeable peace descends upon them. Third, they are eternally united with God who embraces and kisses them so passionately "that I am they and they are me, and we two shall remain a single one forever and ever."[4] When this occurred, the servant was graced with what Meister Eckhart calls "breakthrough." If one is able to die to all things—and especially to oneself—one becomes so lost in God that he has "no consciousness of self except by perceiving self and all things in their first origin."[5]

Suso synthesized in a creative and unique way the "spiritual philosophy" of the Desert Fathers (as handed down by the monks and mendicants), the courtly tradition of the love between God and the soul, Eckhart's mysticism of the ground, and the prevailing spirituality that emphasized an almost literal participation in the sufferings of Christ. The spiritual philosophy of the Desert Fathers was a true love for genuine wisdom, that is, a loving-knowledge acquired from and for authentic living. In Suso's view, "spiritual philosophy" was attained through both speculative and practical knowledge, contemplation and action, meditation on Christ's passion, and even through visions and raptures.

Wisdom had instructed Suso to go beyond all things seen because he had "been brought up differently in our spiritual philosophy"[6] and because he was a mirror of the Godhead in whom God could be seen more clearly than in any other creature. "You are an image of the Trinity," Wisdom informed him, "because his image can shine back in you."[7] A vision of a "handsome young man" who read from an "ancient tome" appeared to Suso to enable him to understand "the lives of the holy fathers and their conferences, contained in the book that many now neglect as old and discarded, although experience can see with complete certainty that in it are the core of all perfection and the true knowledge of Christian philosophy."[8] This Dominican's "higher philosophy" centered on knowing Christ and him crucified. In one of his prayers, Suso petitioned Christ: "Put my philosophy in your wounds, my wisdom in your stigmata, so that from now on I may advance in You, the only book of love, and in your death."[9]

Following in Eckhart's footsteps, Suso accepted the view that the highest forms of consciousness required sinking into the soul's ground. Unlike his mentor, however, Suso emphasized that conformity to Christ is necessary for "breaking through" to the ground. Appearing to the servant in the form of a seraph with six wings, the crucified Christ stressed the necessity of following him willingly and patiently in his sufferings. Everything that Christ was, did, and said had one purpose: "to teach his beloved friends and lead them inward into the pure ground, into the service of truth."[10] The servant was instructed to read Christ's crucified body as the "open book" and to write this book in his heart. Christ emptied himself out "so fully from [his] marks of love that one could not have put a pin's point on [his] martyred body without touching one's own mark of love."[11] The "bitterness" of Christ's saving passion, in Suso's view, is the only sure way into the ground—and one that transforms a person into a "highly learned master" who finds everything there.

Union with the naked Godhead, Suso taught, cannot be reached by bypassing or surpassing the role of the crucified Christ. As with the towering Beguine Hadewijch, Suso admonished those who want to be God without being man; one must be first formed in Christ before being transformed into God. Wisdom instructed the servitor: "You must fight your way through by means of my suffering humanity if you are really to come to my pure Godhead."[12]

Suso dismissed with horror and disgust the beliefs of "the men and women of the spirit" (Brethren of the Free Spirit) and called them "the most perverted group of people on earth."[13] He borrowed the odious figure of "the nameless wild one" from his treatise, *The Little Book of Truth*, to designate them. "The nameless wild one" buzzes around like a "confused bee," does wrong and calls it right, revels in licentiousness, is enslaved by every impulse, and identifies himself with God without distinction. Suso exclaimed that annihilating one's consciousness "as if I wanted to perform all my material actions with no distinction between God and myself, as though uncreated Being were performing them, that would be a mistake to end all mistakes."[14] The wild one also claimed to have become Christ. Suso taught, however, that only Christ is the image of the eternal Father. His mystical theology is exemplary, didactic, and polemical.

Suso strongly disagreed with Eckhart's contention that undifferentiated or indistinct union with God was more than a mental state. "Do you not realize," Suso wrote, "that being powerfully transported from self into the Nothing completely eliminates all difference, not of essences but rather in how we perceive, as has been said?"[15] The distinction between God and the creature may disappear in a mystically drunken consciousness, but it nevertheless remains in reality. Suso also departed from Eckhart's view that the creature's virtual existence is more noble than its actual existence. He wrote, "The being of a creature in God is not a creature, but each creature's created nature is nobler and of more advantage to it than the being it has in God."[16]

Suso's mysticism of the ground focused upon dying to self and finding oneself in God, "where the soul arrives at abandonment of self and all creatures in the naked Nothingness of the Godhead."[17] Redolent of the language of the courtly tradition, he confessed to "uncovering" his heart so that, naked of all creatures, he might embrace God's "bare divinity." On the "marvelous mountain" of the Godhead, "the pure soul finds a preparatory cliff which is the entrance to the hidden Nameless One and to the incomprehensible Estangement."[18]

The spirit, now unconscious of itself, "crosses over" into the "nameless existing No-thing" to find rest in the dark stillness of the "No-thing of unity," an "unfathomable abyss, the ground of God." In this abyss, full of playfulness, the spirit tastes what is intelligible to God alone, hidden from everything not God—except from those with whom God wants to share himself. During this "breakthrough," the spirit dies, and loses awareness of the difference between itself and "the naked simple Unity." "Exhilarating bliss," he wrote, "is the portion of those who enter into this completely supernatural 'where,'"[19] the Where without a where or a why.

Suso experienced "three uplifting fantasies." During the first illuminating fantasy, the servant opened his inner eyes to the countless number of creatures, and, like a drunken choir leader, urged them to sing and to raise their hearts to God. During his second fantasy, he pondered the deep joys and peace experienced by those whose hearts belong to God alone as well as the sufferings and turmoil of those fettered by "transitory love." The third was a "friendly appeal" to those spiritually enslaved and "inwardly confused," those who are halfhearted in their love both of God and of the world. The servant's request: totally renounce self, all creatures—and, "lift up your hearts to God."

Suso wrote of a cosmic mysticism through which he had experienced how all creation praised God: the heavens, the seasons, the angels, the "croaking frogs,"—everything, "they all cry out to my ears the rich tones of boundless praise of you."[20] Moreover, praise of God would flow from the servant, no matter where he was—whether in purgatory or even in hell. As he exclaimed, "then from the lowest pit of hell fair praise would rise up from me, penetrating hell, earth, air and all the heavens, until it came to Thy Divine face."[21] And yet, never was greater praise given "in the eyes of my Father as when I [Christ] hung in death's agony on the cross."[22]

# Walter Hilton

## (ca. 1343–96)

*"I am nothing; I have nothing; I desire nothing but the love of Jesus alone."*[1]

Very little is known about the life of Walter Hilton, a fourteenth-century mystical giant. Historians are certain that he received a higher education in canon law—most probably at Cambridge University—and that he renounced going on for his doctorate in order to lead the eremitical life for several years. Around the year 1375, Walter became a canon of the Augustinian Priory of Thurgarton near Southwell, Nottinghamshire.

Although Hilton lived in a period of tremendous religious and political upheaval—the Great Western Schism, the middle of the Hundred Years' War, the Peasants' Revolt of 1381, the Lollard movement, and the Augustinian battles versus the disciples of Wycliffe—his writings exhibit an almost ethereal serenity. His works, however, do manifest a concern for upholding orthodox faith and church practices, especially against those who professed a so-called "liberty of spirit" by denigrating the sacramental life, religious life, and the veneration of images. His writings also criticize the undue emphasis on the somatic manifestations of contemplation by "enthusiasts" who had misread the works of Richard Rolle. It also says much that Walter Hilton was held in such high esteem by Carthusians and Carmelites.

Hilton's treatise *The Letter on the Mixed Life* is addressed to a wealthy married layman with "worldly" responsibilities, who felt called to a deeper interior life. Although Hilton urges him to foster his spiritual life with devotions appropriate to the "active life," it nevertheless counsels him against trying to imitate the life of vowed religious. Written in the same spirit, his Latin text *Letter to Someone Wanting to Renounce the World* is addressed to a lawyer who, after imprisonment,

had experienced a religious conversion. Hilton discourages him from
entering religious life—for which he judges him unsuitable—but urges
him to continue some of his spiritual practices. Another work, *The Goad
of Love*, teaches that one need not withdraw from the world to seek
Christ, who can be found especially among the sick. His *Commentaries
on Psalms 90 and 91* are also worth mentioning.

His most famous work, *The Scale of Perfection*, has been called the
most lucid, balanced, and complete treatise on the interior life of the
late Middle Ages. It also offers an almost complete guide to the spiritual life of the fourteenth-century English mystics. This text shows
the hand of a pragmatic, ardent, shrewd mystical master of life who
offers sound advice on living one's baptismal life to the heights of
mystical consciousness. Because of its practical advice for even non-
mystics, this work became an immediate favorite of the laity when
it was first published in 1494. Moreover, this treatise testifies to Hilton's finesse in creatively transposing the precision of the classical
Latin tradition into exact and clear vernacular expression.

*The Scale of Perfection* actually comprises two books. Book 1 was
written for an anchoress and for anyone vowed to the contemplative
life, which, in Hilton's view, is the preserve of vowed religious. The
contemplative life consists of three parts. In the first, one attains
knowledge of things spiritual and of God through reason. This do-
main belongs to the learned, to those who come to this knowledge
through the intense study of scripture. However, "it has no spiritual
savor of God," our canon writes, "or that inward sweetness of love
no one can feel unless he is in great charity."[2]

The second part of contemplation belongs to the simple and un-
lettered, whose affection for God is without understanding of spiritual things. The lower degree of this contemplation consists mainly
of varying degrees of intensity and duration of deep emotions. However, only people of interior and exterior quiet acquire the higher
degree of this contemplation that consists of delight in prayer and
meditation.

A person, enlightened by the Holy Spirit and reformed to the
image of the trinitarian Christ, attains "the knowing and perfect loving of God,"[3] which is contemplation's third part. This more inward,
more spiritual contemplation involves the spiritual senses—not the
bodily ones—and is a foretaste of the beatific vision. Hilton understands it as a singular gift, with both cognitive and affective elements,

that is sometimes given to people in the active life through a special grace. However, only those living a solitary, contemplative life can have it to the full.

Hilton denies that he himself has this gift: "Not that I can experience and practice it in the way that I talk about it."[4] He writes to encourage those who do possess this grace to work diligently and humbly to develop their gifts. In Hilton, therefore, one finds an exceptional mystical theologian and mystagogue, but perhaps not a mystic.

Hilton's warm, Christ-centered mysticism permeates this text. As with many other mystics in the tradition, he emphasizes "carnal knowledge of God" through meditation on Jesus' sacred humanity as the only way to the higher states of mystical consciousness. "No man may come to the contemplation of the Godhead," he writes, "unless he is first reformed by humility and charity to the likeness of Jesus in His humanity."[5]

The ardent desire to know and love Jesus, in Hilton's view, casts the person into a "glowing darkness" that extinguishes the false lights of the world. The more one "thinks of nothing"—except the desire for Jesus—the more one experiences the light of his love. Diverting one's attention from worldly things and calling upon Jesus' name produce an inner darkness that opens the spiritual eye. If one suffers the pain of this state of dark nothingness, "right inside this nothing," Hilton teaches, "Jesus is hidden in his joy, and you cannot find him by your seeking unless you pass through the darkness of this nothing."[6] As Christ's true light intensifies, it extinguishes the light from earthly things, then eliminates all darkness, and finally clothes the contemplative in illuminating and blazing light because love of Jesus is both a "blessed night" and a "true day."

Book 2 of *The Scale of Perfection* focuses on reforming the soul, the image of the trinitarian Christ, which was damaged by sin. The "ordinary" Christian reforms this image "in faith alone" through baptism and the confession of sins, but without understanding the things of God, and without a heart truly set on spiritual progress. The second way "in faith and feelings" is for "perfect souls and contemplatives." "This spiritual opening of the eyes of the spirit to the knowledge of the Godhead," Hilton writes, "is what I call *reform in faith and feeling*."[7] This reform destroys the sinful feelings rooted in the corrupted image. The Holy Spirit transforms the image and brings about "gracious feelings." When the spiritual senses are awakened to the inner workings of grace, then one has this reformation in faith and feelings by becoming connatural to the triune God in Christ. Perhaps to contrast himself with those of his day who emphasized bodily feelings (Rolle?), Hilton underscores the spiritual nature of the feelings experienced in understanding and love.

Book 2 describes the three kinds of love of God by which one is "rightly reformed to the image of Jesus." The first and lowest sort of love of God is through faith alone. The second consists in what the soul feels through faith and meditating on Jesus' humanity. The third and highest form of love flows from "spiritual sight" of Jesus' divinity. Because the blessed light of the *God*-Man—*as he is*—cannot be seen in this life, Jesus makes some sort of "inward beholding" of his divine light possible by "tempering" it with his humanity. The true Christian lives, therefore, in "the shadow of his humanity." Just as a shadow is produced by a light and a body, so a "spiritual shadow" is made by the transforming light of the divinity and the humanity united to it and shown to the contemplative person. In Hilton's view, the spiritual shadow cast by the God-Man also protects the pilgrim on his mystical journey from the blazing sun of worldly loves.

Jesus, in Hilton's view, is the very life of the soul and the sight of Jesus *is* heaven. If one lives as if nothing else existed but Jesus, then one will come to experience brief, ravishing sightings of what will be a full and continuous sight of him in everlasting life. The contemplative in earthly life does not see *what* Christ as the *God*-Man is—but only *that* he is an immutable being. However, because the Holy Spirit strengthens and illuminates the contemplative, he does come to see Christ "with great reverence and ardent joy, more clearly and more fully than can be described."[8] This way of seeing the God-Man far surpasses the "obscure, abstract" sight of God attained by theological reason. More than once Hilton teaches that the sublime presence of Christ is better known by experience than by books.

In one of the most quoted chapters in Hilton's text (II, chap. 21), he speaks of the person's contemplative ascent as a pilgrim's journey to Jerusalem. Jerusalem, in his view, means "sight of peace," that is, contemplation as the perfect loving-knowledge of God. Again and again, this Augustinian refers to contemplation as nothing other than seeing Jesus, our true peace, heaven itself.

To reach Jerusalem, one must have both humility and singular love. Humility says that I am and have nothing; love, that I desire

Jesus and him alone. Through unreserved love of Jesus, one dies to the world and enters into that "good night" wherein a "holy idleness," "most busy rest," and "luminous darkness" reign. One hears the "sweet spiritual whispers" of Jesus' hidden voice. The secrets of the scriptures are unlocked because "the mystery of holy scripture is closed under key, sealed with a signet of Jesus' finger, which is the Holy Spirit."[9] One is illuminated to see God's wonders working in "holy Church," Christ's mystical body.

Hilton teaches that the inner eyes of a pure soul transcends all creation and sees first, Jesus' glorious humanity, and then his blessed divinity. Finally, one attains some perception of God's triune unity. His message is simple: renounce all that is not Jesus in order to have a "clearer sight and a purer love of Jesus, in whom is all the blessed Trinity."[10]

# Julian of Norwich

## (1342–ca. 1423)

*"For we do not fall in the sight of God, and we do not stand in our own sight."*[1]

During an illness thought to be fatal, on May 13, 1373, a thirty-year-old "holy woman" (*sancta*, as such women were called) received sixteen "showings" (revelations) centered on Christ crucified. In her youth, she had prayed for "bodily sickness," a deep appreciation of Christ's passion, and for the "wounds" of "true contrition," of "loving compassion," and of "longing for God." This mysterious woman exemplifies the new and complex relationship between illness, suffering, visions, and mystical states emerging in her times.

The visionary described her experience this way: "And in this time, suddenly I saw the red blood running down from under the garland, hot and fresh, plenteous and life-like, just as it was in the time that the garland of thorns was pressed down on his precious head."[2] The God-Man informed her that he, the one who had suffered for her, bestowed this revelation upon her "without intermediary." The Trinity also appeared in all her revelations, which led her to comprehend that not only was the entire Trinity at work in Christ's passion but also "where Jesus appears the blessed Trinity is understood, as I see it."[3] Insights into the Incarnation, the union of the soul with God, and "many fair shewings of endless wisdom and teachings of love"[4] were also given in three different modes: (1) through bodily visions, (2) through spiritual visions, (3) by words formed in the understanding. The visionary character of her mysticism makes this *sancta* unique among the English mystics, except for Margery Kempe, who was a generation younger.

"Our courteous Lord" revealed his passion to this holy woman in five ways: the bleeding of the head, the discoloration of the face, the profuse bleeding from the scourging, the body's desiccation, and "the joy and bliss" she should experience from it. Her emphasis upon the joyful aspects of Christ's sufferings distinguishes her from the more "doloristic" mystics who focus upon the sorrowful aspects of the passion. She was also shown that because of the strength of Christ's humanity due to its union with the divinity, he was able to suffer more out of love for us than the entire combined sufferings of humanity.

Christ's humanity was revealed to her as consisting of three heavens: of "joy," because the Father was pleased with him; of "bliss," because the Son was honored; and, of the "endless delight of the Holy Spirit." All revelations ceased after this approximately twelve-hour period—"I saw no more after this"[5]—but "partial and blessed" touches from the Holy Spirit continued. The Lord instructed her, too, that what she had seen was "no hallucination" and that nothing could overcome her. What this holy woman had called her "doomsday" became not only the day in which her health was restored but also the day when she came to understand prayer as the "sight and vision of him to whom we pray, to be wholly united to him, to live where he lives, to enjoy his love, and to delight in his goodness."[6]

Commanded by the Lord to write, this mystic penned one of the few firsthand accounts of someone at death's door, a work known as the *Short Text*. Perplexed by and desiring to comprehend better what had been revealed, she prayed over and contemplated her showings for almost twenty years to obtain deeper "spiritual understanding"— the result, the *Long Text*.

Neither the birthplace nor even the name of the person who wrote one of the Christian tradition's most appealing mystical texts is known. Because she came to live the solitary, enclosed life of an anchoress in a "cell" adjoining the parish church of St. Julian in Conisford at Norwich (opposite the house of the Augustinian friars), the name "Julian" was probably adopted in honor of the saint of the church to which the hermitage was attached. However, it is not even known when, or how, Julian came to recognize her vocation to the life of an anchoress, or whether the decision was made before or after the revelations—which may have been granted her while she was still living in her mother's house or may have come to her in the anchorhold. It seems logical to assume that at least the *Long Text* was written while she was enclosed, but this too is disputed by scholars.

Based upon the evidence in Julian's book, scholars surmise that she had come from a family of means, entered a religious order, and there received an excellent education. Norwich, moreover, was known for its splendid libraries. Her text evinces a solid knowledge of the classical spiritual writers, the Latin Vulgate, and a mastery of the rhetorical arts. She has been compared with Geoffrey Chaucer and called the first woman of letters in the English language.

Julian experienced all her showings as signs of God's "familiar," "homely," "courteous," and intensely personal love. Her relatively well-known vision of something "no bigger than a hazelnut" in the palm of her hand illustrates a paradox experienced by most Christian mystics: the nothingness of creatures and the greatness of God's goodness. "I marveled," she wrote, "that it continued to exist and did not suddenly disintegrate; it was so small."[7] That God made, loves, and preserves even the tiniest speck of his creation astonished her. However, Julian also emphasized that "no soul is at rest until it has despised as nothing all things which are created."[8] Because God is everything that is good and comforting, God alone satisfies the human heart's immense longing.

The salient feature of Julian's mysticism stresses Jesus' blood as a way to attain union with the triune God. Blood as the redemptive presence of Christ himself was omnipresent in the religious passion art and spirituality of her day. Julian's "spiritual understanding" comprehended that Jesus' blood overflowed the earth, descended into hell to break its power, and ascended into heaven to nurture the risen life of the new Jerusalem. Her blood mysticism is also a form of Sacred Heart mysticism. She saw Christ look "merrily and cheerfully" into his pierced side and say, "My child, if you cannot look at my divinity, see here how I suffered my side to be opened and my heart to be split in two and to send out blood and water, all that was in it."[9] This is the precious blood with which her soul and all the souls of the saved were washed.

Julian's visionary mysticism grappled with the Pauline mystery: where sin abounds, grace abounds all the more (Rom 5:20). Her theological dilemma: how could she reconcile what was revealed to her about the intensity, familiarity, and universality of God's love with what she knew from faith about the mystery of sin, evil, damnation, and God's wrath?

Adam's sin, as Julian knew from Church teaching, caused the "greatest harm" ever done—and we participate in this sin—that she experienced as "unclean," "unnatural," the "sharpest scourge," the "deepest pain," and "more vile and painful than hell." The anchoress understood sin as everything that is "not good," as having "no sub-stance," and why she became "despicable" in her own eyes. More important, because sin causes both *our* wrath and anger toward self, others, and even God, she confessed that she would rather suffer all the pains of earth, death, purgatory, and hell than commit sin. The Lord revealed to her "most gently," however, that although sin was all she was capable of from herself, it is something "necessary."

The Trinity revealed in the showings God's complete victory over sin in the crucified and risen Christ. She heard these comforting words—a refrain that is perhaps the most famous in the mystical tradition: "I may make all things well; I can make all things well, and I will make all things well, and I shall make all things well; and you shall see for yourself that all manner of things shall be well."[10] The "may," Julian attributed to the Father; the "can," to the Son; the "will," to the Holy Spirit; the "shall," to the unity of the blessed Trinity. When she asked how this were possible—since our faith teaches that bap-tized sinners, the unbaptized, and the demons are damned—the Lord replied, "What is impossible to you is not impossible to me."[11]

Julian found this so puzzling that she begged God for a revelation of purgatory, of the damned, and of hell. Because God was silent on this point, she complained that she could speak only of the saved. It was shown her, however, that God eternally damned the devil and also those "of the devil's condition in this life." Still, God called her attempt to contemplate the damned "folly," instructed her to "look away," and to pay close attention to him, her savior and salvation. He was all she needed to know. Thus, the showings revealed God's unconditional goodness and love, but "little mention" was made of evil. Even in those revelations in which sin was mentioned at all, God said to her: "All will be well."[12]

Julian came to comprehend the mystery that the redeemed sinner is and lives. "For we shall see verily in heaven, without end," she wrote, "that we have sinned grievously in this life; and notwithstand-ing this, we shall see that we were never hurt in his love, nor were ever the less value in his sight."[13] The paradox of redemption intensi-fied in her showings because it was revealed to her that sin was not only "no shame" but also that it would be an "honor to man." King David, the apostles Peter and Paul, Mary Magdalene, and a host of others were known as sinners, but "shame is no more in the bliss of heaven—for there the tokens of sin are turned into honors."[14] To the degree that sin caused pain here on earth, it causes a corresponding bliss for it in heaven. In fact, the "manifold joys" that await the redeemed sinner in heaven will greatly exceed "what he would have had if he had not sinned or fallen."[15] If sin is not important and even leads to greater bliss and honor in heaven, should one not sin more? "Folly" and "from the fiend," Julian deemed such a view.

Julian's emphasis upon the Trinity's goodness, love, mercy, and forgiveness as shown through Christ's death and resurrection comes to light in its most theologically satisfying—and challenging—way in her teaching on "wrath." In her view, wrath is the *human* perversity and opposition to love and peace, the anger at our impotence to do good—an anger and tribulation that God himself abates and dispels. "It is quite clear that where our Lord is," she confessed, "peace reigns and anger has no place. I could see no sort of wrath in God, however long I looked."[16] She even dared to write that God cannot forgive because it is impossible for love to become angry. And if, impossibly, God did become wrathful, even briefly, our life and being would be annihilated.

Julian's confusion intensified because she knew from Church teaching and her own experience the weight of guilt hanging upon humanity from Adam onward. "This then was my difficulty," she wrote, "that I saw our Lord displayed no more blame toward us than if we were as clean and holy as the angels in heaven."[17] Why the "courteous Lord" acted in this way was revealed to her "very mysteriously" through a "doubly shown" vision of "the Lord and the servant." Having been instructed to pay attention to *every* detail and having been given "spiritual understanding," Julian contemplated and pondered this revelation for over twenty years—which is the heart of her mystical doctrine. The Lord God "looks on his servant [Adam/Christ] very lovingly and sweetly and mildly."[18] The servant's "good will" prompted him to rush out in loving service of his Lord, but he fell and was injured. The worst part of the fall of Adam/Christ was his inability to turn his face to see the Lord's gaze of love.

Julian's critics point out that the scriptures clearly teach the real cause of Adam's fall: pride, disobedience—not his love and goodwill. This anchoress was instructed, however, that the Lord God is unconditional love who looks upon Adam and the entire human race as "one man" because "in the sight of God everyman is one man, and one man is everyman."[19] Because of the Father's "joy and bliss" at the fall of "his dearly beloved Son," the Father looks with compassion and pity upon Adam and "everyman." Because Christ took upon himself all sin and blame, the Father attributes no more blame to us than he does to his own Beloved Son. "Therefore," Julian wrote, "this meaning was shown for understanding of Christ's humanity. For all mankind which will be saved by the sweet Incarnation and the Passion of Christ, all is Christ's humanity, for he is the head."[20] Because of Adam's "happy fault," we were given such a marvelous redeemer that Julian chose Jesus as her "heaven" and would have accepted any amount of suffering rather than enter heaven in any way other than through Christ.

Origen, the third-century genius, held a view that was eventually condemned: apocatastasis, that is, the belief that everyone will be saved. Two twentieth-century theological titans, Karl Rahner and Hans Urs von Balthasar, subscribed to a theory of *benign* apocatastasis, that is, that one can *hope* that everyone will be saved. Julian saw clearly that all who will be saved are saved through Christ and that "one man is everyman," that is, Jesus Christ. Which form of apocatastasis Julian actually held is still being debated. One might note, too, that although the Catholic Church has canonized saints, it has never said definitively that anyone is "in" hell.

The profoundly trinitarian nature of Julian's showings also focused on the motherhood of God. She stressed that the Trinity is our "maker," our "protector," our "everlasting lover," and "our salvation." Not only is God almighty "our loving Father" but "all wisdom" is also our "loving Mother," and "loving goodness," the Holy Spirit. The Trinity is our Mother from whom we have our substance. "Wherefore it follows that as verily as God is our Father, so verily is God our Mother. Our Father wills, our Mother works, our good Lord the Holy Ghost confirms."[21] And because of what Christ wrought through his passion, death, and resurrection, we are his "crown" in which the Father has "joy," the Son "honor," and the Holy Spirit "delight."

In Julian's view, Christ is also our Mother from whom we have our "sensuality"—our true Mother in nature by our first creation, in grace by his assuming our created nature. One dimension of Julian's Sacred Heart mysticism brings out the motherhood of Christ. "Our tender Mother Jesus," she wrote, "can lead us easily into his beloved breast through his sweet open side, and show us there a part of the godhead and of the joys of heaven, with inner certainty of endless bliss."[22] It is "our precious Mother Jesus" who will sprinkle us all "with his precious blood." (Julian also spoke of the motherhood of the Blessed Virgin.) Mystics before Julian had written of the motherhood of God and Christ, but she was able to explicate this view in a more profound and complex way.

It seems fitting to conclude this chapter with the Lord's ultimate revelation about his "meaning": "And from the time that it was revealed," Julian wrote, "I desired many times to know in what was our Lord's meaning. And fifteen years after and more, I was answered in spiritual understanding, and it was said: 'You would know our Lord's meaning in this thing? Note well. What was his meaning? Love. Who showed it to you? Love. Why did he show you? Love. Why did he show you? For love. Hold onto this and you will know and understand love more and more. But you will not know or learn anything else—ever!'"[23]

# The Anonymous Author of
## *The Cloud of Unknowing*
### (ca. 1345–ca. 1386)

*"For it is a darkness of unknowing that lies between you and your God. . . . Just as a cloud of unknowing lies above you, between you and your God, so you must fashion a cloud of forgetting beneath you, between you and every created thing."*[1]

This fourteenth-century mystical giant has been identified only as an anonymous Carthusian recluse from a monastery in the East Midlands, England. His mystical depth, theological acumen, psychological shrewdness, and soundness of spiritual direction are such that he has been called the English equivalent of St. John of the Cross, whom not a few scholars consider to be the Church's greatest mystic and mystical writer. If I were asked to recommend one work to someone who knew nothing about Christian mysticism, I would unhesitatingly recommend this gem, *The Cloud of Unknowing*.

This monk also penned *The Pursuit of Wisdom*, *The Discernment of Spirits*, *The Assessment of Stirrings*, *A Letter on Prayer*, *A Letter of Private Direction*, and *The Book of Privy Counseling* (his most mature work). These treatises may be the first works in Middle English about the mystical quest for God. The same author also translated and adapted into Middle English Pseudo-Dionysius's *Mystica Theologica* (English version: *Denis's Hidden Theology*), Richard of St. Victor's *Benjamin Minor*, and two of Bernard of Clairvaux's sermons. His texts offer a vigorous defense of the coenobitic and eremitical ways of life and contend that the contemplative life is the royal road to Christian perfection—superior to the life of "ordinary" Christians.

Possessing both considerable literary beauty and practicality, this Carthusian's books evince his personal experience, his love of scripture, and his masterful assimilation of the Western mystical tradition.

However, he does not merely repeat the tradition, offer a compilation of it, or simply recount his own mystical experiences. With a sure touch and serēne authority, he transposes the Western tradition and his own mystical wisdom into a competent guide for the seeker of the contemplative way to God. He towers as a mystic, mystical theologian, and mystagogue.

The anonymous author wrote for a highly selective audience, not for "clever clergy, or layfolk either," but for those who experience in their deepest interiority the Spirit stirring them to love. More specifically, he addressed his treatises to a young Carthusian who had previously led the "common" way of Christian life, that is, a day-to-day mundane existence with his friends, and one far from God. Called to become God's friend, the young man then entered the "special" way of a deeper and more interior life. Finally, God attracted him to the "singular" manner of living at the deep solitary core of his being and directing his loving desire toward the highest way of life that is called "perfect," that is, union with God in consummate love—begun in this life, but fulfilled only in the next.

Because this anonymous monk focuses mainly on the dark, silent, mystical contemplation characteristic of the apophatic tradition, he says very little about the premystical stages of prayer. However, he does emphasize that the intelligent savoring of scripture and "sweet meditations" upon one's own sins, Christ's passion, and God's goodness provide the best foundation for deeper, mystical contemplation. "Day prowlers" and "night thieves" are his names for those who seek exotic shortcuts and go astray.

Our author fully expects that "spiritual insight" and "blind desire" will arise, if one is faithful to one's daily devotions. With various nuances, commentators have called this the "prayer of simplicity," the "prayer of simple regard," the "prayer of the heart," "active recollection," "active quiet," "acquired contemplation," and the highest stage of prayer possible without God's special intervention. It is called "active" or "acquired" contemplation because it can be reached through God's "ordinary" grace.

The Carthusian sharply distinguishes premystical prayer from mystical contemplation, which, in his view, is a qualitatively superior form of prayer that requires a "special" grace. Although the monk is the one more likely to receive this gift, it is offered to people from all walks and stations of life. Even sinners might experience this mysterious, inner attraction because it is given neither for innocence nor withheld because of sin. (He alerts his readers to the fact that he did not use the word "withdrawn.") On the other hand, even the very awareness of and desire for "contemplation" in his sense is strictly God's exceptional gift.

The anonymous author insists that special signs must be present for a person to move from "ordinary" meditations to mystical contemplation. If a growing desire for contemplation constantly intrudes into one's daily spiritual exercises and renders meditation impossible and one's usual devotions very difficult; if a kind of "blind longing of the spirit" and a lingering "spiritual sight" are experienced that both renews the desire and increases it—these are "interior" signs that one may be called to the mystical life.

In addition to this "interior sign," the Carthusian speaks of an "exterior sign": the experience of joyful enthusiasm whenever one hears or reads about contemplation. Although this attraction must be more than a fleeting glow that vanishes with the many distractions of life, even the genuine desire for contemplation may disappear for a while. However, this absence leaves the aspiring contemplative sad and confused. If, once the gift returns, the joy and love that are felt totally override the previous sorrow and intensify the desire for contemplation even more deeply, then this is one of the most obvious and clear signs that a person has a contemplative vocation. The inner and outer signs should occur together and mutually confirm each other.

The deeply interior attraction toward mystical prayer that interferes with so much in the person's interior and exterior life is already the start of what some authors call the "passive prayer of quiet." It is called passive prayer because, according to this anonymous Carthusian, "God alone is the chief worker and he alone takes the initiative, while man consents and suffers his divine action."[2] To enkindle the "tiny flame of love" arising at the core of the contemplative's being, he recommends firmly rejecting *everything* that comes into the mind in order to create a "cloud of forgetting" between oneself and all created things.

A "cloud of unknowing," that is, the absence of knowledge, will then arise between the contemplative and God. In the darkness of unknowing, he must direct his "dart of desire," "naked intent," and "blind desire" toward God. This blind contemplation will allow the person to rest quietly in the loving awareness of God as he is. Only a love—a desire—shorn of all knowledge (hence, "naked") can penetrate the cloud between God and the contemplative. Required now is only the willing offering to God in joyful love of the contemplative's blind awareness of his naked being so that grace can make him spiritually one with God.

To facilitate raising the heart to God in a gentle motion of naked love, the Carthusian recommends selecting a short meaningful word—such as "God," "love," or "sin"—fixing it in one's mind, but not pondering its meaning. This monosyllabic word facilitates the quieting, binding, and emptying of the restless mind and imagination to bring about what he calls "spiritual sleep." This Christian mantra enables the contemplative to drive away distractions and to remain poised and alert in naked love at the fine point of his being. And, at times, this word will arise from the contemplative's spiritual center and be a prayer that expresses his entire being in love.

The Carthusian is an outstanding example of the Christian apophatic mystical tradition, which stresses that only love, not knowledge, can comprehend God. Preferring to speak about what God is not, this author still contends that mystical love engenders a negative knowledge and comprehension of God. His highly introspective form of mysticism emphasizes finding God first and foremost in the depths of the "mirror" of darkness, that is, the soul emptied of *everything* except naked love. Paradoxically, if this is accomplished, the contemplative's inner eye will also find God in all things.

When "naked love," that is, love shorn of all concepts and images, takes hold at the root of the contemplative's being, it torturously causes all the sins of his life to arise. Eventually, he suffers not from the painful remembrance of past sins but from the acute realization that he is a sinner, a "lump of sin." As the tiny flame of love heals the scars of past sins and removes the "lump," the contemplative suffers from not being able to forget his or her self. *Self-awareness* is experienced as a "cross" between oneself and God. In time, one agonizes over not being able to love as much as one is loved. This entire process cleanses the contemplative of all sinfulness, removes disorder, and increases his capacity to love. It comprises all that the later tradition has called the dark night of the senses and the spirit.

Ecstatic revelations of God's superabundant goodness and beauty punctuate the darkness, and the splendor of spiritual light blinds but yet opens the inner eye to God "as he really is." Naked love causes such a radical union between God and contemplatives that they are as close to God "by grace" as God is to himself "by nature." However, they experience that as much as God is their being, they are not God's being. In short, the goal of the contemplative life is mystical union, wherein God and the contemplative become one yet remain two.

Although emphatically theocentric and apophatic, the mysticism of this anonymous Carthusian remains inextricably linked to the person of Jesus Christ. He tacitly assumes that all grace is the grace of Jesus Christ who calls all who are deeply committed to follow him into the inmost depths of contemplative love. In this monk's view, bearing "the cross of self"—and the concomitant self-emptying requisite to destroy self-awareness—is the contemplative's way of sharing deeply in Christ's passion and death. Moreover, if the contemplative receives the special graces for "full and final self-forgetting,"[3] he will find himself clothed in Christ as the garment of love.

This anonymous Carthusian concurs with those in the mystical tradition who interpret Jesus' ascension to the Father as the theological grounds for shifting the contemplative's gaze away from Christ's humanity to his divinity. Employing the typology of his day, he also presents Mary Magdalene, sitting lovingly at Jesus' feet, as the ideal contemplative. (It was actually Mary of Bethany.) The Magdalene had learned to love Jesus "without seeing him in the clear light of reason"[4] and without feeling his presence in sensible delights. Her contemplative love was apophatic, "naked," that is, shorn of thoughts, of discursive reasoning, and of the "tokens of grace" of emotional consolations. She gave no heed whatsoever to any aspects of his humanity, but was "totally absorbed in the highest wisdom of God concealed in the obscurity of his humanity."[5] To the Carthusian's way of thinking, through the "cloud of unknowing" of Jesus' humanity, Mary had reached in naked love his very divinity.

However, just as "sweet" love existed between Jesus and Mary Magdalene; just as she ardently loved him at the foot of the cross and sought him at the tomb, so, too, does this warm love and ardent desire for Jesus Christ permeate this Carthusian's works. An unabashed devotional love of Jesus Christ is the inseparable ambiance and matrix for our monk's dark, silent, mystical love. Meditation upon Jesus' humanity is the sole way to authentic contemplation; he is the "door" to the blind stirring of mystical love. Although the distinction this monk makes between meditations on Christ's humanity and the contemplation of his divinity may be too tidy and ultimately unacceptable for some, he never teaches that a genuine contemplative—to attain some higher form of mysticism—must forget or cast aside the person of Jesus Christ. Mary Magdalene, the ideal contemplative, and this Carthusian remain firmly in the presence of Jesus Christ and they often cry out, "Jesus, sweet Jesus."

The anonymous Carthusian also offers valuable insights into the "pseudo-contemplation" of the "devil's contemplatives." The desire for "experiences" seems to be the root cause of pseudo-contemplation. Bogus contemplatives refuse to heed the advice of an experienced spiritual director and go off on their own. Presuming they can begin contemplation without having passed through the ascetical purification and the instructive lessons to be gleaned only through meditation, they also pay no attention to the signs required to pass from meditation to contemplation and substitute brute force for the gentle stirring of love. These "slaves of the devil" strain their senses, imaginations, and minds. They fall prey in this way to fantasies, daydreaming, frenzies, morbid introspection, mental aberrations, and physical deterioration.

Thinking they know God's will for everyone, they harshly and imprudently reprimand others with unchecked and misguided zeal. They rage against the saints, the sacramental system, and lawful Church authority. Although they pretend to be holy, they are hypocrites whose eccentric, grotesque mannerisms and affectations betray them. Often seen staring into the heavens vacantly like madmen, their eyes become like "wounded sheep near death." They may whine, whimper, utter shrill sounds, speak in a "halting coy voice," "whisper cravenly," and gape with their mouths open. In this monk's view, pseudo-mystical manifestations can take on as many forms and appearances as there are individual temperaments and dispositions.

This master of the contemplative life also teaches that naked love may sometimes manifest itself ecstatically. More often, however, it is a gentle, peaceful, silent love permeating all the contemplative's daily activities. The blind awareness of one's naked being united to God's being does not contend with either the highest or even the most lowly of the monk's activities. Naked love permeates the monk's eating and drinking, sleeping and waking, going and coming, speaking and listening, lying down and getting up, standing and kneeling, running and riding, and working and resting. Contemplation in daily life is, therefore, an element of his genuine apophatic mysticism. Moreover, for this monk, mystical contemplation itself is apostolic and the best form of love we can give others, the "souls in purgatory," and ourselves.

The experience of this blind stirring of love for God is a salient feature of the anonymous Carthusian's teaching on the discernment of spirits. It may first gently prod one's heart to do this or that. If resisted, the "tiny dart of love" becomes like a needle in the heart that points to and insists upon a certain course of action. As he says, this love "will first gently move you to speak or to do the natural ordinary thing, whatever it is. And if you fail to do it, this awareness will wound you as sorely and painfully as if your heart were pierced and let you have no peace until you do it."[6]

The anonymous author contends that neither silence nor speaking, neither fasting nor eating, neither solitude nor companionship is God—nor any other pair of opposites. God hides between them and is found only by the heart's love, not by anything the soul does. Neither thought nor reasoning nor understanding can capture God. But he can be loved and chosen by the true, loving will of the heart. "This little love is the essence of a good life and without it no good work is possible."[7]

# Catherine of Siena

## (1347–80)

*"In the name of Jesus Christ crucified and of gentle Mary, I, Caterina, servant and slave of God, send you my greetings in the precious blood of God's Son, which is permeated with the fire of his blazing charity. This is what my soul desires: to see you in this blood. I want you to shut yourself up in the open side of God's Son, that open hostelry so full of fragrance that sin itself is made fragrant. There the dear bride rests in the bed of fire and blood. There she sees revealed the secret of the heart of God's Son."*[1]

That a young woman with no formal schooling who died at thirty-three years of age could be so influential in her times and so renowned in the later Christian tradition; that she could also be designated a saint, Doctor of the Roman Catholic Church (a title she and Teresa of Avila were simultaneously the first women to bear), and a patron saint of Italy and Europe—all this testifies to both the exceptional power of grace and the spiritual depths of Catherine of Siena. Born the twenty-fourth (and a twin) of twenty-five children of a wool-dyer and a poet's daughter, Caterina di Giacomo (or Iacopo) di Benincasa was gifted with piety and visions from a very early age.

Because of a visionary experience when she was about six years old, Catherine vowed her virginity to God and took on severe ascetical practices that would eventually render her incapable of eating normally and ruin her health. When Catherine was sixteen years of age, her favorite sister died. Seizing upon this tragedy to defy her parents' wishes that she marry, Catherine cut off her hair and deliberately scalded herself in nearby hot mineral springs, and almost died. At eighteen years of age, she became a *Mantellata*, a member of the Dominican Third Order, a loose federation of women—usually widowed—who lived at home, took the habit, received spiritual direction from Dominican friars, and cared for the poor and the sick. However, this ascetic continued to live in a tiny room under the kitchen stairs in her parents' home, where she retreated into solitude, silence, and even harsher austerities.

When approximately twenty-one years of age, Catherine experienced something typical of ecstatic women: mystical marriage with Christ and an exchange of hearts with him. This event transformed her from an overly ascetic solitary into an *apostola*, that is, a woman whose charitable work brings God's good news of mercy, love, and peace to the wider community. Rejoining the life of her family and helping the *Mantellate* in their practical works of mercy, Catherine now embraced a way of life not only of unusual austerity and silent contemplation but also of vigorous social work for the poor, sick, and dying. At the age of twenty-three, she experienced her "mystical death," a four-hour God-given ecstasy in which her body seemed to be dead. She also maintained that she had received the stigmata, though only she could see them.

Raimondo of Capua, the distinguished Dominican reformer, whom Catherine considered to be both a "father and son" given her by "gentle Mary," became her confessor and spiritual director. During the last five years of her life, Catherine was involved in the religio-political problems of the Italian city-states and barely escaped assassination. Highly influential in mitigating the antipapal forces in her region, she also preached in favor of a crusade, and the reform of the clergy, and worked for the return of the Avignon papacy to Rome. Her prophetic gifts and letters actually played a role in Pope Gregory XI's decision to move back to Rome. His successor, Urban VI, sought Catherine's support for his legitimacy as pope and called her to Rome in 1379 seeking her help in a vain attempt to win back the schismatics. The Great Schism was the saddest disappointment in her life.

Her masterpiece, *The Dialogue*, offers a comprehensive summation of her thought on the mystical ascent to God. "About two years before her death," her confessor Raimondo wrote, "such a clarity of truth was revealed to her from heaven that Catherine was constrained to spread it abroad by means of writing, asking her scribes to stand ready to take down whatever came from her mouth as soon as they noticed that she had gone into ecstasy."[2] Entrusting "my book"—as she fondly referred to it—to Raimondo, she later bequeathed this compendium of her teachings to her numerous lay and clerical followers who accepted her spiritual authority and even called her "mama."

In this text, Catherine addresses four petitions to God: for herself, that she be allowed to suffer in atonement for sins; for the reform of the Church; for the whole world; for divine providence in all things, but specifically in regard to a "certain case that had arisen." God grants each of these petitions while she is in ecstasy, to which she responds with thanksgiving.

Catherine teaches that God is "First Truth" and charity itself, who is madly in love with us. Drinking from the fountain of "gentle First Truth," in her view, is the best way to attain self-knowledge and knowledge of God. God is the "sea pacific" in which we must drown. Because Christ's open heart is the revelation of God's heart, it reveals that we were created out of and for an eternal, boundless love. She also describes the incarnation as the "engrafting" of God into human nature. On the day of his circumcision, Catherine teaches, Christ espoused the entire human race with the ring of his flesh. Catherine also depicts Christ as a nursing mother. As she perceives it, the way to God is a lived dynamic of knowledge of and love for the crucified Christ whose sufferings reveal God's "incomprehensible exaltedness." Christ's redeeming, healing, bathing, nourishing, and binding blood is, perhaps, the most important symbol in her writings. Experiencing this blood taught Catherine that the summit of the mystical life combines both union with God and an insatiable hunger for the salvation of others. Mystical marriage must be apostolically fecund.

Because Catherine uses a layered logic that seems repetitious—yet adds new meanings and shadings as she progresses—her book is difficult but rewarding to read. By using Christ as a "bridge" and as a "door," one meets God—the "sea pacific"—in the heart, in ecstasy, and in helping one's neighbor. The bridge, which has three stairs, is the "only begotten Son." Christ built two of the stairs from the wood of the cross; the third he constructed "even as he tasted the great bitterness of the gall and vinegar they gave him to drink."[3]

These three stairs have their corresponding spiritual stages. On the first stair, the soul lifts her feet from earthly affections and strips herself of sin. On the second stair, the soul dresses herself in the love of the virtues. On the third, she tastes peace. This bridge must be used to cross the threatening waters of evil and sin to reach not dry land but God, the sea pacific in which one drowns.

Catherine also writes of six kinds of tears that correspond to six steps to mystical union. Five of these involve literally weeping. First, there are the tears of those dead in sin; second, is the fearful crying of those who know their sins will bring them punishment; third, is the imperfect weeping of those who have transcended fear and attained love and hope; fourth, are the tears of those whose only desire is to will what God wills; fifth, the tears that occur when "the soul is united with Truth and the flame of holy desire burns more fiercely within her."[4]

After the five types of physical tears, the sixth kind are mystical "tears of fire" that consume a person in love. "Such a soul," Catherine writes, "would like to dissolve her very life in weeping out of self-contempt and for the salvation of souls, but she seems unable to do it. I tell you, these souls have tears of fire. In this fire the Holy Spirit weeps in my presence for them and for their neighbors."[5]

Perfect weeping is given only to those whom Christ has washed in his blood, a washing that also gives rise to the "sweet taste" of God's love. Paradoxically, perfect weeping requires the disinterested love of both God and neighbor, yet also brings it about. Spirit-inspired longings of love cause "tears of fire," that is, the desire to belong totally to God. At the stage of "unitive tears," one longs only to have Christ crucified as the pattern for one's life. Catherine depicts the crucified Christ as the "nipple" of the divine breast that one suckles to be filled with the milk from the "high eternal Godhead." In the stage of unitive tears, Catherine hears God say, "She is another me, made so by the union of love."[6]

Perhaps more important than her dramatic mystical experiences is the way Catherine's life of service nourished her mysticism, which, in turn, expressed and fulfilled itself sacramentally in social and political activity. The extreme asceticism of her youth that ravaged her health became in her mature years a mere instrument of discipline, and one now wholly subject to the demands of love and service. Instructed by God to love her neighbors without self-seeking, profit, or thanks, she came to understand that, in this way, she could do for them what she could not do for God. In line with many others in the Christian tradition, Catherine's mysticism and apostolic activity are two sides of the same coin, the systole and diastole of her mystical heart.

Catherine has also bequeathed to the Christian tradition some 382 letters addressed to people from all walks of life, from popes to prostitutes. Dictated—often ecstatically—in her Tuscan dialect, they reveal a woman with a strong pastoral sense and acting with enormous inner freedom. They also disclose her salient themes: the person as image of the Trinity, Jesus Christ as redeemer, the unity of the love of God and neighbor, the centrality and inseparability of truth and love, the twofold knowledge of God and self, the Church as the continuation of Christ's life on earth, and the mystery of God's providence. What dominates the letters, however, is her desire that everyone be united to God "without anything in between." Catherine had been taught that God wanted everyone to be transformed and to be united to him by eliminating "any medium, anything that gets in between—except divine charity, which is a sweet and glorious medium that doesn't separate but unites."[7]

Catherine's letters almost always begin with the phrase "my greetings in the precious blood of God's Son" and then by exhorting the reader to drown in Christ's blood. She saw Christ's blood flowing from his gashed side, the place where the "bride rests in the bed of fire and blood." She experienced this blood as the divine wine that warmed and inebriated her. When she asked Christ why he wanted his side opened, he replied that this was the supreme way to reveal the secrets of his heart—a heart that "held more love for humankind than any external physical act could show."[8] Her blood mysticism is a form of a mysticism of the Sacred Heart of Jesus.

In one particularly striking epistle, Catherine distinguished between baptism by water and baptism by blood and fire, the baptism granted to the martyrs. "This fire," she wrote, "is the love that is the Holy Spirit, for love was the hand that pierced God's Son and made him shed his blood. [The fire and the blood] became one, and so perfect was their uniting that we cannot have fire without blood, nor blood without fire."[9]

Catherine spent the last few years of her life in ever-declining health, but still laboring for Church reform and unity. Most of her recorded prayers come from this time. While dictating to her secretaries, conducting business, or even during conversations, she often burst into prayer because of ecstatic transports. The daily liturgy, her biblical reading, her daily concerns—especially the specific needs of the Church and "of those she had been given to love with a special love"—suffuse her prayers.

Especially striking is the contrast she depicts between herself as the "stench of sin," "death," "the one who is not," "terrible twisted-ness," and God as the "fragrance of grace and virtue," "life," "the one who is," and "absolute directness."[10] In a prayer to the Trinity, she praises God for the God-Man whose humanity was the "hand" that held the "key" to the Godhead "because the Godhead could not open it without the humanity that had locked it with the sin of the first man, nor could the simple humanity open it without the Godhead."[11]

In the beginning of 1380, Catherine became so sick that she could not eat; she refused water as well. Incessant prayer, mystical ecstasies, and self-oblation became her apostolate for the Church. In what is perhaps her last recorded utterance, she confessed that she had noth-ing to give God except what God had given her. She prayed that God accept the sacrifice of her life "within this mystical body of holy Church." She implored this mercy of God in virtue of the Son's most sweet blood. "Blood! Blood! Father, into your hands I surrender my soul and my spirit."[12]

# Thomas à Kempis

## (1380–1471)

*"A lover of Jesus and of truth and a true internal man that is free from inordinate affections, can freely turn himself to God and in spirit elevate himself above himself, and rest in enjoyment."*[1]

The late fourteenth to middle fifteenth century Low Countries saw the rise of what quickly became known as the *Devotio Moderna*, a "renewed" spirituality with roots in scripture, the Desert Fathers, and the best of the tradition they engendered. It contrasted with both the highly scholastic and speculative mysticism rooted in Eckhart and Tauler and the more pedestrian, popular piety of the time. To combat the cooling of Christian ardor among the Catholics of the Low Countries, the renewed devotion—permeated with Cistercian and Franciscan emotion (but not "charismatic" or "enthusiastic" in the contemporary sense)—emphasized a radical imitation of Christ, a deep love for his humanity and passion, the Eucharist, and a "sweet," ardent love of God.

The *Devotio Moderna* also taught that the avoidance of vice, the practice of virtue, self-abnegation, solitude, separation from the world, humility, purity of heart, and a devotional reading of scripture and "raparia" ("snatchings," collected excerpts from the spiritual and mystical tradition) produced a devout, interior person of compunction. Spiritual "exercises" were also a salient feature of this renewed devotion. One of the most influential letters on such exercises urges its readers: "Hold the works of Jesus Christ before your eyes [and] assimilate yourself to them in true charity, deep humility, ready obedience, and complete denial of yourself, in modesty, piety, peace, patience, in contempt of all temporal matters and in modification of your own nature."[2]

The followers of this movement were known as the "Brothers and Sisters of Common Life"; in most cases, simply, the "New Devout."

These pious people lived communally on the basis of their labor, their ecclesiastical incomes, and their own contributed wealth. Not a few worked as copyists and as translators of texts, which indicates their high degree of literacy. Many of them were held in high regard because of their skill in a variety of crafts and trades.

This renewed way of living was open to all social classes (a novelty then) but its followers came mostly from the minor clergy, the laity of both genders, and their communities were usually made up of local people. Nothing was required of them other than a willingness to give up all personal property and an ardent resolve to live a deeply religious life. They took no vows and participated in the sacramental life offered by their local parish churches. Making wide use of the vernacular in their reading of scripture and meditations, they often gathered with interested students and townspeople for "collations," that is, informal sermons, homilies, shared prayer, and reflection. These remarkably self-governing people were accepted relatively rapidly by their contemporaries because they sustained an edifying, contemplative way of life outside of cloister and alongside their parishes, eschewed the begging and crude fund-raising that had come to characterize the mendicant orders, taught no esoteric doctrines, practiced fraternal correction, showed no signs of anticlericalism, were obedient to their bishops, and were humble and unassuming. Their "ordinariness" contrasted not only with the saints depicted in medieval hagiography but also with the urban patricians, lordly monks, and mendicants of their own times.

Out of this movement came the greatest classic of Catholic spirituality, *The Imitation of Christ*, a book second only to the Bible in popularity in the Western Church. More than seven hundred extant manuscripts of this work and translations into more than fifty languages attest to its status as one of the most famous Christian devotional books in history. Numerous statesmen, philosophers, poets, founders of religious orders, saints, and mystics have regarded it as their favorite book.

Since the sixteenth century, the authorship of the *Imitation* has been the subject of much controversy, and no less than forty individuals have been named as its author. But contemporary scholarship tentatively holds that Thomas à Kempis wrote thirteen short and independent Latin treatises, brought them together into one codex, and later rewrote each one of them. Four treatises were eventually copied together, considered as one work, and given the title *The Imitation of Christ*, based on the opening words of the first treatise: "These are the words of Christ . . . that we must imitate his life and manners."[3] When the four treatises finally came to be printed, this same tradition was employed. Thus, the better scholarly hypothesis, to my mind, is that the four treatises were written by Thomas but that neither the book itself in its familiar form nor the title goes back to him.

Thomas à Kempis has been called the outstanding representative of the *Devotio Moderna*. Born Thomas Hemerken in Kempen (thus, Thomas à Kempis) near Düsseldorf in the Rhineland diocese of present-day Cologne, Germany, he was educated in Deventer under the direction of Florentius Radewijns, the successor of the famous Geert Groote, founder of the Brothers of the Common Life and father of the *Devotio Moderna*. Instead of joining the Brothers as planned, Thomas entered the newly founded monastery of the Canons Regular of St. Augustine at Mount St. Agnes (Agnietenberg), near Zwolle, where his older brother was prior. Except for three years, he spent the rest of his life transcribing manuscripts—even an entire Bible—and writing numerous works.

The *Imitation* illustrates the relationship that can exist between deep piety and mysticism—and how difficult it sometimes is to distinguish between the two. The New Devout neither spoke of bridal union with God and Christ nor used sexual language to express their desired inwardness and interiority. Definitely mystical, however, was their often direct and immediate consciousness of God and Christ—engendered by their single-minded resolve to live in Christ and to be bound to God in "delightful" love. The eucharistic mysticism of the *Imitation* highlights this: "Ah! Lord God, when shall I be wholly united to you and absorbed in you and altogether forgetful of myself? Thou in me and I in you and altogether forgetful of myself?"[4]

The first treatise of the *Imitation* focuses on renouncing all that is vain, illusory, and pleasing to the senses. One must seek humility, desire to be unknown, and desire only the eternal. As the text states, "If we were perfectly dead to ourselves, and in no way entangled in our interior, then might we be able to relish things divine and experience something of heavenly contemplation."[5]

The second treatise—the shortest—teaches that since the kingdom of God is within, it cannot be attained by the senses or by mere human knowledge. "Learn to despise exterior things," Kempis wrote, "and give yourself to the interior, and you shall see that the kingdom of God will come into you."[6] Submitting to God's will through humility and purity of heart bring inner peace. To obtain familiarity with and to show one's love for Christ require the unconditional embrace of his cross. "Why then are you afraid to take up your cross, which leads to a kingdom?" wrote Kempis. "In the cross is infusion of heavenly sweetness; in the cross is strength of mind; in the cross is joy of spirit."[7]

The third treatise—the longest—repeats the same themes as the first two, but says more about grace and love. It is written as a dialogue between Jesus, the soul's beloved, and the single-minded disciple of Christ crucified. It emphasizes that only those who are empty of self can be filled with God. The futility of "vain learning" for attaining true knowledge and lasting peace is also a salient theme. Only the words of Christ "inflame the heart and enlighten the mind." In Kempis's words: "I [Christ] am He who teaches men knowledge, and I give a more clear understanding to little ones than can be taught by man. I am He that in an instant elevates a humble mind to comprehend more reasons of the eternal truth than could be acquired by ten years' study in the schools. I teach without noise of words, without confusion of opinions, without ambition of honor, without contention of arguments. I teach to despise earthly things, to loathe things present, to see and relish things eternal, to flee honors, to endure scandals, to repose all hope in Me, to desire nothing out of Me, and above all things, ardently to love Me."[8]

The fourth treatise focuses on the Blessed Sacrament as the key for obtaining the fruit in the first three. The desired union with God can be obtained sacramentally by participating in Jesus' eucharistic supper and sacrifice. Therefore, one should make adequate preparation for the frequent reception of the Lord's great gift to us. "Empty vessels" profit most from this grace. The dignity of the priesthood in relationship to the Mass is underscored. This treatise also stresses the New Devout's desire for union: "Oh, that with your presence you would inflame, burn, and transform me into Yourself, that I may be made one spirit with you, by the grace of eternal union, and by the melting of ardent love. What marvel if I should be wholly set on fire by You, and should die to myself; since You are a fire always burning—and never failing; a love purifying the heart and enlightening the understanding!"[9]

# Nicholas of Cusa

## (1401–64)

*"Therefore, in every such love in which a person is carried into God, knowledge enters in, although it does not know the essence that it loves. There is, therefore, a coincidence of knowledge and ignorance, or a learned ignorance."*[1]

Although relatively unknown in the English-speaking world, Nicholas of Cusa (Cusanus) was one of the remarkable and enigmatic geniuses of the fifteenth century. Born in present-day Kernkastel-Kues on the Mosel, he studied at the universities of Heidelberg, Padua, and Cologne, and became a doctor of canon law.

Ordained priest in 1430, he soon distinguished himself in the affairs of Church and empire. Participating in the conciliarist views of his age, he attended the Council of Basel, but later became a papal champion against the German princes. Given the red hat, he was appointed bishop of Brixen in the Tyrol, where he worked tirelessly for monastic, clerical, and lay reform. His reforming efforts caused such severe tensions—especially with one abbess—that he abandoned his diocese and fled to Italy.

In 1433, he wrote a masterful treatise, *De Concordantia Catholica*, in which he outlined a comprehensive program for the reform of Church and empire. Attaining a reputation as a peacemaker and reconciler, he also became papal legate for the German-speaking countries. In addition to his ecclesiastical endeavors, this mystical theologian managed to pen over fifty works—one, a Christocentric evaluation of the Qur'an. His heart is buried in a hospice he founded at Kernkastel-Kues for the elderly—extant to this day, and containing a vast manuscript collection from his own library.

In this gifted theologian's most famous treatise, *On Learned Ignorance*, Cusanus claims that his two most significant principles, "learned ignorance" and the "coincidence of opposites"—and a way of speaking about them—came not from learning but from divine illumination. In a covering letter to Cardinal Julian Cesarini concerning this book, Cusanus writes that the "Father of Lights" graced him with the ability to embrace incomprehensibles incomprehensibly in learned ignorance, by transcending those incorruptible truths that can be humanly known. "In union with Him who is the Truth," he writes, "I have now set forth the learning that is ignorance in these books, and these can be reduced or enlarged from the same source."[2] In this same letter he speaks of the divine simplicity in which all contradictories coincide.

That "God is known to God alone" grounds this dark, yet learned and holy, ignorance—an ignorance both experiential and speculative. Human knowledge, by contrast, is relative and complex, and at best only approximate. The way to Truth is a not-knowing that is beyond reason, beyond the principle of contradiction, and beyond both ignorance and knowledge. The highest stage of intellectual apprehension accessible to the human intellect forces it to acknowledge its own limitations because Truth—which is absolute, one, and infinitely simple—cannot be comprehended by the human mind. The more one comprehends God to be incomprehensible, the more one attains God.

Learned ignorance flows from a kind of spiritual seeing through which the person rejoices in having attained "the knowledge of ignorance by a more certain experience."[3] This experience transcends all vision and produces a darkness beyond both what is and what is not. Although Cusanus contends that knowledge enters into every love that transports a person into God, nevertheless, knowledge of the essence of what is loved remains impossible. Knowledge and love coincide in such a way that learned ignorance fulfills knowing through the realization that what the person loves and is loved by is beyond comprehension. One should speak of learned ignorance as a connatural loving-knowledge of God that flows from participation in God.

God, in Nicholas's view, is not the coincidence of opposites. Rather, opposites coincide in God, who, as absolute simplicity and the absolute maximum, precedes opposites. God is the *non aliud*, the "not other," who is paradoxically wholly other and without opposites and contradiction. God is the "Absolute Infinity," that which nothing greater IS, and also beyond Being. Only intuition can grasp God, in whom all contradictions meet. This means that God is at once infinitely great and infinitely small, the center and the circumference of everything created, everywhere and nowhere, and the crushing darkness of Light—but really none of these.

Cusanus views the coincidence of opposites not as the goal of the journey to God but only as the limit to all conceptual thinking found at "the wall of paradise." The "spiritual eye" looks beyond this wall into paradise at its "secret love and hidden treasure." However, it remains ineffable, incomprehensible, and hidden, even after it is found. Only the love revealed through the Trinity enables the leap over this wall to meet God in wordless rapture in the garden of paradise.

Cusanus understands "mystical theology" as the entry into "Absolute Infinity" because God is the Absolute Infinite. Infinity alone can express the "coincidence of contradictories, that is, the end without end, and no one can see God mystically save in the darkness of coincidence that is infinity."[4] The language of coincidence is partially able to enunciate what otherwise fails the sciences and language. The language of coincidence overcomes the limits of discursive reasoning, surpasses both affirmative and negative language, and renders infinite concepts understandable and describable without violating their incomprehensibility and illimitability. Still, silence is the best way to speak about God; ignorance, the most effective knowing. Cusanus's mystical theology aims at arousing, kindling, and stirring the soul to receive God's presence in intellectual rapture.

Cusanus speaks of God as the "Absolute Maximum" and the world as the "Contracted Maximum," because the world is the "all." Jesus Christ is the "Absolute and Contracted Maximum," the God-Man who is the supreme example of the coincidence of opposites. Because humanity can exist only in a contracted way and be this or that, Cusanus argues that it is not possible for more than one genuine human being to "ascend to union with maximumness." This being, moreover, would be a human in such a way as to be God and God in such a way as to be a human. The one Jesus Christ, therefore, is the door to the wall of coincidence, the icon of icons in whose light learned ignorance becomes sacred ignorance. The God-Man resolves two issues: first, how the incomprehensible God is known; second, how one can speak about God theologically. The "coincidence" of Christ's divine and human natures is both the criterion and the model for Cusanus's iconographic theology.

The treatise *Dialogue on the Hidden God* was written as a theological conversation between a "Christian" and a "Pagan" (actually, anyone who supposes that he "knows" God) and celebrates God's utter simplicity and incomprehensibility. In it the Christian surprises the pagan when he states that neither he nor anyone knows God. Everything that can be conceived and known is not like God because God transcends them all. When the pagan presses him about what he will say of God, Cusanus replies that God is neither named nor not named, nor is God both named and not named. God's infinity means that all that can be said disjunctively and unitively, whether by means of agreement or contradiction, does not correspond to God, for God is the one beginning prior to every idea that can be formed of God. When the pagan asks why the Christian worships God so reverently, he replies, "It is because I do not know that I worship."[5] This treatise is a paean to God's hiddenness. It underscores that we participate in a God who can never be comprehended.

In reply to the charge of pantheism by John Wenck, professor of theology at Heidelberg, Cusanus wrote his *Defense of Learned Ignorance*. His more contemplative work, *On Seeking God*, exhorts the reader not to know God but to seek the one who is even beyond all interiority. It emphasizes an ignorance illuminated from within by *God's* knowing within us. Cusanus urges the reader to lift himself to God—the light of the human intellect—because "in God's light is all our knowledge, so that it is not we ourselves who know, but rather it is God who knows in us."[6]

Cusanus's devotional classic, *On the Vision of God*, is an attempt to describe the marvels that are revealed beyond all sensible, rational, and intellectual sight. He illustrates the divine-human relationship by using an analogy based on an all-seeing icon of the face of Jesus that seems to gaze directly at the viewer—no matter where he stands. In a way reminiscent of Eckhart, Cusanus says, "In beholding me You give Yourself to be seen of me, You who are a hidden God."[7] One "sees" "Absolute Reason" by means of a sweet, mental tasting (Cusanus does make liberal use of the spiritual senses) that leaps across the "wall of invisible vision," a "wall of coincidence of the hidden and the revealed," which is "at the same time all things and nothing."[8]

The "mental rapture" that sees God is never satisfied because what satisfies the intellect is not what the intellect understands. Only what it understands by not understanding satisfies it. The infinite

God can never be fully "consumed" by the human mind. Paradoxically, too, only the person who possesses self can possess God. "Hence, I now perceive that, if I hearken to Your Word, which does not cease to speak within me, and continually enlightens my reason, I shall be mine own, free, and not the slave of sin, and You will be mine own, and will grant me to behold Your face, and then I shall be whole."[9]

Nicholas's most controversial work, *On the Summit of Contemplation*, is written as a dialogue between the "Cardinal" and "Peter" Erkelenz, a canon in Aachen. It presents a theology beyond negation, affirmation, and even the coincidence of opposites. When Peter asks the Cardinal what he is seeking, the Cardinal replies that whoever seeks is seeking *what*. Unless one were seeking something or *what*, one would not be seeking at all. "What" is another name for God, in Cusanus's view, and what everyone seeks. He confesses that "in some way or other many both have seen it and in their writings left behind their vision of what they have seen."[10] In short, Nicholas himself sees and experiences that about which he writes.

Cusanus uses the term *Posse Ipsum* for the whatness subsisting in itself. The highest form of contemplation focuses upon "Possibility Itself," God's fecundity, God's "pure boiling"—that which appears in all things. Christ is its perfect appearance. In this treatise, *On the Summit of Contemplation*, Cusanus moves from a preference for a Dionysian mysticism of dazzling darkness to a mysticism of light. He confesses that he once thought that "Possibility Itself" could be best found in darkness. He slowly came to realize that "Possibility Itself" blazes forth with light, "shouts in the streets, [and] shows itself easily to be seen."[11] However, just as learned ignorance transcends intellectual comprehension, the mind's ability (*posse*) to see transcends its ability to comprehend.

Cusanus views all things as nothing but appearances of *Posse* Itself. However, all things exist for the sake of the mind, "the living intellectual light," which exists for the sake of seeing *Posse* Itself. When the mind sees that its own *posse* is not the *Posse* of every *posse*, it grasps that it is a mode of appearance of *Posse* Itself. And it likewise sees that *Posse* exists in all things. "All things that the mind sees," Cusanus writes, "are modes of appearance of the incorruptible *Posse* Itself."[12] This grounds Cusanus's mysticism of finding God in all things and finding all things in God.

# Catherine of Genoa

## (1447–1510)

*"If, of that which this heart of mine is feeling, one drop were to fall into hell, hell itself would become all eternal life."*[1]

Looking at the times and achievements of this mystic, married lay-woman, and heroic servant of Genoa's plague-ridden and poor, one can easily understand why Catherine is often called the only genius of her age. Serving as a bridge between the mystics of the late Middle Ages and those of the sixteenth and seventeenth centuries, she had considerable influence on later French mysticism, German Romanticism, nineteenth-century American Protestants, and prominent Anglican converts to Catholicism. Catherine's greatest single historical contribution may well be the spiritual birth she gave to Ettore Vernazza, the father of the Oratory of Divine Love. Composed of laity and clergy, this highly influential movement focused on the care of the poor as well as on individual and Church reform. She was canonized saint on May 18, 1737.

The youngest of five children in the noble Fieschi family, the spiritually precocious Catherine desired to enter an Augustinian convent when she was thirteen years old, but was refused entry because of her age. When she was sixteen years of age, her family—for financial and political advantages—married her off to the dissolute Giuliano Adorno. Bitter loneliness eventually caused her to seek solace in dissipation and frivolities.

During a Lenten confession on March 22, 1473, Catherine had both a sudden, ecstatic experience of God as Pure Love and a penetrating contrition for her sins. A ray of God's flaming love wounded her heart. This experience—"beyond intellect, tongue, or feeling"—ecstatically established her in divine love. From then on, pure love became her state of soul, which also awakened in her a profound sense of her sinfulness and ingratitude. Overwhelmed with self-loathing and near despair, she was tempted to confess her sins publicly. "And Catherine's soul cried out, 'O Lord, no more world, no more sins!'"[2]

In contrast to the many mystics who were only gradually purified by, illuminated by, and united to Pure Love, Catherine's transformation into God seems to have occurred almost instantaneously. Catherine contended that the ray of God's burning love so united her to him that from that time on nothing could separate the two of them from one another. Now *nothing* but Pure Love meant anything to her to such an extent that she would reject any love that would be *for* or *in* God because "pure love loves God who is Pure Love without a why or wherefore."[3]

God as pure, incomprehensible love is the salient feature of Catherine's mysticism. "All that can be said about God is not God," she taught, "but only [the] smallest fragments which fall from His table."[4] She often ecstatically experienced the "Living Fountain of Goodness," a bounty of divinity "without any kind of participation."[5] Two questions came to her mind: why did God create? Out of a Pure Love that asks only that creatures acknowledge their creation out of and for this love was the answer given her. The second question: how pure and strong is this love? The reply: if one drop of what her heart felt of this love were to fall into hell, hell itself would become all eternal life.

Christ crucified ("it seemed that his body rained blood") appeared to Catherine in the aftermath of this conversion. An inner voice told her that Christ's blood had been shed out of love to atone for her sins. Jesus pulled himself to her with such a wound of love that it transformed every fear she had into joy. From that day on, she felt the "pull of Holy Communion," and received it daily—an unusual practice in her day.

Catherine subsisted solely on water and daily Eucharist for approximately twenty-three years during Advent and Lent. These long, mysterious fasts did not diminish her energy, and she continued to give herself fully both to an intense spiritual life and to the needs of the poor and sick. Commenting on this unusual phenomenon (commonly called "inedia"), she claimed that she neither willed these fasts nor considered them important. "This not-eating of mine," she confessed, "is an operation of God, independent of my will, hence I can in nowise glory in it."[6]

Catherine experienced that God alone is the all good; God alone is the person's true center. True self-love, to her way of thinking, consists in loving God. Just as food is transformed into what consumes it, Catherine spoke of herself as God's food being transformed into himself—who eliminates all waste products in the process. "My *Me* is God," she cried out, "nor do I recognize any other *Me* except my God Himself."[7] In her view, her being was God's being and God's being was her being, and "not by simple participation but by a true transformation of [her] being."[8]

Catherine taught that sin is a turning away from Pure Love, an auto-idolatry, a false self-love, a love that always reeks of self. She deemed her very own self—"the very opposite of God"—to be her worst enemy. The slightest deviation from Pure Love caused her intense suffering; she discovered that her self-will was so subtle and so deeply rooted that it obeyed only itself—no matter how hard she tried to outwit it. The penetrating awareness of her spiritual corruption became so intense at times that she would have despaired and then died—had God not lessened the duration of this experience.

Catherine's ecstatic, mystical love expressed itself in her identification with the poor, sick, and suffering of Genoa. She eventually convinced her debauched husband to reform his ways, to adopt a life of mutual continence, and to assist in her charitable work. From that time on, they were both consumed with busy hospital administration work in Genoa's Pammatone Hospital and with work with the poor.

Although Catherine underscored as "most bitter" the battle between pure love and self love, she stressed another kind of war: the one between body and soul. Experience had taught her that the body is a "veritable purgatory" because of the soul's desire to depart from it in order to be with God. Although the soul has a natural instinct for God, it "finds itself bound to a body entirely contrary to its own nature."[9] Thus, Catherine held the infelicitous view that the body "chains the soul to earth." This unfortunate understanding of the body-soul relationship may have emerged from Catherine's long years of illness that terminated in an excruciating death. It is ironic that her body was found to be almost perfectly preserved when exhumed several months after burial.

Catherine's austerities outstripped the rigors of any convent. Her fasts were perhaps nothing compared to her labors with the plague-ridden, the poor, and the dying of Genoa. One tends to forget what "hospitals" were like in her day. To these hardships, one must add her penitential "holy follies," such as eating lice and kissing the sores of syphilitics—extreme penances that some saints willingly undertook to express their gratitude and joy for God's self-emptying love.

Although Catherine wrote no works, her confessor and confidant, Cattaneo Marabotto, and her spiritual son, Ettore Vernazza, faithfully recorded her adages and instructions and added their own comments and interpretations. Catherine's work *Purgation and Purgatory* is a collection of her sayings and teachings about spiritual purgation both here and in the next life. Her other text, *Spiritual Dialogue*, is an account of her inner journey. It is written like a mystery play in which various figures—Soul, Body, Self-Love, Human Frailty, and Spirit—represent different aspects of the same person. There is nothing academic about her mystical wisdom. "The things that I speak about," she says, "work within me in secret and with great power."[10]

The book *Purgation and Purgatory* contains some of the most captivating passages on purgation and purgatory in the Christian mystical tradition. Catherine taught that God does not place a soul in purgatory or hell. When the person dies, in her view, the soul seeks its "own place" based on the nature of its sins. If the soul in mortal sin did not find itself "in hell," it would experience a still greater hell than the one due it. So it is with purgatory: "Should the soul find that the assigned place is not sufficient to remove its impediment, then it would experience a hell far worse than purgatory."[11]

Catherine understood purgatory as the God-given spiritual purification process that may happen partially or fully in this life or—for most of us—at a "place" in the afterlife. One suffers most "in purgatory," in her opinion, from the awareness that something in the person displeases God. However, purgatory is nothing more than God's cleansing, healing, and transforming "fiery love" so that "our being is then God."

Catherine emphasized that nothing she says can compare to what she felt about the "correspondence of love" between God and the soul. As the soul returns to its original purity through purgatory's cleansing action, God draws and unites the soul to himself with a burning love that seemingly annihilates it. God transforms the soul into "that pure state from which it first issued"[12] so that it knows nothing other than God. Feeling itself melting in the fire of God's delicious love and then stripped of all imperfections, "the soul rests in God with no characteristics of its own. Our being is then God."[13]

# Ignatius of Loyola

## (ca. 1491–1556)

*"May He by His infinite and sovereign goodness grant us abundant grace to know His most holy will and perfectly to fulfill it."*[1]

Ignatius of Loyola is one of the Christian tradition's profoundest mystics and perhaps its greatest mystagogue. Born in the austere castle of the Loyolas in the Basque region of northern Spain, Iñigo López de Oñaz y Loyola grew up in a noble Catholic family that prided itself on its military past and its fidelity to the king. He began his "worldly" career as a courtier, a gentleman, and a soldier. Women, gambling, dueling, and a tremendous desire for glory dominated his life—until he underwent a profound religious conversion, catalyzed by the severe leg wounds he received during the battle of Pamplona in 1521.

Soon after his recovery, Ignatius became a wandering pilgrim "for the sake of Christ" and attained heroic sanctity. For apostolic purposes, "to help souls," he decided to study in order to become a priest. He gathered together a group of companions in Christ; founded the Society of Jesus ("Jesuits"); established colleges, universities, and charitable institutions; and always kept his hand in directly pastoral activity. He directed a vast missionary network, and undertook sensitive diplomatic appointments.

Ignatius also authored the text *The Spiritual Exercises*, which transformed the history of spirituality from the sixteenth century to the present day. His other major work, *The Constitutions of the Society of Jesus*, is a foundational document for not only the Society of Jesus but also for many other religious orders and congregations. His thousands of letters demonstrate his far-reaching sociopolitical involvement. However, his apostolic successes, as well as those of the Society of Jesus from his time to the present, have overshadowed the importance of his mysticism.

Misplaced emphasis by historians and commentators upon the ascetical and pragmatic aspects of his spirituality further obscured the importance of Ignatius the *mystic*. It is one of the ironies of history that the man who in the early years after his conversion had difficulties with the Inquisition because he seemed to have something in common with the heretical "enlightened ones" (*Alumbrados*) of his age, quickly became portrayed as an overly rigid, ascetical martinet. In yet another historical paradox, his *Spiritual Exercises* were initially attacked for being too mystical; later, for being too ascetical, too centered on mechanical meditation, and an actual barrier to mystical prayer.[2]

Ignatius wrote his *Spiritual Exercises* on the basis of his own experience and made the unusual claim that these exercises would enable a person to seek and to find God's specific will for him or her. Not some secondary agent, he maintained, but "the Creator and Lord" himself would "deal directly" with the person by inflaming his soul with love and "disposing it for the way that will enable the soul to serve him better in the future."[3] Ignatius's mysticism is primarily one that seeks, finds, and carries out God's will.

The *Spiritual Exercises* are essentially meditations on and contemplations of the life, death, and resurrection of Jesus Christ. One must contemplate the Christian mysteries as if one were actually there witnessing these events. The one engaged in these exercises ("the exercitant") must daily recall, sum up, repeat, and linger over those aspects of the Christian mystery in which he finds "interior understanding and savoring." The evening exercise, the "application of the senses," requires the exercitant to see, hear, touch, taste, and feel "in imagination" the essential aspects of the mystery contemplated that day. This dynamic, creative "method" renders the Christian mystery contemplated in this way to become more simplified and even transparent—ways of praying that are a far cry from the frequent caricature of so-called "Jesuit prayer." The exercitant may even be drawn "wholly to the love of his divine majesty," through what Ignatius calls a "consolation without previous cause." In short, Ignatius's sacramental, iconistic ("kataphatic") mysticism neither requires nor recommends forgetting the Christian mysteries.

Four foundational mystical events stamped Ignatius's life. The first took place at Loyola during his long, boring recuperation from the shattering leg wounds received at the battle of Pamplona. Daydreaming for hours on end about the stories of courtly love he had previously found in the trashy literature of his day, he also pondered what he now read in the only literature at hand—the lives of the saints in *The Golden Legend* by Jacopo da Voragine and the *Life of Christ* by Ludolf of Saxony. Daydreaming about "worldly matters" quickly vanished and left him "dry and unhappy."[4] Reveries about imitating the saints in their holy follies not only consoled him, "but even after they had left him he remained happy and joyful."[5] The insight that some thoughts left him sad while others consoled him caused him to understand that joy is from God and sadness from the devil: "Little by little he came to perceive the different spirits that were moving him; one coming from the devil, the other coming from God."[6] From this seed grew his famous rules for the discernment of spirits.

The second significant mystical experience also occurred during his recuperation at Loyola: a vision of the Virgin Mary holding the Child Jesus. This transformative vision instilled in Ignatius such a disgust for his past life—especially for sins of the flesh—that it seemed to erase all the images that had been previously imprinted on his mind. From that hour, he wrote, "he never again consented, not even in the least matter, to the motions of the flesh. Because of this effect in him he concluded that this had been God's doing."[7] It would be difficult to overemphasize the importance of Ignatius's transformative visions for understanding his mysticism.

An intense sense of his sinfulness awakened at Loyola and Ignatius feared that no penances would suffice "to give vent to the hatred that he had conceived against himself."[8] Nonetheless, "on fire with God," he "felt within himself a strong impulse to serve Our Lord."[9] Recovering from his wounds, he went to Manresa, where for almost a year he indulged his thirst for severe penances and long hours of prayer. Severe depression, doubts, temptations, and scruples—alternating with deep spiritual joys—filled his soul. So painful were the tortures from the scruples about his past sins that Ignatius almost committed suicide. And ill health from the severity of his penances brought him to the brink of death.

Ignatius later claimed that at Manresa God had treated him like a "schoolboy" in order to deepen his desire for selfless service of the "Divine Majesty." It was here that indescribable and unforgettable mystical visions of the Trinity, Christ's humanity, Christ's presence in the Eucharist, and how the world was created indelibly penetrated his soul. These experiences contained such purity and certitude that Ignatius confessed, "if there were no Scriptures to teach us these matters of faith, he would still resolve to die for them on the basis of what he had seen."[10]

The third—and most important—event in Ignatius's life took place on the banks of the nearby river Cardoner, where "the eyes of his understanding began to open" and he was infused with a comprehension of many things pertaining to both faith *and learning*. His understanding was enlightened to such an extent "that he thought of himself as if he were another man and that he had an intellect different from the one he had before."[11] Ignatius would claim only a few years before his death that the clarity he received in his understanding on this one occasion surpassed the sum total of all the numerous and astonishing mystical gifts he had received throughout his entire life.

The fourth salient mystical event took place several years later when Ignatius and several of his companions were on their way to Rome to place themselves at the pope's disposal. In a small chapel at La Storta, some six miles north of Rome, Ignatius had a vision of the eternal Father with his cross-bearing Son. Ignatius heard the Father speak interiorly to his heart, saying, "I shall be favorable to you [plural] at Rome," and to the Son, "I want you, my Son, to take this man as your servant." Then Christ said to Ignatius: "I want you [singular] to serve *us* [Father and Son]." The graces at La Storta confirmed Ignatius's trinitarian, Christ-centered, and ecclesial mysticisms, all directed to the service of God and neighbor.

Ignatius's *Spiritual Journal*[12]—"one of the purest examples of direct reporting of mystical experiences in Christian history" (Bernard McGinn)—gives evidence that he is perhaps the most profound and most explicitly trinitarian mystic in Christian history. At Manresa, he noted, "his understanding was raised on high, so as to see the Most Holy Trinity under the aspect of three keys on a musical instrument."[13] This trinitarian experience remained with him for the rest of his life. When writing the Constitutions, Ignatius often prayed: "Eternal Father, confirm me; Eternal Son, confirm me; Eternal Holy Spirit, confirm me; Holy Trinity, confirm me; My One Sole God, confirm me."[14] Not infrequently during Mass, Ignatius had an experience that he described by saying, "I knew or felt or saw that on speaking to the Father and seeing that He was One Person of the Blessed Trinity,

I felt moved to love all the Trinity especially as the other Persons were all in the Trinity by their very essence: the same feeling when I prayed to the Son and to the Holy Spirit."[15]

Mystical encounters with the Father often led Ignatius to his Son, Jesus Christ. In his jottings about what often transpired at Mass, for example, he wrote, "I could not turn myself to the other Persons, except insofar as the First Person was the Father of such a Son; then I began to exclaim spiritually: 'How He is Father, how He is Son.'"[16] During Ignatius's preparation for Mass he frequently experienced that "it seemed in some way to be from the Blessed Trinity that Jesus was shown or felt, and I remember the time the Father placed me with the Son."[17] Under Jesus' "shadow," Ignatius often mystically felt Jesus "placing him in the presence of the Trinity" and then "toward the Blessed Trinity, a respect of submission more like a reverential love than anything else."[18]

Ignatius's spirituality and mysticism remain firmly anchored to Jesus Christ, the God-Man. The *Journal* contains numerous entries referring to his experiential visions of Christ's humanity and to his mystical comprehension of "Jesus being completely my God."[19] He often "saw and felt" all creatures "bathed in the blood of Christ" and was convinced that nothing could separate him from Christ. Numerous times his inner eye saw how Jesus is present in the Blessed Sacrament. Many of Ignatius's mystical experiences occurred during Mass. His mysticism is both eucharistic and priestly.

Ignatius's writings abound with references to his mystical communion with the Holy Spirit. This is the Holy Spirit he often "saw or felt in a dense brightness." Before, during, and after Mass he frequently "felt the impulse to weep and felt or saw the Holy Spirit himself; complete submission."[20] Powerful visitations by the Holy Spirit gifted him with mystical tears and intense consolations. He often sensed mystically when he should pray to the Spirit and when his profound spiritual consolations "terminated" in this Divine Person. Ignatius's writings clearly show that he linked the Holy Spirit with his experiences of consolation, discernment, judgment, decision making, and confirmation of his decisions. One example: when Ignatius came to the realization that his gift of mystical tears was undermining his health, he judged them to be deleterious, and firmly decided that they cease. And cease they did! He would later relate to a few of his companions that it was the Holy Spirit through whom he had received his most important graces and that toward the end of his life, he was able to experience the Holy Spirit almost at will.

Ignatius's instructions on how to make the sign of the cross offer a good summary of his trinitarian mysticism. He writes:

> When we make the holy Sign of the Cross, we place our fingers first on the head; and this is to signify God our Father, who proceeds from no one. When we touch our breast, this signifies the Son, our Lord, who proceeds from the Father and who descended into the womb of the Blessed Virgin Mary. When we place our fingers on both shoulders, this signifies the Holy Spirit, who proceeds from the Father and the Son. And when we fold our hands together again, this symbolizes that the Three Persons are one single substance. And finally, when we seal our lips with the Sign of the Cross, this means that in Jesus, our Savior and Redeemer, dwells the Father, the Son, and Holy Spirit, one single God, our Creator and Lord— and that the divinity was never separated from the body of Jesus, not even at His death.[21]

Another salient feature of Ignatius's mysticism is its ecclesial aspect. At Manresa, he received a "sublime understanding and very lively feelings" with respect to the Church, the "true Spouse of Christ our Lord, our Holy Mother, the hierarchical Church."[22] Therefore, Ignatius wrote, "we should love the whole body of the Church in her head, Jesus Christ."[23] The full sacramental expression of Ignatius's felt-knowledge of Christ is his "Rules for Thinking and Feeling with and in the Church,"[24] a felt-knowledge with and in the Church.

When Ignatius and his Paris companions were studying for the priesthood with the intent of more effective apostolic service, they decided to bind themselves more closely in a fellowship of love dedicated to Christ's service by taking private vows of chastity, of poverty (to be observed once they finished their studies), and of going to the Holy Land to labor for the conversion of the Turks. If unable to go or to remain in the Holy Land, "they would return to *Rome* and offer themselves to the *Vicar of Christ* so that he could use them wherever he judged it would be for the greater glory of God and the good of souls."[25] And since the Venetian-Turkish wars prevented their trip to the Holy Land, they did end up going to Rome. More than one commentator has called this aspect of Ignatius's mysticism "hyperpapal."

No other Christian mystic has given such prominence to tears in his or her writings as Ignatius did. The first part of his *Journal* mentions tears approximately 175 times; in the second part, every single entry speaks about tears. Uncontrollable tears and sobbing often accompanied Ignatius's numerous graces. Ignatius had admitted to his early companions that he felt deprived of consolation unless he shed tears at least three times during Mass.

Ignatius's *Journal* also indicates that he experienced a variety of tears. Some seemed to overflow from the very center of his soul into his eyes; others were not so profound. The *Journal* is replete with entries concerning tears that led to mystical experiences of the Trinity, of one of the Persons in the Trinity, of the God-Man, and of Mary. In fact, the frequent references to tears in the *Journal* are in part Ignatius's shorthand way of remembering the occasion, the nature, and the circumstances of other mystical graces.

In a letter to Francis Borgia, Ignatius chided him for his penitential excesses and urged, "Instead of trying to draw blood, seek more immediately the Lord of all, or what comes to the same thing, seek His most holy gifts, such as the gift of tears."[26] To Ignatius's way of thinking, tears were often nothing less than God's very own *self-communication*.

In time, however, Ignatius realized that tears were destroying his eyesight, his overall health, and reducing his apostolic effectiveness. This judgment led to a decision never to consent to tears again. They ceased and Ignatius received even more consolation. He taught later in life that the gift of tears should not be asked for unconditionally. If a person has true compassion and actively seeks to relieve the sufferings of one's neighbor, tears are not necessary. As he wrote in a letter to one of his Jesuit confreres, "even if it were in my power to allow this gift of tears to some, I would not give it, because it would be no help to their charity, and would harm their heads and their health and consequently stand in the way of every act of charity."[27]

Several entries in Ignatius's *Journal* mention a highly mysterious mystical gift that he called *loquela*, that is, "voices," "speech," "language," or "discourse." Some *loquela* came slowly, gently, silently, and ineffably from Ignatius's deepest core; other *loquela* were more superficial—emerging more quickly, more brusquely, and with "notable movements." They are almost always mentioned in the *Journal* in conjunction with his experience of the presence or absence of tears during Mass. They both brought him profound peace and helped him in discerning God's will.

Long before Ignatius experienced *loquela*, he had heard in spirit various types of mystical words. At La Storta, for example, the Father and the Son spoke to his soul in a transformative way. He knew from experience that it "frequently happens that our Lord moves and urges the soul to this or that activity. He begins by enlightening the soul; that is to say, by speaking interiorly to it without the din of words lifting it up wholly to His divine love and ourselves to His meaning."[28]

What is most striking about Ignatius's *loquela*, however, is that they consist of inner words, pregnant meaning, tone, rhythm, and music. Ignatius sometimes chided himself for paying more attention to the tone and music and not enough to the spiritual meaning they contained. Although he never questioned their divine origin, he did carefully examine the "relish" and the "sweetness" they brought for possible signs of the evil spirit. In some mysterious way, both *loquela* and tears instructed him in finding God's will.

The demand by some Jesuits for long hours of prayer sparked the first major crisis in the Society of Jesus. Ignatius forbade lengthy prayer and spoke instead of "mortification" and of finding God in all things. This highly circumspect and prudent Basque even maintained that over 90 percent of those who pray for long periods of time are in delusion. When someone spoke of a certain holy Jesuit as a "man of prayer," Ignatius retorted, "No, he is a mortified man." In his letter to Jesuits studying for the priesthood, he underscored that the time and energy requisite for studies leave little time for formal prayer. "Over and above daily Mass," he wrote, "an hour of vocal prayer and examen of conscience, and weekly confession and Communion—they should practice the seeking of God's presence in all things, in their conversations, their walks, in all that they see, taste, hear, understand, in all their actions."[29]

To be with the trinitarian Christ so as to serve in his Church with discreet love is a good summary statement of Ignatius's spirituality and mysticism. Another can be found in one of Ignatius's key exercises, the "Contemplation to Obtain Divine Love." "The second prelude," he wrote, "is to ask for what I desire. Here it will be to ask for interior knowledge of all the great goods I have received, in order that, stirred to profound gratitude, I may be able to love and serve the Divine Majesty in all things."[30]

# Francisco de Osuna

(ca. 1492–ca. 1540)

*"He who labors always to be recollected, his heart still, like a snail bearing his house with him or a turtle withdrawing beneath the shell, walks in the ways of his heart."*[1]

Francisco was born in Osuna (Seville) at a time when Spain's political and mystical golden ages were to coincide. A prolific author of more than five hundred works, and the first to write mystical treatises in Castilian, he forged a bridge between the earlier Spanish giant Ramon Llull and the later mystical titans Teresa of Avila and John of the Cross—who quickly overshadowed him.

Osuna wrote what may well be the Spanish masterpiece of Franciscan mysticism, *The Third Spiritual Alphabet*. Teresa of Avila speaks of it as the book given her by uncle Don Pedro, which was to lead her and so many of her nuns into the life of mystical prayer. Franciscan graciousness and emotion permeate its wealth of material on the ascetical-mystical life. Somewhat arbitrarily organized, the book's first treatise begins with the letter "A," the second "B," and so on— thus the reason for the title.

In the midst of the controversy over the nature of genuine mystical prayer that raged during the 1520s between the proponents of recollection (*recogimiento*) and those who advocated abandonment to God's will (*dejamiento*), Osuna accomplished two things. First, his conviction that all evil comes from a distracted heart inspired him to explain with unusual subtlety and perspicacity the nature of authentic recollection. Second, he exposed the Quietist tendency in *dejamiento*, which overemphasized passivity. The extreme form of *dejamiento* rejected all effort during prayer, ridiculed the sacramental life, averred that abandonment bestowed impeccability, and had no fear of sexual licentiousness.

Osuna emphasized that humility is the foundation for the entire spiritual-mystical life. It has nothing to do with pusillanimity and cowardice, but everything to do with magnanimity and the flight to "sublime, spiritual graces." Humility is truth, which understands that the more excellent a creature is, the greater its corresponding nothingness. Thus, in order to be filled with God, one must be emptied of self. Humility is the cornerstone of sanctity, because it was Christ's "first step" in this world.

One of the Christian tradition's most striking paeans to humility is found in the nineteenth treatise of Osuna's *Alphabet*. It describes humility as the mother of all virtues—the virtue that deepens the heart, enlarges it to receive God, conquers demons, and wins praise from God. Even pride—humility's bitterest foe—attempts to cloak itself as humility. Humility "magnified" the greatest of all men, Jesus Christ, and condemned the angels who did not love this virtue. Humility "can turn the house of God upside down, making the last first and the first last."[2]

Osuna wrote his book mainly to emphasize that friendship and communion with God are possible in this life of exile and best attained through recollection, which is a gift of God open to everyone. Much more than a technique, recollection is a way of life involving an organic process of prayer wherein one enters into self, rises above self, and unites with God.

Recollection, in Osuna's view, requires three types of silence. The first kind of silence arises from quieting the exterior senses and then emptying the mind and heart of all images, fantasies, and thoughts. The second type of silence flows from a "spiritual idleness," a "holy laziness," during which the soul does nothing except to remain alert and to contemplate itself as being recollected. The soul acts like a sentry on duty during a quiet night who is alert not only to every sound but also to his need to be alert. The third kind of silence flows from the simple remembrance of and desire for God alone. With the soul's powers united in love to its "highest" part where God's image dwells, it falls asleep but is awake in God.

Spiritual repose, in Osuna's view, is attained by "tasting," not through understanding. Wisdom comes only from the experience received in prayer and surpasses everything found in learned books. If all the knowledge and good qualities in the world could be found in one teacher, the "master of experience," that is, the recollected person, would still outmatch him. One must moderate the desire for knowledge and heed the biblical warning that the more learned one is, the more angry (Eccles 1:18). This does not imply that learning is of no value; it does imply, however, that everything understood must also be tasted and that tasting transcends understanding.

"Learned ignorance" (*docta ignorantia*) is a salient feature of Osuna's mysticism. In order to "taste" God, the understanding must be as blind as a bat in the noonday sun, the memory dumb, and the will deaf to all created things, yet silently awaiting God in the heart. God becomes the eyes of a soul that knows that God cannot be understood nor comprehended.

Osuna suggested quieting the understanding and stirring the will to fashion a "brief prayer" that immediately penetrates the heavens. He calls it a "brief prayer," not because of its transient nature, but because this prayer uses only love to reach God and is capable of immediate union with him. Quieting the understanding, however, does not mean stilling what Osuna calls "pure intelligence," or "intelligence-will," that can actually see the "invisible invisibly and essentially." When both creatures and understanding are abandoned, the "intelligence-will" enters into what is most secret and tastes the divine sweetness. Moreover, when the soul receives the "sublime and nourishing knowledge of experience," the understanding not only knows nothing but is also stunned and overwhelmed.

Paradoxically, the understanding is occupied during this experience but understands nothing of the intelligence-will's loving. This is the highest and most sublime form of understanding, a learned ignorance that comes from the real experience of spiritual things. The soul becomes like that of a simple and uneducated old man, whom Osuna knew, who loved to listen to learned sermons because the preacher's voice was like the sound of an organ that delighted his soul. Although he understood nothing, "his soul played in counterpoint to them, praising the Lord in music he could feel but not explain to others."[3]

"Fix your mind on recollecting yourself more completely," Osuna wrote, "for to constrain your heart is to embrace God, which is better effected solely by love. He often wishes us to be silent and leave him to work."[4] However, he contradicted the teaching of those who held that perfection can be attained by thinking nothing (*no pensar nada*) and that recollection can be equated with pure privation. In line with the orthodox apophatic mystical tradition, Osuna maintained that to think of nothing is to think of everything. Silencing the understanding and imagination subtly attunes the heart to God alone—with whom it is in fact united. Because the soul is aware of its enjoyment and the understanding "watches" what is occurring, "a tiny spark" of understanding always remains—until raptures take it away and the soul prays without awareness and enjoys God in a secret, obscure way.

Osuna distinguished speculative from mystical theology. By way of reasoning and argumentation, scholastic theology attains a "cold and penetrating" understanding of God as the highest truth. Mystical theology, on the other hand, proceeds by exercising the moral virtues and loves God as the person's highest good. Because this "holy devotion" is simply desire and the heart's innermost movement, anyone can possess this "supreme and perfect knowledge"—not just the learned. On the other hand, Osuna deems four kinds of people "useless on the battlefield of recollection": those who have entered religious life only physically, greedy clerics, the newly wed, and cowards who will not even attempt this devotion.

Osuna stressed that the goal of recollection is mystical theology by which the soul's highest power, intelligence-will, not only comes to desire and love what it ponders but also transcends itself in "transport." Like boiling water overflowing its pot, the soul becomes aflame with the loving heat of mystical theology, spills over, and is carried beyond itself. Only in this way does speculative knowledge become loving-knowledge, wisdom, the "sweet science" of mystical theology, which knows the truth by loving goodness. Osuna also called mystical theology "the art of love" and a "hidden theology" that only Christ can teach and who reserves to himself "the ministry of secretly teaching the hearts where that theology lives hidden like a divine science, more excellent by far than the other theology known as speculative."[5]

Osuna calls mystical theology a "profundity" because it discovers God in the depths of the human heart; a "concealment," because God hides in the heart's secret recesses; and "abstinence," because it withdraws a person from sin, from love of earthly things, and from all thoughts and images. It proudly wears these names: "drawing near" to one's greatest good, "enkindling" of love, "spiritual ascension," "arrival of the Lord," and "adoption" as a child of God. However, the most suitable name for this devotion, in Osuna's view, is "recollection," which connotes "union," that is, becoming one in spirit with God.

Osuna alerted his readers to the somatic effects that often accompany recollection. The limbs lose strength as the body contracts toward the breast. As this devotion empties the heart of all created things to fill it with God, a painless, "unbearably sweet" fire arises—which one wishes would burn forever. The mounting heat in the heart forces the recollected person to "explode" in groans and cries, otherwise his breast would burst.

Spiritual movements in the soul's highest part, in Osuna's view, may produce grimaces, bodily gestures, and even an unwanted, forceful raising of one's head. Deep sighs for something incomprehensible, penetrating cries, and unpremeditated, indistinct words come forth from the person's deepest center, "the heart." If one attempts either to stop or to conceal this "jubilation," the mouth and nose may bleed. The energy expended during recollection sometimes causes violent headaches and watering of the eyes—a condition that cannot be endured for very long.

Spiritual and bodily pleasures arise during recollection in other ways. For example, the person's entire psychosomatic structure is drawn inwardly, which produces a "marvelous dilation, whereby the soul is expanded like a glove into which one blows."[6] Even the breast seems to be so pleasantly filled that it expands far beyond its natural capacity to provide room for grace. Osuna claimed that he once knew "a recollected man who was awakened from peaceful sleep by hearing his own soul sing in a delicate treble which arose from his breast and seemed to mount to heaven."[7] To his way of thinking, in order to receive the grace to be truly recollected even during sleep, one should never go to bed sleepy but always remain wide awake in the desire for God.

Osuna maintained that the tears, which often accompany recollection, both justify and sanctify a person. They also "overpower God," just as a child's tears may overpower its mother. Beginners enjoy the first degree of tears when they weep for the "absent Beloved." The proficient savor the second degree of "hot and soundless" tears and weep like a "heated still" that constantly drips hot distilled water without any noise or effort. In the third degree of tears, the perfect become like an inexhaustible fountain; their tears originate in the joy they feel from God's abundant graces and from seeing themselves loved by God. Their souls utter a constant hymn of thanksgiving, which makes their hearts melt into God's love like ice exposed to bright sun.

Osuna stands out in the Christian mystical tradition as one of the most ardent—yet nuanced—proponents of interior and bodily delights. Because of their value in converting sinners and promoting love of God, he urged everyone to seek divine sweetness and consolations. Better love of God tinged with delectable self-love than seeking the pleasures of "the world, the flesh, and the devil." The truly recollected person, however, will never be satisfied with seeking consolation for its own sake but always as a means to increasing love and service of the Lord. God will eventually wean from self-love those fervent in their search for the things of God. Osuna offered wise counsel when he wrote, "If you delight in God, your soul possesses the best possible sign of the supreme love of God; therefore, let no one frighten you by saying that it is self love."[8]

On the other hand, Osuna was very wary of people who only stand at the door of recollection, never enter in, but imagine that what they feel comes from God. Such people also cry out, groan harshly, make noises, weep profusely, tremble, gesture strangely, and even fall to the ground as if dead. Although he did not view such actions as necessarily sinful in themselves and as sometimes even resulting from genuine spiritual desire, he nevertheless insisted that "everything like this is open to suspicion of being evil."[9]

Silence and restraint are, in Osuna's view, usually the wiser course of action. He urged his readers to be prepared to temper from the outset the above-mentioned outbursts and to remain praying in "deep quiet." The people he considered experienced and wise in recollection always tried to conceal the somatic manifestations of their most interior experiences. On the other hand, he admired a holy man who taught that "God denies himself in secret to those who deny him in public, and in order not to lose his hidden communication we must not crush that which he seeks to work in us publicly, so he may be glorified in all things."[10] Thus, only a person of deep discernment can decide whether to hide or to reveal the bodily manifestations of interior fervor.

As one would expect especially of a Franciscan mystic, Osuna's teaching on recollection never lost sight of the God-Man, Jesus Christ. From the very beginning of the book, he emphasized that Jesus' "blessed Humanity" in no way hinders or impedes even the highest states of mystical consciousness. Through Christ's body, the "hidden water" of "secretly communicated" graces are channeled to the world.

If all created things can move us to love and contemplate God, then Jesus' "Sacred Humanity overwhelms us and almost forces us to it."[11] Osuna considered the daily one-hour contemplation of Christ's passion by the monks of Mont-Dieu to be a "mark of perfection."

Osuna judged Christ's injunction to follow him as his "most frightening teaching" and spoke of imitating him as man and as God. The first way he compares to running; the latter, to flying, which is, of course, less demanding and tiring. To Osuna's way of thinking, the "exterior man" is born to run after Christ in self-denial, penance, and poverty; the inner man, the soul, is "superior," "a very swift bird," and born that it may fly to divinity. However, following the divinity may be a "grand thing," but it is known by few and practiced by fewer still. Because the human person is body-soul and Christ the God-Man, Osuna maintained that "your soul ought not to desire to follow Christ's divinity unless your body seeks to imitate his humanity; the one is source of the other."[12]

# Teresa of Avila

## (1515–82)

*"The silkworm is like the soul. When full-grown it starts to spin its silk and to build the house in which it is to die. This house may be understood to mean Christ. When the soul is truly dead to the world, a little white butterfly comes forth."*[1]

Teresa of Avila is considered by not a few commentators to be the greatest mystic among Christian women. Such was her mystical and mystagogical prowess that on September 27, 1970, Pope Paul VI solemnly declared her a Doctor of the Church—a title she and Catherine of Siena were simultaneously the first women to bear. To attain this designation, a person must possess notable sanctity, distinguished learning, and be proclaimed Doctor by either a pope or an ecumenical council. Because this title is associated with the Church's own teaching office and had been bestowed only upon men, some theologians assumed that a woman could not hold the title.

Teresa insisted that her eminent learning came from God—not from a formal education—which, in any case, she lacked. So directly and powerfully did God speak to her that she claimed that "the soul suddenly finds itself learned, and the mystery of the Most Holy Trinity, together with other lofty things, is so clearly explained to it that there is no theologian with whom it would not have the boldness to contend in defense of the truth of these marvels."[2] When valued books on prayer were placed on the Church's Index of Forbidden Books, the Lord himself said to Teresa: "Don't be sad, for I shall give you a living book"[3]—the book of her inner and outer life that she both understood and expressed with profound subtlety and detail. She wrote, "I shall speak of nothing of which I have no experience, either in my own life or in the observation of others, *of which the Lord has not taught me in prayer.*"[4]

Born to a family of Jewish origins, Teresa de Ahumada entered the Carmelite Monastery of the Incarnation near Avila at the age of twenty. The severity of conditions there and her own interior struggles led to a three-year paralytic condition that brought her to death's door. She claimed to have been cured through St. Joseph's intercession. After a struggle with the life of prayer for the next eighteen years, Teresa's definitive conversion took place "after nearly twenty years on a stormy sea," that is, when she was about forty years old.

A few years later, Teresa set out to correct the diminishment of fervor in Carmelite life and in 1562 founded the first convent of the new Carmelite reform. She wrote of the next five years at the Monastery of St. Joseph as "the most restful years of my life." In 1567, she met John of the Cross and persuaded him to initiate a similar reform for Carmelite men. Although she called John the father of her soul, recent studies have shown that his spiritual influence upon her was much less than once assumed. After twelve years of hostilities, opposition, and successes, the Carmelites of the Primitive Rule were given independent jurisdiction from the other Carmelites. Teresa continued the work of the reform, traveled widely to establish new foundations, and eventually succumbed to the ill health that she had suffered most of her life.

In what may be Teresa's most personal and captivating volume, *The Book of Her Life*, Teresa discusses the first fifty years of her life. The first section focuses upon her family life, her sins, her graces, and her desire to serve God perfectly. The second section is a magnificent treatise on prayer that likens the soul to a garden. She compares hauling water with buckets to the labor involved in meditative prayer; watering by way of a windlass, to the restful prayer of recollection and quiet; watering by way of an irrigation ditch, to the prayer in which the soul's deepest part enjoys God's undisturbed presence, while the soul's faculties "sleep"; and finally, the watering by torrential rains, to the prayer of union in which the soul dies to itself and finds itself alive in God.

In the book's third and fourth parts, she describes some of her salient mystical experiences: ecstasies, raptures, wounds of love, a vision of her place in hell, visions of Christ's humanity ("his great beauty"), mystical marriage, and spiritual fecundity. Because of Bernini's famous statue of Teresa in ecstasy, her "transverberation" experience is relatively well known: "I saw in his [a seraph angel] hands a large golden dart," she writes, "and at the end of the iron tip I seemed to see a point of fire. With this he seemed to pierce my heart several times so that it penetrated to my entrails. When he drew it out, I thought that he was drawing them out with it and he left me completely afire with a great love for God."[5]

Teresa's text *The Way of Perfection* offers practical advice on the life of prayer to her Carmelite nuns. This book contains one of history's most striking commentaries on the Our Father. Another text, *The Book of Her Foundations*, narrates events connected with the founding of many Carmelite monasteries, as well as writings on the perfect contemplation and many mystical favors given to her nuns. Her minor work *Meditations on the Song of Songs* (actually, only on a few verses of it) depicts the Song of Songs as a paradigm of what transpires between God and the soul, and also illustrates Teresa's penetrating knowledge and skillful use of scripture.

Her masterpiece, *The Interior Castle*, describes the human soul as an extremely beautiful diamond castle. The Teresian mystical journey consists in entering the castle, making one's way through seven stages of "dwelling places" (each containing innumerable rooms), in order to encounter the King in the central mansion. No one person will pass through all the rooms of the castle, nor does Teresa attempt to describe them all because of the impossibility of the task.

One enters the castle through vocal and mental prayer, which, in Teresa's view, is "nothing else than an intimate sharing between friends; it means taking time frequently to be alone with Him who we know loves us."[6] Prayer restores the lost knowledge we should have of ourselves as made in God's image. It also begins to heal our spiritual "paralysis" that is caused by too much interest in the body, which is only a "diamond's rough setting."

The first three dwelling places of the interior castle describe the premystical stages of prayer. Those with good desires, who sometimes pray, and who attempt to avoid even venial sins can be found in these dwelling places. As they increase in virtue, however, they often become impatient with God, if they find themselves without consolation.

A long tradition distinguishes between a level of prayer that can be attained through "ordinary grace" ("acquired contemplation") and another that can be received only through exceptional graces ("infused contemplation"). Teresa's fourth dwelling places use a variety of terms for this type of prayer that is totally beyond human effort: "supernatural" prayer, "the prayer of quiet," and "the second degree of prayer." The person in these dwelling places now drinks living water directly from the divine source—unlike those who must use the buckets of meditation to haul water from the divine well.

"Supernatural prayer" effects a deep consciousness of Christ entering the soul to utter "whispers of love through the din of a crowd." As this prayer arises from the person's deepest core, it causes the soul to dilate and permeates both the inner and outer person with a delicate, ineffable joy and peace. Although this "prayer of quiet" does not unite the memory and intellect to God (thus, the "din"), they are to some extent absorbed in and amazed by the divine activity in the will. The person realizes that the core of her will has been satisfied for the first time in her life—that, until now, happiness had reached only the will's "rind." So powerful can this prayer of quiet be at times that it absorbs, engulfs, and plunges the person into a "holy madness" and a "divine intoxication." It is as if a spark of the Holy Spirit has become a conflagration and effects an inner and outer swoon in which the body willingly partakes. If the soul is not so absorbed, however, the prayer of quiet may be somewhat arid, but still fruitful.

Teresa called attention to a bogus quietude produced by the devil to lead to the person's ruin. However, even this pseudo-quiet may profit a person—for a time—because it increases one's eagerness to pray. A deleterious quiet afflicted some of her nuns, who easily fell into sleeplike absorption during prayer because of their physical weakness and excessive penances. Although these nuns called this languor "rapture," Teresa judged it to be "foolishness" because it eventually destroyed physical and spiritual health. Her advice: less penance and prayer, and more food, sleep, and physical activity.

In her description of the fourth dwelling places, Teresa distinguished between "sweetness in prayer and spiritual consolation." Sweetness arises from our own nature and ends in God; spiritual consolation arises from God but terminates in us. Sweetness is the natural result of meditation, the natural joy that doing good work produces, and may be compared to drinking the divine water "downstream." Teresa identified spiritual consolation with the prayer of quiet and compared it to drinking water directly from the divine source.

The fifth dwelling places describe the "prayer of union," which Teresa also calls the "sleep of the faculties." God enters the soul's deepest center and suspends the memory, intellect, and will. For a period of time rarely exceeding thirty minutes, the soul seems to have withdrawn from the body. Love alone remains awake during this sleep and, upon reawakening, the person is left with an unshakeable certitude that God was there.

Teresa compares the characteristics of the prayer of union to pre-betrothal activity of lovers. This specially God-given prayer engenders abnegation, a contempt for worldly vanities, a deep wish for penances and suffering, solitude, solid virtues, a voracious hunger for God, and a desire that God be known by all. The living water is now up to the "soul's neck," causing spiritual delights that far exceed those given during the prayer of quiet. The total surrender of the will to God during this prayer is what matters—not the pleasures.

People who suffer from severe illnesses, ridicule, persecution, distrust from one's confessor, spiritual darkness, and the seeming absence of faith and of God populate the sixth dwelling places. One finds in these dwelling places a description of the apogee of Teresa's dark night of the soul: the excruciating vision of her place in hell—a tiny hole at the end of a long, narrow passageway, filled with snakes and sewage. Worst of all, she confessed, "I felt myself burning and crumbling; and I repeat the worst was that interior fire and despair."[7]

The other experiences that occur in the sixth dwelling places, however, are "raptures" that confirm the soul's mystical betrothal. The soul seems drowned by the torrents of living water produced by this "irresistible contemplation." Spiritual locutions enkindle the soul's union with God and are often so powerful that if God said, for example, "be at peace," the soul would immediately be peaceful.

Raptures usher in spiritual inebriation and the certitude that the person lives only for and in God. It is as if God has become the soul's soul or that the soul has even become God. "For the love which it knows His Majesty has for it," Teresa wrote, "makes it forget itself and it thinks it is in Him, and that He and it are one and the same thing, without any division, and so it talks nonsense."[8]

Most striking in the description of the supremely mystical sixth dwelling places is Teresa's return to the topic of *meditating* upon Christ's sacred humanity. When she first began to enjoy the delights of the prayer of quiet, Teresa admitted that no one could have persuaded her to meditate upon Christ's sacred humanity. However, as she came to realize the dangers of too much absorption in prayer, she judged this period of prayer without meditations upon Christ's life, death, and resurrection as an unwitting "act of high treason."

Because learned and spiritual people taught an apophatic prayer, namely, one that casts all images and thoughts—including that of Christ's humanity—into a cloud of forgetting, Teresa grudgingly conceded that in some sense it must be all right. If God, for example, suspends the intellect and memory, as is done in the prayer of quiet, then so be it. But she remained adamant: "Nevertheless, they will not make me admit that such a road is a good one."[9] In fact, she warned her nuns not to believe anyone who told them anything different. Insisting still further, she wrote "that we should skillfully and carefully accustom ourselves to avoid striving with all our strength to keep this most sacred humanity always present (and please the Lord it would be present always), this, I say, is what I don't think is good."[10] In fact, without Jesus as "Guide," one will never enter the last two dwelling places.

Teresa also distinguished between reasoning with the understanding and having the memory represent the Christian mysteries to the understanding. When one is advanced in the spiritual life, the soul understands the mysteries of Christ's life, death, and resurrection more simply and profoundly because they have become connatural with the soul. Because these mysteries are special signs of God's love for us, they act like sparks to enkindle the soul in love. She recommended, therefore, a prayer of simple regard, a simple "dwelling" on these mysteries, or a simple recollection of Christ within. Teresa confessed that thinking about Christ's passion on occasion was simply too painful because of what may be going on in one's life but she asked, what is to prevent us from being with Christ in his risen state?

Almost every page in Teresa's collected works speaks of Christ as "good Jesus," "our Companion," both "God and man," "Divine Guest" of our souls, "the good Lover, Jesus," "your true Friend and Spouse," "our Teacher," "such a Son" of the Father, the "very Master" who taught the Lord's prayer, and the "Pattern" of our lives. Teresa called genuine contemplatives "soldiers of Christ" who must be ready for spiritual combat. She preferred, however, to call her nuns "brides of this great King" and "brides of such a Spouse" who belong to "Christ's communities." Those in religious life must learn from and have a special reverence for the apostles who belonged to the "College of Christ."

The seventh dwelling places describe what occurs during mystical marriage, or transforming union. Christ himself brought Teresa into his own dwelling and removed the "blindfold" that had covered the eyes of her soul during the prayer of union and rapture. An intellectual vision of the Trinity illuminated her soul, disclosed to her the meaning of the divine indwelling promised in John 14:23, and imparted an understanding of how the three Divine Persons are one substance and one power. From that point on Teresa constantly experienced the triune presence and comprehended that the seventh dwelling places were now its permanent home.

The distinction between the soul's higher and lower aspects—which Teresa called "spirit" and "soul"—was also revealed to her. She experienced the highest aspect of her soul, "spirit," as permanently united to God and as continually enjoying the divine presence. Firmly anchored to God, her spirit enjoyed unassailable peace and joy. What were once transient experiences became permanent states. The soul's lower aspect, which she called "soul," however, was free to engage fully in daily activity and to suffer the trials and aridities of daily life. The harmony that existed between "spirit" and "soul," or Mary and Martha, enabled Teresa to be perfectly contemplative in action.

"Imaginary" visions of Christ—which, to Teresa's way of thinking, are more profound and trustworthy than bodily visions and allowed her, to some extent, to describe Christ's appearance—also marked Teresa's mystical marriage. "Intellectual visions" of Christ—that bypass the imagination, intellect, or will—occurred in her soul's center, just as he had once appeared to the disciples behind locked doors. Christ made her soul inseparably one with himself and enabled her to enjoy "secret communications" with him. Just as two wax candles may become one light, or rain falls into the ocean to become one water, Teresa's soul became one with Christ. This union gave her experiential evidence of what St. Paul meant when he wrote, "it is no longer I who live, but Christ who lives in me" (Gal 2:20).

Transforming union imparted to Teresa the profound awareness that she was to impart to others the divine life she lived. The mystically married are also spiritually fecund. Almost one-fourth of her autobiography is taken up with describing the fruitfulness of her life of service, especially her practical reforms of the Carmelite communities. Teresa taught that love of God and neighbor is the only lasting foundation for and genuine result of the life of mystical prayer.

Teresa's life sharply contradicts the view that mysticism, Church, and authority are intrinsically irreconcilable. Her experiences, her teachings, her practical love, and her reforms reinforce the view that mysticism is essentially the intensification and full-flowering of authentic ecclesial, religious life. As she wrote, "If anyone were to see that I went against the slightest ceremony of the Church in a matter of faith, I myself knew well that I would die a thousand deaths for the faith or for any truth of Sacred Scripture."[11] An intellectual vision infused her with an understanding of scripture and a determination to carry out its least demands. One of the greatest trials in Teresa's life occurred when the demons so stormed her understanding and imagination that she could not remember the truths of the faith.

The exacting congruence between Teresa's mysticism and "Church" must not be misunderstood. She was always one to plead her cause—especially in matters concerning the Carmelite reform—with firmness, determination, and a subtle sense of ecclesiastical politics. This shrewd, pragmatic, self-possessed woman did not demur in overcoming, in some issues, the hesitations of St. John of the Cross, in reining in the often-impolitic Jerome Gratian (one of her key collaborators in Teresian reform, who frequently embarrassed her), or in outmaneuvering bishops and secular authorities, when God's will indicated a certain line of action. So often and so convincingly did she argue her case on matters of reform before those in authority that she could write—and not only in this case: "Some of the things I said made them afraid, but this Father Rector never doubted that I was being led by the Spirit of God. In short, after hearing these numerous reasons, they did not dare to risk hindering me."[12]

# John of the Cross

## (1542–91)

*"This dark night is an inflow of God into the soul, which purges it of its habitual ignorance and imperfections and which contemplatives call infused contemplation or mystical theology. Through this contemplation, God teaches the soul secretly."*[1]

John of the Cross has long been considered to be the outstanding mystic in the Christian tradition. His mystical experiences, poetry, and mystical theology offer such a skilled guide to the life of perfection that he is judged in many circles to be the normative teacher of the mystical ascent to God. One senses throughout his apophatic writings that John had reached in, through, and beyond images, symbols, and concepts to experience in naked faith the mystery of the ever-greater God who both indwells and transcends all things. Thus, in 1926, Pope Pius XI bestowed upon him the title "Doctor of the Church."

Juan de Yepes y Alvárez was born about twenty-five miles north of Avila in Fontiveros, Spain. John's father, Gonzalo de Yepes, had been disowned by his wealthy Toledo silk-merchant family because he married a woman not of his social class. Moreover, when John was only two years old, his father died—leaving him and his mother in poverty.

When John was twenty years old, he entered the Carmelite Order at the monastery of Santa Ana in Medina del Campo, attended the University of Salamanca a year later, and was ordained priest in 1567. The following year, John helped Teresa of Avila to restore austerity to her Carmelite convent, and then founded a Discalced Carmelite monastery in 1569. Because of his success in restoring the Primitive Rule to the friars of the Mitigation, John is considered—along with Teresa of Avila—to be a cofounder of the Discalced Carmelites.

Because the reform movement created resistance as well as much political and ecclesiastical intrigue, turmoil filled much of John's life thereafter. Kidnapped in 1578 by disgruntled members of his own order, John was held captive for approximately nine months in Toledo, where he wrote some of his famous lyric poetry. After his escape, however, he rose to positions of responsibility in his order and showed remarkable skill as an administrator. Later clashes within the reform movement forced him out of office and into retirement at the La Peñuela monastery in Andalusia. Soon becoming ill, he went to Ubeda because no one there knew him, and, before long, he succumbed to his illness.

John's major works came to fruition in the last fourteen years of his life, that is, after he had attained intellectual, spiritual, and mystical maturity. The mystical life, in John's view, progresses from an entrance into a twilight of the senses (by which one transcends the world of appearances) to a total night of the spirit (by which the self is transcended) to a mystical dawn and journey toward the noonday sun involving spiritual betrothal and marriage. (In his mystical poetry he frequently uses primordial words, such as "Oh" and "Ah," which he calls "expressions of love arising from mystical understanding."[2]) Blending his poetry with discursive commentary, John systematically unfolds the classical purgative, illuminative, and unitive stages of mystical ascent that culminate in the "highest degree of perfection one can reach in this life (transformation in God)."[3]

His treatise *The Ascent of Mount Carmel—The Dark Night* was written for the Reformed Carmelites and their lay associates, that is, for those already somewhat detached from the world and seeking to love God. Because the mystical journey cannot be undertaken without competent guidance, this work aims to instruct travelers on this journey, especially those being led astray on the mystical path by incompetent guides, whom he called "blacksmiths hammering on the soul." This allegorical classic describes the lover singing of her good fortune in having departed "one dark night" to be united with her beloved.

The work explains three signs that indicate that a contemplative is being graced to progress from "meditation" (prayer characterized by a discursive, step-by-step use of reason, memory, imagination, and will) to mystically infused contemplation. First, *nothing* consoles the person—neither creatures nor the things of God. Second, although the person during this period has a heightened awareness of God's presence, it produces only a dread that one is not serving God well. Third, because God now weans the person from the milk of sensual satisfaction during prayer in order to feed him with a spiritual bread, the person can no longer meditate.

This stage demands that the one making spiritual progress be satisfied with a loving and quiet attentiveness to God and live without the effort or the desire to taste and feel his presence. Because "contemplation is nothing else than a secret and peaceful and loving infusion from God, which, if permitted, enkindles the soul with a spirit of love,"[4] the contemplative should neither struggle to pray nor place obstacles in the way of God's inner activity.

Only God, in John's view, can thoroughly purify a person's capacity to love, and thus increase it. God's loving inflow into the soul, which he calls both "infused contemplation" and "mystical theology," rather than causing sweetness and delight instead produces pain and suffering because of the soul's weakness and sinfulness. As the owl is blinded by gazing into the noonday sun, so the soul is blinded by the flood of God's light into a bitter "dark night" of purgation.

Infused contemplation, to this Carmelite's way of thinking, awakens the person not only to his most secret sins and hidden resistance to God but also to his own nothingness and radical distance from God. Feeling as though bound, gagged, and thrown into a prison, he is unable to move or to cry out for either earthly or heavenly assistance. Mystical theology, as purgative, plunges the soul into a profound darkness that seems to dissolve it in a cruel spiritual death. The experience of the "shadow of death" brings the contemplative to the brink of physical death—which would occur in a few days, if God did not lessen the intensity of the loving influx.

The "sorrows of hell" penetrate the contemplative's soul. He sees damnation open up before him and feels as if he were going into hell alive. The remembrances of past graces further deepens his suffering. Although he loves God with all his strength, the worst pain comes from the feeling that God no longer loves him and has justifiably rejected him. The feeling of being despised by friends and by all creatures adds to his intense sense of rejection. Nothing—not prayer, nor advice from a confessor or spiritual director, nor even the truths of the faith—can remove the sufferings from one in the dark night of the spirit. (I would add that contemporary psychiatry and pharmacology can offer no genuine help to the person undergoing these spiritual trials.)

The complexity of trials during the dark night of the spirit is such that John complains that he has neither the time nor the energy to describe their variety and the numerous scriptural passages he could use to illustrate them. Full purification and expansion of one's capacity to love, moreover, usually require many years of this night. Even the transient periods of consoling light and love that remove the sufferings do not eliminate the feeling that the enemy is still "sleeping within."

God's primary purpose in this process is not to cause suffering but to cleanse the person so "that he may reach out divinely to the enjoyment of all *earthly* and heavenly things, with a general freedom of spirit in them all."[5] The divine inflow that both purifies and expands the soul brings about psychosomatic wholeness—*apatheia*, to use the ancient term. The contemplative's consciousness, preconsciousness, and even his unconscious become consonant with the divine will. The soul is, John writes, "as it were, divine, deified, so that in even its first movements it has nothing which stands contrary to God's will, insofar as it can understand."[6] To John's way of thinking, therefore, the contemplative's entire being—memory, intellect, will, interior and exterior senses, sensory and spiritual appetites—operates from and in divine love.

Directed at the most advanced of contemplatives, John's treatise *The Spiritual Canticle* describes in lyric verse the exchange of love that transpires between the soul and Christ, its bridegroom. It explains contemplation as a special grace through which God begins to communicate and to show himself to the soul in this life to such an extent that only a "thin veil" may come to separate the soul from the beatific vision.

John's work *The Living Flame of Love* focuses upon an even deeper and more nearly perfect love in this state of transformation. It distinguishes—among other things—between a "union of love alone" and a "union with an inflaming of love." The Holy Spirit's activity in the soul is far greater in the union with an inflaming of love than in the union of love alone. The union of love alone resembles glowing embers in a fireplace, whereas the union with an inflaming of love is similar to embers that not only glow but also have become so hot that they shoot forth a living flame. "So great is this union," John writes, "that even though God and the soul differ in substance, in glory and appearance the soul seems to be God and God seems to be the soul."[7]

The treatise *The Living Flame of Love* also describes some of the "awakenings" of God in the soul. So numerous and complex are these awakenings that John admits that he cannot explain them all. The most sublime and profitable awakening in the soul occurs when God's Word "moves" in the soul's substance. When this happens, "all the virtues and substances and perfections and graces of all created things shine forth and make the same movement together and in unison."[8] The soul experiences a cosmic drama in which it finds all things in God, God in all things, and sings: "My Beloved is the mountains and solitary wooded valleys, strange islands and sonorous rivers, the whisper of the amorous breezes, the tranquil night at the time of the rising of the dawn, silent music, sounding solitude, the supper that refreshes and enkindles love."[9] Comprehending the distinction between God and creatures, the contemplative now knows creatures better in God's being than in their own being: "And this is the great delight of this awakening: to know creatures through God and not God through creatures."[10]

To understand John's somewhat austere "all and nothing" mentality, it is imperative to read his works in the context of the awesome descriptions of the deepening of loving union with God found in the work *The Living Flame of Love*. This masterpiece on mystical marriage should be read *before* attempting his more intimidating work, *The Ascent of Mount Carmel—The Dark Night*. Too many people read the imposing and seemingly impossible *Ascent—Night* but never get to *Living Flame*. The hollowing-out process described in *Ascent—Night*, however, can be understood only in terms of the being-filled-with-God process described in *The Living Flame of Love*.

John's single-minded spirituality and mysticism are highlighted by his comparison of the contemplative to a "turtledove," a bird that never lands, perches, rests, eats, drinks, or enjoys companionship until it has found its mate. The following quotation sets the tone of his entire mystical enterprise: "To reach satisfaction in all, desire satisfaction in nothing. To come to possess all, desire the possession of nothing. To arrive at being all, desire to be nothing. To come to the knowledge of all, desire the knowledge of nothing."[11]

When underscoring the importance of complete detachment, John teaches that it matters little whether a bird is tied by a thin thread or by a cord. He also insists that the bodily senses help the contemplative's spirit only if—at the first stirring of any sensuous delight—he "immediately" directs his thoughts and affections to God, receives more satisfaction in the thought of God than in the sensible objects that caused it, and finds no gratification in the senses, save for God.

As do many mystics in the Christian tradition, John uses the scriptures as his guide for describing and explaining the mystical journey. Despite the prohibition by the 1559 Valdés Inquisition of even a partial use of scripture in the vernacular, John's masterpieces breathe forth the scriptures and are practically a Castilian Bible. Less focused on the salvation history of the people of Israel, John concentrates on those archetypal individuals in the Old Testament—such as Abraham, Moses, Job, and the prophets—who were haunted and even tortured by their experiences of the living God.

Although John refers much more often to the Old than to the New Testament, his theocentric emphases are solidly rooted in the person of Jesus Christ. The mystical life, to this friar's way of thinking, *is* the life of Jesus Christ. Because the Father spoke everything to us at once in his one and only Word, he has nothing more to say. John's evocative ink drawing of the crucified Christ—from the Father's perspective, that is, from one looking down upon Christ—is an excellent summary of his Christocentrism.

By choosing what is harshest and most difficult, and by desiring to be stripped both inwardly and outwardly of all things, the contemplative imitates Christ and enters the dark night. In imitation of Christ's self-sacrificing death, the contemplative must abandon all consolations, experiences, and feelings to live the "exterior and interior death of the cross"[12] and follow Christ most closely by taking "the narrow path of obscure contemplation."[13]

As the contemplative progresses toward transforming union, he desires to go to the "high caverns in the rock," for this rock is Christ. Just as Moses took shelter in the rock and saw God's "back" when he passed, the contemplative discovers that God's "back" is Christ's humanity. The divine Word's union with his humanity is the paradigm of the contemplative's union with God. Entering into the heart of the Incarnation, he becomes a "Son by participation" and is transformed into the "beauty of the union of the Word with His humanity."

John urges the contemplative, as he advances in the mystical life, to continue to perform acts of love consonant with both the active and the contemplative life. When union of love with God is attained, however, John counsels the contemplative not to engage in any activity—no matter how important—that might hinder in any way his loving attention toward God. The slightest bit of pure contemplative love, in John's view, is more precious to God, to the Church, and to the contemplative—even though bridal sleep seems to be a "spiritual idleness"—than all apostolic activities put together. "Great wrong," he writes, "would be done to a person who possesses some degree of this solitary love, as well as to the Church, if we should urge him to become occupied in exterior things, even if the works are very important and demand only a short time."[14] Contemplation, in John's view, surpasses every other activity and is the greatest of all gifts because contemplative attentiveness to God *is* love—out of which and for which we were created. Contemplation, to this Carmelite's way of thinking, is deeply apostolic and the superior way of life.

# Johann Arndt

## (1555–1621)

*"It is not enough to know God's word; one must also practice it in a living, active manner. Many think that theology is a mere science, or rhetoric, whereas it is a living experience and practice."*[1]

Johann Arndt stands out as one of the most influential mystical theologians of the Protestant tradition. Born of a village pastor and his wife in Edderitz bei Köthen (Saxony), "the father of German Pietism" launched his career by studying medicine in Helmstedt. Falling ill after two years there, he gave up these studies and began to read theology and the mystical classics. In time, he married Anna Wagner and became the Lutheran pastor of Badeborn—and aroused Calvinist hostility because of his uncompromising Lutheranism.

Arndt lived at a time when Lutherans were both politically and territorially secure, but plagued by severe, internal theological controversies. Lutheran Orthodoxy had armed itself with the weapons developed by sixteenth-century scholasticism, which itself became part of the intra- and interdenominational disputes. Arndt assessed this Orthodoxy as dry, polemical, intolerant, and irrelevant to the development of Christian life and virtue.

Arndt published the four books of his work *True Christianity* between 1606 and 1610. Protesting against the decadence he saw in Christian society and the divorce between faith and life, he made use of the ancient threefold itinerary of progress to God to argue his case. Christian life has three stages that are analogous to the childhood, adulthood, and old age periods of natural life. Spiritual "childhood" begins with repentance, the first step in Christian life. Through prayer, contemplation of divine things, and suffering, one arrives at the "middle age" of illumination. The perfection of Christian "old age" consists in a full union with God through love—which St. Paul calls "mature manhood," the coming to "the measure of the stature of the fulness of Christ" (Eph 4:13).

Book 4 of Arndt's opus treats of God's work in the macrocosm of the world and the microcosm of the human person. Instantly popular, this work saw twenty editions prior to Arndt's death—and some 125 editions before 1800. Two more books were added in later editions— book 5 contains some of Arndt's mystical treatises, and book 6 is a reply to his critics. He also wrote a popular prayer book called *The Paradise Garden Full of Christian Virtues*. These treatises and his editions of the *Theologia Deutsch* had a significant impact on the rise of the Pietistic movement of spiritual and theological reform in the seventeenth and eighteenth centuries.

Arndt distinguishes sharply between intellect and will, especially between knowledge and love of Jesus Christ. Without love, knowledge of Christ is useless. The "learned ones," through their study and disputations, become puffed up with pride and never become lovers. The "saintly ones," in contrast, grow to be humble, attain wisdom and understanding through prayer and love, and thus find their "inner treasure."

Arndt teaches that genuine justification by faith alone must give rise to good works. Unlike most of his contemporaries, he saw much more in the medieval Church and the monastic tradition than the "commercialization of grace" and "popish doctrines." He also did not hesitate to draw upon the rich resources of the late medieval mystical tradition. Because of this, because of his repeated attacks on Lutheran Orthodoxy, and because of his emphasis on repentance, on individual growth in holiness, and on religious experience, he was denounced as a heretic.

Arndt maintained that since the human person is made in God's image and likeness, the kingdom of God is within. Insisting that every likeness gives birth to love—and love results in attraction and union—he taught that God binds nothing more firmly and lovingly to himself than his image and likeness in which he dwells. Because the person has his "All" within himself, he must die to the world and rest in the "quiet Sabbath of the heart."

Drawing upon the teachings of Johannes Tauler, Arndt wrote of an active and a passive way to God. In the active way, the person seeks God through the duties and practices of Christian life; in the passive way, God himself seeks the person. When God acts in this way, he draws the person into the ground of his heart to become aware of the kingdom of God within. An inner light often reveals God instantaneously in the soul's ground. There, Christ, the Father's Word, is heard, and the Holy Spirit raises the soul above all things in prayer.

"Oral prayer," to Arndt's way of thinking, is the best way to indicate that we are given speech to praise God; "interior prayer," to show that we are spiritual beings in order to lift our souls to God. In "supernatural prayer," however, the created spirit melts and sinks into God's uncreated Spirit "so that everything happens in an instant."[2] Because of such teachings, Albert Schweitzer deemed Arndt to be the "prophet of interior Protestantism."

Arndt has also been called "the second Luther." Although Luther was not a mystic, he did prefer some mystical writers to the dry scholastic theologians he had read. Union with Christ, mystical marriage, and deification are a few of the themes about which Luther wrote. Mystical union, in his view, is an ever-present union of the Christian with Christ and the beginning of the believer's incorporation into the Body of Christ.

Luther "democratized" the term "mystical union" by applying the language of mystical theology to it. Although this seems at first glance to be radically different from the way mystical union is understood in Catholicism—perfection coming at the *end* of the mystical process—in many ways it is not. The Catholic tradition insists that union with Christ and the trinitarian indwelling is first established in baptism. However, the mystic becomes more explicitly, more directly, and more intensely conscious of this union and indwelling than so-called "ordinary" Christians. The link between perfection and mystical consciousness is disputed among Catholic theologians to this day.

Book 5 of Arndt's opus treats the incarnational foundation for the mystical union freely intended by God from the beginning of a Christian's life. This total gift of grace is announced by the external word of scripture and the internal word in the heart. In order to describe this union, Arndt employs the bridal imagery used by many in the Christian mystical tradition. Inspired by St. Paul's paean to the self-emptying of Christ described in Philippians 2:5-11, Arndt delights in the angelic world's "marvel" at the "love of the Bridegroom," who cast aside so easily the prerogatives of his divinity to dwell in a "breakable vessel," "as a humble man enduring all insult and as a needy man with a poor bride."[3] The ultimate manifestation of the unitive life of faith, therefore, is imitation of Christ's love directed to God and his self-emptying service to his neighbor. And spiritual joy crowns this union.

Christian perfection, in this Lutheran's view, does not consist of profound meditations and exalted spiritual joys, but in a denial of self-will, a carrying out of God's will, and a deep knowledge of one's nothingness. One must have a "burning love for neighbor," Christ-like compassion, and a love totally centered on God—insofar as this is possible in the weakness of earthly life.

Arndt may have fully agreed with Luther's emphasis upon faith, but his view that one may also have a transforming *experience* of mystical union was expressed in language that might well have sounded to Luther like those of the speculative mystics he so vehemently opposed. When one considers Arndt's appreciation and extensive use of medieval texts (especially those of Angela of Foligno and Johannes Tauler), one can also better understand why he was the object of such fierce opposition from his Lutheran and Calvinist contemporaries.

Although both Luther and Arndt had assimilated and incorporated into their own thinking some of the views of medieval mystical writers, the so-called chasm between "Reformation" and "mysticism" quickly arose and has lasted, in some ways, right down to recent times. For example, Walter T. Stace (d. 1967), the influential British philosopher, bluntly claimed that there were no Protestant mystics. Many Protestants still agree with Stace, although some have added the qualification that even if there were Protestant mystics, there should not be any. (On the other hand, some have recognized members of the Society of Friends [Quakers] as mystics.)

Twentieth-century dialectical theologians, influenced by Albrecht Ritschl (d. 1889), Christian mysticism's fiercest opponent, exemplify this bias against mysticism. Karl Barth (d. 1968), for example, wrote of mysticism as a "blind alley," an "esoteric atheism," which is as opposed to the gospel as are "law" and the evils of the Pharisees.

Rudolf Bultmann (d. 1976), considered to be the most influential Protestant theologian of the twentieth century, denounced mysticism because it supposedly keeps a person under the law and living out of himself instead of in Christ. In his view, the mystic attempts to convert God's word into his own human word, which he can hear in the depths of his own soul, in order to replace revelation and historical existence with immediate contact with God. Most serious of all, he judged mysticism to be a "work."

Arndt and the many mystics in this volume stand as a critical corrective to the views of these dialectical theologians. In fact, a case can be made that Arndt—and especially the titans of the Christian mystical tradition—had insights that go far beyond what Ritschl, Barth, and Bultmann had to say about scripture, faith, and grace.

# Benet of Canfield

## (1562–1611)

*"One must not turn inward because one must never be turned outward. One must live continually, with all constancy, in the abyss of God and in the nothingness of all things."*[1]


William Fitch was born in the Essex village of Little Canfield about thirty-five miles northeast of London, the third of four sons, in a family of prosperous landed gentry. From an early age he mourned the death of "true religion" and spoke of having been "infested" with the Calvinistic doctrines advanced by the Puritan party. At the Middle Temple of the London Inns of Court where he studied from 1580–86, William acquired an exceptional grasp of law and liberal arts, came into his first contact with Catholics, and was also exposed to the religious controversies of his day.

After reading a Jesuit book of spiritual exercises, William resolved to turn to God. A bit later, he received a prophetic vision of horses (a symbol of concupiscence) and two sets of poor men in different religious garb. The ones who beckoned wore the habit of the Capuchins, the order that combines the eremitic-contemplative with the apostolic life, and the one that William eventually joined. During a vision a short time later, he was imparted an "inexplicable" illumination that gave him a "perfect insight" and "sure knowledge" of God's "most pure religion."

On August 1, 1585, the day after this vision, William was received into the Roman Catholic Church and departed for the continent. The outward "majesty, beauty, and magnificence" of the Catholic Church in Paris overpowered him. In March 1587 he became a Capuchin friar at the convent of St. Honoré in Paris and was given the religious name Benoît (Benedict) de Canfield. However, he preferred and used the older English form "Benet."

Profound mystical experiences filled Benet's novitiate period. Then, studying at the Capuchin school in Venice (1588–92), he acquired an almost encyclopedic knowledge of scripture, theology, liberal arts, and languages. Returning to France in 1592, he became novice master in Orleans, but returned to Paris in 1594, and came to associate with a group there surrounding the ecstatic Madame Acarie, the future Blessed Marie of the Incarnation, cofounder of the French Discalced Carmelites.

Forced to leave Paris in 1599 because of his involvement in an exorcism that triggered a dispute over whether Parliament and its secular magistrates had jurisdiction in such spiritual matters, Benet returned to England and was immediately incarcerated because being a priest was considered to be an act of treason. Imprisoned until approximately 1603, he wrote his lesser known work, *The Christian Knight*, and was then banished to France, where he later became novice master in Rouen.

An ecstatic experience during his novitiate period granted Benet the key insights for what was to become his masterpiece, *The Rule of Perfection*. Composed during his years in Venice as a "perspicuous abridgement" of the essential oneness of the spiritual life, his treatise maintains that the way to perfection is simply obedience to God's will—a way, moreover, that is open to all persons—no matter what their state of life.

Benet's masterpiece is also a paradigm of the so-called "logic of opposites" because he teaches that, in the mystical life, God is known through a pair of extreme opposites, the all and the nothing. God and his will are all; everything else is nothing. The person must come to know the divine All, one's own nothingness, and the nothingness of all creation in three ways: (1) "reasonably," in active annihilation; (2) "imaginatively," through the contemplation of Christ's passion; and (3) "experientially," in passive annihilation.

The introductory remarks to Benet's work focus on two ways to God: the way of speculation and the way of abnegation. Although speculation, to his way of thinking, is the most satisfying and pleasing, it is not open to everyone. Abnegation, on the other hand, is the "most profitable and stable," and open to everyone with good desires. The *Rule* teaches the second way. He also warns the reader of a flawed version of his text in circulation that was printed without his knowledge or consent.

The *Rule* is divided into three major parts. Part 1 deals with God's "exterior will," known to beginners through law and reason, which enlightens the person's will "from without." Describing God's will as a "spiritual sea," Benet writes that the boats of beginners set out into the shallow waters of the exterior will through renouncing sin, eradicating defects, and the practice of prayer and virtue. The active life demands practice, not speculation.

Because God's will and self-will cannot coexist in the same person, progress in the spiritual life requires that the "dark land of self will" yields to the waters of the divine will until one sees nothing but the divine ocean. The contemplative tyro must therefore focus on God's will alone.

Benet describes a "most secret deception," a state of mind that distinguishes what one does in daily life from the divine will. Both the work and the divine will, in his view, "are but one." Through a lively faith and "fixed contemplation," one must learn to see by the light of God's will that every required exterior or interior "work" is not just a human work but God's will. This manner of living and acting eventually annihilates self-interest. Then one discovers that the active and contemplative life are one, "not separated (as many take it to be)."

Part 2 of the *Rule* describes the contemplative life in terms of God's "interior will." The progressive purification of one's intention in the active life slowly brings about an "experiential internal knowledge" that awakens the mystical senses to see, taste, feel, hear, and even smell the divine will. When the contemplative sets his boat out into "the deep waters of God's inner will," "the abyss of inaccessible eternal light" so floods the soul that it does not feel that its will is its own, but that it is God's will in whom alone it sees and feels itself. Prayer at this stage becomes a simple waiting at the foot of the cross—a waiting without any exterior or interior activity. In Benet's view, this is the perfection of the "supereminent life."

The contemplative may be now tempted to see nothing outside of himself nor anything greater than himself. However, God's inner will intervenes to bring about "very profound but very secret and subtle acts of humility"[2] so that the soul will be proportioned to God and not God to the soul. Comprehending its own nothingness, the soul somewhat "sees" God's infinite being, swoons, and breaks into "secret words." In line with the ancient Fathers of the Church, Benet writes of the birth of Christ in the soul. Obedience to the divine will unites the soul with God and it "becomes the mother of Jesus Christ."[3]

Benet teaches that "pure and perfect contemplation" must be apophatic, that is, imageless and free of concepts. Any and all images and divisions of the divine will—which is one—must be rejected. In addition, one must never abide in the feelings one has of God's will, but repose only in the divine will. This demands the utmost abnegation that, in his view, consists of two things: renunciation and contentment. One should "rest" only in the first, never the second. The act of resignation to the divine will also has two aspects: "the resignation and the savor that comes from it." One must cling fast to the first, but never to the second.

Benet never consented to the many requests that part 3 of the *Rule* be published. However, a highly defective version had been printed and circulated widely. Given the subtle and profound nature of its contents, his superiors judged it necessary that the correct version (written some fifteen years prior) see the light of day. Benet yielded to the desires of his superiors, but insisted that part 3 be read only with the consent of one's spiritual director or confessor.

Part 3 focuses on God's "essential will" (which, in Benet's view, is identical with God) and its correlative, the "supereminent life." Benet subscribes to the view already seen in this volume that because the human soul exists eternally in the mind of God and was one with God in its precreational existence, the soul's goal in this life is "superessential union" with God—that is, to be as united with God in this earthly life as it was in its precreational existence. "The soul is to be as it was before it was." He insists—with the apophatic mystics before him—that one must be united to God "without means" by contemplating God "without images," "seeing God as much as he can be seen in this life," through an "essential denuding of the spirit," "inner annihilation," and "holy idleness."

This Capuchin explains that just as our interior will must be born of God's exterior will, our essential will must issue from God's interior will. The "interior will" is a "means," "unitive," and "has some images"; the "essential will" is an "end," "intimate," "transforming," and "wholly naked." Because the essential will is God himself, it is totally beyond human comprehension. Only a "means without means" can attain it, that is, insofar as "God's naked essence" permits itself to be experienced or comprehended in any way.

God allows his essential will to be attained in two ways. In the first way, all the soul's acts are "sweetly annihilated" in order to simplify and to transform the soul into God. In the second way, the person works with great subtlety to silence every movement of the soul and to strip it naked. The first way is for those who have "fervor and devotion"; the second, for those who have "only a bare and reasonable devotion."[4] Benet deems the first way to be an inferior path because it allows delightful feelings to bathe the "intellectual powers." In the second way, the contemplative transcends sense and intellectual activity, sees and embraces God, and possesses him in naked love—that is, in a love shorn of all feelings, images, and concepts.

The two ways impart a very "subtle" (one of Benet's favorite words) knowledge of the soul's secret faults, which, in his view, are anything that distracts the soul from its "great spiritual longing." These include the least disordered affection, any movement of the senses, and "the most detached image *except of the Passion*."[5]

Benet claims that not only is contemplation of Jesus' passion and crucifixion compatible with annihilation but it is also absolutely necessary for a genuine "superessential life." Paradoxically, God sends his light to facilitate the contemplation of Christ's passion, not the divinity. However, because Jesus is the God-Man, both the divinity and the passion must be comprehended *as one*. In the active life one must grasp both God's will and the cross "without any multiplicity." In the "supereminent life," one must contemplate God and his cross "with a single glance."[6] "The knot and secret of this whole practice,"[7] in Benet's view, is to grasp "in one simple sight" the divinity who emptied himself to the point of death on a cross. Perfect faith will always have Christ's cross in view, yet, paradoxically, will swallow it up and annihilate it.

Saint Paul insists that he had been taken up as a man in Christ to the "third heaven" and even into "paradise" (2 Cor 12:3). However, he decided that all he desired to know was Christ and him crucified (1 Cor 2:2). Benet underscores this apophatic-kataphatic mystery lived by the apostle Paul, Francis of Assisi, Bonaventure, Teresa of Avila, and many others, who never removed the cross from the contemplation of God's naked essence. "In this matter [of imageless contemplation]," Benet writes, "I always exempt the image of the sacred Passion of Jesus Christ"—even in the "supereminent life." The self-emptying death of the incarnate Word, in Benet's view, reveals that God is more amazing outside of himself than within himself. To penetrate the ultimate mystery of Christ's crucifixion is to penetrate to the heart of God's identity as self-emptying love.

Benet urges his reader not to imagine Christ's passion as something that occurred far off in Jerusalem ages ago, but to contemplate and feel it in oneself. What strips and grieves the most, what is the "inner bitterness," "the sharp point of affliction," is, to his way of thinking, the key that opens the door "of the sacred chamber of the treasures of divine wisdom and the deep mysteries of this Passion."[8] When one strives to find the passion perfectly in oneself, one sees only one unique passion—that of the one Christ suffered in himself and now suffers in us. One then sees all the "stations of the Passion together," without the hindrance of images, because one sees only God in them all. However, to desire or to consent to any sensible consolation in this practice ruins it.

Our Capuchin criticizes those who attempt to transport their spirit directly to the divine by avoiding the contemplation of Christ crucified. With Ruusbroec before him, he writes of these "deceived souls" who remain trapped in their own spirit in a "false and evil idleness." This "abstraction" of the spirit is more often natural than supernatural—"a benumbing of nature and repose in a human spirit instead of in the divine."[9] The soul becomes stupid, dark, and bereft of virtue in a spiritual death grounded in love of self.

Benet calls attention to both a passive and an active annihilation, which serve the two loves that embrace the entire spiritual life: an enjoying love and a working love. Passive annihilation, which only God can bring about, extinguishes every act of the soul—but in God—so that the soul's activity becomes God's activity. Active annihilation takes place by a natural and supernatural light of the understanding, in which one comprehends the nothingness of oneself and all creation. Passive annihilation bestows experiential knowledge; active annihilation, intellectual knowledge. In his view, the latter is more perfect because it annihilates all things when they remain present and when they have vanished. The person becomes contemplative in action because no activity—neither outer nor inner—hinders it. As Benet writes, active annihilation—known to few and practiced by fewer—"annihilates things not only when the soul is raised above them, but even when she is among them."[10] This nonclinging awareness grounds Benet's practice of a genuine superessential mysticism of daily life inextricably rooted in the crucified Christ.

During the period of illness before his death, Benet was in an almost constant state of ecstasy, while his eyes remained continually fixed on the crucifix at the foot of his bed. The writings, life, and death of this mystic, mystical theologian, and mystagogue express the Pauline paradox of a man rapt to the third heaven but who nevertheless wanted to know only Christ and him crucified. The manner in which he died is a summary of what is his most profound teaching: "When [we] contemplate the Passion, [we] should plunge into it more deeply until [we] find this great God clothed in mortal flesh, scourged, and cruelly nailed to the cross, and until the soul is made to cry out in astonishment and, as it were, go outside herself."[11]

# Francis de Sales

## (1567–1622)

*"The second mark of a true ecstasy is the ecstasy of work and life,
a life elevated and united to God by denial of worldly lusts and
mortification of [one's] natural will and inclinations through interior
gentleness, simplicity, and humility, and above all through constant
charity."*[1]

Francis de Sales exemplifies the manner in which seventeenth-century
France dominated the profound renaissance of spirituality and mysti-
cism, which accompanied the reforms throughout the Catholic
Church during this period of the Counter-Reformation. Mystic, saint,
Doctor of the Church, "devout humanist," and "the master and re-
storer of sacred eloquence," he is "the heavenly patron of all writers,"
and one who contributed much to the development of the modern
French language.

He was born the eldest of thirteen children at the castle of Sales
in Savoy, some thirty miles south of Geneva. When only four years
of age, Francis uttered prophetically, "God's and my mother's love
I hold most dearly." At Annecy, Paris, and Padua, he received the
education befitting a Renaissance gentleman destined for a brilliant
secular career. Although he received a doctorate in canon and civil
law, his life was soon to take another turn because his student life in
Padua had brought him into contact with a Jesuit who gave "spiritual
exercises" to students.

In an atmosphere darkened by Calvin's teaching on predestination, Francis believed that he was doomed to hell where his greatest
suffering would be not being able to love God. Release from this
spiritual torment began to arrive when he prayed, "Whatever may
happen, O Lord, I will love you always. At least in this life will I love
you, if it is not given me to love you in eternal life."[2] One day, while

praying the Memorare before a statue of Our Lady of Good Deliverance, he experienced profound healing.

However, the predestination issue continued to plague our Savoyard, but it never shook his resolve to live in "disinterested love" for God. While kneeling before the statue of the Black Madonna in the Parisian church of St. Étienne, Francis heard in his heart the words that undid the eternal decree: "I do not call myself the Damning One; my name [Jesus] is the one who saves." Like "leprous scabs," the dark weights in his soul fell away, and the victorious optimism of joyful love of God was born in the depths of his spirit.

After strong initial opposition, Francis's parents blessed his desire to become a priest and he was ordained in 1593. Burning with a Counter-Reformer's missionary ardor, he undertook the task of reclaiming for Catholicism the Chablis, an area on Lake Geneva's southern shore that had been forcibly converted to Calvinism. Enduring many hardships and often exposed to danger (even armed attacks against his life), Francis reconverted the Chablis with his holiness, personal charm, eloquent preaching, skilled debating, and a series of short, popular writings, known as the *Controversies*. His lesser known work, *The Standard of the Cross*, also dates from this period.

In 1602, Francis became bishop of Geneva, where he remained—despite better offers—until he died. A zealous pastor, he drew people to God by love and gentleness. Everything Francis did flowed from his deep tasting of God as love, which was shaped and matured by his labors for the Church. Contrary to the strong Calvinistic currents of the times, Francis insisted that God desires the salvation of everyone and predestines no one to hell. God as Savior, not God as Judge, filled his sermons and writings. Central to his vision is the "correspondence" between God—the source of love—and the *free* human person, created out of and for love. He labored to win the hearts of his people, for he knew that to win the heart was to win the entire person. It has been said of him that he sweetened everything but attenuated nothing. Moreover, this bishop both preached and lived his famous motto, "Live Jesus! Live, Jesus."[3]

Francis's influential book *Introduction to the Devout Life* was the fruit of his pastoral activity, especially his gifts as a spiritual director. His more than two thousand letters witness to this. Madame de Charmoisy, one of the many persons he directed, showed the written instructions he had given her to a Jesuit, who then urged that they be published. This classic has been praised for the originality, symmetry of thought, penetrating psychology, clarity, and systematic way it explains the purgative, illuminative, and unitive aspects of the spiritual life. Affective love of God—which flows into effective love of neighbor—requires mortification of one's entire self, keeping Christ before one's eyes, and ceaseless attention to uniting one's will with that of God's.

The *Devout Life* presupposes that everyone is called to a holiness of total dedication to Christ. Its lucidity, warmth, charm, and optimism about the goodness of human nature led many to devotion in a manner that contrasts with the more militant spiritualities of the Counter-Reformation. Francis addresses his book to "Philothea" (lover of God) and urges her to look to heaven, and not to give heaven up for earth; to look down into hell, and resolve not to throw herself into hell for the sake of transient things; to gaze at Jesus, and not to deny him for the world; and when the spiritual journey becomes difficult, to sing with St. Francis of Assisi, "all pains grow sweet, all labors light. Live, Jesus!"[4] That his treatise was translated into the major European languages during his lifetime speaks for itself.

In 1610, Francis and Jeanne de Chantal, a young widow and spiritual friend, cofounded the Order of the Visitation of Mary, a congregation of women originally without enclosure. Francis taught that God acts in ordinary human relationships and that spiritual friendship is necessary for a full Christian life. Another fruit of his association with her and the Visitation community is our bishop's masterpiece, *Treatise on the Love of God*. Written for those "advanced in devotion," this work emphasizes affective and effective love and illustrates (along with his numerous letters) why Francis has been called the teacher of a lived theology of the heart. This book and his life exemplify what he teaches about the Church: in it, all is by love, in love, for love, and of love.

Francis remains solidly rooted in the kataphatic mystical tradition, which stresses that knowledge is required for love and that true contemplation does not demand abandoning images and concepts. Although he emphasizes human passivity in relationship to God's action in the depths of the soul, Francis nonetheless urges his reader to be a "mystical bee," that is, to ponder God's holy mysteries "in order to extract from them the honey of divine love."[5] In fact, meditation in his view is not a beginner's preoccupation but the "mystical rumination" needed to inflame the will to holy affections and to discover reasons for love.

Meditation, to Francis's way of thinking, gives birth to contemplation when it "produces the honey of devotion."[6] He views meditation as the mother of love, and contemplation as its daughter. Contemplation is a simple loving attention of the mind to "the things of God." Because both prayer and mystical theology speak only of God, with God, and in God, they are the same. Because the conversation between God is "heart to heart" and "altogether secret," it is called "mystical." Both prayer and mystical theology are the soul's loving conversation with God in order to be united with God's goodness.

The contemplative—in contrast to one who meditates—is like someone smelling the united aromas coming from water containing a perfume that is made up of a great variety of flowers. This effects an effortless, sacred inebriation that moves him "out of himself to raise him above himself."

In contemplation, God often acts like a skilled beekeeper, who uses aromatic herbs, honeyed wine, and pleasant sounds to change the course of his wayward bees. God may also secretly instill the depths of the heart with a delightful "suave feeling" that witnesses to his presence. Then the exterior senses and the powers of the soul secretly agree to turn inward where their most lovable and most cherished spouse is found.

Using yet another analogy for what he and Teresa of Avila call the "prayer of quiet" or the "sleep of the powers" (of the soul), the soul often acts like a hungry child who eventually falls asleep at its mother's breast but still continues to suckle in an almost imperceptible way. The quieted soul takes delight in God's presence effortlessly, without need for thought, using the "will's highest part" as a spiritual "mouth" to drink in and enjoy the divine presence. And when the contemplative empties himself of all self-interest, he becomes "like an immobile stature in a hollow niche," and partakes of this "pure and supremely excellent quiet."

Francis's opus contains some of the most striking images used in the Christian mystical tradition to depict the soul's union with God: ivy grasping and penetrating the bark of a tree, a nursing infant at its mother's breast, honeybees attracted to sound and smell, "imperial water" infusing one's entire body as soon as it is drunk, and precious ointment permeating a ball of cotton. He uses these images to describe the experience of God's holy presence intimately penetrating the soul and expanding it lovingly. This experience occurs at "the summit and supreme point of the spirit where God's love reigns and carries out its principal exercises."[7]

By underscoring both the person's complete dependence upon God and the different ways in which the person must cooperate with and consent to God's grace, Francis criticizes indirectly the Quietism of some of the spirituality and mysticism of his day. Quietism, broadly speaking, is the mystical heresy that exaggerates the role of interior passivity in contemplation, teaches that interior recollection can be a single, continuous act in the soul, and eschews external practices.

De Sales describes various degrees of holy union with God during prayer. Sometimes union occurs without the contemplative offering any resistance. God at other times causes this union by drawing the will alone or all the soul's faculties. Francis describes a type of union that he compares to the way a large, heavy mass will press deeper and deeper into the soil because of the force of gravity. If the heart, for example, is united to God and nothing draws it away, it may consent to allow itself to sink deeper and deeper until it is wholly in God. Finally, when Francis was asked whether a sleeping saint or a contemplative during the prayer of union is more closely united to God, he replied that the saint is *already* united to God; the other is *being* united.

Francis is known as the teacher of "holy indifference," that is, of a total and loving abandonment of self-will and an embracing of God's will, as it is manifested in one's life. To live the good news of Jesus Christ, one must have radical trust in God's loving providence and surrender totally to God's guidance and dispensation. Central to Francis's vision is that "God's will is God's love," and that one must love God for God's sake, not for one's own. Even during what he describes as "loving ecstasy," the will must rest in God and not in its own contentment.

In his mature years de Sales taught a profound and orthodox view of "holy indifference." Contradicting the belief of his day that only someone who has absolutely no concern about his or her salvation can be said to have "pure love," Francis taught, "Yes, [the soul] would prefer hell to paradise *if* it knew that it would find a little more of God's good pleasure in hell than in heaven. Therefore, *to imagine something impossible*, if the soul knew that damnation would be a little more pleasing to God than salvation, it would forsake salvation and run after its own damnation."[8]

The highest type of union with God, in Francis's view, is "inhesion" or "adhesion." So united is the human spirit to God that only a painful force can separate them. He uses the analogy of the rapt attention often given by those playing a "foolish game of cards." This "adhesion" is often called "transport" when the experience is brief; "rapture," when prolonged. He also speaks of intellectual, affective, and active ecstasies. Cold ecstasies, that is, ecstasies that affect the intellect more than the will, are immediately suspect because an abundance of knowledge is not always followed by surplus of love.

Francis calls attention to powerful raptures during prayer that *seem* to empty the contemplative and to plunge him into God, yet do cause an "ecstasy of work and life." Raptures that do not result in interior and exterior gentleness, humility, constant charity, and the conquest of worldly lusts and self-will are "extremely doubtful and dangerous." There were many saints, in his view, who were never ravished yet lived the most sacred ecstasy of all, the "ecstasy of work and life." Renunciation and self-denial by true imitation of the crucified Christ—who came in sacrificial love to serve, not to be served—is the genuine rapture, the "ecstasy of work and life" that deracinates the contemplative from self and plants in him the love of God and neighbor.

# Pierre de Bérulle

## (1575–1629)

*"And just as there is a God worthy of being adored, served and loved, so there is also in you, O Jesus my Lord, a God adoring, loving and serving him eternally . . . without any defect in this adoration, and a God who adores, without detracting from his divinity!"*[1]

Often called the father of the French school of spirituality, Pierre de Bérulle lived during France's Catholic Golden Age. Born of an old, distinguished, and deeply religious family at Chateau de Sérilly (about sixty miles due south of Paris), he was considered a master of the spiritual life at age seventeen. Educated at the Jesuit College of Clermont and at the Sorbonne, ordained a diocesan priest in 1599, he went on to found the enormously successful French Oratory in 1611. He later established numerous colleges to train the clergy for pastoral work and to prepare the laity to fulfill their own priestly office—all in accord with the decrees of the Council of Trent. After arduous negotiations, Bérulle succeeded in establishing the Carmelite nuns of the Teresian reform in France, of whom the pope appointed him perpetual visitor. Desiring only to devote himself to spiritual direction, to reforming religious communities, and to reuniting Catholics against Protestant reformers, he repeatedly refused pressing offers of significant prelacies and bishoprics.

A powerful influence for good at court, Bérulle undertook sensitive diplomatic missions for the king and finally accepted the red hat in 1627. The formidable Cardinal Richelieu wanted Bérulle banished from France because of their frequent clashes, but succeeded only in bringing him into "official disgrace." Approximately a month after this humiliation, Bérulle died on October 2, 1629, and thereafter his reputation for holiness was enhanced by the many miracles attributed to his intercession.

The "abstract mysticism" of the circle of his cousin, Madame Acarie (often called the "conscience of Paris"), attracted the young Bérulle.

This French version of radically apophatic mysticism stressed God's absolute transcendence, the divine-human congress in the spark of the soul, and the indistinct union of the soul with the naked Godhead. This type of mysticism, akin to Eckhart's mysticism of the ground, required the contemplative to set aside all creatures, abandon all images and concepts, and even to "bypass" Christ's humanity in order to attain an indistinct unity with God. Spiritual "annihilation" (*anéantissement*) was its hallmark. Thus, in 1597, Bérulle wrote his *Short Discourse on Interior Abnegation*. For this book, Pope Urban VIII named Bérulle "the apostle of the Incarnate Word."

Early in this thirties, however, Bérulle underwent a profound Christological conversion—due perhaps to Carmelite and Jesuit influences. He came to see Jesus Christ as the "totally uncreated light subsisting in the Godhead" who became incarnate to become the "world, a splendid world" and also the "true sun" around which the world revolved. From then on Bérulle was to emphasize that one cannot seek God apart from the "only one Man-God and one God-Man."[2] In his view, "Jesus is the object of the science of salvation and the science of Christians."[3] Every relation between the Father and humanity must pass through Jesus, the perfect adorer of the Father. Thus, Bérulle rejected emphatically the abstract school's well-known "bypassing" of Jesus' humanity.

Until the coming of Jesus Christ, in our cardinal's view, God was neither properly served nor properly adored. There had been an infinitely adorable God from all eternity, but no infinite adorer; there had been a God infinitely deserving of being loved and served, but no man, no infinite servant capable of rendering infinite service and love. Bérulle resolves this matter by emphasizing Jesus Christ as the "only one Man-God and one God-Man," with his "deified humanity" and his "humanized divinity." (The last two expressions violate the Council of Chalcedon's definition of Jesus' inseparable but *unmixed* human and divine natures.) Because of Jesus, God is now not only the infinitely adorable God but also the infinite adorer, a God adoring. One finds in Bérulle's writings one of the most striking paeans in the entire Christian tradition to Jesus as the Father's perfect servant and adorer, "a God who adores, without detracting from his divinity!"[4] No mystical theologian has written as eloquently as Bérulle of a God adored and a God adoring.

The term "state" (*état*) plays a key role in Bérulle's mystical theology. The mysteries of Jesus' life, death, and resurrection are permanent conditions and aspects of his being, not just transitory historical events. Jesus' foundational "state," his entire being, *is* to be the perfect contemplative and adorer of the Trinity. Bérulle's desire for union with and participation in Christ's being finds its source in Jesus' state as the perfect adorer. Loving, sacrificial adoration is one of the salient aspects of this cardinal's mysticism.

From approximately 1615 to 1623, Bérulle was embroiled in the so-called "vows controversy" because of his attempt to impose upon Carmelite nuns and the Oratorians special vows of servitude to Mary and Jesus. This move aroused the opposition of many Carmelites and Jesuits, and ended his friendship with Madame Acarie. In fact, a defective copy of the vow was censured by the theological faculties of Louvain and Douai. In his masterful 1623 work, *Discourse on the State and Grandeurs of Jesus,* Bérulle defended his doctrine by showing that the vow is both a logical consequence of one's baptismal vows and an appreciation of the "servitude" of Christ's human nature hypostatically united to the Word.

The foundation of Bérulle's controversial vow of servitude flowed from his understanding of a "new mystery," namely, the Incarnation as the exemplar of perfect annihilation (*anéantissement*). He marveled that the Word had stripped Jesus' humanity of its "natural subsistence" in order to raise it "supremely" to the "subsistence of the eternal Word."[5] Agreeing with the opinion of Thomas Aquinas, Bérulle maintained that Jesus' humanity is also stripped of its own act of existence: "This humanity then is much more under the power and possession of the eternal Word, which receives it and sustains it in its being, than the slave is under his master's power and possession."[6] Jesus' human nature is so poor and "annihilated" that it has no act of existence of its own but exists by virtue of the Word's own act of existence and is, therefore, the Word's slave. It is in this light that one should understand Bérulle's emphasis upon "adherence" to Christ (another salient feature of his mysticism), which is the voluntary, conscious effort to conform one's entire being and life to that of Christ's, and the "annihilation" (*anéantissement*) of all that is not ordered to God.

Some of the most profound (and controversial) Spirit-centered mysticism and theology in the entire Christian mystical tradition is found in Bérulle's writings. From eternity the Father begets the Son and together they spirate the Holy Spirit. Because the Holy Spirit—despite being Love—neither generates nor spirates another Divine

Person, he is sterile and terminates the divine fecundity. As the divine fecundity *outside* the Godhead, as the Creator and cause of a God outside of God, the Holy Spirit impregnated the Virgin Mary and "produced" the God-Man. The Holy Spirit is the termination of love in the Trinity; Jesus, its termination outside the Trinity—the fecundity of God's Spirit "in the order of grace and glory."

To Bérulle's way of thinking, Jesus is the "perfect image" of the Holy Spirit. (Does he actually mean that Jesus could have said, "He who sees me sees the Holy Spirit?") Bérulle also wrote of a *second* Trinity: Jesus' body, soul, and divinity. Because of the Incarnation, the adored Trinity also becomes the adoring Trinity.

Some of the tradition's most provocative Mariology is found in Bérulle's writings. Just as Christ is united to his Father through birth and nature, he is also "united to the Virgin through production and infusion of a Spirit in her soul,"[7] the Spirit that the Son and the Father spirate from all eternity. In the wondrous mystery of the fetal Jesus, the "Man-God," "Word-Child," "Child-God" actually contemplates the Mother of God. The mystery of the Incarnation growing in Mary's womb in turn enraptures her, making her the supreme contemplative of the Word made flesh.

So intimate is this union between Mary and the incarnate Word that Bérulle suggests that she may have had "clear vision of the divine Essence and the Person of the incarnate Word within her."[8] In his view, however, if the Virgin did not have this supreme vision, she still uniquely "possessed" the Divine Person in her, and their union *adores* the bond between Christ and the eternal Trinity. Thus, Christ is closer to Mary than to any other human person. Then, of all humanity, only the Mother truly knows the Son—and, she is the Son's perfect image, joined to him "through both nature and grace."

Just as Bérulle emphasizes that Jesus' human nature exists by virtue of the Word's act of existence, he also daringly suggests that Mary exists by virtue of Christ's act of existence. By stating that "in a way, [Mary] lost her own life and personal subsistence in order to live in him who is life and her life as well,"[9] he comes dangerously close to positing a second hypostatic union and agrees with those theologians who claim of the Blessed Virgin that she attained "the very boundaries of the Godhead."[10] The unique unity between Mary and her Son caused her heart to be pierced just as her son's was. A salient aspect of Bérulle's spirituality and mysticism is devotion to the pierced hearts of Jesus and Mary, who are "host-victims" for the forgiveness of sins. The Bérullian journey to perfection is through Mary to Christ, and through Christ to the Trinity.

Although Bérulle confuses Mary Magdalene, Mary of Bethany, and the sinful woman who washed Jesus' feet with her tears, his meditation on "Mary Magdalene" is one of the loveliest in the tradition. He calls her the masterpiece of Jesus' grace whom he raised to the "heights of perfection" through an "interior and invisible" miracle wrought by his Spirit in her soul—just as he had raised Lazarus from bodily death *for her sake* through an "exterior and visible" miracle. Her greatness? Not to have any other purpose in life than to live, love, and desire in the love of Jesus. When she washed Jesus' feet with her tears and wiped them with her hair, a "sacred, seraphic love" took place, "a new difference in the order of grace and in the order of love."[11] Such is her dignity and greatness that the first words used by the risen Christ were directed to Mary, calling her by name, making her an apostle of life, glory and love, and an apostle to the apostles.

Bérulle subscribes to a tradition that claims that, after Jesus' ascension, Mary Magdalene withdrew to the desert to do penance for her sinful life. In his view, love became her penance, her desert, her solitude, her love, her cross, her languish, and her death: "I see only love in Magdalene. I see only Jesus in her love. I see only Jesus and love in her desert."[12]

After his death, Bérulle was soon overshadowed by his disciples, Jean-Jacques Olier (founder of the Society of Saint-Sulpice), John Eudes, and Charles de Condren. Nonetheless, Bérulle's heart and mind had indelibly stamped Olier, Sulpician seminaries, Eudes, Condren, and the Oratory, whose significant impact on Catholic spirituality has endured right up to the present day. The fact remains that this undeservedly neglected cardinal remains one of the significant mystical theologians and mystagogues of the seventeenth century.

# Marie of the Incarnation

## (1599–1672)

*"This was an outpouring of the apostolic Spirit of Jesus which took possession of my soul. Then this adorable Majesty said to me: 'It is Canada that I have shown you; you must go there to build a house for Jesus and Mary.'"*[1]

Despite the encomiums heaped upon Marie of the Incarnation by prominent historians of the Christian tradition, and the declaration of her as "venerable" by the Catholic Church, she remains a relatively obscure figure. Wife, mother, widow, Ursuline nun, and the first woman missionary to the New World, she ranks as one of the outstanding mystics in the Christian tradition. In terms of her intense mystical life, an absorbing exterior apostolate, and her sense of being a "victim of love for the salvation of souls," few can compare with her. Given the apostolic-missionary dimension of her astounding mystical life, the title given her—the "Teresa of Avila of the New World"—may not quite do her justice.

Marie (née Guyart) was born the middle child of a baker and his wife in Tours, France, at the time when the Edict of Nantes had brought about a "veritable mystical invasion" (Henri Brémond) in France's resurgent spiritual life. When only seven years old, Marie experienced a life-transforming dream in which Christ embraced, kissed, and asked her, "Will you be mine?" From the moment she replied yes, she was inclined to prayer and virtue.

Although deeply drawn to religious life, Marie acceded to her parents' plans that she marry the local silk merchant, Joseph Claude Martin. After two years of marriage, her husband died, leaving his nineteen-year-old wife with a six-month-old son and a failing business. Reflecting upon this episode in her life, she remembered her husband somewhat unenthusiastically as a "good man," but praised

God joyously for having made her the mother of a son who would become a Benedictine priest.

On March 24, 1620, Marie underwent a transforming vision that opened her "inner eyes" not only to all the sins, imperfections, and faults of her life but also to her immersion in Christ's redeeming blood. Recovering from this ecstatic experience, she confessed to one of the Feuillant fathers in a nearby chapel, and maintained later that she returned home "another person," which even she could not recognize.

Profound mystical experiences—some that seemed to render soul from body—filled the next ten years of her life. God-given premonitions of these gifts, to her way of thinking, were also granted her so that she could prepare herself to receive them. The experience of Jesus' abiding presence—especially in the form of mysticisms centered on the Sacred Heart of Jesus, on Jesus' precious blood, and on the Eucharist—came to dominate her consciousness.

Financial circumstances forced Marie to move into her sister's large household, where she aided with the supervision of the domestic help and attended to household chores. Her brother-in-law's keen business sense quickly alerted him to her exceptional practical skills. As his business assistant, she soon found herself among dockworkers, stablemen, and tradesmen where she supervised loading and unloading, checking invoices, examining goods, and counting money—"worldly" experience that was to serve her well as a missionary in New France. However, throughout this period she also sustained a life of penance and mystical prayer.

One may find it strange that a thirty-two-year-old widowed mother—with a powerful contemplative spirit—would enter the Ursuline teaching Order. To have become a local Feuillant nun (a reformed Cistercian group known for their prayer and penance), or a Carmelite contemplative, or a member of the Sisters of the Visitation (who were accustomed to "unusual" vocations) would have been the more obvious course. The key to her decision: "I wanted to be an Ursuline because they were instituted to help souls, something which powerfully attracted me."[2]

Marie's spiritual director had acceded to the unusual request of this mother of an eleven-year-old son to become a nun because of her profound interior life. Contrary to her maternal instincts, Marie entrusted her son Claude to her sister and entered the Ursuline monastery at Tours on January 25, 1632. There she had to endure both the gossip about her unusual action and her son's nightly pleadings outside the monastery walls: "Give me back my mother!"

Marie's Ursuline life intensified her already considerable mystical gifts and she quickly attained a state in which her soul felt like a battle-field casualty who awakens in a comfortable "bed of sweet-smelling roses." With her soul now at rest, able only to love, absent of any desire to know more than the Holy Spirit revealed, Marie cleaved to the "tender impressions of the Spirit of the Sacred Word Incarnate"[3] who was preparing her soul for yet more marvelous things.

This Ursuline stands out as one of Christianity's foremost trinitarian mystics. During her first major trinitarian experience, God instructed her in the meaning of the triune indwelling in her soul. A second experience led her to bridal union as the spouse of the divine Word. On March 17, 1631, she was enraptured and "in this abyss" received her greatest trinitarian grace: the Father, Son, and Holy Spirit taking complete possession of her soul. From that time on, she always experienced at the soul's center—which she called "spirit"—the eternal Father as her Father, the incarnate Word as her Spouse, and the Holy Spirit as the Soul of her soul.

Marie's life went from a paradise to a hell the following two years. Deep depression, severe temptations (even to suicide), doubts about her mystical graces, aridity, and demonic manifestations plagued her. During one particularly painful experience she felt an evil spirit penetrate her bones into the marrow and nerves to destroy and annihilate her. Despite these severe trials, prayer and perseverance brought her to a state in which her crosses became "sweet and easy" to bear.

During the winter of 1633 Marie's darkness lifted after a mysterious dream deepened her union with Christ and Mary and imbued her with deep peace and joy. In this dream, she and a companion witnessed the Blessed Virgin Mary and the Christ Child gazing upon a land that aroused both fear and compassion in them. A short time later, Jesus' "apostolic Spirit" took possession of her soul and transported her in spirit to all parts of the inhabited world where there were "souls who belonged by right to Jesus Christ"[4] because he had redeemed them by his precious blood. Another visionary ecstasy revealed that she must go to Canada "to build a house for Jesus and Mary."[5]

Three years later Marie met the unidentified lady of her winter 1633 dream, Madeleine de la Peltrie, a young widow, with whom she and two other Ursuline nuns would set sail for Canada in 1639. After a parlous sea journey, they landed in Quebec. Despite sickness, poverty, enormous physical hardships—as well as the intimidation and murder by hostile tribes of missionaries and the indigenous people entrusted to their care—Marie and her companions established a monastery and founded a school to educate the girls of these people. Having mastered Algonquin, Montagnais, Huron, and Iroquois, Marie also wrote catechisms and dictionaries in these languages.

Marie's son, Dom Claude Martin, had become a famous Benedictine who later published four volumes of her writings. At his request, she wrote two spiritual autobiographies, known as *The Relation of 1633* (an account of her inner life from childhood up to 1633) and *The Relation of 1654* (the same, but up to 1654). The latter is considered to be her masterpiece and, of all her writings, reveals the most about her captivating mystical and apostolic life.

Several things stand out in this account. First, only someone who has passed through all the mystical stages and attained spiritual maturity could have written this document. Second, her thirteen states of prayer do not fit the "classical" pattern of mystical ascent.

For example, when she was in her forties—long after mystical marriage—she suffered another eight years of the dark night of the spirit. Often tempted to despair, she wanted to throw herself into hell. Consonant with a growing seventeenth-century theological view, she expressed the belief that she deserved hell and that God's justice would not err in hurling her into the abyss. "I had a strong desire for this," she wrote, "although I would never want to be deprived of the friendship of God."[6]

The slumbering disorders of her lower nature reawakened and brutally assaulted her. Severe impulses to hate, feelings of bitterness toward others, suicidal tendencies, unspecified humiliations, thoughts of being the vilest and most debased of God's creatures—in short, a significant variety of spiritual, psychological, emotional, and physical turmoil and temptations—filled her life. She even lost confidence in the advice given by her most trusted spiritual directors and confessors—one of the classic signs of the dark night of the spirit. Paradoxically, this spiritual dereliction was experienced only as a "punishment" to be endured, and not as something that ensnares and leads to immoral conduct.

The Holy Spirit also revealed how cunning her corrupt human nature was in hiding her sins and imperfections. She came to realize that God's light alone could shine into every nook and cranny of her soul to purify, heal, and transform it. The Spirit's presence—which previously had been that of embracing love—now became "a sword that divides and cuts with subtle sharpness,"[7] which Marie called a "honing purgatory." Yet, the Spirit's "subtle" and "penetrating" thrusts into her spirit never reached the soul's center, where God is master. The experience of God leaving this center for a while hurled her into a "intolerable void," in which "are born those despairs which would like to throw body and soul into hell."[8]

Except for those brief periods of God's seeming absence, Marie always experienced an intimate peace in the soul's center. "What I was suffering," she wrote, "was contrary to the state that his divine Majesty maintained at the center of my soul."[9] The trials ended, the "garment of darkness" vanished, and peace came flooding into the sensitive part of her soul. The Spirit had graced Marie with what the Desert Fathers called *apatheia*, that is, a psychosomatic wholeness in which the lower appetites instantly obey reason. Peace, the tranquility of order, became her permanent state.

The third salient feature of the anomalous thirteen stages of Marie's mystical journey is that even at the highest states of mystical prayer, the mysteries of Christ's life, death, and resurrection remained present in her consciousness. She admitted to the impossibility of meditating upon them, but the least thought of these mysteries pertaining to the "adorable Word Incarnate" enkindled her soul with their truth, certitude, and holiness. The mystical appropriation of these mysteries continued to deepen, even as she approached the end of her life.

Marie maintained that the Holy Spirit who had led her into the mystery of the incarnate Word had also given her the "key" to scripture. Without study or meditation, she could convincingly explain texts that were being sung or discussed. Her biblical prowess gained her the reputation of conversing with scriptural maxims in ways wholly apposite to even the minutiae of daily living.

Marie's unconditional love of the cross was an integral aspect of her spousal and trinitarian mysticisms that culminated in the state of "the despoilment of the soul, the state of victim, and true and substantial spiritual poverty."[10] She had once received a vision of a magnificent building constructed of crucified bodies. Some of the crucified had only their legs pierced; others were crucified at the waist; still others, their entire bodies: "But it was only those who were entirely attached who bore it willingly."[11] Marie belonged to the latter group, but as an apostolic mystic whose inner and outer life bore all the marks of the "spiritual poverty" of a "victim of love" for the "salvation of souls."

# Blaise Pascal

## (1623–62)

*"All things on earth show man's wretchedness and God's mercy, man's helplessness without God and man's power with God."*[1]

Blaise Pascal was born in Clermont-Ferrand, in the Auvergne region of France. When he was only three years of age, his mother died, prompting his father to become even more devoted to him and to his two sisters. Five years later, his father moved the family to Paris and decided that he alone would educate his children. When Pascal was approximately twenty-three, he experienced what he called his "first conversion" through the influence of several French Jansenists associated with their well-known center at Port Royal des Champs, about eighteen miles southwest of Paris.

In its benign form, Jansenism emphasized the need for evangelical seriousness, conversion, moral severity, total rejection of the world, and wholehearted submission to God. Jansenism also refused to compromise with the humanism and "enlightened" skepticism of its day. In its extreme form, Jansenism was a form of Augustinianism gone sour. Almost fanatically severe, it taught that sin is possible even without interior free choice, that Christ died only for an elect, that the virtues of pagans are only vices, that sinful concupiscence almost completely rules the person, that sexual sins are not washed completely away by the sacrament of penance, and that most people are doomed to damnation.

Pascal's conversion to a seemingly mitigated type of Jansenism awakened him to what he considered to be an unchristian desire for "worldly" renown, so he renounced his scientific work. His Jansenist sensibilities went as far as accusing his sister, Gilberte, of "moral turpitude" because she embraced her children and allowed them to embrace her in return. Serious illness, however, forced him to return to a more "worldly" life but he still remained a frequent visitor at

Port Royal. Pascal then wrote his masterpiece of French irony, the *Provincial Letters*, a mordant denunciation of Jesuit casuistry, a clever defense of Jansenism, and a call to restore Christianity to the austerity of the primitive Church.

Although he was Port Royal's most eloquent voice, Pascal the mystic surpasses Pascal the polemicist in his most famous work, the *Pensées*. These notes were occasioned by what he considered to be the miraculous cure of his niece by a relic of the holy thorn applied to a severe fistula in her eye. This classic text is a defense of the Christian religion that strives to bring people to the living God through Jesus Christ in the Roman Catholic Church. Jansenist emphasis on human corruption and the distinction between the "carnal" and the "spiritual" fill this work. His pessimism about human nature provides a sharp contrast to the exuberant, triumphalistic mood of the Counter-Reformation. However, the *Pensées* also expresses some of the finest sentiments of that movement: an emphasis on mystical experience of God, ardent love of Jesus Christ, and interest in experiential knowledge.

Pascal admired Montaigne for his skeptical exposé of rationalism's pretensions and its attack on Christianity. Against Descartes and those with similar views, Pascal stressed the primacy of religious experience over reason but maintained that religious authority did not substitute for scientific evidence. He stressed the danger of making one of two "fatal errors": excluding reason or relying solely on reason to fathom the mystery of God and of the human. Reason can never penetrate Christianity's supernatural and mysterious dimensions; violating reason, however, reduces Christianity into an absurdity deserving of ridicule.

Pascal's scientific curiosity, moderate philosophical skepticism, awareness of the necessity of moral preparation for the proper use of reason, and firm Christian beliefs are salient elements in his writings. The "science of the human," to his way of thinking, is much more valuable than "the science of things." The two poles of his thought? Human corruption and God's mercy. In what can be taken as a summary of his theology, Pascal wrote, "Man's greatness and wretchedness are so evident that the true religion must necessarily teach us that there is in man some great principle of greatness and some great principle of wretchedness."[2]

The rationalism of his age never seduced Pascal, who was convinced that science could not reach fundamental human truths because it could not probe the mystery of what it ultimately means to be human: a creature haunted by God and redeemed by Christ. To his way of thinking, the "heart" connaturally, intuitively, directly, and prephilosophically knows God with certainty; the heart's reasons are *certainties*, not sentiments. As he wrote, "the heart has its reasons, which reason does not know. I say that the heart naturally loves God, and that it loves itself naturally. It is the heart that is conscious of God, and not reason."[3] Contrary to the common view of his times that a natural knowledge of God was both possible and sufficient, Pascal stressed that religious knowledge is impossible without love and "submission."

After Pascal's death, a piece of parchment was found that had been sewn into his clothing and that he always had with him. The *Mémorial*,[4] as it is called, records the episode of his "definitive conversion"—one of the Christian tradition's best known mystical experiences. It states:

> The year of grace 1654, Monday, 23 November, feast of Saint Clement, Pope and martyr, and others of the Martyrology. Eve of Saint Chrysogonus, martyr, and others. From about half past ten at night until about half past twelve. FIRE! God of Abraham, God of Isaac, God of Jacob, not of the philosophers and scientists. Certainty, joy, certainty, sight, joy. God of Jesus Christ. . . . Your God will be my God. Ruth. Oblivious to the world and to everything except GOD. He can only be found in the ways taught in the Gospel. Greatness of the human soul. Righteous Father, the world did not know you but I knew you. John. Joy, joy, joy and tears of joy. I have cut myself off from him. . . . My God, will you forsake me? Let me not be cut off from him for ever. This is eternal life, that they may know you the only true God, and him whom you sent, Jesus Christ. Jesus Christ. Jesus Christ. I have cut myself off from him. I have fled from him, denied him, crucified him. Let me never be cut off from him. He can only be kept by the ways taught by the Gospel. Sweet and total renunciation. Total submission to Jesus Christ and my director. Everlasting joy for one day's tribulation on earth. I will not forget your word. Amen.

This experience illustrates Pascal's thirst for the "God of Jesus Christ"—the God of Abraham, Isaac, and Jacob—not the God of the philosophers. For him, only the God revealed by Jesus Christ makes the human soul great. Reason alone, declared the intellectuals, could discover a God of natural religion that was to replace the God of traditional Christianity. Pascal's mystical experience underscores his disdain for this shallow rationalism. In his view, deism is even more pernicious than atheism because only the "living God" is the person's true good.

The person of Jesus Christ stands at the center of Pascal's spirituality and mysticism: "Whoever knows him knows the reason for everything."[5] Knowledge of God and knowledge of self are impossible without knowledge of Christ—not only impossible but also useless. We know God and ourselves only through the life and death of Jesus Christ. On the other hand, it is not possible to know Christ without knowing both God and our wretchedness alike.

Pascal's meditation "The Mystery of Jesus"[6] has been called a "tiny masterpiece" of Christ-centered mysticism. It should be read as a summary of Pascal's relationship to Christ and as his rewriting of the gospels' passion narratives. His passion-mysticism underscores both the human and the *divine* sufferings of Christ, especially his loneliness. The horror that Christ endures in the garden is so piercing that he complains—the only time, in Pascal's view, that Christ ever complained. Jesus' sufferings, moreover, are not transient because his agony lasts until the world's end.

How could God have become man, Pascal wonders, and allowed himself to be united with such a "vile" creature? How could he have actually sought the "companionship and solace from men" during his agony? To Pascal's way of thinking, human beings spontaneously—from the depths of their nature—hate each other. On the other hand, because Christ died for our sins, the human person is a redeemed sinner. Just as Jesus was achieving salvation even as his disciples slept, so, too, has Jesus brought about the salvation of the "righteous, while they slept, in nothingness before their birth and in their sins after their birth." This Jesus is our only trustworthy friend, dying for us even when we were "cruel and faithless," and as he is still ready to do "in the Blessed Sacrament."

Pascal's "wager" argument for God's existence is relatively well known. If one bets that God exists, one is betting finite existence against life eternal. What casino would allow gamblers to bet the finite for the infinite? The second aspect of his wager argument: a better human life here and now, if one gambles that God exists. His wager argument for Christianity is less well known: it will one day be disclosed that either Christians or their despisers are wrong. In Pascal's view, those who reject Christianity have much more to dread, if they have erred. His arguments are especially powerful, if placed in his contention that one *must* wager.

Mathematician, scientist, literateur, poet, rhetorician, philosopher, theologian, and mystic, the views of this "sublime misanthrope" permeated much of France's religious atmosphere in the second half of the seventeenth century. Despite his brief life and his unfinished work, Blaise Pascal was a genius who continues to fascinate a significant variety of people. Self-tormented and intellectually restless— evidence suggests that because of an accident, he always saw an abyss on his left side—Pascal delineated in a perennially contemporary way the heart's immense longings, its tangles, the will's powerlessness, human fragility, and the darkness of the "thinking reed" who knows his own misery. This makes the human person among all God's creatures great because this greatness comes from knowing that he is wretched.

In the last years of his life, though very sick, Pascal made great spiritual progress and died in such terrible agony that some considered him to be a Christian martyr. The great desire he had for the Viaticum as he was dying and the piety with which he finally received it speaks volumes of his love for Christ. His witness to the Christian calling is perhaps as significant as his works.

# Angelus Silesius

## (1624–77)

*"How deep the Godhead is, no one may ever fathom;*
*Even the soul of Christ in its abyss must vanish."*[1]

Johannes Scheffler was born in the Silesian capital of Breslau of a well-to-do Lutheran, landowning family, who, for religious reasons, emigrated from Poland. Although his parents died when he was young, they left him financially secure, and thus able to study medicine and philosophy at Strasbourg, Padua, and Leiden. While in Holland, he studied the works of the Silesian mystic Jacob Boehme, the "Teutonic philosopher of Görlitz."

Boehme's noted biographer, Abraham von Franckenberg, urged Scheffler to write down his insights, a practice encouraged further by his exposure to Ignatius of Loyola's *Spiritual Exercises*. His writings indicate that he had also steeped himself in the works of the German speculative mystics, the earlier German visionary mystics, and the Franciscan mystics of the order he eventually joined.

Appointed a court physician by Duke Sylvius Nimrod of Württemburg, Scheffler converted to Catholicism and left his position—apparently because of the court chaplain's intolerance. Returning to Breslau, he entered the Brotherhood of Minorites, a Franciscan group, was ordained priest in 1661, and took the name "Angelus Silesius."

Although Angelus became a vitriolic Counter-Reformation pamphleteer, he lived a life of almost extreme asceticism and spent himself in service to the poor, the sick, and the orphaned. His works, *The Holy Joy of the Soul* and especially his classic *The Cherubinic Wanderer*, have universal appeal because they resound with mystical joy, peace, serenity, and an enthusiasm for the divine-human encounter. When one considers the horrors, turmoil, sufferings, and animosities that existed in his region both during and after the Thirty Years' War, his profound serenity is all the more remarkable.

A new variety of Christian mystical literature appears in *The Cherubinic Wanderer*, which reveals both Angelus's mystical genius and rhetorical skills. By using old French Alexandrine verse, liturgical expressions, and the Silesian Pietists' *paradoxa* (concatenations of seemingly contradictory scriptural verses), Scheffler wrote epigrammatic couplets. By blending images, themes, paradoxes, aphorisms, antithetical statements, and dissonance, these couplets dazzle, delight, and unite both the mind and heart with the object of their longing: the ineffable God. He has been called the one who "speaks forth" (prophet) the Ineffable.

If the "symbol leads to thought" (Paul Ricoeur), these epigrams flow from and return to a profoundly mystical life. His epigrams are sparks from a mystical soul, a mysticism expressed and incarnated in language, rhythm, and music. They illustrate the unity that often exists between the mystical life at a person's core and its psychosomatic expression through all levels of the person's being. These epigrams—much like Japanese *haiku* or a Zen *koan*—baffle the mind, reveal the Ineffable, and exemplify the inextricable unity between the mystical life and its expression.

Many of his couplets underscore the intimacy of the divine-human intercourse, which he describes as the "art of kissing God." Emphasis upon abnegation, emptiness, God as the "Naught," the virgin soul pregnant with God, God and the human soul as the same abyss, and the paradoxical divine-human union illustrates his roots in the German speculative mystical tradition. Some of his epigrams show the influence that German bridal love mysticism (the soul should swoon in the "wounds" of her Lover) and ardent Franciscan incarnational mysticism ("God drinks humanity's milk, leaves His divinity's wine"[2]) had upon him. The illuminative ("cherubinic") and love ("seraphic") aspects of his poetry attempt to enlighten and inflame the spirit with love of the Trinity, Christ, the cross, and Mary.

Angelus has been called a pantheist because a number of his epigrams blur the distinction between the human and the divine. He wrote, for example, "Tell me, which holy soul will not be God in God?"[3] Such poems indicate, however, that Silesius subscribed to the views of those mystics who emphasized the oneness of all things in God *prior* to creation. One clear example: "The rose which here on earth is now perceived by me, has blossomed thus in God from all eternity."[4] Why did God become man? Silesius asked: "Because I once was He."[5]

His couplets are redolent of theological exemplarism. For example, why has God created us in his own image? Silesius replied, "I say because He has simply no other one."[6] Two other salient features in these epigrams: (1) the necessity of becoming a son in the Son for the return to God; (2) one is reborn by seeing reality as Adam saw it before the Fall and by participating in the language with which Adam conversed with God prior to the Fall.

Silesius's epigram "How God Dwells in the Holy Soul"[7] has been called his most beautiful. The Word lives in us like many suns drenching the world with light. It is like the bridegroom who comes in the night, like a king ruling in his realm, or like a father to his son. The Word lives in us like a hidden treasure, an "honored guest," "and like sweet music at an evening meal."[8]

It seems apposite to conclude this section the way Silesius ends his work: "Reader, it is enough. But if you still would read more, then you yourself be the book, in thought, word, life, and deed."[9]

# George Fox

## (1624–91)

*"Now the Lord God opened to me by his invisible power that every man was enlightened by the divine light of Christ, and I saw it showing through all."*[1]

George Fox, the founder of Quakerism, was born in the strongly Puritan village of Drayton-in-the-Clay (now, Fenny Drayton), Leicestershire, England, of a well-to-do weaver—whom his neighbors called "righteous Christer"—and of a mother "of the stock of the martyrs."[2] Strict adherents of the established religion, his parents destined him for the Church. From early childhood, however, "dear George" (as his followers were affectionately to call him) had a strong aversion to what he judged to be a "hireling ministry." Christ, he thought, later reinforced this loathing by "opening" to him that an Oxford or a Cambridge "breeding" was insufficient to qualify men to be suitable ministers of Christ.

From early childhood Fox was of a serious, religious disposition. God had instructed him from his youth in "purity and righteousness" and on how to be faithful "inwardly to God" and "outwardly to man." In order to maintain his health—but more to avoid becoming "wanton"—simple food and drink were his daily fare. After only a rudimentary education, he became apprentice to a shoemaker, who also dealt in wool and cattle. Because of his innocence, honesty, native abilities, and practical skills, George proved to be rather good for his master's business, who was "blessed" when Fox was with him, but "broke and came to nothing" after he left him.

When he was nineteen years of age, he was so shocked by an invitation to join his two "professor" (nominal Christians) friends in a drinking bout after a fair, that he hastily left for home. During prayer that night, the Lord instructed him about the young rushing toward "vanity," and the old "into the earth." Fox was then commanded to forsake everything and to be "as a stranger to all."[3]

Taking the Lord's injunction literally, Fox left family and friends in July 1643 to search for light. Temptations and severe depression bordering on despair drove him to seek the counsel of renowned "professors." These "miserable comforters" advised him to marry, or to sing psalms, or to take up smoking. The "Ranters" disgusted him with their "empty high notions" of being God or Christ. He ridiculed members of a sect for their belief that women did not have souls. However, "kindred souls" among the "dissenting people" (mainly Baptists and Congregationalists) provided him with some comfort.

Obtaining no satisfaction from the members of the Church of England or from those in the innumerable sects who flooded the land, Fox was thrown back upon his own resources. He often fasted, haunted solitary places, sat in hollow trees reading his Bible, and walked much of the night in sadness. In his words, "I was a man of sorrows in the first working of the Lord in me."[4] It was during this period, however, that he had "great openings of the scriptures."[5]

When approximately in his mid-twenties, Fox had his first significant "awakening": the realization that no one and nothing of this world could "address his condition," followed by a loud voice that rang out: "There is one, Christ Jesus, that can speak to your condition."[6] From that moment on he knew experientially that Jesus was the "bishop" of his soul and the light in which he was to see everything. In his view, he came to know Christ—not from the scriptures or the preaching of others—but from experience, an inner revelation.

In the wake of this experience, he understood that "two thirsts" drove him: the first, toward the world, which could do him "no good"; the second, toward the Creator and his Son, Jesus Christ. A bit later on, the love of God so overpowered him that all he could do was to admire it. During this event, it was also "opened" to him that "all was done, and to be done, in and by Christ."[7]

The salient element in Fox's mysticism is the divine light of Jesus Christ. The Lord God "opened to him," with a power that could not be doubted, "that every man was enlightened by the divine light of Christ, and I saw it showing through all."[8] This foundational truth, the primary datum of his experience, is the context for understanding dear George's mysticism, spirituality, charismatic personality, and apostolic drive. The "divine light" of Jesus Christ also became the discerning principle in which the darkness of temptation, sin, unrighteousness, and death became evident to him.

Fox was later enraptured "through the flaming sword, into the paradise of God,"[9] which made all creation "smell" differently. He experienced that because Jesus Christ is transforming everything into God's image, purity, innocence, and righteousness permeate all creation. It was also at this time that he elected to follow Jesus and to abandon his strong desire to practice medicine.

Fox found resonance with his own view of the importance of inner stillness in the German theosophist Jacob Boehme (d. 1624), that the Holy Spirit guides those who "stand" in inner quiet in the soul's still point. Both he and Fox taught that silent worship witnesses to Christ's authority and that silent waiting upon the Lord is also a means of serving one's fellow brothers and sisters.

Walking in Christ's light and obeying his speaking within the soul were for Fox a genuine Christian's supreme and only duties. Creeds, churches, councils, rites, and sacraments were discarded as outward things. Even the scriptures were to be interpreted by the inner light. And from this light, Fox concluded that one should never take an oath, never take part even in a defensive war, never tip one's hat or bow respectfully to anyone, and never give or accept titles of honor. Art, music, drama, field-sports, and dancing were rejected; simplicity of dress and absence of ornament were mandated.

Impelled by frequent "revelations," Fox began the public preaching of his novel tenets in 1647. It was not his intention to increase the religious confusion of the time by the addition of a new sect. What quickly marked him and his followers out for persecution was not so much the theory of the inward light or the rejection of rites and sacraments; it was the refusal to pay tithes, to take the oaths prescribed by law, and to have anything to do with the army. What the authorities found especially galling was the unwillingness of Fox and his followers to uncover their heads in court or to address the judges as "thee and thou."

Fox's first imprisonment centered on his "blasphemous" denial that the sacraments of baptism and the Lord's Supper were commanded by God. When arrested by the authorities and questioned, he said, "I told them they were not to dispute of God and Christ, but to obey Him."[10] This sentence, in a nutshell, sums up Fox's entire theology.

In 1669, Fox married Margaret Fell, the widow of his wealthiest patron, the former vice-chancellor of the duchy of Lancaster. Through Margaret, "the nursing mother of Quakerism," he secured for his followers a valuable rallying-point in the seclusion of Swarthmoor Hall, Lancashire.

The "Society of Friends," as they are now called, initially saw themselves as "Children of Truth" and the "Children of Light." However, they were soon derisively dubbed "Quakers." Justice Gervase Bennett of Derby—who had sentenced Fox to prison as a blasphemer—was the first to call him and his followers "Quakers" because Fox had the audacity to command him to "tremble" at God's word. It seems likely that the judge was using a familiar term of derision for sects—labeled "Quakers"—in which shivering and shaking were part of their so-called experience of the Holy Spirit.

With Margaret's able help, "dear George" expanded his ministry, undertook tours of North America and the Low Countries, and spent the final decade of his life working in London to organize the rapidly expanding Quaker movement. He and his followers had to endure disdain, ridicule, hostility, and even severe persecution. However, William Penn and Oliver Cromwell admired and respected them.

His journal, subtitled *An Account of the Life, Travels, Suffering, Christian Experience and Labor of Love in the Work of the Ministry of George Fox,* was published in 1694, after editing by Thomas Ellwood (a friend and associate of John Milton), with a preface by William Penn. Like many works of its time, the journal—most of it dictated—was written years after the events it described and was heavily edited. Rufus Jones (d. 1948), perhaps the best-known Quaker of the twentieth century, compared it to Augustine's *Confessions.* Hundreds of Fox's letters—mostly intended for wide circulation—along with a few private communications were also published.

In the fields of education, charity, and philanthropy, the Friends have occupied a place disproportionate to their numbers. For example, many important colleges in the United States were founded by Quakers. Long before other Christian denominations, they denounced slavery and would not permit any of their members to own slaves. Widely admired for their pacifism, they are also exemplary in the care of the poor and the sick and have been eminently solicitous for the welfare and fair treatment of Native Americans.

Walt Whitman (d. 1892), an American poet raised by parents inspired by Quaker thought, wrote, "George Fox stands for something too—a thought—the thought that wakes in silent hours—perhaps the deepest, most eternal thought latent in the human soul. This is the thought of God, merged in the thoughts of moral right and the immortality of identity. Great, great is this thought—aye, greater than all else."[11]

# Crises in Mysticism

*"These articles are condemned as heretical, suspect, erroneous,
scandalous, blasphemous, offensive to pious ears, reckless, and
particularly weakening, subversive and seditious of Christian
discipline."*[1]

The first significant Christian mystical heresy was Gnosticism. The
1945 Nag Hammadi discovery of lost Gnostic texts produced a surge
of scholarly and popular interest in the so-called "lost books" of the
Bible. "The Gospel of Judas," a recently discovered and published
ancient Gnostic document, produced nothing short of a media frenzy.
N. T. Wright, a noted New Testament exegete, claims that the sensa-
tionalism surrounding this document highlights an unfortunate feature of American life in the last few decades: namely, a longing for
new evidence to undermine orthodox Christianity.

Gnosticism, broadly defined, is a dark dualism that views the
world as thoroughly evil. It understands this world as created by an
evil god who is either the son or an angel of a totally unknown and
unknowable God. Relentlessly hostile to the main lines of ancient
Judaism, it emphasizes that salvation is attained through deliverance
from the material cosmos to a purely spiritual upper world by secret
knowledge imparted to the elite by a noncorporeal savior. Because
it considers the highest part of the human soul to be innately divine,
Gnosticism as a mystical theology emphasizes the identity of the
unknown God and the human soul.

The second century witnessed the emergence of a variety of Gnostic groups, most of which considered themselves to be followers of
Jesus Christ. These "people of knowledge," the *Gnostikoi*, professed
Jesus to be a noncorporeal redeeming spirit who revealed a saving
knowledge, gnosis, to a select core of believers. Their teaching about
self-denial centered on sexual purity, not on moral progress and

personal integration—and they judged women as inferior because they were supposedly less spiritual.

The Gnostics maintained that new and ongoing revelations superseded the revelation found in the canonical biblical texts. Their own exegetes often interpreted these texts in ways contrary to that of the apostles, their successors, and the Fathers of the Church, that is, in ways contrary to the "rule of faith." One of Gnosticism's most important effects was to render esotericism of any sort suspect to the wider Church community, especially that based on secret modes of scriptural interpretation and on books outside the canon of scripture.

Orthodox Christianity, on the other hand, stresses the good God of the book of Genesis who creates everything—including the human soul—and pronounces his creation to be "good." Revelation ended with the "death of the last apostle," although the Church's historical life fosters deeper insights into God's revealed and normative word. Christianity's good news is open to all, not just to an elite.

Paul's First Letter to Timothy 6:20 is apposite here: "Avoid the godless chatter and contradictions of what is falsely called knowledge [gnosis], for by professing it some have missed the mark as regards the faith." The Fathers of the Church accepted as valid mystical and even allegorical interpretations of scripture—but only if they were congruent with the orthodox message of salvation authoritatively taught by the rule of faith of the "Great Church." They also viewed genuine Christian gnosis as the authentic loving-knowledge of the crucified and risen Christ, which must bring about personal transformation and love of neighbor.

Heresies of a mystical nature also became prominent during the second half of the thirteenth century. The adherents of the various "Free Spirit" movements maintained that the Holy Spirit enlightened them to the extent that everything they did flowed from divine inspiration. Some even maintained that a higher knowledge of God that they reached through the spiritual annihilation of their created wills made them aware of their identity with God. A practical outcome of this belief was that they could neglect Christian practices and indulge in licentious behavior.

Some in these movements stressed that gospel freedom allowed them to neglect the sacraments. Moreover, if contemplation supposedly becomes so pure that it results in one continuous act of adoration, what need is there for other Christian practices, even obedience to civil and ecclesiastical authority? Not a few claimed to have reached such a state of inner "quietude" and "pure and disinterested love" that they were indifferent to everything, even to their own salvation. Stated more daringly, could one really love God in such a way so as to be gladly damned, if God so willed?

Ninety-seven erroneous articles were collected in the 1260s from those suspected of the views of the Brethren of the Free Spirit and sent to Albert the Great, a prominent Dominican theologian at the University of Paris. As one would expect, he condemned their esotericism, antinomianism, libertinism, attacks on the institutional Church, and their claims to impeccability and to having identity with God. For example, against article 58, he said, "To say that a person may become equal to the Father and surpass the Son is not only heretical but even diabolical." Against article 94, he said, "To say that a person in this life can attain a state where he is not able to sin is a lie against the true teaching."[2]

The earliest official use of the term "Free Spirit" is found in the letter of Pope Clement V dated April 1, 1311, in which he wrote that a bogus liberty of spirit "allows them to do whatever they want." In that same year the Council of Vienne was convened to investigate erroneous forms of mystical beliefs. The resulting decree, "Ad Nostrum," listed eight errors attributed to "an abominable sect of malignant men known as Beghards and faithless women known as Beguines," that is, to groups of men and women who lived a semireligious community life but without vows. The views pronounced heretical are (1) only the imperfect practice the virtues, (2) one can become impeccable, (3) one can attain a natural beatitude in this life, (4) the "light of glory" is not necessary to elevate the soul for the beatific vision, (5) showing respect to the Eucharist or to Christ's passion requires descending from the heights of contemplation, and (6) pay no heed to sexual licentiousness. One example of the strange teachings circulating at that time expressed the belief that "the kiss of a woman, since nature does not incline to it, is a mortal sin; but the act of intercourse, since nature does incline to it, is not a sin, especially when strongly tempted."[3] These fourteenth-century condemnatory documents established a template upon which later suspicious forms of mysticisms were to be judged.

Jean le Charlier de Gerson (d. 1429), the renowned chancellor of the University of Paris—a formidable mystical theologian in his own right—also entered the dispute. His trenchant criticisms of German-

Flemish mystical views on indistinct union with God, especially those of the highly orthodox John Ruusbroec, added to the increasingly antimystical atmosphere.

The Spanish "Alumbrados," the "Illuminati" ("enlightened ones"), also subscribed to some of the tenets of the Free Spirits, especially the view that everything they did was inspired by the Holy Spirit. Even the well-known mystics, Ignatius of Loyola and Teresa of Avila, came under suspicion.

Quietism is the most salient heresy of early modern mysticism. Broadly speaking, this erroneous view exaggerates the role of interior passivity in contemplation, teaches that recollection can be a single, continuous act of the soul, and eschews external practices. It also insists on the "holy indifference" of "pure love" that abandons all concerns—even for one's own salvation. More narrowly, Quietism signifies the errors attributed to Miguel de Molinos (d. 1696), Jeanne-Marie Bouvier de la Motte-Guyon (d. 1717), and Abbé François Fénelon (d. 1715), which precipitated what is frequently called "The Eighteenth-Century Crisis of Mysticism."

The situation came to a head in Rome because of Miguel de Molinos, a celebrated confessor and spiritual director, who wrote an influential book, *The Spiritual Guide* (1675). Because of his alleged unorthodox teachings of what he called the "mystic science"—and the rumors that came to surround his name—the "Father of Quietism" was put on trial and imprisoned. Although he recanted when his teachings were formally condemned in 1675, he was nonetheless sentenced to lifelong imprisonment on charges of the gravest moral depravities. Because of the Molinos drama, public opinion became increasingly hostile to mysticism.

Pope Innocent XI, in his document, "Coelestis Pater" (November 20, 1687), condemned sixty-eight propositions attributed to Molinos and brought fresh life to previous decrees against the Alumbrados. The first proposition denounced the salient feature of the Quietism supposedly taught by Molinos, namely, that the genuine "inward way" demands that a person annihilate his spiritual powers and abandon himself entirely to God, thereafter remaining as a lifeless body. The thesis that God wishes to work "in us without us" may well sum up his teaching on the interior life.

The decree also denounced the views that (1) by doing nothing the soul annihilates itself and returns to its source, God's essence.

There it is transformed, divinized, and permanently indwells. (2) The inward way demands that one thinks neither of reward nor of punishment, neither of heaven nor of hell, neither of death nor of eternity. (3) Resigned to God's will, the soul must remain inactive so that God alone works in it. This state of resignation demands that the soul offers no active resistance to temptations. (4) Perfect prayer requires that a person remain quietly in "obscure faith" and forgets every distinct thought about God and all else. And finally, (5) to seek sensible devotion is to seek oneself and not God. In fact, every sensible effect experienced in the spiritual life is "abominable, filthy, and unclean."

One of the key characters in the Quietism controversy was Jeanne-Marie Bouvier de la Motte-Guyon (Madame Guyon, as she is most often called), a widow who had been initiated into the secrets of the mystical life by Père François Lacombe, a Barnabite priest. Deeply influenced by Molinos's writings, Lacombe guided Madame Guyon from a deep sense of God's presence to a "mystical death," and then to a state in which she no longer possessed God but in which God possessed her.

Now totally in God's hands, she claimed to have become like an automaton—able to write remarkable things without preparation and without reflection. From this point on, all her actions flowed from God who brought her into an "apostolic state," which consisted not in preaching the Gospel but in advancing the mystical life—the theory of which she presented in a work inspired mostly by her own experiences, *A Short and Easy Method of Prayer* (1685).

Another one of her books, *The Torrents* (1682), focused on the vehemence of pure love, the bitterness of passive purification, and a spiritual annihilation through which one loses oneself in the divine essence. Jeanne-Marie also undertook an exposition of the entire Bible, an astonishing undertaking for anyone, especially for a woman of that day.

Madame Guyon then set out to gain adherents for her mystical theories, but the moment was ill chosen. Louis XIV, who had recently striven to have the Quietism of Molinos condemned at Rome, was by no means pleased to see gaining ground, even in his own capital, a form of mysticism, which, to him, resembled that of Molinos's teachings. By the king's order, Père Lacombe—who had defended Guyon, especially through his short treatise "An Analysis of Prayer"— was imprisoned in the Bastille.

During a period in which he was enduring severe spiritual trials, Abbé François Fénelon (the future archbishop of Cambrai) befriended Madame Guyon, who was able to lead him into a state of "holy indifference" and mystical prayer. In his view, she was the embodiment of "pure love," which he considered the essence of mysticism. As her teachings came under increasing suspicion, Fénelon attempted to defend her by writing the *Explanations of the Maxims of the Saints on the Interior Life* (1696), a tome that gave undue importance to holy indifference.

Fénelon had also participated in the 1695 conference at Issy, which promulgated thirty-four articles on orthodox mysticism. These articles restated earlier views on the authentic mystical life and also sought to clarify what truly Christian "holy indifference" is. For example, number nine states, "A Christian is not allowed to be indifferent with regarded to his salvation, nor to the things related to it. Holy indifference pertains to the things of this life (not including sin), and to the giving of spiritual consolation or of aridity."[4]

Although both Fénelon and Guyon consented to these articles, she was accused of bad faith because she continued to propagate her own views of passive prayer and pure love. The formidable bishop of Meaux, Jacques-Bénigne Bossuet (d. 1704), entered the fray and worked to have them both condemned. Almost totally incompetent to discern genuine from false mysticism, Bossuet mounted a blistering attack on mysticism in his book *Instructions on the States of Prayer*, which did not spare even John of the Cross.

This Parisian "Battle of the Olympians"—as it is sometimes referred to—focused on three issues. The first concerned passive prayer, which Bossuet considered miraculous and granted to very few. Fénelon, on the other hand, understood passive prayer as the full flowering of the life of sanctifying grace, which required only the Christian's total and peaceful cooperation. The second and third issues centered on Fénelon's thesis that pure love demands total and absolute indifference, even to one's own salvation.

Bossuet was a master of pamphleteering and had powerful political connections. Publishing the private correspondence between Guyon and Fénelon, the bishop portrayed Guyon as a half-mad visionary and Fénelon as the "Montanus of this Priscilla."[5] On March 12, 1699, Pope Innocent XII condemned twenty-three propositions from Fénelon's *Maxims* in his brief "Cum Alias." One of the condemned articles states,

"Pure love alone constitutes the whole interior life; and from it arises the one principle and the one motive of all the acts that are deliberate and meritorious."[6] Although not condemned for heresy as his enemies had wished, Fénelon accepted the mitigated denunciation of his teachings and his own exile from court, but remained attached to Guyon to the end. Fénelon, the great champion of mysticism, had been disgraced—and mysticism with him.

Guyon was tried, imprisoned for approximately seven years in the Bastille, and then exiled to a village in the diocese of Blois, where she later died. Despite the defamation of her character, her morality appears to have been beyond reproach. Even her sworn enemy Bossuet said as much before the full assembly of the French clergy, though he had defamed her on other grounds. It is remarkable, too, that her disciples at the Court of Louis XIV were always persons of piety and exemplary life.

The wider context for this dispute, of course, was the Enlightenment, the so-called Age of Reason. Enlightenment beliefs had reduced the Judeo-Christian God of revelation to the watchmaker God, who created, wound up his watch-like creation, and had no further dealings with it. Hostile to Orthodox Christianity, the proponents of the Enlightenment rejected authority and considered truth to be a matter of experimentation, observation, and reason in the narrowest sense of clear and distinct ideas. The Age of Reason rejected mysticism as so much "Dionysian balderdash," "sheer daydreaming," and even madness. The eighteenth century witnessed an attack against Catholic mysticism that, without causing its complete disappearance, led to a deep suspicion of and decline of mystical life and thought from then on well into the twentieth century.

The controversial terms that were salient in these disputes—"annihilation," "detachment," "abandonment," "quieting the soul's faculties," "deification," "conformity to God's will," and "pure love"—have a long and noble history in orthodox spirituality and mysticism. Some commentators maintain that Molinos, Guyon, and Fénelon stressed *only* those elements. To this way of thinking, *exclusiveness* marks the emphasis placed on certain aspects of Christian spirituality and mysticism that have long been present. This doctrinal exclusiveness may well be the hallmark of Quietism. On the other hand, contemporary scholarship tends to rehabilitate these controversial figures and their teachings.

# Viscount Charles-Eugène de Foucauld

## (1858–1916)

*"Think that you may die a martyr, despoiled of everything, stretched on the ground, covered with blood and wounds, violently and painfully killed. Wish this to happen today."*[1]

Viscount Charles-Eugène de Foucauld was born in Strasbourg, France, of aristocratic parents who both died when he was only six years of age. Entrusted to his maternal grandfather—who was fiercely proud of his service to cross and crown—Charles eventually entered the military academy of Saint-Cyr, plunged headlong into frivolities and debauchery, and resigned his commission because of "Mimi." Renewed Arab hostility in Algeria prompted Foucauld to rejoin his old cavalry unit, in which he distinguished himself as a fearless officer. Resigning his commission yet again, he became the first Westerner to explore Morocco—earning for his work a gold medal from the French Geographical Society.

Exposure to Muslim piety was the catalyst for his conversion. In the fall of 1886 in Paris, he sought out the famous confessor and spiritual director Abbé Huvelin, made his confession, received Communion, and left the church determined to give himself totally to God. He later wrote, "As soon as I believed there was a God, I understood that I could not do anything other than live for him. My religious vocation dates from the same moment as my faith."[2]

Renouncing his fortune, Charles went to the Holy Land, entered the Trappists, and spent the next seven years in a monastery in Syria. Desiring an even deeper life of poverty and imitation of Jesus' hidden life, he obtained a dispensation from the Trappists and moved to Nazareth to spend three years as a servant at a convent of Poor Clare nuns. At the urging of mother superior that he become a priest, he left for Paris and was ordained in 1901. Returning to Africa to live as a hermit in a small Arab settlement near the Algerian oasis of Béni-Abbès, he devoted himself to caring for the local Arabs and ministering to the French garrison troops. Then this forty-two-year-old seeker discovered that his true mission, his true "Nazareth," was to adopt an even more eremitical life at Tamanrasset, in the isolated, rugged Hoggar region. Accepted by the seminomadic Tuareg tribes of devout Muslims as a *marabout* ("holy man"), he ministered to their needs and wrote grammar books and dictionaries of their language.

The desire of "Brother Charles" (as he preferred to be called) "to reproduce the hidden life of Our Lord as St. Francis of Assisi reproduced his public life"[3] sums up his spirituality and mysticism. A pioneer of enculturation, he dressed and lived as a poor Arab, practicing an evangelism of presence. Of his move to Tamanrasset, he wrote, "I no longer want a monastery which is secure. I want a small monastery, like the house of a poor workman who is not sure if tomorrow he will find work and bread, who with all his being shares the suffering of the world."[4]

Foucauld spent his life accomplishing nothing in the eyes of the world. Although he wanted followers, he remained alone to the end. His former abbot—with whom he maintained cordial relations—said of him that with his excessive mental concentration he would drive any disciple mad before killing him by excessive austerities.

"Annihilation," to Charles's way of thinking, was the most powerful means we have of uniting ourselves with Christ. He wished to live as if he were to die a martyr's death at any moment. Approximately nine years before his violent death at the hands of Senoussi Muslim extremists, he wrote that Jesus had spoken to him: "Your thought of death: Think that you may die a martyr, despoiled of everything, stretched on the ground, covered with blood and wounds, violently and painfully killed. Wish this to happen today."[5]

Beatified in 2005 by Pope Benedict XVI, Foucauld is considered by many to be a martyr. The circumstances of his death, however, are too complicated for a certain judgment of martyrdom. His solitary life and mystical spirituality centered on the hidden life of the eucharistic Christ inspired the posthumous foundations of the Little Brothers of Jesus by René Voillame and the Little Sisters of Jesus by Madeleine Hutin.

# Thérèse of Lisieux

## (1873–97)

*"Then, in the excess of my delirious joy, I cried out: O Jesus, my Love. My vocation, at last I have found it. MY VOCATION IS LOVE!"*[1]

Although Thérèse of Lisieux was a respected member of her Carmelite community, few nuns noticed anything remarkable about her. However, when her autobiography was published about a year after her death at age twenty-four, the worldwide reaction to "the very little Sister Thérèse of the Child Jesus and the Holy Face" produced a "hurricane of glory." Thousands of letters poured into Lisieux to sing her praises. So evident was she a "miracle of virtues and a prodigy of miracles" that the Holy See waived the normal fifty-year waiting period; Pope Pius XI solemnly canonized her on May 17, 1925, with a half million pilgrims in attendance in St. Peter's Square.

Thérèse never traveled much beyond her hometown, except for one brief trip to Italy. Nevertheless, she lived her vocation to "suffer for souls" so radically that a few years later Pius XI declared her the "principal patroness, equal to St. Francis Xavier, of all missionaries, men and women, and of the missions in the whole world." Then, on May 4, 1944, Pope Pius XII proclaimed her to be France's second patroness and "the equal of St. Joan of Arc."

One hundred years after her death on October 19, 1997, Pope John Paul II declared Thérèse to be a "Doctor of the Roman Catholic Church," the third woman to be so honored. To attain this distinction, one must bear witness to the Church's ancient tradition in an outstanding way. Thus, the nun who had often called herself a "grain of sand" has come to be known as "the greatest saint of modern times" (Pope Pius X)—and looms in popular piety, perhaps second only to St. Francis of Assisi.

Born in Alençon, France, Marie Françoise Thérèse Martin was the youngest of nine children born to Louis Martin, a skilled watchmaker, and Zélie Guérin, a successful craftswoman. Not only had both parents seriously considered entering religious communities but they had also lived together as brother and sister for almost a year after their marriage. The Martins reared their children by using the saints as both educational models and as sources of entertainment. The family led an active Catholic sacramental life—unusual for that period of severe Jansenism—and engaged in the service of the poor and the sick. Family life was of extreme importance to the Martins, and Thérèse was later to recall how God had surrounded her life with love from her first memories. This may also account for her easy familiarity with God.

When Thérèse was four years old, her mother died. Pauline, her elder sister, became her "second mother"—and, later, the superior of the Carmelite community Thérèse was eventually to enter. Shortly thereafter, the family moved to Lisieux, where she experienced eight years of weariness, hypersensitivity, and even religious scrupulosity. For three months in 1883 during this "winter of trial," Thérèse suffered from an illness that produced convulsions, hallucinations, and comas. She claimed that she was instantaneously and miraculously cured while praying before a statue of Our Lady of Victories.

Thérèse later wrote that she had received the grace of leaving her childhood by experiencing a "complete conversion" after Christmas Eve Mass in 1886. During what she called "the third period" of her life, she experienced charity entering her soul and the need to forget herself for the sake of others. A few days later, while looking at a picture of the crucified Christ, a "great thirst for souls" consumed her. She also comprehended that she was being asked to pour upon "souls" the blood of Christ flowing from "one of the divine hands." This thirst was partially slaked when she heard the news that the unrepentant murderer Henri Pranzini kissed the crucifix three times immediately before his execution. Thérèse referred to him, even in her last years, as her "first child"—convinced that her prayers had led to his conversion.

With an ardent desire to suffer for God and to pray for sinners, Thérèse wanted to enter the Carmelite monastery in Lisieux when she was fourteen years of age, but was told to wait until she was twenty-one. However, when she, her father, and her sister Céline pilgrimaged to Rome, Thérèse personally asked Pope Leo XIII to intervene. He said, "If it is God's will, you will enter." Unmoved by his response, she had to be removed from his presence by the papal guards. However, she did enter Carmel at the age of fifteen.

For the next ten years—until her slow, excruciating death from tuberculosis before she was twenty-five years old—Thérèse lived her famous "Little Way," an attitude of soul that stamped her entire relationship with God. The "greatest thing" God had done for her, in her view, was to have revealed her "littleness, her impotence." Concomitant with this awakening was the insight that one should not become discouraged if one falls because little children often fall, but they are rarely injured. With perfect confidence in and total abandonment to God, she lived expecting everything from God alone. In fact, Thérèse's life is a commentary on St. Paul's: "when I am weak, then I am strong" (2 Cor 12:10).

The power of Thérèse's Little Way flows from the living out of her favorite quotation from St. John of the Cross: "Love is repaid by love alone." She measured sanctity not by heroic deeds but by the quality of love with which anything is done. "Pure love," to her way of thinking, was of more value to the Church than all the works that have ever been done. Her Little Way, therefore, is essentially the martyrdom of filling ordinary life with extraordinary love. She wanted to cast at Jesus the "flowers of little sacrifices" filled with love. To desire and to succeed in filling each moment with perfect love is not a little way but the full flowering of Christian life.

The Little Way can also be described as her vocation. Although a Carmelite nun and despite her "littleness," she also felt interiorly the vocation of the warrior, the priest, the apostle, the doctor, and the martyr. Contemplating St. Paul's famous twelfth and thirteenth chapters in his first epistle to the Corinthians, Thérèse apprehended that "LOVE COMPRISED ALL VOCATIONS, THAT LOVE WAS EVERYTHING, THAT IT EMBRACED ALL TIMES AND PLACES. IN A WORD, THAT IT WAS ETERNAL! Then, in the excess of my delirious joy, I cried out: O Jesus, my Love. My *vocation*, at last I have found it. MY VOCATION IS LOVE!"[2]

In its profoundest dimension the Thérèsian Little Way is one of the "Holy Face," love's victim-face of Isaiah's Suffering Servant. Isaiah's words describing the "no beauty" and "no comeliness" in the Suffering Servant was the foundation for all her piety: "I, too, have desired to be without beauty, alone in treading the winepress, unknown to everyone."[3]

Thérèse of the Holy Face lived an intense suffering-servant, or "victim-soul," mysticism. Victim souls are not those who experience the cross as the setbacks encountered in apostolic undertakings but the ones who manifest God's hand even in life's apparent absurdities: natural failings, physical defects, sickness, old age, and death. More important, they are the ones who have also grasped the redemptive value of suffering, that is, how even hidden, sacrificial love is apostolic. As Thérèse wrote, "My 'little life' is to suffer; that's it."[4] The victim-soul mystic is the prime example of the person who passionately desires to suffer like Jesus for the world's redemption by filling each moment with total and radical self-emptying love.

Hans Urs von Balthasar, the distinguished Swiss theologian, held the view that Thérèse was not a mystic because her Little Way seems incompatible with mysticism's heights. He seems to have confused the genuine mystic with the ecstatic—and with those who experience a variety of secondary mystical phenomena.

Although Thérèse was not an ecstatic mystic, it would be difficult to find a person in the Christian mystical tradition whom God had so radically purified at such an early age—if, indeed, she needed such purgation. From the age of three, she claimed that she never refused God anything. The least trace of imperfection or infidelity horrified her. In time, her only joy was to suffer for Christ, and she rejoiced that "this *unfelt* joy is above every other joy."[5]

It is also true that Thérèse neither desired nor experienced many secondary mystical phenomena. For example, she said explicitly, "I can nourish myself on nothing but truth. This is why I've never wanted any visions."[6] On one occasion, however, she did experience a "flight of the spirit" that cast a veil over all created things. "It was as if someone had lent me a body," she wrote. "I remained that way for one whole week."[7] She was convinced that at one point God had flooded her soul with a transforming light and revealed that she would become a great saint—once her posthumous glory became evident.

From the age of fourteen, Thérèse experienced "transports of love" that consumed her and reached their zenith in her "Oblation to Merciful Love" on June 9, 1895, when she offered herself totally as a "victim of holocaust" for the salvation of others. A violent love for God seized her like an all-consuming fire: "Oh! What fire and what sweetness at one and the same time! I was on fire with love, and I felt that one minute more, one second more, and I wouldn't be able to sustain this ardor without dying."[8]

Thérèse wrote of enjoying a "living faith," a very "clear faith," that made the thought of heaven the main source of her happiness. But an all-consuming trial of faith accompanied her sufferings from tuberculosis the last year and a half of her life. The "thickest darkness" invaded her soul and transformed the thought of heaven from something so "sweet" into a "cause of struggle and torment." The sense that heaven did not exist tortured her because, to her way of thinking, "it is upon heaven that everything hinges. How strange and incoherent this is!"[9]

To describe her experience of spiritual dereliction, Thérèse imagined growing up in a land of thick fog where one never experienced sunshine. A new land captured her imagination, one transformed and drenched by brilliant sunlight to which she would someday go. Just as Christopher Columbus had a presentiment of a new world, Thérèse always knew in "lively faith" that a heavenly "Fatherland" existed. However, as time went on, the fog in her soul became thicker and the darkness spoke mockingly: "Advance, advance: rejoice in death which will give you not what you hope for but a night still more profound, the night of nothingness."[10]

Unlike God's crucifying absence—one of the characteristics of the classical dark night of the spirit—Thérèse agonized over having her natural satisfaction in desiring heaven destroyed. Her "veil of faith" became a "wall" that caused her to lose the "joy of faith." She professed to Jesus, however, that she was willing to shed her blood to the last drop to witness to her faith in heaven's existence.

Thérèse insisted that she *wanted* to believe and no longer had any desire except that of loving to the point of dying from love. This seeming absence of faith actually deepened her faith: "Since the time He permitted me to suffer temptations against the *faith*, He has greatly increased the *spirit of faith* in my heart."[11] Her dark night of the soul also revealed heaven's real attraction for her: "Oh! It's Love! To love, to be loved, and to return to the earth to make love loved."[12]

Thérèse's remarkable God-consciousness puts her mysticism into sharp focus: she never passed more than a few minutes without thinking of God. It is also instructive how often the words "God alone" and "Jesus alone" appear in her writings. "I delivered myself totally to Jesus" is another refrain in her mystical life. She was nothing less than a God-haunted, God-possessed woman with a steely determination to be nourished on Truth alone and to fill each moment with self-emptying love. Her crucifying desire and ability to love God and Christ alone, her steadfastness during long periods of spiritual dereliction, her thirst for souls, and her radical suffering-servant mysticism amply illustrate that Thérèse had attained mystical maturity through the fullness of her Christian faith, hope, and love. Despite von Balthasar's opinion, a strong case can be made that Thérèse is one of the outstanding mystics in the Christian tradition.

Thérèse's prioress, Mother Agnes (who was her older sister Pauline), convinced her to write about her life, which resulted in the book now known as *The Story of a Soul*. Controversy continues to surround the book—as well as Thérèse's poems, letters, and plays—because her texts were emended by her sister to conform better to the ideals of nineteenth-century bourgeois piety. The unexpurgated manuscripts, eventually published, reveal a much less saccharine figure than the "Little Flower" of traditional piety—in fact, one far stronger and even somewhat darker.

Some readers find Thérèse's flowery and childlike language a major obstacle to appreciating her spiritual and mystical profundity. Even the unedited texts indicate that she sometimes used the "precious" religious language of her times. And she did write mainly for family, community members, and friends—not for the general public. The fact remains that her writings reveal someone who has gone to the heart of and lived the Christian gospel.

Only a few months before her death, she prayed that her mission in heaven would be to teach her Little Way, to make others love God as much as she loved him. Moments before her death, Thérèse said, "Never would I have believed it was possible to suffer so much! [She didn't receive a single injection of morphine.] Never! Never! I cannot explain this except by the ardent desires I have had to save souls."[13] She did not fear death because, as she said, "*I am not dying; I am entering into life!*"[14]

# Gemma Galgani

(1878–1903)

*"Listen, Jesus, to what the Confessor asks me: 'What do you do, Gemma, when you are before Jesus?' What do I do? If I am with Jesus Crucified I suffer, and if with Jesus in His Sacrament, I love."*[1]

Jesus Christ was faithful to the promise he made to Maria Gemma Umberta Pia Galgani in a vision that she would travel the entire mystical journey. The frequency and variety of arresting mystical phenomena that transformed and filled the life of this "daughter of the Passion" stand out as the salient feature of her mysticism. Perhaps no one in the entire Christian mystical tradition experienced more unusual mystical manifestations—and in such a short time—than Gemma Galgani. Numerous trinitarian, Christ-centered, Marian, and eucharistic illuminations—as well as raptures, ecstasies, seraphic wounds of love, visions, locutions, the *complete* stigmata, bloody sweat, tears of blood, mystical effluvia (perfumed bodily secretions), and satanic attacks—filled her daily life. Never has the extraordinary been so ordinary.

On March 12, 1878, Gemma Galgani was born the fourth of eight children of fairly well-to-do parents at Camigliano, near Lucca, in Tuscany. When her mother died in 1886, the "seraphic virgin of Lucca," as she is called, attended the school run by the sisters of St. Zita but soon terminated her education because of ill health. Her father's eventual bankruptcy and then death in 1896 exposed the family to extreme poverty. A few years later, Cecilia Giannini asked Gemma's brother to allow her to live with the Giannini family in Lucca, where she spent her remaining four years of life. She and Cecilia Giannini, the family matriarch, became close friends and confidants.

Illness prevented Gemma from becoming a Passionist nun, a vocation that attracted her because of this order's emphasis upon reparation and propitiation by "filling up what is lacking in Christ's sufferings" through one's own. She did take a vow of chastity, later took privately the vows of Passionist nuns, and not long before her death, worked toward establishing a Passionist convent in Lucca. Dying an agonizing death on Holy Saturday, April 11, 1903, the "Daughter of the Passion" was canonized May 3, 1940. Her fame spread quickly, mainly because of the publication of her correspondence with her spiritual director, Germano di San Stanislao Ruoppolo, C.P.

Gemma possessed uncommon spiritual gifts even as a child. Before she was five years old, she spent time methodically meditating upon God and Christ's passion. Effortless prayer that absorbed her soul into God and powerful light-filled visions of Christ—"not seen with the eyes of the body"—soon became her daily fare. "I have been in the presence of Jesus," she related. "I said nothing to Him and He said nothing to me; we both remained in silence; I looked at Him and He looked at me. But if you only knew how delightful it is to be thus in the presence of Jesus."[2]

Even when Gemma was a child, a concomitant sense of sin permeated her prayer—to the point that she believed she would die. Even the presence of Christ often intensified the awareness of her transgressions: "Oh, how I blush and tremble at seeing myself so unclean in His (Jesus') presence."[3] Many mystics have testified that the deeper one's experience of the holy, the more trenchant the experience of even one's slightest fault. However, it is highly unusual to find this phenomenon in one so young.

When Gemma made her First Communion at nine years of age, she experienced mystical union with Christ. Especially on the anniversary of this day, she remembered ecstatically what had transpired between her and Jesus. She spoke of the tabernacle as "paradise" and suffered greatly from her intense desire to receive Jesus as "food." Her eucharistic mysticism experienced the sacrament of Jesus' Body and Blood as the "academy of love," wherein one learns how to love. "The school is the supper-room," she said, "Jesus is the master, the doctrines are his flesh and blood."[4]

Many mystics have been graced with the ability to find God in all things. A divine light that penetrated, illuminated, and animated all things is a salient feature of Gemma's mysticism. Another was her gift of constantly experiencing Christ's presence through what is now called an "exchange of hearts": "The Heart of Jesus and my heart are one and the same thing."[5] The exchange nurtured a "new life," in which she experienced a vocation to imitate "Calvary's victim" by living for love alone and by making reparation for the sins of the world.

During a vision of Christ crucified, Gemma understood that the nails, the cross, and the blood were all the works of love of the "sacrificing priest." She, in turn, experienced herself also as a victim and desired that she "be suffering itself"—so that *everyone* might be saved. When it seemed to her that Jesus had used the word "abandon" with respect to a known sinner, she offered herself as a willing victim for him and even chided Jesus: "In your mouth, who are mercy itself, that word 'abandon' sounds badly; you must not say it."[6] With respect to another sinner, she offered years of her life in exchange for his conversion. "Jesus," she prayed, "I give you three years of my life; convert him for me."[7] Her harshest recorded words were directed at her spiritual father because he spoke of cutting off contact with an obdurate penitent. Witnesses attest, too, that she often had ecstatic conversations with "Divine Justice," pleading for the conversion of a known sinner.

Once on the eve of the feast of the Sacred Heart, Christ appeared and opened his wounds, from which came flames of fire. "In an instant," Gemma related, "those flames came to touch my hand, my feet and my heart. I rose to go to bed, and became aware that blood was flowing from those parts where I felt pain."[8] During Holy Week 1899, she had a vision of Christ crucified, accompanied by a mysterious "exhausting and consuming"—but "delightful"—inner fire, which moved throughout her body as the weeks went on, and left in its wake *all* the marks of Jesus' passion: the bloody sweat, the crowning with thorns, the scourging, the shoulder wound from carrying the cross, the bruised knees from falling under the weight of the cross, the nail holes in the hands and feet, the thirst on the cross, the lance wound in the side, and the overall agony of Gethsemane and Calvary. I know of no one else in the entire Christian mystical tradition for whom this claim has been made.

Gemma described her increasing physical and spiritual dereliction as the "wrath of my divine Father" and of "being in hell." Severe temptations often plagued her—the worst being the "satanic" suggestion that Christ had rejected her. Yet, Christ revealed to her during an ecstatic vision that Satan would be unleashed to put the "last touch" to Christ's work in her, which would fortify her in his war against Satan. Gemma claimed that Satan often physically beat her and the bruises were attested to by some in her household. The Desert Fathers wrote of this phenomenon, but its precise nature is still a matter of theological and psychological debate. Satan also taunted her for praying to "Christ the malefactor," "who makes all who love Him suffer."[9]

The frequency of her visions of and conversations with a "guardian angel" makes Gemma unique in the Christian mystical tradition. Early in her life, Gemma's guardian angel assured her that Jesus would be her "guide and inseparable companion." She complained on occasion that her angel was a "little severe," but said that she was "glad of it." During one appearance, her guardian angel instructed her to restrict her "conversation" to him and Jesus and to converse with no other creature.

Gemma's mystical life underscores the fact that God's purifying, illuminating, and transforming self-communication—"infused contemplation," to use an older terminology—often cannot be distinguished clearly from the astonishing phenomena she received. It was often through these unusual occurrences that she both received and expressed God's loving self-communication. If past studies tended to overemphasize unusual experiences at the expense of "infused contemplation," contemporary studies tend to distinguish them too sharply.

Some contemporary commentators dismiss unusual phenomena as insignificant, as "other-worldly," and as detracting from genuine Christian living. Not a few consider them to be "miraculous." Unusual mystical phenomena are perhaps best viewed as the echoes, reverberations, radiations, shock waves, and aftereffects of God's purging, illuminating, and unifying self-communication as it is refracted into the mystic's full body-person. Gemma's psychosomatic structure adjusted to God's self-communication at her deepest core by means of these phenomena. God purified, illuminated, transformed, and integrated Gemma's entire body-person into his life by means of these psychosomatic phenomena.

These phenomena also express symbolically the way Gemma's deepest mystical life reached her surface mind, various levels of her psyche, and her body. They should be compared, therefore, to the poetry, literature, music, paintings, and sculptures of the world's great artists. As such, they can be no more dismissed as "irrelevant" to the mystic's life than can dreams be considered irrelevant to one's psychological life. Gemma's mystical life, her sanctity, her heroic virtue, and her passionate desire to participate in Christ's redemptive work cannot be understood without them.

The Christian mystics unanimously teach that such phenomena may be caused by autosuggestion, by the demonic, or by God. If they come from the self, they produce aridity, not transformation. Phenomena of demonic origin lead a person away from holiness and cause deformation. However, genuine God-induced unusual phenomena leave behind in their wake faith, hope, love, humility, heroic virtue, and peace. The enhancement of life at all levels of the person's being—full Christian transformation—attests to their authenticity. They both flow from holiness and increase it.

From early childhood, Gemma rejoiced that time passed by so quickly because she wished to spend less time in this world, where nothing attracted her. The day before her agonizing death, she had called out to a friend who wanted to leave so that she could rest a bit: "Don't leave me until I am nailed to the Cross. I have to be crucified with Jesus."[10] Her last words: "Now it is indeed true that nothing more remains to me, Jesus, I recommend my poor soul to you, Jesus!"[11] She is indeed the "Daughter of the Passion" whose heaven is the crucified and risen Christ.

# Elizabeth of the Trinity

## (1880–1906)

*"I leave you my devotion to the Three, to 'Love.' Live within Them in the heaven of your soul; the Father will overshadow you, placing something like a cloud between you and the things of this earth to keep you all His. The Word will imprint in your soul, as in a crystal, the image of His own beauty; the Holy Spirit will transform you into a mysterious lyre, which, in silence, beneath His divine touch, will produce a magnificent canticle to Love."[1]*

Despite dying at the young age of twenty-six, Elizabeth of the Trinity not only attained the heights of sanctity but is also acknowledged as one of the greatest mystics of the twentieth century. Called the apostle of the indwelling Trinity, she was beatified by Pope John Paul II in 1984. Born Elizabeth Catez at a military camp in France where her father was stationed as a military officer, she developed into a vivacious, socially successful, iron-willed girl who loved sports, nature, and won first prize for piano at the Conservatory in Dijon.

Reminiscing about her spiritually precocious childhood, Elizabeth wrote, "I was very fond of prayer, and I loved God so much that even before my First Communion, I could not understand how it was possible to give one's heart to anyone else. From that time on, I was determined to love Him alone and to live only for Him."[2] The day of her First Communion, she met Mother Marie of Jesus, the prioress of the nearby Carmel of Dijon, who explained that the name "Elizabeth" meant "House of God." Even then, "Sabeth," as she was called, knew that she housed the three Persons of the Blessed Trinity. The key phrase throughout Sabeth's writings, "in the heaven of my soul," summarizes her doctrine and inner life.

When fourteen years of age, Elizabeth began to think seriously of a vocation to the local Carmelite monastery and took a vow of perpetual virginity. She asked permission to enter Carmel when she was only seventeen, but her mother insisted that she wait until she was twenty-one. Thus, in the intervening years, she lived the Carmelite life as much as she possibly could at home. A year before her entrance, she met Père Gonzalve Vallé, a well-known Dijon Dominican preacher, who explained with theological sophistication what she already experienced: the mystery of the triune indwelling in the soul.

The salient feature of Sabeth's spirituality and mysticism was her profound awareness of being plunged ever more deeply into the trinitarian abyss. The soul, to her way of thinking, is a crystal that reflects the Trinity, a mirror in which the Trinity loves to contemplate its beauty. As a "mystical bride," Elizabeth experienced "the Father, the Word, and the Spirit possessing the soul, deifying it, consuming it in the One by love."[3]

In one of Elizabeth's best-known prayers, she adored the Trinity as the "Unchanging One," begged the Father that she be further plunged into his Mystery, implored the "Eternal Word" that she spend her life listening to him, and beseeched the Holy Spirit to come upon her, create in her a kind of incarnation of the Word so "that I may be another humanity in which He can renew His whole Mystery."[4] When Sabeth surrendered to the Three as their "prey," she discovered that it was in them that she could love herself properly.

As a member of the zealous Dijon Carmelite community under the able leadership of Mother Germaine, Elizabeth deepened her already considerable gifts for silence, recollection, and prayer in the "little cell of her heart." In a short time, she understood that her vocation was "to live by love," to be a "praise of Glory," to be "always giving thanks," and to be a silent soul that is like a delicate musical instrument "under the mysterious touch of the Holy Spirit."[5] She learned that the silent soul simply "gazes" at God in faith and simplicity in order to become a "bottomless abyss" into which the Trinity can flow and expand.

Carmelites view their vocation as a *life* of prayer. Sabeth understood prayer not as the mechanical recitation of many prayers but as a relaxation in which the soul bathes in the trinitarian "Ocean." Faith in the Trinity's love—not feelings—is what is of supreme importance to her. The Trinity, in her experience, flows into the soul and the soul flows into the Trinity through what she calls a "heart-to-heart" exchange.

"Since He is always with me," she writes, "prayer, the heart-to-heart exchange should never end! I feel Him so alive in my soul. I have only to recollect myself to find Him within me, and that is my whole happiness."[6] In Sabeth's view, prayer is as simple as doing everything in the presence of the "Three Guests" in her soul.

Sabeth understood the Carmelite life not only as contemplative but also as apostolic. One must stay "buried in the contemplation" of the gospel "Mary"—whom she confused with Mary Magdalene—even when duty calls to perform the busy tasks of gospel "Martha." (Elizabeth had been baptized on the feast day of the Magdala [July 22] and had deep devotion to her because Mary loved and felt loved by Christ.) By "staying at the Source," Carmelites radiate God and give him to "souls." Contemplative love is itself apostolic, to her way of thinking, and the greatest good one can do for others. Love, giving God to others through contemplative prayer, is the Church's greatest apostolate because through this activity one does what one will do for all eternity—love. "I wish," she wrote, "to be wholly silent, wholly adoring, so that I may enter into Him ever more deeply and be so filled with Him that I can give Him through prayer to these poor souls who are unaware of the Gift of God."[7] Two words summarize Elizabeth's view on holiness and the apostolate: "Union and Love."

In Elizabeth's view, the life of the Virgin Mary from the annunciation to the nativity is the perfect exemplar of the interior life. In fact, the goal of Carmelite life is to be an Advent to prepare for God's Incarnation—not only in oneself but also in others. She desired to be so thoroughly transformed that the Father would recognize only Christ when he looked at her. In line with an ancient tradition, she prayed for the Son to be born in her heart just as the Word pours forth from the Father's bosom.

Elizabeth understood that a Carmelite is one who has "gazed" (one of her favorite words) on the crucified Christ offering himself to his Father as a "victim for souls." The Pauline admonition to be configured into the pattern of Christ's death and to fill up what is lacking in his passion played a significant role in why she understood her vocation as apostolic. Having become a "prey" of the Trinity's love and bathed in Christ's blood, she experienced them saying Mass with her as "the little sacrifice," the "host," and "the victim of the praise of God's glory." She wanted nothing less than mystical death, to have her whole substance consumed, to feel her being distilled drop by drop—as an oblation for the salvation of others. Thus, one sees in Elizabeth another example of "suffering-servant" and "victim-soul" mysticism in which one is emptied like Christ so that others may be filled with eternal life.

Although Elizabeth lacked a formal education and received no specific theological training, she did write several short treatises in the last few months before her death: *Heaven in Faith*, *Last Retreat*, *The Greatness of Our Vocation*, and *Let Yourself Be Loved*. Her more than three hundred extant letters to people from many walks of life reveal much about her spiritual journey and her gifts of discernment.

Elizabeth's suffering-servant mysticism reached its peak in those final months of her short five years in Carmel. "Everything passes!" she wrote. "In the evening of life love alone remains."[8] She was convinced that her spiritual motherhood, her mission, would continue even after death: "I think in heaven that my mission will be to draw souls by helping them to go out of themselves in order to cling to God by a wholly simple and loving movement, and to keep them in this great silence, which will allow God to communicate Himself to them and to transform them into Himself."[9] The mysterious beauty of the truth of the communion of saints—that the deeper one enters into the trinitarian life, the deeper one enters into the lives of all those God loves—was for her an experiential reality. Her last intelligible words: "I am going to Light, to Love, to Life!"[10]

# Pierre Teilhard de Chardin

## (1881–1955)

*"No one, I think, will understand the great mystics—St. Francis and Blessed Angela and the others—unless he understands the full depth of the truth that* Jesus must be loved as a world."[1]

No person in the Christian mystical tradition has the credentials of Pierre Teilhard de Chardin: Jesuit priest, distinguished member of the French Academy of Science, paleontologist, world traveler, poet, visionary, and mystic. It is difficult to find someone who lived such an intense spiritual and mystical life as Teilhard and yet was so passionately in tune with the secularity of his era. Intense love for science, the world, and their projects filled his soul. He claimed that because he was a priest, he wished with all his strength to be the first to become aware of what the "world" loves, seeks, and suffers. "I desire," he wrote, "to be . . . the first in self-fulfillment, the first in self denial—I want to be more widely human in my sympathies and more nobly terrestrial in my ambitions than any of the world's servants."[2]

As scientist, Teilhard considered himself to be a "priest performing a holy task"; as Jesuit, a missionary to the world of science. For him, science itself is a mysticism, a search for absolute meaning, a quest to understand and comprehend the universe as a whole. "The scientist's quest," he wrote, "however positivistic he may claim it to be is invincibly animated, fundamentally, by a mystical hope."[3] Teilhard desired to help others to discover the mystical vibration inherent in genuine scientific discovery, that God can be found in the very act of scientific endeavor. He also wished to disclose to scientists the ultimate meaning and coherence of the universe that is both personal and loving because of "the science of Christ through all things."[4]

Teilhard speaks of two supreme loves, the natural and the supernatural, which seem to pull the human heart toward either the mastery of the earth or toward the kingdom of heaven. These only seemingly contrary loves, in his view, are reconciled through an impassioned quest for the cosmic Christ: "It is *through the fulfillment of the world*," he writes, "that we reach Jesus."[5] Uniting and reconciling in himself the two worlds of science and Christianity, the religions of earth and heaven, Teilhard's genius consists of transforming within himself—without deformation—the "God of the Gospel" into the "God of evolution" by explaining how evolution is a "christifying" process with "Christ the Evolver" at the heart of the evolutionary process.

Born of a gentleman farmer and a devout mother in Sarcenat, France, Teilhard entered the novitiate of the Society of Jesus at Aix-en-Province in 1899 and was ordained priest in 1911. Throughout his long years of Jesuit training in the classics, philosophy, and theology, he was attracted to the natural sciences, especially to geology and paleontology. His "naturally pantheistic soul" found matter "intoxicating." At the very core of the ocean of matter, Pierre had discovered what he called the "Great Stability." Resonating passionately with this Great Stability, he experienced himself as having become "pure light" and understood the mystic as the one who lives "to give place in his experience to this aureole."[6]

After serving as a stretcher-bearer in World War I, Teilhard completed his doctorate in paleontology at the Sorbonne in 1922. For almost twenty-five years, he worked in China, took part in numerous scientific expeditions to Central Asia, India, and Burma, and gained a notable reputation as a paleontologist. Returning to Paris to continue his research and writings in 1946, he subsequently undertook an archeological expedition to South Africa in 1951. After that, he settled as a research scholar at the Wenner Gren Foundation in New York City and died there on Easter Sunday, April 10, 1955.

During his lifetime, Teilhard had been unable to obtain permission from his religious superiors to publish his controversial philosophical, spiritual, and theological writings. Thus, his only published works had been scientific papers. But from 1955 on, all his writings were published, and the response to his daring, brilliant, and creative synthesis of science and religion was exceptional. The essence of his scientific-mystical ideas may be found in his books, *The Phenomenon of Man*, *The Divine Milieu*, *Writings in Time of War*, *The Future of Man*, *Hymn of the Universe*, *The Heart of Matter*, *The Making of a Mind*, *Science and Christ*, and numerous other works.

Teilhard's is a mysticism of "seeing" that evolution permeates everything and literally converges on the person of Jesus Christ. In his view, nothing is profane for the one who knows how to see. "I believe that the universe is an evolution," Teilhard writes. "I believe that evolution proceeds toward spirit. I believe that *in man*, spirit is fully realized in person. I believe that the supremely personal is the Universal Christ."[7] As expressed in his neologisms, "cosmogenesis" (the coming to be of the universe) is "biogenesis" (the coming to be of life) is "anthropogenesis" (the coming to be of man) is "Christo-genesis" (the coming to be of the one cosmic Christ).

Teilhard never had the least difficulty during his entire lifetime in addressing God as a "Supreme Someone."[8] His emphasis, however, was upon a "Christo-cosmic" mysticism that stressed "the God who makes himself cosmic and an evolution which makes itself a person."[9] The Christian tradition, in his view, understood more in the "total Christ" than "just" God and man. Saint Paul, for example, wrote of Christ as the one in whom all creation holds together. Teilhard maintained that everything in the universe converges on Jesus' "theandric being," which he called (controversially) Christ's "third nature," a nature neither human nor divine but cosmic. If St. Bruno emphasized Christ the poor Man; St. Dominic, Christ the Truth; St. Ignatius, Christ the eternal King—Teilhard proclaimed Christ the Evolver, the cosmic Christ.

During a meditation on an image of the Sacred Heart of Jesus, Teilhard realized that the metallic nature of the strange patch of crimson and gold at the center of Christ's breast allowed "a way of finally *escaping* from everything that so distressed [him] in the complicated, frail, and individual organization of Jesus' body."[10] The "historical difficulties" attached to the gospels made "the face of the historical Jesus" difficult for Teilhard to grasp. "My basic disposition?" he wrote. "What is past and dead no longer interests me."[11]

The meditation of the Sacred Heart of Jesus, however, awakened Teilhard to a "Christic milieu" beyond the limitations of the historical Jesus. Only in this Christic milieu can one approach what Teilhard called God's "heart." He professed belief in Jesus' divinity *"insofar as, and in the form in which* that divinity is historically and biologically included in the reality of the universal Christ to whom his faith and his worship are more directly attached."[12] Moreover, given the scientific knowledge of a vast universe replete with billions of galaxies and the statistical necessity of intelligent life on other planets, he argued that Jesus of Nazareth is only "one face" of the cosmic Christ.[13] The Christ of St. Paul and St. John cannot be smaller than the cosmos.

Teilhard preferred to view Jesus Christ as the "universal Christ," the "total Christ," the "cosmic Christ," the "super-Christ," the "privileged central axis of evolution," the "Soul of the world," the "Evolver," the "Christic nucleus" of an evolving cosmos that surpasses any prophet or Buddha. It is little wonder that some commentators have called Teilhard's view a "Christian pantheism," a "panchristic monism," a "Christo-monism," a "panchristism"—even a "Christo-fascism."

Paradoxically—and inadequately thought out in Teilhard's writings—his enthusiasm for the cosmic Christ of an evolving universe did not diminish his love for Jesus of Nazareth. "However far we may be drawn into the divine space opened to us by Christian mysticism," he wrote, "we never depart from the Jesus of the Gospels."[14] To his way of thinking, only a contemporary Gnostic would attempt to divorce the cosmic Christ from the historical Jesus. Orthodox reasoning also demands that the cosmic Christ remains inextricably linked to the historical Jesus, "otherwise the historical Jesus would not be truly inserted into the cosmos."[15]

Despite Teilhard's controversial emphasis upon the cosmic Christ, he did not contend that Jesus' human reality dissolved into something superhuman to vanish into the cosmos. "If it is indeed true that it is through Christ-Omega that the universe in movement holds together," Teilhard wrote, "it is from that Man of Nazareth, that Christ-Omega (both theoretically and historically) derives his whole consistence. The two terms are intrinsically one whole, and they cannot vary, in a truly total Christ, except simultaneously."[16] Saint Paul said little about the historical details of Jesus' life, death, and resurrection, but never separated his Christ from the actual Jesus of testimony; this is also true of Teilhard.

The historical Jesus and the cosmic Christ remain linked in Teilhard's thinking for yet another reason. Although he maintained that creation, incarnation, and redemption must be understood as more of a cosmic process than an instantaneous act, he wrote that they do "take the form of particular *expressive* facts such as the historical appearance of the human type (creation), the birth of Christ (incarnation), and his death and resurrection (redemption)."[17]

In Teilhard's relatively well-known work "The Mass of the World," he described finding himself in the desert without bread and wine to say Mass. As substitutes, he offered all the world's efforts, accomplishments, sufferings, and deaths—as well as his own—as the elements to be transubstantiated into the Body and Blood of Christ. He wrote, "Over every living thing which is to spring up, to grow, to flower, to ripen during this day say again the words: This is my Body. And over every death-force which awaits in readiness to corrode, to wither, to cut down, speak again your commanding words which express the supreme mystery of faith: This is my Blood."[18]

The Teilhardian vision sees the eons-old "Eucharist of evolution" gradually consecrating all the elements of the cosmos into the one cosmic Christ. Looking upon the cosmos as one immense host, Teilhard understands the Eucharist to be the axis of evolution through which Christ produces a cosmic transubstantiation of all things into himself. "At every moment," Teilhard writes, "the Eucharistic Christ controls— from the point of view of the organization of the Pleroma—the whole movement of the universe. As our humanity assimilates the material world, and as the Host assimilates our humanity, the eucharistic transformation goes far beyond and completes the transubstantiation of the bread on the altar. Step by step it irresistibly invades the universe."[19] Only one thing is happening throughout the cosmos: the incarnation-birth-passion-death-resurrection "event" that completes itself in each individual and society through the cosmic Eucharist.

Because of Teilhard's views on christifying evolution through developing one's talents to the utmost in order to build a better world, he criticized certain traditional notions about suffering and the cross. The crucified Christ, to his way of thinking, is the "supreme paradigm of progress," not "a symbol of sadness, of limitation, and of repression."[20] Jesus on the cross both realizes and symbolizes the immense human labor over the millennia that is slowly bringing about the cosmic Christ. Jesus on the cross "represents in a true sense creation, upheld by God, as it ascends the slope of being, sometimes clinging to things for support, sometimes tearing itself away from them in order to pass beyond them, and always compensating, by physical suffering, for the setbacks caused by its moral downfalls."[21]

Teilhard understood suffering as an evolutionary energy that promotes Christogenesis. In a letter to his invalid sister, Marguerite, he wrote of traveling the world, giving himself "soul and body to the positive forces of the universe," while she was stretched out on her bed of pain, "silently, deep within [herself], transforming into light the world's most grievous shadows. In the eyes of the Creator, which of us will have had the better part?"[22] This is Teilhard's contemporary transposition of a suffering-servant mysticism.

Contemplative prayer and purity of heart, to Teilhard's way of thinking, are also the means through which the cosmos is healed, directed, and christified. He was fond of a story by Robert Hugh Benson in which a visionary enters an out-of-the-way chapel, finds a nun praying, and sees the axis of the universe passing through the chapel and all the elements of the cosmos reorganizing themselves around it. "All at once," Teilhard writes, "he sees the whole world bound up and moving and organizing itself around that out-of-the way spot, in tune with the intensity and inflexion of the desires of that puny, praying figure."[23] Because of this nun's contemplative faith and purity of heart, she is an energy center that spearheads the evolutionary process. Her efficacious and transformative contemplation gives life to, or "sur-animates," the universe. To paraphrase a well-known Zen saying, the Christian mystic contemplates for the universe.

The mysticisms of the major world religions had long fascinated Teilhard. His cosmopolitan and ecumenical spirit disposed him to learn as much as possible from the richness and diversity of other cultures. With high hopes Teilhard traveled to distant lands but he was soon disappointed by what he found. In China he found "nothing but the absence of thought, senile thought or infantile thought. Mongolia seemed to me asleep—perhaps dead."[24] Most of Islam he simply dismissed as a "backward-looking revival of Judaism that offers itself today as a principle of fixation and stagnation."[25] Hinduism, in his view, offered nothing more than the "numbing and deafening effect of a religion obsessed by material forms and ritualism."[26] The Hindu yogi tries to become a pure subject without the world of phenomena and ends up a "lonely Titan" swallowed up in a fruitless solipsism and egoism. "The Buddhist *denies* himself," he wrote, "in order to kill desire (he *does not believe* in the value of *being*)."[27]

All these religions failed because they did not come to grips with contemporary life. "No one," he wrote, "who has been deeply influenced by modern culture and the knowledge that goes with it can sincerely be a Confucian, a Buddhist, or Muslim (unless he is prepared to live a double life, or profoundly to modify for his own use the terms of his religion)."[28] They all led to a diminishment of consciousness and personhood because they did not "adhere" to evolution's "upward helical spiral." Despite trenchant criticisms of his understanding of what Teilhard called the "Road of the East," he never wavered from his negative assessment: "I still believe that *logically*, Eastern religions and contemplation kill action."[29]

Japanese mysticism fascinated Teilhard because of its grasp of the power of the "collective"—but it lacked an appreciation for the individual. Marxism also attracted him because of its appreciation of "collective man, humanity, the earth" and had awakened humanity to the power of politics, science, technology, evolution, the future, and the *human* ability to create a more humane world. On the other hand, because it essentially ignores the person to favor an abstract collective and also internationalizes hatred, Marxism demolishes the only basis for a solid humanism: love and compassion. Its rejection of personal immortality and real transcendence dooms humanity to this world and falls prey to the false hopes of an earthly utopia.

Teilhard was convinced that "Christianity alone saves the essential aspiration of all mysticism: *to be united* (that is, to become the other) *while remaining oneself.*"[30] Christianity, in his view, is the major axis for the development of the mysticism and religion of the future because it "extracts *all* that is sweetest and strongest circulating in all the human mysticisms, though without absorbing their evil or suspect elements."[31]

Because of Christian mysticism's excessively otherworldly communion with God that too quickly bypassed the desires of this world, however, Teilhard did not see it—as it had been or as it existed in his day—to be the mysticism for the contemporary age. He called for a "new mysticism," a future mysticism based not only upon a *"Christianity faithfully extended to its utmost limits,* but also upon a Christianity which surpasses itself."[32] Rejecting both the facile syncretism and the sterile "common core" views of so much of contemporary thought, Teilhard saw the major religions of the world "converging" upon and synthesizing around Christianity as the "principal axis" of evolution to bring about this new mysticism, a mysticism of convergence.

In summary, by focusing upon the cosmic Christ, Teilhard's "new mysticism" looks to a synthesis of three universal elements: the cosmic, the human, and the Christic. It blends in effect what he called

"Hindu totality," Western technology, Christian personalism—and brings together a faith that loves the earth, science, humanity, and Christ.

Teilhard's new mysticism also seeks to incorporate, sublate, and transform the pantheistic and dehumanizing tendencies of Eastern mysticisms, Marxist faith in humanity, and Christianity's traditional faith in a transcendent, personal God into a Christianity that surpasses itself. The legitimate aspirations of pantheistic Eastern mysticisms, Marxist humanism, and traditional Christianity are satisfied and fulfilled in the cosmic Christ in whom the All, evolution, and personality converge so that God will be All in all. "Jesus must be loved as a world."

# Edith Stein

## (1891–1942)

*"God is truth. All who seek truth seek God, whether this is clear to them or not."*[1]

German Jewish atheist and disciple of the philosopher Edmund Husserl, Edith Stein's written musings about him after his death say much about her spirituality: "It has always been far from me to think that God's mercy allows itself to be circumscribed by the visible church's boundaries. God is truth. All who seek truth seek God, whether this is clear to them or not."[2]

After reading the autobiography of Teresa of Avila, she converted to Catholicism and entered the Discalced Carmelite monastery in Cologne. To her way of thinking, the fundamental premise of Carmelite life—and all religious life—was "to stand in proxy for sinners through voluntary and joyous suffering and thus to cooperate in the salvation of humankind."[3] The contemplative life, in her view, was as simple as allowing oneself to be drawn into God and out of self (the word "ecstasy" often appears in her writings) so as to carry divine life to the world. Because nothing in Christ's being or in his decisions resisted perfect love, he was her model.

Stein took the name "Sister Teresa Benedicta of the Cross" to express her solidarity with the Jewish victims of Nazism: "By the cross I understood the destiny of God's people which, even at that time, began to announce itself. I thought that those who recognize it as the cross of Christ had to take it upon themselves in the name of all."[4]

Her masterpiece, *The Science of the Cross*, refracts the Nazi horrors of her day through the prism of the love mysticism of John of the Cross. Christians, to her way of thinking, must assimilate the truths of faith that shaped their lives, calling this "the science of the saints."

330

"If the mystery of the cross," she wrote, "becomes the inner form [of one's life], it grows into the science of the cross."[5] If we accept in faith that Christ's passion and death consumed our sins, we accept the whole Christ to walk the path of the imitation of Christ, which will lead us through his passion and cross to the glory of the resurrection. "This is exactly what is experienced in contemplation," she wrote, "passing through the expiatory flames to the bliss of the union of love. This explains its twofold character. It is death and resurrection. After the Dark Night, the Living Flame shines forth."[6]

Pope John Paul II's 1988 apostolic letter, The Dignity and Vocation of Woman, owes much to Edith Stein's pioneering work on this subject. She died in the Auschwitz gas chambers, and was canonized in 1998.

# Maria Faustina Kowalska

## (1905–38)

*"I saw a great radiance and, in the midst of it, God the Father. Between this radiance and the earth I saw Jesus, nailed to the cross in such a way that when God wanted to look at the earth, he had to look through the wounds of Jesus. And I understood that it was for the sake of Jesus that God blesses the earth."*[1]

During a particularly difficult period in her novitiate year of 1926–27 in Krakow, Maria Faustina Kowalska had a mysterious dream in which St. Thérèse of Lisieux assured her that the issues troubling her would soon be happily resolved. Faustina then asked if she would become not only a saint but also a canonized one, to which Thérèse replied, "yes, but you must trust in the Lord Jesus." On April 20, 2000, Faustina Kowalska was canonized and became the first saint of the new millennium.

On February 22, 1931, Faustina received the foundational revelation of her life: a vision of Jesus wearing a white garment, one hand held up in a gesture of blessing, and the other touching his breast. Two large rays—one red, the other pale—emanated from beneath the garment, slightly drawn aside at the breast. Jesus then instructed her to paint the image—with the signature "Jesus, I trust in You"—and to make known his desire that the image be venerated first in her chapel and then throughout the world. Faustina was also commanded—an injunction repeated several times throughout her life—to have this image blessed on the first Sunday after Easter, which was to become the "Feast of Mercy."

Faustina stands in a long line of mystics in the Christian tradition whose mysticism contains a "prophetic" dimension. These mystics received divine revelations, including a message for the universal

Church that its members must heed. This phenomenon also indicates that the line between "mystic" and "prophet" should not be too sharply drawn.

The Devotion to Divine Mercy spread rapidly (but not without setbacks) first in Poland and eventually to many foreign countries. In addition to the reverence shown to the painted image of Christ, Faustina's revelation led to praying the rosary in a particular way (the Divine Mercy "chaplet") in order to obtain the grace of a merciful death. After her death it led to the founding of a religious congregation devoted to Divine Mercy (established by Faustina's director, Rev. Professor Michael Sopocko). It is no coincidence that Pope John Paul II's 1980 encyclical, On the Mercy of God (*Dives in misericordia*), was influenced by Faustina's vision. The devotion to Divine Mercy saw its crowning point when he inaugurated the universal celebration of Divine Mercy Sunday in the year 2001.

"The Apostle of Divine Mercy" was born Helena Kowalska on August 25, 1905, in the village of Glogowiec, near Lodz, Poland. After a devout childhood, and without completing her elementary school education, Helena began doing household work in Aleksandrow, and then in Lodz, when she was only fourteen years old. Entering the Congregation of the Sisters of Our Lady of Mercy in 1925, she took the religious name Mary (Maria) Faustina, and worked mainly at domestic tasks in various houses of her congregation. Plagued with ill health from the time she entered religious life, she died from tuberculosis on October 5, 1938, in Krakow.

Outwardly, Faustina lived the "ordinary" life of an untalented and dedicated nun. In fact, her superiors had judged her to be "no one special." She kept a diary because her confessors, the Rev. Michael Sopocko and Father Joseph Andrasz, S.J. (the confessor and retreat director who set her completely at peace "for the first time"), commanded her to do so. Furthermore, Christ himself had ordered her to write so that after her death others might derive strength and consolation from what she had recorded about Divine Mercy.

Her diary, *Divine Mercy in My Soul: The Diary of the Servant of God Sister M. Faustina Kowalska, Perpetually Professed Member of the Congregation of Sisters of Our Lady of Mercy*, is one of the most striking examples of direct reporting of mystical experiences in Christian history and reveals a person who traveled the entire mystical path. The richness and variety of the mystical graces, states, and phenomena that she experienced are impossible to summarize in a short space. Thus, a few examples must suffice.

When Faustina was only twenty-four years old, she received "one of the extraordinary graces" of her life: a vision of Christ in which he tied around her waist the golden cincture he was wearing. "Since then," she wrote, "I have never experienced any attacks against this virtue [purity], either in my heart or in my mind."[2] Mystically "infused chastity," as we have seen, was also given to both Thomas Aquinas and Ignatius of Loyola.

Faustina valued prayer so highly that she claimed every single grace comes to the soul through it—an exaggeration many mystics would contradict. Her striking experiences of intimacy with God during prayer prompted her to confess that she could not live without God. One hour spent before the Blessed Sacrament, even in the "greatest dryness of spirit," meant more to her than hundreds of years of "worldly pleasures."

Her diary reveals the normal life of private, communal, and liturgical prayer practiced in religious orders and congregations. The eucharistic dimension of her spirituality, however, is especially salient. Claiming that the Sacrament nested in her heart, she confessed that it was only the Eucharist that enabled her to endure periods of unusual trials.

Ravishing prayer and "flashes of light" in Faustina's soul made hours of prayer seem like only minutes. The mere thought of contemplation plunged her more deeply into it and even the recollection of graces received this way caused her to lose herself in God. Uttering Jesus' name sometimes caused her to swoon; his "fiery love" transformed her into himself; and an interior fire enkindled her with such a love of God that she seemed to be dying. A "strange fire" and a "strange silence" entered her soul and effected an "utterly spiritual" communion with God and an "imperturbable silence." Staccato bursts of total absorption in God and complete self-forgetfulness led her to believe that God and the soul had merged. These brief periods of what she called a "higher form of prayer"—which rendered normal life seemingly unreal and dreamlike—produced such lasting effects that Faustina compared them to the happiness of the blessed in heaven.

Yet, Faustina wrote that neither her ecstasies nor this higher form of prayer interfered with her regular duties. Contemplative in action,

Faustina was able to "see God in everything" and to find God "every-where," even in "the most hidden things."[3]

Faustina's Divine Mercy mysticism is a further shaping of her spirituality of the Sacred Heart of Jesus, a devotion that was highly popular at that time. She promised that she would hide herself in the open wound of Christ's heart and prayed that the Father would view her sacrificial heart through the wound in Jesus' heart. She often beseeched Jesus to hide her in him as a drop of his own blood. During prayer before the Blessed Sacrament, she worshiped each of Jesus' five wounds and often "saw Jesus, nailed to the cross in such a way that when God wanted to look at the earth, he had to look through the wounds of Christ. And I understood that it was for the sake of Jesus that God blesses the earth."[4]

Faustina's diary indicates that she was a trinitarian mystic. Her desire to drown in God led to her union with the Three Persons, to a deeper "understanding" of the Trinity, to living in the "bosom of the Most Holy Trinity," and to being "immersed in the love of the Father, the Son, and the Holy Spirit."[5] With the eyes of her soul, she saw the Three Divine Persons—"but Their Essence was One." She experienced that when she was united to one Person, she was equally united to "the Second and to the Third."[6] In one remarkable passage, Faustina testified that *Christ's* "Trinitarian Being" enveloped her entirely and with such intimacy that her heart was married to his and she could "feel the faintest stir of His Heart and He, of mine."[7]

In a manner reminiscent of Ignatius's experience on the banks of the river Cardoner, God imparted to Faustina intellectual clarity and infused knowledge. Claiming that she rarely had apparitions, she contended, however, that her communion with God led to seeing all creation as God sees it and to understanding many mysteries of the faith, although she had not studied. She was also convinced that God had imparted "one mystery" that united her to the Trinity in such secrecy that "not even angels" knew of it. She lived by this mystery, which, she claimed, distinguished her "from every other soul here on earth or in eternity."[8]

No mystic has a romantic view of the life of prayer. Faustina's diary is replete with her trials, large and small: bone-marrow depression, discouragement, dryness, spiritual torpor, boredom, temptations, and the fear of illusion. Ill health, accusations of delusion, snide remarks and various harassments from those less dedicated to prayer, the deterioration of her body, and the final assaults of the spiritual dark night totally purified her.

A series of purifying illuminations left Faustina terrified and unable to pray as she had before; paradoxically, they also heightened her sense of God's mercy. When God's palpable presence disappeared, her every fault seemed to raise its ugly head. A horrible coldness seized her soul, her power to pray disappeared, and nothing could comfort her: not God, nor her confessor, nor any creature. Both her craving for God and the sense of her own misery intensified. Suspecting her of illusion, community members scornfully nicknamed her "dump."

In what Faustina experienced as Satan's most painful assault, he claimed boldly that he now possessed her and said, "You have been rejected by God!"[9] The word "rejected" became a fire that penetrated her entire being and caused her to cease looking for help anywhere. Her soul shrank into itself and lost sight of everything: "it is as though it has accepted the torture of being abandoned."[10] The experience of God's utter rejection and of her own utter sinfulness became her daily fare.

Faustina, however, never lost her desire to "save souls" and her readiness to die for them. She came to see her severe trials as an invitation from the Trinity to make reparation for the world's sins and to be the vehicle of God's mercy to hardened sinners (especially at the hour of their death). Accepting her vocation as filling up in a special way what is lacking in Christ's sufferings, this victim soul felt "transconsecrated." Her conviction that God had taken total possession of her soul became "a conscious reality that nothing can obscure."[11]

When Christ asked Faustina to be a living "host-sacrifice," she consented: "My name is to be 'sacrifice.'" Just as the priest consecrates the "white host," Christ the priest "transubstantiated" her in such a way that the "shell of her body" hid the sacrificial host her soul had become for sinners. Christ rendered Faustina selfless in yet another way: he asked for what was hers alone—her misery. From now on, she could claim absolutely nothing as her own—not even her misery.

Faustina willingly accepted her vocation as a suffering servant, to have "no other life but that of sacrifice." Through her identification with the crucified Christ, he would bless the world. Because Christ now lived a second passion in her heart, her apostolate was to suffer and to save more souls through her prayer and sacrifice than "a missionary through his teachings and sermons alone."[12] Not living for herself, she would live only for the Church and for the salvation of others.

Faustina understood her victim-soul mysticism in terms of the Father exercising his "justice" upon "pure and innocent souls." "These souls," she wrote, "are the victims who sustain the world and who fill up what is lacking in the Passion of Jesus. They are not many in number."[13] In her view, such persons are chosen for a higher form of holiness, and God demands greater love from them than he does from others. "The soul which is specially marked by God," she wrote, "will be distinguished everywhere, whether in heaven or in purgatory, or in hell."[14] Faustina had responded to this special calling wholeheartedly and distinguished herself as a "disciple of a crucified Master." This first saint of the new millennium is well called the Apostle of Divine Mercy.

# Karl Rahner

## (1904–84)

*"The devout Christian of the future will either be a 'mystic,' one who has experienced 'something,' or he will cease to be anything at all."*[1]

Karl Rahner is often called the theological titan of the twentieth century. Four thousand written works (paperback sales in excess of one million copies) and three volumes of television, radio, and newspaper interviews make up his bibliography. In addition, he engaged in backbreaking editorial work on theological encyclopedias, journals, and reference books. His writings evince his skill not only as a theologian but also as a spiritual director, a master of St. Ignatius's *Spiritual Exercises*, a gifted preacher, and a teacher of prayer. A dedicated ecumenist, he entered into dialogue with atheist, Buddhist, Jewish, Marxist, Muslim, Protestant, and scientific thinkers the world over. He has been called a Church Father and the quiet mover of the Catholic Church in the twentieth century.

Rahner was born in Freiburg in Breisgau, Germany, on March 5, 1904, and entered the novitiate of the Upper German Province of the Society of Jesus in 1922. After completing two years of novitiate and taking his Jesuit vows, Rahner began the normal course of studies for Jesuits. He went on for doctoral degrees in philosophy at Freiburg—where he studied under Martin Heidegger, the famous German philosopher—and then in theology at Innsbruck.

The beginning of the winter term at Innsbruck in 1937 was for Rahner the start of his thirty-four-year career as professor of theology. Only a year after his arrival, however, the Nazis took over the university and banished Rahner to Vienna. In 1948 he began to teach in the reconstituted theology faculty at Innsbruck and launched his extraordinarily prolific period of writing, lecturing, and publishing. In October 1962, he was appointed one of the official *periti*, or theological experts, of the Second Vatican Council (1962–65), a council whose theological outlook he significantly influenced.

In March 1964, he became the successor to Romano Guardini in the Chair of Christian World-View (*Weltanschauung*) at the University of Munich. In April 1967, he was appointed to what was to be his final teaching position, as professor of dogmatic theology at the University of Münster, where he taught from 1967 until his retirement in 1971. Living at the Jesuit writers' house in Munich from 1971 to 1981, and afterward with the Jesuit community in Innsbruck, Rahner continued his unrelenting worldwide lecturing, writing, and pastoral activity. Becoming ill a few days after the celebrations of his eightieth birthday, he died on March 30, 1984.

This simple, holy Jesuit priest is well known as a profound and prolific speculative theologian. However, he was without a doubt also the twentieth century's most important mystical theologian. Central to his thinking was the view that what haunts every human heart and is every person's deepest experience is of a God whose mystery, light, and love have embraced the total person. "In *every* human being," he wrote, "there is something like an anonymous, unthematic, perhaps repressed, basic experience of being orientated to God . . . which can be repressed but not destroyed, which is 'mystical' or (if you prefer a more cautious terminology) has its climax in what the older teachers called infused contemplation."[2] Thus, Rahner understood the human person as *homo mysticus*, as "mystical man."

In Rahner's view, everyone is conscious of God, not as the "predicamental" object of one's consciousness, but as the "transcendental horizon" of consciousness itself. This "implicit," "unthematic" form of God-consciousness—an actual mystical consciousness—forms the ambience, the undertow, or the basal spiritual metabolism, of daily life. The mystical experience of God, in Rahner's view, is really not *an* experience but the deepest aspect of all human experiences. When an interviewer said to Rahner, "I have never had an experience of God," Rahner quickly retorted, "I don't believe you; I just don't accept that. You have had, perhaps, no experience of God under this precise label *God* but you have had or have now an experience of God—and I am convinced that this is true of every person."[3]

Rahner held the view that everyone—even the agnostic or atheist—who lives moderately, selflessly, honestly, courageously, and in silent service to others lives what he called the "mysticism of everyday life." The courageous, total acceptance of life and of oneself—even when everything tangible seems to be collapsing—is perhaps the primary mystical "experience" of everyday life. Anyone—Hindu, Buddhist, Jew, Christian, Muslim, agnostic, atheist—who does this accepts at least implicitly the holy Mystery that fills the emptiness both of oneself and of life. Surrender to the depths of one's humanity, to the depths of life, to Mystery itself—fostered either without or with explicit Christian faith, hope, and love—is the key to Rahner's notion of mysticism.

Rahner often spoke of the "mystical" dimension of Christianity and of the mystical depths of the human being. Because "we do have an immediate, preconceptual experience of God through the experience of the limitless breadth of our consciousness," he wrote, "there is such a thing as a mystical component to Christianity."[4] "Mysticism as the experience of grace"[5] grounded not only this view of the ordinary Christian's life of faith, hope, and love but also that of anyone surrendering, however implicitly, to the Mystery that embraces one's life. This provides the context for understanding what Rahner wrote and said on numerous occasions, namely, that "the devout Christian of the future will either be a 'mystic,' one who has experienced 'something,' or he will cease to be anything at all."[6] He fully expected that the Christian of the future will be more explicitly aware of what is only latent, implicit, and even repressed in the consciousness of most people.

The mysticism of everyday life normally appears in the grayness and banality of daily life and can encompass even the most humble aspects of our daily routine. Rahner wrote, for example, of a mysticism of working, sleeping, eating, drinking, laughing, seeing, sitting, and walking around. The mysticism of everyday life becomes more apparent, however, in the lives of "unknown saints": "I still see around me living in many of my [Jesuit] companions a readiness for disinterested service carried out in silence, a readiness for prayer, for abandonment to the incomprehensibility of God, for the calm acceptance of death in whatever form it may come, for total dedication to the following of Christ crucified."[7] Rahner signaled out as an exemplar of this type of mysticism his friend Alfred Delp, who had signed his final vows with chained hands and then went to his death in Berlin for anti-Nazi activity; a Jesuit unknown to Indian intellectuals because of his humble work with the poor; a Jesuit student chaplain, beaten by police along with his students, but without the satisfaction of considering himself a revolutionary; a hospital chaplain whose daily work with the sick and dying made even death a "dull routine"; a prison chaplain appreciated more for the cigarettes he brings than for the Gospel he preaches. Rahner's mystic of everyday life, his unknown saint, is the "one who with difficulty and without any clear evidence of success plods away at the task of awakening in just a few men and women a small spark of faith, of hope and of charity."[8]

Because God is experienced most clearly and most intensely in our ordinary and banal everyday existence "where the graspable contours of our everyday realities break and dissolve,"[9] Rahner argued that even non-Christians, agnostics, and atheists are called to the mysticism of everyday life. God's presence becomes transparent when the "lights which illuminate the tiny islands of our everyday life go out."[10] The most telling moment, Rahner wrote, is when everything that props up our life fails. Then we are forced to ask if the inescapable darkness engulfing us is absolute absurdity or a blessed, holy night.

In addition to the mysticism of everyday life, Rahner described what he oddly called "mysticism in ordinary dress," or a "mysticism of the masses."[11] This designates the "mysticism" of those in contemporary charismatic movements, of those who claim to be intoxicated with the Holy Spirit, experience dramatic faith conversions, speak glossolalia, publicly and loudly proclaim their faith, prophesy, experience swooning or "slaying" in the Spirit, healings, and the like. This mysticism occurs more ostentatiously than the mysticism of everyday life and more commonly than the extraordinary mysticism of the saints. Although Rahner considered himself to be a "sober" Christian, he took seriously charismatic phenomena as a real and concrete expression of Christianity—*when* they deepen Christian faith, hope, and love.

However, Rahner's writings indicate that he was uneasy with and suspicious of "mysticism in ordinary dress." Insofar as charismatic experiences disrupt "everyday religious consciousness," he understood them as psychosomatic language that could both point to and "disguise" the person's primordial experience of God. He never viewed them—even when genuine—as "the unadulterated operation of the Holy Spirit," nor did he dismiss them—as some of his contemporaries did—as so much "rubbish" or as "skewed religious emotions."

In contrast to an "elitist" tendency by some in charismatic groups to identify every emotional twitch as a sign of the Holy Spirit, Rahner recommended "a mysticism of daily life, the finding of God in all things, the *sober* drunkenness of the Spirit mentioned by the Church Fathers and ancient liturgy, which we dare not reject or disdain just because it is *sober*."[12] He much preferred people who prayed, received the sacraments, and experienced only what he called a "wintry spirituality," that is, one closely allied with the torment of atheists, though obviously people who practice it are not atheists.

Rahner was one of the few twentieth-century theologians to incorporate into his theology the mystical writings found in the Christian tradition. He found in the "classical masters" irreplaceable sources for a contemporary theology and mystagogy because of their special ability to make "intelligible the personal experience of God."[13] They had experienced "most clearly and with the least distortion the relationship which exists between the human subject and the reality we call God."[14]

In this increasingly secular and self-sufficient age—an age in which God is seemingly absent—the special ability of the mystics to intensify, clarify, and explain the experience of the God-human relationship could give rise to a new mystagogy that can awaken people to *the* experience of God "at the heart of human existence." Because the classical mystics interpreted their experiences of God according to the thinking of their age, their writings must be made contemporary, "transposed"—and "such a transposition," Rahner wrote, "could be fruitful, because the depth and radicality of the experience of God which the classical authors describe are not so commonplace that we could discover in ourselves the buds and traces of this experience of God just as easily without their help as with it."[15] Moreover, a theology and mystagogy drawn from the experiences of the outstanding Christian mystics would help Christians in their dialogue with Eastern religions.

In contrast to a long-standing Christian tradition that views mysticism as requiring a "special grace," Rahner maintained the controversial theory that it is something "natural," fundamentally learnable, and belongs to the person's *natural* ability for concentration, contemplation, meditation, submersion into the self, self-emptying, and other psychomental techniques often associated with Eastern mysticisms.

Rahner rejected any elitist interpretation of Christian life "which can see man's perfection only in the trained mystic."[16] Yet, in no way is Christian mysticism deprecated by understanding its essentially natural foundation. "For example," he wrote, "feeding the hungry, giving drink to the thirsty, clothing the naked, and the like—though natural acts in themselves—can be of extreme significance for salvation."[17] This mystical theologian also stressed that to all who love their neighbor unselfishly and therein experience God, the New Testament "awards that final salvation in God's judgment, which is not surpassed even by the highest ascent or the deepest absorption of the mystic."[18] "Any other theory of Christian mysticism," he wrote, "would undoubtedly be either gnosticism or theosophy and either an overestimation of mysticism or else a fundamental underestimation of the real depth of the 'ordinary' Christian life of grace."[19]

A contemporary mystical theology based on Rahner's distinction between different types of mysticism is much needed. "God-mysticism" purifies, intensifies, and makes more explicit the ever-present, transcendental experience of God. Mysticisms of the "self" (yoga?) heighten and make more transparent the human spirit's "presence to itself" in every act of consciousness. Nature-mysticisms (Zen?) nourish the experience of one's "pancosmic" unity with all creation. Finally, "psychic-mysticisms" (Shamanism?) make more explicit the experience of one's id and psychic archetypes. In Rahner's view, psychic mysticisms may account for some of the paranormal phenomena often associated with mysticism.

Rahner maintained that because the human person is spirit-in-world, there can be no Christian mysticism that is either purely apophatic or purely kataphatic. Insofar as the mystic is *spirit*-in-world, mysticism must contain an apophatic dimension that experiences God as "not this," "not that," as beyond definition and incomprehensible. Insofar as the mystic is spirit-in-*world*, mysticism must contain a kataphatic dimension that finds God in all things, especially in the Father's supreme kataphatic expression, Jesus Christ. "He who sees me sees the Father."

In Rahner's view, Christian mysticism must ultimately embrace dying to all created things to surrender totally to loving Mystery to make all things new. The death and resurrection of Jesus Christ—the perfect, enfleshed mystical Word—is the paradigm of perfect mysticism. His death is the paradigm of perfect detachment from all created things required for perfect surrender to Mystery. "In earthly man," Rahner wrote, "this emptying of self will not be accomplished by practicing pure inwardness, but by real activity which is called humility, service, love of neighbor, the cross and death. One must descend into hell together with Christ and lose one's soul, not directly to the God who is above all names, but in the service of one's brethren."[20] Christ's bodily resurrection is the paradigm of Mystery's acceptance of total self-surrender and confirmation that dying to self and to all created things is not ultimately absurd but brings about the new heavens and the new earth.

I know of no better way to conclude this chapter than by quoting from Rahner's essay "Ignatius of Loyola Speaks to a Modern Jesuit."[21]

> "But now," Rahner wrote, "I must speak about Jesus. Did what I say before sound as if I had forgotten Jesus and his blessed Name? I have not forgotten him. He was intimately present in everything I said before, even if the words I addressed to you could not say everything at once. I say *Jesus*. There is no Christianity which can bypass Jesus to find the incomprehensible God. This Jesus I thought about, loved, and desired to follow. And this was the way in which I found the real, living God without having made Him a figment of my own unbridled speculation. A person gets beyond such speculation only by dying a real death throughout life. This death succeeds only if the person inwardly accepts—resigned with Jesus—the abandonment by God embedded in it. This is the ultimate 'wayless' mysticism."

# Bernard J. F. Lonergan

## (1904–84)

*"As the question of God is implicit in all our questioning, so being in love with God is the basic fulfillment of our conscious intentionality. . . . Being in love with God, as experienced, is being in love in an unrestricted fashion. Just as unrestricted questioning is our capacity for self-transcendence, so being in love in an unrestricted fashion is the proper fulfillment of that capacity."*[1]

Bernard J. F. Lonergan is a distinguished Canadian-born Jesuit philosopher and theologian, who taught at the Gregorian University in Rome (1953–65), at Harvard Divinity School (1971–72), and at Boston College (1975–83). The reader may find it strange that a person who was not a mystic nor a mystical theologian nor a mystagogue has found his way into this book. However, in a small work written in 1982,[2] I maintained—and still hold the conviction—that Lonergan's "cognitional theory" can provide an unshakable foundation for the successful transposition of classical spiritual and mystical theology into a much-needed contemporary framework.

Under Lonergan's influence, some contemporary scholarship has already shifted the study of mysticism away from the category of "experience" to that of "consciousness," and from the merely "descriptive" to the "explanatory." The term "experience," a highly complex concept, lends itself to a misunderstanding of mysticism as particular feeling or sensible perception that is too easily separated from understanding, judging, deciding, and loving—what forms the full range of the human person as a self-conscious and free subject. The long-standing distinction between mystical experience and mystical theology, therefore, is seemingly misleading and reduces mysticism to what can be found in autobiographical accounts of the experience of God.

The shift toward the category of "consciousness" engenders a view of mysticism as more than unusual sensations. It helps to underscore that mysticism brings about new ways of knowing and loving that involve a transformative decision about how one lives. These new ways of knowing and loving are based on states of awareness in which God is present to our inner acts, not as an object to be comprehended, but as the direct and transforming center of our lives. One might say that God is what is ultimately experienced in all experience, what is ultimately understood in all understanding, what is ultimately judged in all judgments, and what is ultimately decided upon in all decisions.

Lonergan's cognitional theory distinguishes between "intentionality," which makes objects present to us, and "consciousness," which makes us present to ourselves. In knowing any "object," the human mind also co-knows itself through its intelligible and loving presence to itself. Contained in the presence of the human spirit to itself is a dynamic loving knowledge of God. Expanding this understanding of implicit consciousness of self and of God in every explicit consciousness of an "object" is a task, in my view, for a future mystical theology.

Cognitional theory asks simple but foundational questions: (1) What am I doing when I am knowing? (2) Why is doing that knowing? (3) What do I know when I am doing it? By becoming aware of and attending to consciousness, I (1) explicitly experience my experiencing, understanding, judging, and deciding; (2) understand the unity and relation of my experienced experiencing, understanding, judging, and deciding; (3) affirm the reality of my experienced and understood experiencing, understanding, judging, and deciding; and (4) decide to operate in accord with the norms immanent in the spontaneous relatedness of my experienced, understood, and affirmed experiencing, understanding, judging, and deciding.

Cognitional theory articulates the basis of all human inquiry because it makes explicit what is implicit in every act of human knowing. It focuses on the human person's self-appropriation of what it means to know in order to disclose what all the sciences and disciplines have in common: fidelity to the "transcendental precepts," that is, the basic dynamisms of the mind—which Lonergan calls the "native spontaneities and inevitabilities of our consciousness"—to be attentive, intelligent, reasonable, and responsible.

Unrestricted questioning, in Lonergan's view, is our capacity for self-transcendence. The dynamism of the human spirit, frequently catalyzed by its encounter with evil, contains the question of ultimate intelligence, reason, and value. Because the question of God is intrinsic to all questioning, "being in love with God is the basic fulfillment of our conscious intentionality."[3] Being in love with God in the unrestricted sense as an active experience, to Lonergan's way of thinking, is identical with religious consciousness as such, a consciousness that is directed to God as the goal of one's being and life.

Falling in love with God without reservations gives rise to faith, to loving-knowledge, which Lonergan defines as "the knowledge born of religious love."[4] If, in the usual course of events, knowledge precedes love, in religious matters love precedes knowledge. The loving-knowledge of faith results from God's love flooding our innermost being. Faith as the eye of religious love is "the knowledge reached through the discernment of values and the judgment of value of a person in love."[5] If the heart has its reasons, which the mind does not know, these reasons are the reasons of faith.

Lonergan understands mystical consciousness as the passive experience of being in love with God without restrictions—the experience of receiving God's love. The mystic is the one who becomes explicitly aware of the intersubjective union given through the gift of God's love poured into our hearts. (Romans 5:5 is Lonergan's favorite scriptural text.) Influenced by William Johnston's work *The Mysticism of the Cloud of Unknowing*,[6] Lonergan views mystical consciousness as the intensification and clarification of religious consciousness. In experiencing the vital relationship of union between God and the human person, the mystic drops the "constructs of culture," sinks into the "ultimate solitude," and becomes aware of the "mediated immediacy" of his subjective reaching for God.

The "emergence of the gift" of God's love poured into the heart becomes a "differentiated realm" of consciousness that withdraws the mystic from the realms of common sense and of theory—and even from most forms of interiority—into a "cloud of unknowing." In less technical language, the love of God dominates ("differentiates") the mystic's consciousness and is analogous to the way love of the laws of physics dominates ("differentiates") a physicist's consciousness.

The experience of the mystery of God's love usually "remains within subjectivity as a vector, an undertow, a fateful call to a dreaded holiness."[7] It may speak with a loud or a soft voice in any given individual. For the mystic, this voice is so loud that he withdraws "from the world mediated by meaning into a silent and all-absorbing self-surrender in response to God's gift of love."[8] Lonergan contends that this is mysticism's "main component." Explicitly aware of being in love with God, the mystic's "differentiated consciousness" prefers the negations of an apophatic theology. This highlights, in Lonergan's view, that there are no qualifications or conditions on this love.

By grounding his notion of mysticism in the structure of human consciousness as the awareness of the reception of divine love, Lonergan seems to hold the position that all true mysticism, whatever the difference in its mediated content, is essentially the same in the world's major religions. I would maintain, however, that there are different types of genuine mysticisms: (1) mysticisms of "Being"—certain forms of Buddhism?—that intensify the consciousness of the oneness and difference of the silent Creator and his creation; (2) mysticisms of the "self"—certain forms of yoga?—that heighten and make more transparent the human spirit's "presence to itself" in every act of consciousness; (3) nature-mysticisms—certain types of Zen?—that heighten the consciousness of one's "pancosmic" unity with all creation; and (4) "psychic-mysticisms"—certain forms of Shamanistic consciousness (sometimes mimicked in psychedelic drug experiences)?—that make explicit the experience of one's psychic archetypes and id.

"Foundations," Lonergan's fifth "functional specialty," in my view, is a rich area to be mined for mystical theology. "Foundations" explicates the human authenticity resulting from intellectual, moral, and religious conversions. Conversion transforms the person, bestows a new set of roots, alters one's stance toward reality, and changes the meaning of one's life. The person who falls in love with God without reservations experiences a collapse of his previous horizon for knowing, choosing, deciding, and doing. Loving God with one's whole heart, mind, strength, and soul "sets up a new horizon in which the love of God will transform our knowing."[9] When God's gift of love takes over the core of a person's being, it becomes the efficacious ground for all self-transcendence. It changes how a person seeks truth, realizes virtue, and stands vis-à-vis the universe, its ground, and its goal.

To construct a mystical theology in a Lonerganian fashion one might ask, (1) what am I doing when I am loving? (2) why is doing that loving? and (3) what do I love when I am doing that? The transcendental precept "be in love" might be fruitfully expanded through the investigation of what Aquinas meant by *complacentia*, the will's resting in the intellect's truth, the simple harmony that results when the will is adjusted affectively to the good independently of all desire.[10]

Lonergan's cognitional theory attempts to shift certain areas of theology away from the categories of "faculty psychology" (memory, intellect, and will) to those of "intentionality analysis." The basic terms and relations of mystical theology would then be psychological and not metaphysical. General basic terms would name the mind's conscious and intentional operations. This will mean that for "every term and relation there will exist a corresponding element in intentional consciousness."[11]

In conclusion, I maintain that mystical theology finds itself in an age of science, technology, relativity, statistical analysis, psychoanalysis, biofeedback, psychedelic drugs, philosophical and theological pluralism, ecumenical conversations, and the East-West dialogue. Thus, Lonergan's cognitional theory, that is, one based on the inherent dynamism of the human spirit to know and to love without reservations, is one of the best ways to correlate critically and comprehensively religion, science, and culture.

Lonergan identified the desire of faith to surrender itself in unrestricted love as the transcultural dimension of the world's major religions. Rejecting the classicist's claim that there is only one authentic culture, Lonergan argues for many cultures. His transcendental precepts of being attentive, intelligent, reasonable, responsible, and in love remain invariant through cultural change and differences. In any given culture, the authentic person is one who is attentive, intelligent, reasonable, responsible, and has surrendered to the demands of unrestricted love. The basic mystical dynamism of the human spirit can provide, therefore, the basis for fruitful dialogue among the world's major religions. In short, Lonergan has provided the requisite critical foundations for a "new science" of spirituality and mysticism.

# Simone Weil

## (1909–43)

*"Every time that I think of the crucifixion of Christ, I commit the sin of envy."*[1]

Simone Weil was a radical French Jewish activist and thinker who worked for a while in a Renault car factory in order to share the plight of the workers. She also spent time on the front with the Republican army during Spain's civil war. Participating in an Easter week liturgy at the Benedictine Abbey of Solesmes, she felt that Christ's entire passion had entered her soul. She claimed, too, to have "fallen in love" with St. Francis of Assisi as soon as she came to know about him. This may explain why the theme of *malheur* ("affliction") is often found in her writings. While reciting George Herbert's mystical poem "Love," she experienced Christ taking possession of the deepest recesses of her soul. "I never wondered," she wrote, "whether Jesus was or was not the Incarnation of God; but in fact I was incapable of thinking of him without thinking of him as God."[2] She also said of Christ: "For it seemed to me certain, and I still think so today, that one can never wrestle enough with God if one does so out of pure regard for the truth. Christ likes us to prefer truth to him because, before being Christ, he is truth. If one turns aside from him to go toward the truth, one will not go far before falling into his arms."[3] Charity, to her way of thinking, was loving human beings "insofar as they are nothing." This is the way God loves them.

The words of the Lord's Prayer often transported her. A frequent theme in her two works, *Waiting for God* and *First and Last Notebooks*, is "the possibility of loving divine love in the midst of affliction." Although strongly attracted to Catholicism, Simone claimed that she could not bring herself to join a Church with sinful members: "I have never once had, even for a moment, the feeling that God wants me to be in the Church."[4] There is growing evidence, however, that she was baptized shortly before she died.

# Henri Le Saux

## (1910–73)

*"Now that the Christian jñani [enlightened one] has penetrated to
the heart of Saccidananda, the Spirit of Wisdom makes known to him
. . . that Being,* sat, *opens itself at its very source to give birth
eternally to the Son, that being is essentially the mutual
communication of love, that self-awareness,* cit, *only comes to be
when there is mutual giving and receiving, that the supreme and
ultimate felicity,* ananda, *is fullness and perfect fulfillment only
because it is the fruit of love, for being is love."*[1]

Just as Greek culture enriched nascent Christianity's life and development, contemporary Christianity's "Eastern turn" seems to be producing similar fruits. A few scholars have even predicted that when
future historians write about the twentieth century, they will consider
the meeting of East and West on the level of religious experience as
one of its most significant events. To some extent, the Second Vatican
Council (1962–65) has facilitated Christianity's Eastern awakening
through its openness to the holiness, wisdom, and truth found among
the major non-Christian religions.

Long before Christianity's fascination with Eastern religions was
in vogue, Henri Le Saux (Abhishiktananda) was a builder of bridges
between Indian and Christian spirituality and mysticism, between
the oldest Indian monastic tradition and the Christian Desert Fathers.
He desired to make Indian Christians aware of the rich cultural heritage that the Church must integrate into its life for the good of all
Christianity. In contrast to the West's emphasis on rational thought,
science, technology, and doing, India—to his way of thinking—drew
its strength from Being, the experience of life itself, and was more in
tune with the "inner whispering of the Spirit." Because he understood
India from within, he may have succeeded in "Indianizing" Christi-

anity by incarnating it into India's spiritual culture, which established him as one of Christianity's pioneers of enculturation.

Even more significant is the synthesis he achieved in his own person of Benedictine Christianity and Hindu Advaitic mysticism, that is, the nondualistic mysticism at the heart of the Hindu Upanishads. Although Le Saux never denied his Christianity, Hindus acknowledged him as an authentic Hindu *sannyasi* (wandering monk) and as one who had attained true Advaitic enlightenment. So profound was his enlightenment that toward the end of his life, le Saux attained the distinction of being a guru for both Christian and Hindu disciples.

The eldest of eight children, Henri Le Saux was born in Brittany, France on August 30, 1910. Attracted to the priesthood when ten years of age, he first studied at a local minor seminary, then at the major seminary at Rennes, and finally at the Benedictine monastery of St. Anne de Kergonan in 1929. He was solemnly professed and ordained priest in 1935 and remained at St. Anne de Kergonan teaching church history and patristics until 1948. His Benedictine affection for liturgy and Gregorian chant, he often said, had indelibly stamped his life.

A love of India and a desire to root Christian monasticism in the land of the gurus and seers motivated Le Saux to obtain permission to join Abbé Jules Monchanin in founding the ashram of Shantivanam ("Woods of Peace") in Kulittali, southern India. Here he took the name Abhishikleshvarananda ("the joy of the anointed one"), shortened to Abhishiktananda.

Shortly upon arriving in India, he met Sri Ramana Maharishi (d. 1950), a man who Le Saux knew embodied the fullness of self-denial, self-actualization, and the wisdom of India. So powerful was the effect of this great Hindu sage upon Le Saux that he became convinced that Christianity could enrich India spiritually only if and when it could produce mystics like Ramana. Le Saux would later write that he found Ramana's Advaitic mysticism—although something entirely new to him—in harmony with his own Benedictine spirituality.

This led Le Saux to discover the sacred mountain of Arunachala, where Ramana had lived, and where, for several long periods between 1952 and 1955, he lived as a hermit in several of its caves. With the obscurity, silence, and self-renunciation characteristic of a Hindu sannyasi, Le Saux penetrated the mystery of the Advaitic experience of

India's rishis (sages) and saints. During this experience, he was attempting to discover in the "most secret mirror" of his heart the sacred image in whose likeness he was made. The brightness of the "Original" gradually engulfed the reflected image. Descending deeper and deeper in his "true self," "finally, nothing was left but he himself, the Only One, infinitely alone, Being, Awareness, and Bliss, Saccidananda. In the heart of Saccidananda, I had returned to my Source."[2]

This experience brought Le Saux a severe problem of conscience, for it seemed to conflict deeply with his own Christian experience. In his diary, he confessed that he had drunk too deeply of Advaita to return to the "Gregorian" peace of a Benedictine monk and had enjoyed too much "Gregorian" peace not to be disturbed by his Advaitic experience.

Drawn to achieve a synthesis in his person, Le Saux placed himself under the direction of Sri Gnanananda to listen to "the Spirit who never ceases to call within" and to receive "the knowledge of the All."[3] In 1959, he and an Indian Catholic priest pilgrimaged to the source of the Ganges in the Himalayas, an Indian symbol for the inner journey to the source of Being. After taking a ritual bath in the Ganges with Hindu pilgrims and singing verses from the Upanishads, he celebrated what may well have been the first Mass at that Hindu sacred site.

In 1962, Le Saux built a small hermitage in Uttarkashi, not far from the sources of the Ganges in the Himalayas. There he wrote his chief works, undertook many journeys to and from Shantivanam, and participated vigorously in numerous Hindu-Christian ecumenical meetings. With the arrival of Dom Bede Griffiths, O.S.B., in 1968, Le Saux was free to spend the rest of his life in silent contemplation in the solitude of the Himalayas as the only Christian among the Hindu sannyasis. On July 14, 1973, he suffered a heart attack, and though he temporarily recovered—to even greater spiritual enlightenment—he succumbed the following December 7, his faculties and clarity undiminished. He was buried in the cemetery of the Fathers of the Divine Word in Dolda, near Indore.

Dom Le Saux's main contribution to mysticism is not to be found in his books but in the Advaitic and Christian experiences he plumbed and made accessible to others. His view was that the monk has the duty to free his inner Mystery, thereby freeing the self. This is the monk's gift to the world. Because of a powerful desire to make Christ known to the Hindus, he went to India as a giver. However, through the interiority at the heart of the Hindu Upanishads, he claimed that India—better than anything from his Christian background—plunged him more deeply into the mystery of the cosmic Christ.

Le Saux's inner partner in dialogue was the Advaitic, or nondualistic, *experience* of Ramana and Gnanananda. Advaita is essentially a mysticism and a derived theology. It maintains that the ultimate experience is one of undifferentiated unity and that the person's deepest self (*atman*) and the all-embracing absolute Reality (*Brahman*) cannot be two. In short, because *atman* is *Brahman*, one experiences that the self is the Absolute.

The Advaitic mystic strives for the experience of the Absolute in a pure consciousness totally beyond all feelings, desires, images, thoughts, and multiplicity—and has much in common with the Christian apophatic tradition. Nothing less than the experience of the "pure silence" of the absoluteness of Being—the ineffable, "unpersonifiable God" discovered as the self vanishes at the deepest depths of one's being—satisfies the Advaitic mystic.

Le Saux's mysticism is an attractive, Eastern-flavored, image-of-God mysticism, which he understood as true—not because he could find in himself analogies to the divine processions—because he experienced the Son living and revealing himself in him, as well as the divine generation and the divine life operative in him. India calls the image of God in the cave of the heart "Saccidananda," a compound of the Sanskrit words *sat* (being), *cit* (awareness), and *ananda* (bliss). Saccidananda signifies not only God's inmost mystery but also God's presence in the person's deepest core.

Le Saux claimed that by experiencing the "Gospel of the Absolute in the cave of the heart,"[4] he had brought his Advaitic experience into harmony with his Christian experience. He emphasized—not without controversy—the cosmic dimension of Christ's mystery and understood the risen and ascended Lord as one who had left behind all the distinctiveness of the Incarnation "in order to be simply the Man, the One who is present to all, living in all, free of any particularized form and of any limit imposed by the categories of time and space."[5] The mystery of Christ reveals itself, in Le Saux's view, in anyone who awakens to the "divine Presence." "Taken in all its amplitude," he wrote, "the mystery of Christ is in fact this awakening of the Son to the Father in the heart of men, and in the bosom of all creation."[6]

Le Saux contended, too, that Christian trinitarian and Hindu Advaitic experiences enrich and indwell each other. In the Trinity's womb, one finds true Being, the "ineffable First Source which is," and the "abyss of eternal Silence,"[7] which one must address as "Abba, Father." In the Advaitic experience of Saccidananda, Le Saux experienced the Absolute as Being (*sat*), Awareness (*cit*), and Bliss (*ananda*). In *sat*, the Christian experiences the Father as the source of being; in *cit*, the Son as the Father's self-consciousness and Word; in *ananda*, the Spirit of love as the nondual bliss of Father and the Son. From his experience and way of thinking, he maintained that there is no face-to-face encounter with God that is not fulfilled in the beatifying experience of Oneness. "The Son is not," he wrote, "until he attains completion in the Plenitude of the Spirit, the consummation of God in the deepest recesses of the bosom of God. And there is no experience of oneness that does not end up in the face to face from which it springs."[8]

Dom Henri Le Saux learned that in becoming aware of one's self, one becomes aware of God. "By awakening to God," he wrote, "he has awakened himself to self, beyond God and self, in this eternal mystery of the Father, at a point where the Spirit leads this Spirit whom the word of God become man has come to spread all over the world."[9] And to him, this is nothing less than "the experience of the Lord Jesus, the *face to face* of the Father and the Son in the nonduality of the Spirit."[10]

# Thomas Merton

## (1915–68)

*"My monastery is a place in which I disappear from the world as an object of interest in order to be everywhere in it by hiddenness and compassion. To exist everywhere I have to be a no one."*[1]

Thomas Merton was perhaps the world's most famous monk at the time of his sudden and mysterious death while attending an international congress in Bangkok on the future of monasticism. Born of a New Zealand father and an American mother in the Midi region (Prades) of France on January 31, 1915, Merton had a difficult and unhappy childhood. When he was only six years old, his artist mother died. Although loving and caring, his father—also an artist—moved from place to place, and often left the boy alone. Merton was only sixteen years old when his father died.

Merton received a good education in France, England, and then at Columbia University. Not untypical of youth, his teens and early twenties were years filled with sensuality, confusion, a critical attitude toward religion, and intense searching. One evening in his room, he had a vivid experience of the presence of his dead father and wrote trenchantly of his sense of sin and self-loathing: "The whole thing passed in a flash, but in that flash, instantly, I was overwhelmed with a sudden and profound insight into the misery and corruption of my own soul and I was filled with horror at what I saw."[2]

Merton was received into the Roman Catholic Church in 1938, while still a student at Columbia. Three years later he became a Trappist monk at the Abbey of Our Lady of Gethsemani in Kentucky. His autobiography, *The Seven Storey Mountain* (1948), became an international success—not only because of its significant statement about monastic spirituality but also because of its telling account of the spiritual condition of the times.

357

The diverse genres of his writings are indicative of Merton's range and depth. He wrote personal journals (e.g., *The Sign of Jonas*), devotional meditations (e.g., *New Seeds of Contemplation*), theological essays (e.g., *The Ascent to Truth*), reflections on Far Eastern religions (e.g., *Zen and the Birds of Appetite*), biblical reflections (e.g., *Bread in the Wilderness*), poetry (e.g., *Emblems in a Season of Fury*), and collections of essays and reviews (e.g., *Raids on the Unspeakable*). The thousands of letters he wrote to people the world over should also be mentioned. Through these writings, one sees Merton move from the enthusiastic, but somewhat narrow, Catholicism, not untypical of a recent convert, to the creative openness of the mature man, who tapped the resources of other spiritual traditions and of worlds beyond his own monastery.

Merton is a twentieth-century American supplement to the "autobiographical" figures in this volume who were not afraid to reveal their intimate longings, loves, joys, friendships, hopes, and fears. They have attractively described the conversions, syntheses, transformations, paradoxes, and contradictions that filled their inner and outer lives. Moreover, by revitalizing the Christian apophatic tradition, Merton echoes many of the themes favored by mystics of the incomprehensible God: divine darkness, radical emptiness, the wayless path, and the desert experience.

Although more eclectic than original, Merton as writer stands out among the figures already seen because he blended in his writings scripture, the Fathers of the Church, the Desert Fathers, the significant Western mystics, the Russian Orthodox mystics, contemporary Catholic and Protestant theology, contemporary psychology, art, poetry, literature, existentialism, Taoism, and Buddhism—and with a remarkable sensitivity to how all this bears on civil rights, racial discrimination, the peace movement, nuclear disarmament, social justice, urban violence, poverty, ecumenism, and the East-West dialogue. This Trappist monk—dedicated to silence, asceticism, contemplation, and at times, a hermit-like existence—had friends and contacts with persons from almost every walk of life and from many different cultures and religions, to which his thousands of letters bear witness. In this way, he made an enormous contribution to contemporary American spirituality.

As Merton saw it, because everyone shares in Adam's flight from unity with God, all remain in exile not only from God but also from their own deepest selves. Thus, he distinguished sharply between a "true self," a "deep self," a "new self"; and a "false self," a "shadow self," and an "outer self." For the most part, the external, daily self that we seem to know is a fabrication and a distortion of the self made in God's image and likeness. This "worldly self" proclaims itself to be autonomous and to be a god unto itself. Because the true self made in God's image seems the very enemy of the daily, familiar self, the quest for authenticity requires a great battle. The struggle for God is at the same time a struggle simply to be one's genuine self. This, in his view, brings about inner transformation.

Merton valued contemplation as a powerful means of forcing a person below the surface comforts of narcissism to face the hell of the self's lived lie. God is revealed to the contemplative only when he has embraced the "wilderness of the human spirit," the inner desert in which he comes face-to-face with his own nothingness, sinfulness, ignorance, infidelity, helplessness, and need for God. This Trappist understood contemplative prayer as "simply the preference for the desert, for emptiness, for poverty. One has begun to know the meaning of contemplation when one intuitively and spontaneously seeks the dark and unknown path of aridity in preference to every other way,"[3] which begins the transformation process.

Merton compared contemplative prayer to "a mind awake in the dark, looking for a light, not totally reconciled to being out of bed."[4] He held the unusual view that authentic prayer springs from the crises of living and, paradoxically, may even intensify these conflicts. "Christian contemplation," he wrote, "is precipitated by crisis within crisis and anguish within anguish. It is born of spiritual conflict. It is the reconciliation of enemies that seem to be irreconcilable."[5] Contemplation makes the person more sensitive both to sinfulness and to God's gracious love. Still, waiting for God in emptiness and silence may indicate not only that our capacity to receive the divine has been enlarged but also that we are already resting in a God who seeks us first.

Merton belonged to the apophatic tradition that speaks of God as "Emptiness" and "Nothingness. " Congruent with this tradition, Merton wrote of the "infinitely productive darkness of contemplation" and of the monastic life as nurturing "the darkness of contemplation." In his view, contemplation is a plunging into the "luminous darkness," the "dark fire," and the "clear darkness." Aridity, suffering, crises, dread, anxiety, and doubt drive the monk to contemplation and are, in turn, intensified by contemplation. Darkness becomes the inner atmosphere of contemplation that prepares the monk who waits for God in purposelessness, emptiness, and darkness. "In the deepest spiritual darkness, in the most profound night of unknowing, in the purity of naked faith," Merton wrote, "God unites the soul to Himself in mystical union."[6]

Merton's preference for the "darkness of contemplation" may account for his distaste of prayer that manifests itself in dramatic ways. The prayer of the Desert Fathers, he maintained, was so simple and profound that they were not even aware that they were praying. This view overlooks, however, the high regard the Desert Fathers had for the ecstatic and rapturous "prayer of no prayer" and the "prayer of fire."

Merton understood contemplation, in its broadest sense, as "a deep participation in the Christ-life, a spiritual sharing in the union of God and Man which is the hypostatic union."[7] Contemplation, in a narrow sense, is a participation in Christ's solitary prayer on the Mount of Olives before his passion. All Christian prayer, meditation, and contemplation have one goal: loving union with the incarnate Word, through an imitation of Christ's self-emptying. In agreement with many mystics in the tradition, Merton insisted that "no one can dismiss the Man Christ from his interior life on the pretext that he has now entered by higher contemplation into direct communication with the Word."[8]

"Hidden contemplatives," those who practice a type of "masked contemplation" in the midst of busy daily life, fascinated this monk. The temperament, psychology, and calling of "masked contemplatives" lead them to "hectic exterior activity" in identifying with the "least of Jesus' brethren"—not to the monastic life. "Although they are active laborers," Merton wrote, "they are also hidden contemplatives because of the great purity of heart maintained in them by obedience, fraternal charity, self-sacrifice, and perfect abandonment to God's will in all that they do and suffer. They are much closer to God than they realize. They enjoy a kind of 'masked' contemplation."[9]

By branding the desire for exotic experiences and altered states of consciousness as so much "pseudo-mysticism," Merton contradicted some of the loudest voices of the 1960s era. His writings frequently warned against the "spiritual consumerism" of that age: narcissism, self-preoccupation, and a comfortable flight from the world. "To become a Yogi," he wrote, "and to be able to commit moral and intellectual suicide whenever you please, without the necessity of actually dying, to be able to black out your mind by the incantation of half articulate charms and to enter into a state of annihilation, in which all the faculties are inactive and the soul is as inert as if it were dead—all this may well appeal to certain minds as a refined and rather pleasant way of getting even with the world and with society, and with God Himself for that matter."[10] Walled up in the narcissistic seclusion of his own inner darkness, the pseudo-mystic creates the emptiness of a hell that is paradoxically full of self. Even in mysticism, nothing is sometimes only nothing.

Merton criticized not only the pseudo-mystical currents swelling in contemporary life but also what he called "the pseudo-spirituality of activism"—the serious temptation to worship political pressure groups, causes, movements, slogans, and ideologies. The "unregenerate activist," to his way of thinking, lacks authentic inner freedom, contemplative peace, spiritual insight, and the love born from prayer that is required for a genuine transformation of society. Without inner transformation, activists only infect others with their sinfulness, brokenness, egoism, delusions, illusions, obsessions, violence, and hatreds.

The power latent in the Eastern and Western mystical traditions to combat a growing Western materialism interested Merton even in his preconversion university years. Aldous Huxley's books planted the seed that was to develop into Merton's deep appreciation for the values of Oriental mysticisms and religions. Ironically, too, it was his Hindu monk friend, Bramachari, who called Merton's attention to the wealth of *Christian* mystical literature.

After his conversion and entry into the monastic life, however, Merton became initially somewhat critical of Eastern mysticisms. His autobiography, *The Seven Storey Mountain*, argued that the ways of the East do not lead to genuine mysticism. At most, they are natural techniques that promote peace and tranquility but have no value for the supernatural life. They also tend to mix with magic, superstition, and the demonic.

On the other hand, Merton remained convinced that the universal striving for purification, illumination, and transformation could be found in the world's major religions. Rejoicing in the openness to Oriental religions found in the documents of the Second Vatican Council, this Trappist monk began to explore the transformative power of

Eastern mysticisms, especially Zen. Their ancient meditation and monastic practices, in his view, were effective means of destroying the illusions of the false self and establishing the true self in its authentic relationship to the whole of reality. He also came to accept the outstanding religious figures in the Hindu, Buddhist, and Islamic traditions as mystics in the strictly supernatural sense of the word, that is, those who had experienced purification by, illumination by, and union with the God of truth and love.

In 1968, Merton journeyed to the Far East as a pilgrim in search of the special places of Oriental purification, illumination, and transformation. He had already made this trip spiritually. In his *Asian Journal*, Merton wrote, "I come as a pilgrim who is anxious to obtain not just information, nor just 'facts' about other monastic traditions, but to drink from ancient sources of monastic vision and experience. I seek not only to learn more (quantitatively) about religion and about monastic life, but to become a better and more enlightened monk (qualitatively) myself."[11]

Merton rejected both a facile syncretism and a concordist view in his approach to Oriental religions. Mystics the world over, to his way of thinking, neither experience the same thing nor do they transcend in an elitist way the philosophies and theologies of their respective traditions. The mystic—no matter of what religious tradition—is rooted in that tradition and is its full flowering.

The essence of authentic religious experience, to Merton's way of thinking, varied little from religion to religion. Common to monks of every age and culture are the universal elements of dedication, ongoing effort, real discipline, guidance from experienced teachers, the combining of wisdom and technique, a critical distance and detachment from secular life, emphasis upon the experiential dimensions of religious beliefs, a concern for inner transformation, and a recognition that life requires more than ethical and pious attitudes.

The following quotation illustrates Merton's view of the unity-in-diversity found in the world's major religions: "Without asserting that there is complete unity of all religions at the 'top,' the transcendent or mystical level—that they all start from different dogmatic positions to 'meet' at this summit—it is certainly true to say that even where there are irreconcilable differences in doctrine and in formulated beliefs, there may still be great similarities and analogies in the realm of religious experience. Cultural and doctrinal differences must remain, but they do not invalidate the very real quality of existential likeness."[12] When asked what his deepest desire was, Merton replied, "We must contain all divided worlds in ourselves and transcend them in Christ."[13]

# William Johnston

(1925– )

*"Buddhist-Christian dialogue must be based above all on religious experience and, ideally speaking, upon mysticism."*[1]

Born in Belfast, this Irish Jesuit has lived in Japan for the past fifty years as a professor at Tokyo's Sophia University and is well known as a spiritual guide, retreat director, lecturer, translator, and author of numerous books on Christian and Zen mysticism. His background in the incarnational, kataphatic mysticism of St. Ignatius of Loyola has given him an appreciation for a trinitarian mysticism of discernment, service, and action centered on the life, death, and resurrection of Jesus Christ. His early book *The Mysticism of the Cloud of Unknowing*[2] and his editing of the Christian classic *The Cloud of Unknowing and the Book of Privy Counseling*[3] did much to call attention in the English-speaking world to the dark, silent, imageless, apophatic mysticism of the Christian tradition. These studies also provided him with a Christian analogue for entering into conversation with the world of Zen mysticism.

This gentle Irishman embodies an exemplary, contemporary Christian stance: a firm knowledge of and commitment to his Christian identity and an appreciation of the genuine religious values of the East. In a manner reminiscent of Teilhard de Chardin, Johnston has argued in his many books for a "Christianity stretched beyond itself," especially for one that embraces the mystical riches of the East.

Because the human psyche and its aspirations are the same the world over, Johnston maintains that our common human nature provides the foundation for an interreligious dialogue based on the values resulting from meditation: interiority, humility, compassion, nonviolence, peace, and justice. Even though the philosophies and theologies of the world's major religions often differ enormously, he maintains that they can best meet at the level of dark faith and silent love. "Any

Buddhist-Christian dialogue," he writes, "must be based above all on religious experience and, ideally speaking, upon mysticism. The greatest union will be found when Buddhists and Christians meditate together. The deepest union is found in pure and naked faith."[4]

"Mysticism," in Johnston's view, "is wisdom or knowledge that is found through love; it is loving knowledge."[5] Along with Thomas Aquinas, he also defines it as "the simple intuition of the truth." Rejecting the contemporary overemphasis upon the sometimes exotic and ecstatic side of mysticism, this Irishman understands it as a deepened form "of ordinary human experience" not limited to any one religion. Mysticism responds to the call in every human heart to unrestricted love—a love that brings about the enlightenment, supraconceptual wisdom, and the naked, silent, dark faith found in all major religions. Because mysticism fosters a realization of one's poverty, disorder, and nothingness, it engenders love of God, of one's neighbor, of the world, and often promotes practical action.

Christian mysticism, to Johnston's way of thinking, is founded on the trinitarian mystical experiences of the crucified and risen Christ: "Mysticism which arises from, and culminates in, love of God in Christ is Christian."[6] It is also "nothing less than a transformation of the whole person in preparation for that final transformation that takes place through death and resurrection."[7] True Christian enlightenment comes only after death, and the Church canonizes saints for their heroic virtue—not for a mystical consciousness. Inextricably linked to the person of Jesus Christ and proclaiming him as Lord, Christianity does not emphasize a technically developed mysticism to the extent that Buddhism does. Johnston also emphasizes that a "sense of presence" is one of the chief characteristics of Christian mysticism. (My research has already shown, however, that a "sense of absence" is often a significant factor in Christian mystical consciousness.)

Johnston views Zen meditation as a process by which one becomes increasingly present—but with exceptional emotional detachment—to all reality, to the fact that things are. It involves "a process of unification in which the whole personality is harmonized in a oneness which reaches its climax with a complete absence of subject-object consciousness in *satori* [enlightenment]."[8] Its goal is "the simple intuition of the truth" in which the "oneness" and the "suchness" of all reality become luminous to the Zen practitioner. Although such language strikes Western ears as monistic, the Zen practitioner experiences that everything is one, yet not one. Such a meditative view, to Johnston's way of think-ing, can serve as a reminder to Christians of the unity of all things and of our oneness with God. He also stresses that Zen meditation can give Christianity a much-needed "technology" for deeper, richer, simpler prayer rooted in the body.

Johnston explains both Christian and Zen mysticism phenomeno-logically as a process by which the unconscious is brought into and integrated with consciousness. Meditation, be it Christian or Zen, plunges the practitioner into the deepest levels of the psyche, which are beyond reason and discursive thinking, to heal and transform consciousness. Sinking more deeply into the self—or ascending higher into God—requires walking a path of naked faith filled with the "nights" of anguish and spiritual dereliction. Progress in medita-tion bestows a sacramental view of reality, a loving-wisdom, and a compassion for all creatures.

Johnston admits that even psychedelic drugs may help a person to reach the deepest levels of the psyche. Unlike drug experiences, however, genuine mysticism engenders psychic maturity, reform, conversion, and transformation. One must distinguish, in his view, between the authentic mystic in love with the mystery beyond ratio-nal consciousness and the explorer of consciousness interested only in the inner world, "experiences," and "spiritual consumerism." "Meditative states of consciousness," in his view, may also be called "altered states of consciousness," but not all "altered states of con-sciousness" are "meditative states of consciousness."

Meditation-contemplation, in Johnston's view, must always in-volve more than technique. Although he insists that one's "ultimate concern" does not have to be explicitly religious, he distinguishes between contemplation done for the development of human potential and that done with faith, hope, and love—conceding that in practice the dividing line may be rather blurred. The "self-realization" brought about in authentic mystical self-transcendence in faith, hope, and love—regardless of the technique used—must be distinguished from a "self-actualization" brought about by techniques to develop human potential. To Johnston's way of thinking, unless the awareness exer-cises of the East are done in faith, hope, and love, there is no authentic mysticism—only a humanly beneficial "mental jogging." Even deep intellectual and moral conversions, to his way of thinking, are not mystical, unless they are permeated with love.

Johnston calls attention to a new and important partner in the interreligious dialogue: the interest of the empirical sciences in altered states of consciousness. Given the psychological, physiological, and neurological basis of mysticism, science has much to say about and much to contribute concerning the psychosomatic and neurological repercussions of mysticism as a love affair with wisdom. Johnston's book *Silent Music: The Science of Meditation*[9] is an especially compelling attempt at considering the East-West contemplative dialogue, to some extent, under the aspect of what psychoanalysis, the study of brainwaves, and biofeedback can contribute to "the new science of mysticism."

# Mother Teresa

## (1910–97)

*"If I ever become a saint—I will surely be one of darkness. I will continually be absent from heaven—to light the light of those in darkness on earth."*[1]

Mother Teresa was once called "the most powerful woman in the world" by the former secretary general of the United Nations, Javier Perez de Cuellar. This hyperbole notwithstanding, it can be said of this Albanian peasant "Saint of the Gutters" that she is history's best known nun. Appreciated primarily for her service to the "poorest of the poor"—and honored for it through a Nobel Prize—Mother Teresa's unique holiness and mystical depths came to light only a few years ago because of the publication of her private correspondence.

Born Gonxha Agnes Bojaxhiu, of Albanian parents, in Skopje, Macedonia, Mother Teresa possessed both an intense love of the "Sacred Heart of Jesus" and "the love of souls" from the time of her First Communion. She knew from the tender age of twelve that she was destined to serve the poor in a foreign land. Entering the Sisters of Loreto in Dublin in September 1928, she took the name "Teresa" out of devotion to Thérèse of Lisieux and was sent to Calcutta to teach at St. Mary's Medium School for girls.

During this time, Mother Teresa took an exceptional private vow to consider even the smallest voluntary refusal to submit to God's will to be a "mortal sin." Writing later to her spiritual director, she informed him that she often begged Jesus for the grace to do promptly whatever he asked her, however small, and that she would "rather die" than refuse him. This private vow was the motivation behind all that she did and one of "her greatest secrets."

During a train journey to Darjeeling on September 10, 1946, Mother Teresa received the "call within a call" to quench the thirst of the crucified Jesus by serving him in the poorest of the poor. This invitation also initiated a series of further interior locutions in which Christ addressed her as "my own spouse," "my little one." The "Voice" kept pleading with her to carry him into the darkest hovels of the poor and to be his light for them. Thirsting with love for souls as Christ on the cross did, she realized that if she were to serve India's poorest of the poor properly, she must then "live like an Indian with the Indians."

Speaking of herself as a "pencil in God's hands," Mother Teresa considered that September day—later celebrated as "Inspiration Day"—to be the real beginnings of the order she founded, the Missionaries of Charity, to which she later added a contemplative branch. Her so-called "business card" sums up the spirituality of this admirable religious order: "The fruit of silence is prayer. The fruit of prayer is faith. The fruit of faith is love. The fruit of love is service. The fruit of service is peace."[2]

Three visions deepened Mother Teresa's mysticism of enculturation. Her first vision was of a large crowd of poor men, women, and children. Lifting their hands toward her, they all cried out: "Come, come, save us—bring us Jesus." The second vision consisted of the same crowd and of our Lady facing them and asking Teresa to take care of them, to bring them Christ, and to teach them to say the family rosary, assuring her that all would be well, because Mary and her Son would be with them. During the third vision, she saw the same crowd, Jesus on the cross, and our Lady to one side, with her hand on Mother Teresa's left shoulder. Christ reminded her that he, his Mother, and the crowd had requested of her that she take care of them, and then asked, "Will you refuse to do this for me—to take care of them, to bring them to me?"[3] Although she experienced no further visions, Mother Teresa never had the slightest doubt about the genuineness of these three visions.

As certain as Mother Teresa was of her "call within a call" to serve the poorest of the poor in India, she made light of her locutions and visions. In a letter to one of her spiritual directors, Archbishop Ferdinand Périer, S.J., she assured him that she was not interested in "voices and visions." They came unbidden, disappeared, and had not changed her life. Her desire for self-sacrifice in the service of the poor had been just as strong before they came. In line with many in the Christian mystical tradition, this nun neither wished for nor clung to unusual mystical phenomena—even though they did aid her spiritual progress.

Mother Teresa's writings contain only a brief statement about the 1946–47 honeymoon period of her mystical life, during which she experienced so much "union—love—faith—trust—prayer—sacrifice."[4] Reflecting back upon this stage of her life, she felt much nostalgia for the intimacy she had experienced with Christ: "The sweetness and consolation and union of those six months passed by too soon."[5] There were also "oasis moments" of "joy untold" that punctuated her long bouts of darkness, loneliness, and pain of loss. Her spiritual directors later stated that she was on the brink of transforming union.

Mother Teresa's writings are replete with references to desolation, spiritual darkness, interior suffering, spiritual dryness, deep loneliness, an "icy cold" interior, acute feelings of emptiness and of her own nothingness ("what are you doing, God, to one so small?"). Her feelings of love for God, for Christ, and for others—as well as any experience of faith, hope, and love—simply vanished. The bone-marrow sense of God's absence, of God's rejection, of fear that her soul, Jesus, and heaven were illusions, and of a radical longing for God became her "inner hell" for more than half a century.

Mother Teresa's account of her severe trials surpasses even the classical description of the dark night of the soul found in the writings of John of the Cross. The exceptionally long fifty-five-year period of interior dereliction—exceeding even the prolonged years of suffering of St. Paul of the Cross—is unique in the Christian mystical tradition. Her state of mystical martyrdom, as that of several others in this volume, serves as a counterbalance to the popular view of mysticism as consisting of ecstatic experiences and states of rapture. One discovers another anomaly in her writings: an almost complete absence of references to sin and disorder.

It is remarkable that under these circumstances Mother Teresa never wavered in her resolve to live for "God alone, God everywhere, God in everybody and in everything, God always."[6] Experiencing that God was destroying everything in her to fill her with himself, she came to the realization that this darkness—which she called "her greatest secret" (even her closest collaborators knew nothing about it)—allowed her to identify more closely with the poor. "It often happens," she wrote, "that those who spend their time giving light to others, remain in darkness themselves."[7] The true nature of Christ's early and repeated call to her, *"Come, Come, carry Me into the holes of the poor. Come be My light,"*[8] led to her peaceful acceptance and love of her interior darkness as an instrument through which she brought Christ's light to others. In one of the most powerful statements of suffering-servant mysticism ever written, Mother Teresa prophesied: "If I ever become a saint—I will surely be one of darkness. I will continually be absent from heaven—to light the light of those in darkness on earth."[9]

The mysticism of reparation (also called "suffering-servant" and "victim-soul" mysticism) of the "saint of darkness" is a lived commentary on three Pauline texts. In 2 Corinthians 5:21, Paul speaks of the sinless Christ who became sin for our salvation; in 1 Colossians 1:24, Paul rejoices that he is filling up what is lacking in Christ's sufferings. Mother Teresa knew that she, her nuns, and all Christians were called to be "the spirit, mind, heart, eyes, ears, mouth, hands and feet of Christ," to be the God-forsaken man on the cross for the redemption and salvation of others. In this way, she took upon herself the darkness and sufferings of others—even the pain of resisting the temptations that plagued those she saved.

Mother Teresa lived what St. Paul said about himself in Galatians 2:20: "I have been crucified with Christ; it is no longer I who live, but Christ who lives in me." "When outside," she wrote, "in the work—or meeting people—there is a presence—of somebody living very close—in very me."[10] Although she understood that she and her sisters must "more and more be His Light—His Way—His Life—His Love in the slums,"[11] she found the hungry, thirsty, naked, sick, and unwanted Christ "in His distressing disguise"[12] in the slums.

Mother Teresa's spirituality and mysticism are utterly simple: mad, passionate, total love of Jesus Christ. "From childhood," she wrote, "the Heart of Jesus has been my first love."[13] One might add that he was her only love: Christ in the poor and the poor in Christ. Mass and the Real Presence of Christ in the Blessed Sacrament dominated her life. She spoke of herself as leading a eucharistic life, a Calvary life. On her deathbed she rallied when a makeshift tabernacle was brought into her room. Despite years of crucifying darkness, she affirmed that an "unbroken union" with Christ existed because her entire being was centered on him. "I have loved him blindly, totally, only," she wrote. "I use every power in me—in spite of my feelings—to make Him loved personally by the Sisters and people. I will let him have a free Hand with and in me."[14] She spoke of herself and of her nuns not as social workers—whose work she valued—but as contemplatives who are "twenty four hours a day with Jesus."[15]

What a wonderful grace and blessing—to be able to say at the end of one's life: "Jesus, I have never refused you anything."[16]

# Notes

## Preface—pages xi–xiv

1. Elmer O'Brien, *The Varieties of Mystic Experience* (New York: New American Library, 1964).

2. Harvey D. Egan, S.J., *The Spiritual Exercises and the Ignatian Mystical Horizon* (St. Louis, MO: Institute of Jesuit Sources, 1976).

3. Harvey D. Egan, S.J., *Ignatius Loyola the Mystic* (Wilmington, DE: Michael Glazier, 1987).

4. Harvey D. Egan, S.J., *What Are They Saying About Mysticism?* (Mahwah, NJ: Paulist Press, 1982).

5. Harvey D. Egan, S.J., *Christian Mysticism: The Future of a Tradition* (New York: Pueblo, 1984).

6. Harvey D. Egan, S.J., *An Anthology of Christian Mysticism* (New York: Pueblo, 1991).

7. Harvey D. Egan, S.J., *Karl Rahner: Mystic of Daily Life* (New York: Crossroad, 1998).

## Introduction—pages xv–xxi

1. Peter Matthiessen offers a better insight into the effect of such drugs—but still does not get to the heart of the matter—when he writes, "Drugs can clear away the past, enhance the present; towards the secret garden they can only point the way. Lacking the grit of discipline and insight, the drug vision remains a sort of dream that cannot be brought into daily life. Old mists may be banished, that is true, but the alien chemical agents form another mist, maintaining the separation of the 'I' from the true experience of the infinite within us." Cf. "A Reporter at Large: The Snow Leopard I," *New Yorker* (March 27, 1978): pp. 57–58.

2. *Major Trends in Jewish Mysticism* (New York: Schocken, 1954), pp. 6–7.

3. Anne Fremantle, *The Protestant Mystics* (Boston: Little, Brown and Company, 1964). See pp. vii–viii.

4. *The Foundations of Mysticism: Origins to the Fifth Century,* vol. I of *The Presence of God: A History of Western Christian Mysticism* (New York: Crossroad, 1991), p. xvii. Henceforth referred to as McGinn I.

## Mysticism in the New Testament—pages 5–11

1. Karl Rahner, S.J., and Herbert Vorgrimler, "Mysticism," *Dictionary of Theology* (New York: Crossroad, 1981), p. 326.

## Origen—pages 12–17

1. *Origen—An Exhortation to Martyrdom, Prayer and Selected Works* (On First Principles: Book IV, The Prologue to the Commentary on the Song of Songs, Homily XXVII on Numbers), trans. Rowan A. Greer (Mahwah, NJ: Paulist Press, 1979), *Martyrdom*, XXI, p. 55.

2. *Martyrdom*, XXII, p. 56.

3. *Martyrdom*, XIV, p. 51.

## Gregory of Nyssa—pages 18–21

1. *Gregory of Nyssa: The Life of Moses*, trans. Everett Ferguson and Abraham J. Malherbe (Mahwah, NJ: Paulist Press, 1978), II, § 234, p. 115.

2. *The Life of Moses*, II, § 168, p. 96.

3. *The Life of Moses*, I, § 47, p. 43.

4. *Commentary on the Song of Songs*, sermon 12, quoted by Ferguson & Malherbe in *Gregory of Nyssa: The Life of Moses*, p. 22.

## Evagrius Ponticus—pages 22–27

1. *Evagrius Ponticus—The Praktikos and Chapters on Prayer*, trans. John Eudes Bamberger, O.C.S.O. (Spencer, MA and Kalamazoo, MI: Cistercian Publications, 1970), *Chapters*, § 60, p. 65.

2. *The Praktikos*, § 5, p. 16.

3. *Chapters on Prayer*, supplement 4, quoted by F. Refoulé, "Evagrius Ponticus," *New Catholic Encyclopedia* V, pp. 644–45.

4. PG 40:1244A, quoted by John Eudes Bamberger, O.C.S.O., *Evagrius Ponticus— The Praktikos and Chapters on Prayer*, p. xci.

5. *Praktikos*, § 12, p. 18.

6. *Chapters on Prayer*, § 122, p. 75.

7. *Chapters on Prayer*, § 113, p. 74; § 125, p. 76.

8. *Chapters on Prayer*, § 60, p. 65.

9. *Chapters on Prayer*, § 119, p. 75.

## Augustine of Hippo—pages 28–32

1. *Saint Augustine: Confessions*, trans. Henry Chadwick (Oxford, England: Oxford University Press, 1991), I, i (1), p. 4.

2. *Augustine of Hippo—Selected Writings*, trans. Mary T. Clark (Mahwah, NJ: Paulist Press, 1984), *The Confessions*, VII, chap. 17, p. 75.

3. *St. Augustine: The Literal Meaning of Genesis*, trans. John H. Taylor, S.J. (Ramsey, NJ: Newman Press, 1982), II, chap. 11, § 22, p. 191.

## John Cassian—pages 33–36

1. *John Cassian—Conferences*, trans. Colm Luibheid (Mahwah, NJ: Paulist Press, 1985), IX, § 25, p. 116. All references are to this volume.
2. III, § 6, p. 85.
3. X, § 6, p. 128.
4. X, § 11, p. 137.
5. X, § 11, p. 138.
6. X, § 10, p. 133.
7. X, § 10, p. 136.

## Pseudo-Macarius—pages 37–40

1. *Fifty Spiritual Homilies of St. Macarius the Great*, trans. A. J. Mason (Willits, CA: Eastern Orthodox Books, 1974), I, § 2, p. 2.
2. *Pseudo-Macarius: The Fifty Spiritual Homilies and The Great Letter*, ed. and trans. George A. Maloney, S.J. (Mahwah, NJ: Paulist Press, 1992), XV, § 20, p. 116.
3. Homily VIII, § 6, p. 68, Luibheid translation.
4. Homily XV, § 13, p. 112, Luibheid translation.
5. Homily 7, § 3, p. 66, Maloney translation.
6. *Pseudo-Macarius: The Fifty Spiritual Homilies and The Great Letter*, p. 257.

## Pseudo-Dionysius—pages 41–47

1. *Varieties of Mystic Experience*, trans. Elmer O'Brien (New York: New American Library, 1965), *The Mystical Theology*, I, 997A, p. 69.
2. *Pseudo-Dionysius—The Complete Works*, trans. Colm Luibheid (Mahwah, NJ: Paulist Press, 1987), *Letter Four*, p. 265. All references are to this volume.
3. *The Celestial Hierarchy*, III, § 1, 424D, p. 209.
4. *The Mystical Theology*, I, § 3, 1000C, p. 137.
5. *The Mystical Theology*, I, § 3, 1000C, p. 136.
6. *The Divine Names*, VII, § 3, 872A, p. 108.
7. *The Divine Names*, V, § 8, 842B, p. 101.
8. *The Celestial Hierarchy*, III, §§ 1–2, 164D–165A, pp. 153–54, my emphasis.
9. *The Celestial Hierarchy* I, § 1, 376A, p. 198.
10. *Letter Three*, 1069B, p. 264.

## Gregory the Great—pages 48–53

1. *Homily on Ezekiel*, II, v, quoted by Dom Cuthbert Butler, *Western Mysticism* (New York: Gordon Press, 1975, 3rd ed.), p. 70.
2. Epistolae 1.5, quoted by Bernard McGinn, *The Growth of Mysticism: Gregory the Great through the 12th Century*, vol. II of *The Presence of God: A History of Western*

*Christian Mysticism* (New York: Crossroad, 1994), p. 36. Henceforth referred to as McGinn II.

3. *Homily on Ezekiel*, II, V. 17, 9. Quoted by Cuthbert Butler, p. 70.
4. *Moralia in Job*, 24.6.10, quoted by McGinn II, p. 56.


## John Climacus—pages 54–57

1. *John Climacus: The Ladder of Divine Ascent*, trans. Colm Luibheid and Norman V. Russell (Mahwah, NJ: Paulist Press, 1982), step 27, p. 269. All references are to this text.
2. Step 4, pp. 96–97.
3. Step 5, p. 128.
4. Step 30, p. 286.
5. Step 7, p. 137.
6. Step 3, p. 90.


## Maximus Confessor—pages 58–61

1. *Maximus Confessor—Selected Writings*, trans. George C. Berthold (Mahwah, NJ: Paulist Press, 1985), *Chapters on Knowledge*, Second Century, § 37, p. 156. All references in this chapter are to this text.
2. *The Four Hundred Chapters on Love*, Third Century, § 99, p. 75
3. *The Church's Mystagogy*, p. 203.


## Isaac the Syrian—pages 62–64

1. *The Ascetical Homilies of Saint Isaac the Syrian*, trans. The Holy Transfiguration Monastery (Brookline, MA: Holy Transfiguration Monastery, 1984), homily 23, p. 122.
2. Homily 23, p. 115.


## Symeon the New Theologian—pages 65–69

1. *Hymns of Divine Love by Symeon the New Theologian*, trans. George A. Maloney, S.J. (Denville, NJ: Dimension Books, 1976), hymn 25, p. 136.
2. Hymn 50, p. 254.
3. Hymn 19, p. 88.
4. Hymn 23, p. 122.
5. Hymn 50, p. 253.
6. Hymn 18, p. 80.
7. *Symeon the New Theologian—The Discourses*, trans. C. J. de Catanzario (Mahwah, NJ: Paulist Press, 1980), XXXIII, § 4, p. 337.

## William of St. Thierry—pages 70–74

1. *William of Saint Thierry—The Mirror of Faith,* trans. Thomas X. Davis (Kalamazoo, MI: Cistercian Publications, 1979), chap. 4, § 6, p. 18.

2. *William of St. Thierry—On Contemplating God, Prayer, Meditations,* trans. Penelope Lawson, C.S.M.V. (Kalamazoo, MI: Cistercian Publications, 1977), *Meditations* 7:7, p. 137.

3. *On Contemplating God,* § 11, p. 57.

4. *On Contemplating God,* § 3, p. 38.

5. *The Golden Epistle,* XVI, § 263, pp. 95–96.

6. *Meditation* 3:8, p. 106.

7. *The Golden Epistle,* XIV, § 249, p. 92.

## Bernard of Clairvaux—pages 75–80

1. *Bernard of Clairvaux—On the Song of Songs,* trans. Kilian Walsh, O.C.S.O. (Kalamazoo, MI: Cistercian Publications, 1980), IV, S. 74, § 5, p. 89. References to Bernard's eighty-six sermons in the four-volume Cistercian Publications series will be given according to volume, sermon, paragraph, and page number.

2. *Consideration,* 3:492.10–14, quoted by McGinn II, p. 207.

3. *Song* I, S. 6, § 3, p. 33.

4. *Song* I, S. 15, § 6, p. 110.

5. *Song* I, S. 20, § 4, p. 150.

6. *Song* II, S. 43, § 4, pp. 222–23.

7. *Song* I, S. 4, § 1, p. 21.

8. *Song* II, S. 32, § 3, pp. 135–36.

9. *Song* I, S. 8, § 5, pp. 47–48.

10. *Song* IV, S. 69, § 8, p. 35.

11. *Song* II, S. 41, § 6, p. 208.

## Hildegard of Bingen—pages 81–84

1. *Hildegard of Bingen—Scivias,* trans. Mother Columba Hart and Jane Bishop (Mahwah, NJ: Paulist Press, 1990), "Declaration," p. 59. All references are to this work.

2. "Declaration," p. 60.

3. II, Vision 2, intro., p. 161.

4. II, Vision 2, § 9, p. 165.

## Aelred of Rievaulx—pages 85–88

1. *Aelred of Rievaulx—Spiritual Friendship,* trans. Mary Eugenia Laker, S.S.N.D. (Kalamazoo, MI: Cistercian Publications, 1974), 1:70, p. 66. References are to this volume, unless otherwise noted.

2. 2:61, pp. 84–85.

3. 1:65, p. 65.

4. *Aelred of Rievaulx—Mirror of Charity*, trans. Elizabeth Connor, O.C.S.O. (Kalamazoo, MI: Cistercian Publications, 1990), 1.34, p. 106.

5. 3:82, p. 112.

6. Prologue, § 5, p. 46.


## Richard of St. Victor—pages 89–93

1. *Richard of St. Victor—The Twelve Patriarchs, The Mystical Ark, Book Three of the Trinity*, trans. Grover A. Zinn (Mahwah, NJ: Paulist Press, 1979), *The Mystical Ark*, IV, chap. XVII, p. 292.

2. *Mystical Ark*, I, chap. 4, p. 157.

3. *Mystical Ark*, I, chap. 4, p. 157.

4. *Twelve Patriarchs*, chap. 13, p. 65.

5. *Mystical Ark*, IV, chap. 23, p. 306.


## Guigo II—pages 94–96

1. *Guigo II: The Ladder of Monks. A Letter on the Contemplative Life and Twelve Meditations*, trans. Edmund Colledge, O.S.A., and James Walsh, S.J. (Kalamazoo, MI: Cistercian Publications, 1981), *Ladder*, II, pp. 67–68.

2. *Ladder*, V, p. 72.

3. *Twelve Meditations*, I, p. 90.

4. *Twelve Meditations*, IV, p. 100.


## Francis of Assisi—pages 97–100

1. *The Little Flowers of St. Francis*, trans. Raphael Brown (Garden City, NY: Doubleday, 1958), pp. 190–91.

2. Bernard McGinn, *The Flowering of Mysticism: Men and Women in the New Mysticism—1200–1350*, vol. III of *The Presence of God: A History of Western Christian Mysticism* (New York: Crossroad, 1998), p. 342, n. 96. Henceforth referred to as McGinn III.


## Giles of Assisi—pages 101–2

1. *Actus Beati Francisci et Sociorum Ejus*, quoted by Martin Buber, in *Ecstatic Confessions*, ed. Paul Mendes-Flohr and trans. Esther Cameron (San Francisco: Harper & Row, 1985), p. 48.

2. *Actus Beati Francisci et Sociorum Ejus*, quoted by Martin Buber, in *Ecstatic Confessions*, pp. 49–50, my emphasis.

## A Few Women of the New Mysticism—pages 103–12

1. Margaret of Cortona, quoted by McGinn III, p. 41.
2. Quoted by McGinn III, p. 161.
3. Quoted by McGinn III, p. 69.
4. Quoted by McGinn III, p. 137.
5. Quoted by McGinn III, p. 197.
6. Quoted by McGinn III, p. 179.
7. Quoted by McGinn III, pp. 140–41.
8. Quoted by McGinn III, p. 141.

## Hadewijch of Antwerp—pages 113–16

1. *Hadewijch: The Complete Works*, trans. Mother Columba Hart, O.S.B. (Mahwah, NJ: Paulist Press, 1980), *Poems in Couplets*, 16, p. 356. All references are to the Hart translation.
2. Letter 24, p. 103.
3. *Poems in Couplets*, 16, § 45, p. 353.
4. *Poems in Couplets*, 16, § 85, p. 354.
5. Vision 13, § 97, p. 299.
6. Vision 5, § 59, p. 277.
7. *Poems in Stanza*, 33, § 25, p. 222.
8. Vision 11, § 49, p. 290.
9. Letter 30, § 107, p. 118.
10. Vision 30, § 114, p. 118.
11. Vision 30, § 123, p. 118.
12. Vision 11, § 90, p. 289.
13. Vision 7, § 64, p. 281.
14. Letter 29, § 44, pp. 114–15.
15. Letter 17, § 26, pp. 82–83.

## Bonaventure—pages 117–21

1. *Bonaventure—The Soul's Journey into God, The Tree of Life, The Life of St. Francis*, trans. Ewert Cousins (Mahwah, NJ: Paulist Press, 1978), *Soul's Journey into God*, VII, § 3, p. 112. Referred to as Cousins translation.
2. *The Journey of the Mind to God*, ed. Stephen F. Brown, trans. Philotheus Boehner, O.F.M. (Indianapolis, IN: Hackett Publishing, 1991), VII, § 4, p. 38. Referred to as Boehner translation.
3. Cousins translation, *The Life of St. Francis*, prologue, § 3, p. 182.
4. Boehner translation, prologue, § 2, p. 54.
5. Boehner translation, VII, § 6, p. 39.

6. Cousins translation, *The Tree of Life*, 8th fruit, § 29, p. 154.

7. Cousins translation, *Journey*, prologue, § 3, p. 54.

## Thomas Aquinas—pages 122–27

1. Quoted by Jean-Pierre Torrell, O.P., *Saint Thomas Aquinas*, vol. I, *The Person and His Work*, trans. Robert Royal (Washington, DC: The Catholic University of America Press, 1996), p. 289. Henceforth referred to as Torrell I.

2. Torrell I, p. 289, my emphasis.

3. *Summa Theologiae* I, q. 2, a. 1.

4. *De Veritate*, q. 18, a. 104, quoted by Bernard McGinn, *The Harvest of Mysticism in Medieval Germany*, vol. IV of *The Presence of God. A History of Western Christian Mysticism* (New York: Crossroad, 2005), p. 31. Henceforth referred to as McGinn IV.

5. ST Ia, q. 8, a. 3, ad. 3, quoted in Jean-Pierre Torrell, O.P., *Saint Thomas Aquinas, vol. II, Spiritual Master*, trans. Robert Royal (Washington, DC: The Catholic University of America Press, 2003), p. 69. Henceforth referred to as Torrell II.

6. Quoted in Torrell I, p. 284.

7. Quoted in Torrell I, p. 285.

8. *Summa Contra Gentiles*, IV, 22, n. 3585. Quoted by Torrell II, p. 170.

## Jacopone da Todi—pages 128–30

1. *Jacopone da Todi—The Lauds*, trans. Serge and Elizabeth Hughes (Mahwah, NJ: Paulist Press, 1982), § 90, p. 261. All references are to this volume.

2. § 41, p. 144.

3. § 55, p. 177.

4. § 56, p. 178.

5. § 55, p. 176.

6. § 65, pp. 198–99.

7. § 65, p. 200.

8. § 48, p. 165.

9. § 91, pp. 272, 266.

10. § 90, p. 259.

11. § 91, p. 269.

12. § 23, p. 108.

13. § 24, p. 113.

14. § 25, p. 116.

15. § 82, p. 239.

16. § 63, p. 193.

## Ramon Llull—pages 131–34

1. Ramon Llull, *The Book of the Lover and Beloved*, ed. Kenneth Leech, trans. E. Allison Peers (Mahwah, NJ: Paulist Press, 1978), introduction, p. 11.

2. *Blanquerna: A Thirteenth Century Romance*, trans. E. Allison Peers (London: Jarrolds Publishers, 1926), Book 5, XCIX, § 2, p. 410.

3. *The Book of the Lover and the Beloved*, trans. Mark D. Johnston (Warminster, England: Aris & Phillips, 1995), chap. 100, § 3, p. 5.

4. *The Book of the Lover and the Beloved*, trans. E. Allison Peers (New York: Macmillan, 1923), § 95, p. 47.

5. § 3362, p. 108.

6. *Blanquerna*, § 350, pp. 465–66.

7. Peers translation (1978), § 258, p. 79.

8. Peers translation (1923), § 226, pp. 345–46.

9. Johnston translation, § 351, p. 135.

## Angela of Foligno—pages 135–40

1. *Book of Divine Consolation of the Blessed Angela of Foligno*, trans. Mary G. Steegmann (New York: Duffield and Windus, 1909), 8th vision, p. 191. Referred to as Steegmann translation.

2. *Angela of Foligno: Complete Works*, trans. Paul Lachance, O.F.M. (Mahwah, NJ: Paulist Press, 1993), *Instructions* XXXVI, p. 315. References are to the Lachance translation, unless otherwise noted.

3. *Memorial*, VII, p. 192.

4. *Instructions*, II, p. 222.

5. *Memorial*, III, p. 142.

6. *Memorial*, III, p. 142.

7. *Instructions*, XXI, p. 277.

8. *Instructions*, XXI, p. 277.

9. *Memorial*, III, p. 143.

10. *Memorial*, VII, p. 182.

11. *Instructions*, IV, p. 245.

12. *Instructions*, IV, p. 247.

13. *Memorial*, IX, pp. 204.

14. *Memorial*, IX, p. 203.

15. *Memorial*, IX, p. 205.

16. *Memorial*, IX, p. 205.

17. *Memorial*, IX, p. 205.

18. *Memorial*, VI, p. 170.

19. *Memorial*, IX, p. 213.

20. Steegmann translation, 8th vision, p. 191.

21. *Memorial*, IX, p. 214.

22. *Memorial*, VIII, p. 199.

23. *Memorial*, VIII, p. 197.

24. *Instructions*, XXVI, p. 284.

25. *Instructions*, XXIII, p. 280.

## Gertrude the Great—pages 141–44

1. *The Life and Revelations of Saint Gertrude, Virgin and Abbess of the Order of St. Benedict*, trans. M. F. C. Cusak (Westminster, MD: Christian Classics, 1983), chap. 4, p. 80. Referred to as Cusak translation.

2. *Gertrude of Helfta: The Herald of Divine Love*, trans. Margaret Winkworth (New York: Paulist Press, 1993), II, chap. 23, p. 130. Referred to as Winkworth translation.

3. Cusak translation, chap. 39, pp. 93–94.

4. *The Herald of Divine Love*, V, chap. 33. Quoted by McGinn III, p. 272.

5. Winkworth translation, II, chap. 21, p. 126.

6. Winkworth translation, II, chap. 4, p. 100.

7. Cusak translation, chap. 8, p. 89.

8. Cusak translation, chap. 6, p. 86.

9. Cusak translation, chap. 9, p. 91.

## Mechthild of Magdeburg—pages 145–48

1. *Revelations of Mechthild of Magdeburg* or *The Flowing Light of the Godhead*, trans. Lucy Menzies (London: Longmans, Green, 1953), VI, § 43, p. 203. Referred to as Menzies translation.

2. Menzies translation, IV, § 13, p. 108.

3. *Mechthild of Magdeburg: The Flowing Light of the Godhead*, trans. Frank Tobin (Mahwah, NJ: Paulist Press, 1998), III, § 26, p. 96. Referred to as Tobin translation.

4. Tobin translation, I, § 22, p. 50.

5. Tobin translation, IV, § 12, p. 153.

6. Menzies translation, I, § 44, p. 24.

7. Tobin translation, II, § 22, p. 87.

8. Tobin translation, II, § 22, p. 87.

9. Tobin translation, II, § 25, p. 96.

10. Tobin translation, II, § 6, p. 76.

11. I, § 44, p. 62

12. Menzies translation, III, § 10, p. 79.

13. Menzies translation, II, § 44, p. 25.

14. Tobin translation, VI, § 12, p. 156.

15. Tobin translation, VII, § 3, p. 277.

## Marguerite Porete—pages 149–54

1. *Marguerite Porete—The Mirror of Simple Souls*, trans. Ellen L. Babinsky (Mahwah, NJ: Paulist Press, 1993), chap. 135, p. 218. All references are to this text.

2. Chap. 140, p. 222.

3. Chap. 97, p. 171.

4. Chap. 23, p. 106.

5. Chap. 59, p. 136.

6. Chaps. 55–56, pp. 132–33.

7. Chap. 118, p. 190.

8. Chap. 57, p. 134.

9. Chap. 118, p. 190.

10. Chap. 118, p. 193.

11. Chap. 81, p. 156.

12. Chap. 81, p. 156.

13. Chap. 82, p. 158.

14. Chap. 131, p. 213.

15. Chap. 131, p. 214, my emphasis.

16. Chap. 118, p. 193.

17. Chap. 58, p. 135.

18. Chap. 61, p. 138.

19. Chap. 23, p. 106.

20. Chap. 85, p. 160, my emphasis.

21. Chap. 83, p. 159.

## Meister Eckhart—pages 155–58

1. *Meister Eckhart*, trans. Raymond B. Blakney (San Francisco: Harper & Row, 1941), sermon 12, p. 270. Referred to as Blakney translation.

2. Blakney translation, p. 259.

3. *Meister Eckhart—The Essential Sermons, Commentaries, Treatises, and Defense*, trans. Bernard McGinn & Edmund Colledge, O.S.A. (New York: Paulist Press, 1981), sermon 5b, p. 183.

4. *Meister Eckhart—Teacher and Preacher*, ed. Bernard McGinn (Mahwah, NJ: Paulist Press, 1986), sermon 12, p. 270.

5. Blakney translation, sermon 24, p. 211.

6. *Teacher and Preacher*, sermon 86, p. 341.

7. *Teacher and Preacher*, sermon 86, p. 341.

8. Blakney translation, sermon 19, p. 186.

9. *Essential Sermons*, sermon 52, p. 199.

10. *Essential Sermons*, sermon 52, p. 203.

11. Tony Hendra, *Father Joe: The Man Who Saved My Soul* (New York: Random House, 2004), p. 199. Although I have never found this quotation in the Meister's work, it sounds like something he would have written.

12. *Teacher and Preacher*, sermon 10, p. 265.

13. *Essential Sermons*, sermon 22, p. 196.

14. The first of the "Sayings" ascribed to Eckhart and the subtitle of Bernard McGinn's excellent volume *The Mystical Thought of Meister Eckhart: The Man From Whom God Hid Nothing* (New York: Crossroad, 2001), p. 183, note 2.

## John Ruusbroec—pages 159–64

1. John Ruusbroec, *Spiritual Espousals*, trans. Eric Colledge (Westminster, MD: Christian Classics, 1953), II/III, C, d., 2, p. 141.

2. *John Ruusbroec—The Spiritual Espousals and Other Works*, trans. James A. Wiseman, O.S.B. (Mahwah, NJ: Paulist Press, 1985), *Mirror*, II, B, p. 231. Referred to as Wiseman translation.

3. The Jewish philosopher-mystic Martin Buber admitted that what he had once assumed was an experience of God was, in fact, an experience of what he called "the original prebiographical unity" of his soul. This seems analogous to what Ruusbroec says about "natural rest." See Martin Buber, *Between Man and Man* (New York: Macmillan, 1972), p. 24.

4. *Little Book of Clarification*, I, B, p. 256, Wiseman translation.

5. *Little Book of Clarification*, 3, A, p. 263, Wiseman translation.

6. *Espousals*, II, 4, B, p. 129, Wiseman translation.

7. *Little Book of Clarification*, I, B, p. 257, Wiseman translation.

8. John Ruusbroec, *The Spiritual Espousals* (Collegeville, MN: Liturgical Press, 1995), trans. Helen Rolfson, O.F.M., § 848, p. 58. Referred to as Rolfson translation.

9. Rolfson translation, §§ 860, 864, p. 59.

10. *Little Book of Clarification*, III, B, p. 264, Wiseman translation.

11. *Little Book of Clarification*, II, B, p. 259, Wiseman translation.

12. Rolfson translation, §§ b 1340–44, p. 92.

13. Rolfson translation, §§ b 1344–52, p. 92.

14. *Sparkling Stone*, II, D, p. 176, my emphasis, Wiseman translation.

15. *Sparkling Stone*, II, G, p. 183, Wiseman translation.

16. *Sparkling Stone*, II, G, pp. 183–84, Wiseman translation.


## Gregory Palamas—pages 165–69

1. John Meyendorff, ed., *Gregory Palamas—The Triads*, trans. Nicholas Gendle (Mahwah, NJ: Paulist Press, 1983), B., I. iii., §18, p. 36. All references are to this volume.

2. C., I. ii., §§ 7, 8, pp. 45–46.

3. C., I. ii., § 4, p. 44.

4. C., I. ii., § 4, p. 44.

5. B., I. iii., § 23, p. 39.

6. C., II ii., § 12, p. 51.


## Richard Rolle—pages 170–75

1. *Richard Rolle—The Fire of Love*, trans. Clifton Wolters (Harmondsworth, England: Penguin, 1972), chap. 15, p. 93. Referred to as Wolters translation.

2. *The Fire of Love*, trans. G. C. Heseltine (London: Burns Oates & Washbourne, 1935), chap. 15, p. 63. Referred to as Heseltine translation.

3. *The Fire of Love and The Mending of Life*, trans. M. L. del Mastro (Garden City, NY: Doubleday, 1981), chap. 19, p. 164. Referred to as del Mastro translation.

4. Wolters translation, chap. 34, p. 151.

5. *Richard Rolle—The English Writings* (Mahwah, NJ: Paulist Press, 1988), trans. Rosamund S. Allen, *The Form of Living*, chap. 9, p. 173.

6. Wolters translation, chap. 8, p. 60.

7. Del Mastro translation, chap. 37, p. 236.

8. Del Mastro translation, chap. 37, p. 236.

9. Wolters translation, chap. 8, p. 68.

10. Heseltine translation, chap. 21, p. 87.

11. Del Mastro translation, chap. 21, p. 168.

12. Wolters translation, chap. 21, p. 110.

13. Wolters translation, chap. 21, p. 112.

14. Heseltine translation, chap. 39, pp. 173–74.

15. Heseltine translation, chap. 39, p. 170.


## Johannes Tauler—pages 176–81

1. Sermon 56, quoted by McGinn IV, p. 290.

2. Sermon 45, quoted by McGinn IV, p. 240.

3. *Johannes Tauler: Sermons*, trans. Maria Shrady (New York: Paulist Press, 1985), sermon 29, p. 104. Referred to as Shrady translation.

4. Sermon 26, p. 97, Shrady translation.

5. Sermon 28, p. 107, Shrady translation.

6. Sermon 41, quoted by McGinn IV, p. 263.

7. Sermon 45, quoted by McGinn IV, p. 264.

8. Sermon 64, quoted by McGinn IV, pp. 255–56.

9. Sermon 64, quoted by McGinn IV, p. 256.

10. Sermon 50, quoted by McGinn IV, p. 292.

11. Sermon 37, p. 128, Shrady translation.

12. Sermon 15, quoted by McGinn IV, p. 271.

13. Sermon 40, p. 139, Shrady translation.


## Henry Suso—pages 182–88

1. *Little Book of Eternal Wisdom and Little Book of Truth*, trans. James M. Clark (London: Farber and Farber, 1953), *Little Book of Eternal Wisdom*, I, chap. 13, pp. 97–98.

2. *The Life of Blessed Henry Suso: By Himself*, trans. Thomas Francis Knox (London: Methuen, 1913), chap. 1, p. 5.

3. *Henry Suso—The Exemplar, with Two German Sermons*, ed. and trans. Frank Tobin (Mahwah, NJ: Paulist Press, 1989), *The Life of the Servant*, I, chap. 1, p. 65.

4. *Life of the Servant*, Tobin translation, I, chap. 32, p. 129.

5. *Life of the Servant*, Tobin translation, I, chap. 32, p. 130.

6. *Blessed Henry Suso: Wisdom's Watch Upon the Hours. The Fathers of the Church: Medieval Continuation*, vol. 4, trans. Edmund Colledge, O.S.A. (Washington, DC: The Catholic University of America Press, 1994), I, chap. 9, p. 155.

7. *Wisdom's Watch Upon the Hours*, I, chap. 9, p. 155.

8. *Wisdom's Watch Upon the Hours*, II, chap. 3, p. 264.

9. Quoted by McGinn IV, p. 205.

10. *Sermons*, Tobin translation, 4, p. 371.

11. *Little Book of Eternal Wisdom*, Clark translation, I, chap. 4, p. 38.

12. *Life of the Servant*, Tobin translation, chap. 13, p. 84.

13. *Life of the Servant*, Tobin translation, chap. 28, p. 131.

14. *Life of the Servant*, Tobin translation, chap. 46, p. 176.

15. *Little Book of Truth*, Tobin translation, chap. 5, p. 320.

16. *Little Book of Truth*, Tobin translation, chap. 3, p. 311.

17. *The Exemplar: Life and Writings of Blessed Henry Suso, O.P.*, vol. 1, trans. Sister M. Ann Edward, O.P. (Dubuque, IA: Priory Press, 1962), chap. 52, P. 174.

18. *The Exemplar*, p. 174.

19. *The Exemplar*, p. 174.

20. *The Exemplar*, p. 174.

21. *Little Book of Eternal Wisdom*, Clark translation, chap. 24, pp. 153–54.

22. *Little Book of Eternal Wisdom*, chap. 24, p. 288.

## Walter Hilton—pages 189–93

1. *Walter Hilton: The Scale of Perfection*, trans. John P. H. Clark and Rosemary Dorward (Mahwah, NJ: Paulist Press, 1991), II, chap. 22, p. 231. Referred to as Clark-Dorward translation.

2. Clark-Dorward translation, I, chap. 3, p. 79.

3. Clark-Dorward translation, I, chap. 8, p. 82.

4. *The Scale of Perfection*, trans. Dom Gerard Sitwell, O.S.B. (London: Burns Oates, 1953), I, chap. 93, p. 138. Referred to as Sitwell translation.

5. Sitwell translation, I, chap. 92, p. 138.

6. Clark-Dorward translation, I, chap. 54, p. 125.

7. Sitwell translation, II, chap. 33, p. 246. Hilton's emphasis.

8. Sitwell translation, II, chap. 32, p. 241.

9. Clark-Dorward translation, II, chap. 43, pp. 295–96.

10. Clark-Dorward translation, II, chap. 32, p. 261.

## Julian of Norwich—pages 194–200

1. *Julian of Norwich—Showings*, trans. Edmund Colledge, O.S.A., and James Walsh, S.J. (Mahwah, NJ: Paulist Press, 1978), chap. 82, p. 339. Referred to as Colledge-Walsh translation.

2. *The Revelations of Divine Love of Julian of Norwich*, trans. James Walsh, S.J. (New York: Harper & Brothers, 1961), chap. 4, p. 51. Referred to as Walsh translation 1961.

3. Colledge-Walsh translation, chap. 4, p. 181.

4. *Revelations of Divine Love Shewed to a Devout Anchoress by Name Julian of Norwich*, trans. Dom Roger Huddleston, O.S.B. (Westminster, MD: Newman Press, 1927), chap. I, p. 1. Referred to as Huddleston translation.

5. Colledge-Walsh translation, chap. 68, p. 315.

6. *Julian of Norwich: Revelations of Divine Love*, trans. Clifton Wolters (London: Penguin Books, 1966), chap. 43, p. 129. Referred to as Wolters translation.

7. Wolters translation, chap. 5, p. 68.

8. Colledge-Walsh translation, chap. 5, p. 184.

9. Colledge-Walsh translation, chap. xiii, p. 146. Lowercase Roman numerals for chapters refer to the *Short Text*.

10. *Julian of Norwich: Revelation of Love*, trans. John Skinner (New York: Image Doubleday, 1997), chap. 31, p. 61. Referred to as Skinner translation.

11. Colledge-Walsh translation, chap. 32, p. 233.

12. Colledge-Walsh translation, chap. 34, p. 236.

13. Huddleston translation, chap. 61, p. 126.

14. Colledge-Walsh translation, chap. xvii, p. 154.

15. Colledge-Walsh translation, chap. 38, p. 242.

16. Wolters translation, chap. 49, p. 138.

17. Skinner translation, chap. 50, pp. 98–99.

18. Colledge-Walsh translation, chap. 51, p. 267.

19. Wolters translation, chap. 51, p. 270.

20. Colledge-Walsh translation, chap. 51, p. 276.

21. Huddleston translation, chap. 59, p. 122.

22. Colledge-Walsh translation, chap. 60, p. 298.

23. Wolters translation, chap. 86, pp. 211–12.

## The Anonymous Author of *The Cloud Of Unknowing*— pages 201–7

1. *The Cloud of Unknowing and the Book of Privy Counseling* (Garden City, NJ: Doubleday-Image, 1976), ed. William Johnston, S.J., *Cloud*, chaps. 4–5, p. 53. Referred to as *Cloud* and *Counseling*.

2. *Counseling*, chap. 17, p. 179.

3. *Counseling*, chap. 12, p. 172.

4. *Cloud*, chap. 16, p. 70.

5. *Cloud*, chap. 17, p. 71.

6. *The Pursuit of Wisdom and Other Works*, ed. and trans. James A. Walsh, S.J. (Mahwah, NJ: Paulist Press, 1988), *The Assessment of Inward Stirrings*, p. 142.

7. *Cloud*, chap. 49, p. 111.


## Catherine of Siena—pages 208–13

1. *The Letters of St. Catherine of Siena* I, trans. Suzanne Noffke, O.P. (Binghamton, NY: Medieval and Renaissance Texts and Studies, 1988), Letter 31 (June 1375) to Frate Raimondo da Capua, p. 108.

2. *Legenda Major* III, iii, quoted by Suzanne Noffke, O.P., trans., *Catherine of Siena—The Dialogue* (Mahwah, NJ: Paulist Press, 1980), p. 12.

3. *Dialogue*, § 26, pp. 64–65.

4. *Dialogue*, § 90, p. 167.

5. *Dialogue*, § 91, pp. 168–69.

6. *Dialogue*, § 96, p. 181.

7. Letter 58 (1376) to Monna Melina, p. 180.

8. Letter 84 (October–November 1376) to the monks of the Monastery of San Girolamo at Cervaia, p. 254.

9. Letter 84 (October–November 1376) to the monks of the Monastery of San Girolamo at Cervaia, p. 255.

10. *The Prayers of Catherine of Siena*, ed. Suzanne Noffke, O.P. (Mahwah, NJ: Paulist Press, 1983), prayers 10 and 11, pp. 82, 89.

11. Prayer 20, p. 189.

12. Letter 371 and a letter to Sister Catherine Petriboni, quoted by Noffke, *Prayers*, pp. 228–29.


## Thomas à Kempis—pages 214–17

1. *My Imitation of Christ*, trans. Msgr. John J. Gorman (Brooklyn, NY: Confraternity of the Precious Blood, 1982), II, chap. 1, § 6, p. 106. References are to this volume, unless otherwise specified.

2. *Devotio Moderna: Basic Writings*, trans. John van Engen (Mahwah, NJ: Paulist Press, 1988), "On the Life and Passion of Our Lord Jesus Christ, and Other Devotional Exercises," pp. 188–89.

3. I, chap. 1, § 1, p. 5.

4. IV, chap. 13, § 1, p. 437.

5. I, chap. 11, § 3, p. 33.

6. II, chap. 1, § 1, p. 103.

7. II, chap. 12 § 2, p. 145.

8. III, chap. 43, §§ 2–3, pp. 304–5.

9. IV, chap. 16, § 3, p. 449.

## Nicholas of Cusa—pages 218–22

1. "Letter of Nicholas of Cusa to Kaspar Ayndorffer (September 22, 1542)," *The Essential Writings of Christian Mysticism*, ed. Bernard McGinn (New York: Modern Library, 2006), p. 271. Volume referred to as McGinn, *Essential Writings*.

2. "Letter of the Author to the Lord Cardinal Julian," in *Of Learned Ignorance*, trans. Father Germain Heron, O.F.M. (Westport, CT: Hyperion Press, 1954), p. 173.

3. *Apologia doctae ignorantiae* (h II. 3), quoted by H. Lawrence Bond, trans., *Nicholas of Cusa—Selected Spiritual Writings* (Mahwah, NJ: Paulist Press, 1997), p. 31. Volume referred to as Bond translation.

4. "Letter of Nicholas of Cusa to the Monks of Tegernsee" (September 14, 1453), McGinn, *Essential Writings*, p. 274.

5. *Dialogue On the Hidden God*, § 1, Bond translation, p. 209.

6. *On Seeking God*, II, § 36, Bond translation, p. 225.

7. *The Vision of God*, trans. Emma Gurney Salter (New York: E. P. Dutton, 1960), V, p. 19. Referred to as Salter translation.

8. Salter translation, XII, p. 55.

9. Salter translation, VII, pp. 32–33.

10. *On the Summit of Contemplation*, § 3, Bond translation, p. 294.

11. *On the Summit of Contemplation*, § 5, Bond translation, p. 295.

12. *On the Summit of Contemplation*, § 24, Bond translation, p. 302.

## Catherine of Genoa—pages 223–26

1. *Vita*, quoted by Friedrich von Hügel, *The Mystical Element of Religion as Studied in Saint Catherine of Genoa and Her Friends*, second ed. (Westminster, MD: Christian Classics, 1961), p. 159. Referred to as *Vita*, von Hügel translation.

2. *Catherine of Genoa: Purgation and Purgatory, The Spiritual Dialogue*, trans. Serge Hughes (Mahwah, NJ: Paulist Press, 1979), p. 109.

3. *Vita*, von Hügel translation, p. 268.

4. *Vita*, von Hügel translation, p. 277.

5. *Vita*, von Hügel translation, p. 260.

6. *Vita*, von Hügel translation, p. 264.

7. *Vita*, von Hügel translation, p. 265.

8. *Vita*, von Hügel translation, p. 265.

9. *Vita*, von Hügel translation, p. 273.

10. *Purgation and Purgatory*, Hughes translation, p. 86.

11. *Purgation and Purgatory*, Hughes translation, p. 77.

12. *Purgation and Purgatory*, Hughes translation, p. 79.

13. *Purgation and Purgatory*, Hughes translation, p. 80.

## Ignatius of Loyola—pages 227–34

1. *Letters of St. Ignatius of Loyola*, ed. and trans. William J. Young, S.J. (Chicago: Loyola University Press, 1959), Letter of July 29, 1547 to the College of Gandia, p. 146. Referred to as *Letters*.

2. John Philip Roothaan, S.J. (d. 1853), "the general who rebuilt the Jesuits," wrote a short and highly influential book, *Method of Meditation* (*De ratione meditandi*). The method he described quickly became known as "Jesuit prayer," which it definitely is not. Neither do the contents of this small work represent the best and deepest aspects of Roothaan's spirituality.

3. *The Spiritual Exercises of St. Ignatius*, trans. George E. Ganss, S.J. (St. Louis: Institute of Jesuit Sources, 1992), § 15, p. 25.

4. *A Pilgrim's Journey: The Autobiography of Ignatius of Loyola*, trans. Joseph N. Tylenda, S.J. (Wilmington, DE: Michael Glazier, 1985), § 8, pp. 14–15. Referred to as *Autobiography*.

5. *Autobiography*, § 8, p. 15.

6. *Autobiography*, § 8, p. 15.

7. *Autobiography*, § 10, p. 16.

8. *Autobiography*, § 12, p. 18.

9. *Autobiography*, §§ 9, 11, pp. 15, 17.

10. *Autobiography*, § 29, p. 38.

11. *Autobiography*, § 30, pp. 38–39.

12. Ignatius's *Journal* consists of only two small surviving notebooks from a much larger packet of jottings that the saint probably burned. The first notebook is a diary covering the period from February 2 to March 12, 1544. During this time, Ignatius was deliberating on the degree of poverty to be observed by the churches of the Society. The second notebook covers the period from March 13, 1544, to February 27, 1545. It contains much shorter entries, many algebraic symbols, abbreviations, and cryptic notations. These two notebooks belong together with the most beautiful and most striking pages that Christian mystics have set down on paper.

13. *Autobiography*, § 28, pp. 36–37.

14. *Iñigo: Discernment Log-Book, The Spiritual Diary of Saint Loyola*, ed. and trans. Joseph A. Munitiz, S.J. (London: Iñigo Enterprises, 1987), § 48, p. 33. Referred to as *Log-Book*.

15. *Log-Book*, § 63, p. 35.

16. *Log-Book*, § 72, p. 37.

17. *Log-Book*, § 67, p. 36.

18. *Log-Book*, § 83, pp. 38–39.

19. *Log-Book*, § 87, p. 39.

20. *Log-Book*, § 169, p. 51.

21. *Monumenta Historica Societatis Jesu. S. Ignatii Epistolae XII*, ed. M. Lecina, V. Augusti, F. Cervos, D. Restrepo (Madrid, 1911), p. 667.

22. *Exercises*, § 353.

23. *Letters*, Letter of July 23 and August 7, 1553, to the whole Society, p. 301.

24. *Exercises*, §§ 352–70.

25. *Autobiography*, § 85, p. 98.

26. *Letters*, Letter of September 20, 1548, to Francis Borgia, p. 181.

27. *Letters*, Letter of November 22, 1553, to Nicholas Gaudano, p. 312.

28. *Letters*, Letter of June 18, 1536, to Sister Teresa Rejadell, p. 22.

29. *Letters*, Letter of June 1, 1555, to Father Antony Brandao, p. 240.

30. *Exercises*, § 233, p. 94.

## Francisco de Osuna—pages 235–41

1. *Francisco de Osuna—The Third Spiritual Alphabet*, trans. Mary E. Giles (Mahwah, NJ: Paulist Press, 1981), treatise 15, II, p. 390. Referred to as Giles translation.

2. *Francisco de Osuna—The Third Spiritual Alphabet*, trans. a Benedictine of Stanbrook (Westminster, MD: The Newman Bookshop, 1947), treatise 19, V, p. 404. Referred to as Benedictine translation.

3. Giles translation, treatise 21, IV, p. 562.

4. Benedictine translation, treatise 21, VII, p. 457.

5. Giles translation, treatise 6, II, p. 161.

6. Giles translation, treatise 18, III, pp. 485–86.

7. Benedictine translation, treatise 9, VI, p. 188.

8. Benedictine translation, treatise 12, VI, p. 249.

9. Giles translation, treatise 18, IV, p. 491.

10. Benedictine translation, treatise 9, VI, p. 265.

11. Giles translation, prologue, p. 41.

12. Benedictine translation, treatise 17, V, p. 366.

## Teresa of Avila—pages 242–49

1. St. Teresa of Avila, *The Interior Castle*, trans. and ed. E. Allison Peers (Garden City, NY: Doubleday, 1961), chap. 2, §§ 3–6, pp. 105–6.

2. *The Autobiography of St. Teresa of Avila*, trans. and ed. E. Allison Peers (Garden City, NY: Doubleday, 1960), chap. XXVII, p. 252.

3. *The Collected Works of St. Teresa of Avila I*, trans. Kieran Kavanaugh, O.C.D., and Otilio Rodriguez, O.C.D. (Washington, D.C.: Institute of Carmelite Studies, 1976), *Life*, chap. 26, § 5, p. 172.

4. *Way of Perfection*, ed. and trans. E. Allison Peers (Garden City, NY: Doubleday, 1964), prologue, p. 40, her emphasis.

5. *Autobiography*, chap. XXIX, pp. 274–75.

6. *Collected Works I*, *Life*, chap. 8, § 5, p. 67.

7. *Collected Works I*, *Life*, chap. 32, § 2, p. 214.

8. *Autobiography*, chap. XXXIV, p. 324.

9. *The Collected Works of St. Teresa of Avila II*, trans. Kieran Kavanaugh, O.C.D., and Otilio Rodriguez, O.C.D. (Washington, D.C.: Institute of Carmelite Studies, 1980), *Interior Castle*, VI, chap. 7, § 5, p. 399.

10. *Collected Works I, Life*, chap. 22, § 9, p. 147.

11. *Collected Works I, Life*, chap. 33, § 5, p. 222.

12. *Autobiography*, chap. XXXIII, p. 315.

## John of the Cross—pages 250–56

1. *The Collected Works of St. John of the Cross*, trans. Kieran Kavanaugh, O.C.D., and Otilio Rodriguez, O.C.D. (Washington, D.C.: Institute of Carmelite Studies, 1976), *The Dark Night*, bk. II, chap. 5, § 1, p. 335.

2. *Collected Works*, Kavanaugh-Rodriguez translation, *The Spiritual Canticle*, prologue, § 1, p. 408.

3. *Collected Works*, Kavanaugh-Rodriguez translation, *The Living Flame of Love*, prologue, § 3, p. 578.

4. *The Complete Works of Saint John of the Cross* I, trans. and ed. E. Allison Peers (Westminster, MD: The Newman Press, 1949), *Dark Night*, bk. I, chap. 10, § 6, pp. 380–81.

5. *Collected Works*, Kavanaugh-Rodriguez translation, *Dark Night*, bk. II, chap. 9, § 1, p. 346, my emphasis.

6. *The Complete Works of Saint John of the Cross* II, trans. and ed. E. Allison Peers (Westminster, MD: The Newman Press, 1946), *Spiritual Canticle*, stanza 27, § 7, p. 339.

7. *Collected Works*, Kavanaugh-Rodriguez translation, *Spiritual Canticle*, stanza 31, § 1, p. 531.

8. *The Complete Works of Saint John of the Cross* III, trans. and ed. E. Allison Peers (Westminster, MD: The Newman Press, 1946), *Living Flame of Love*, stanza 4, § 4, p. 209.

9. *Complete Works* II, Peers translation, *Spiritual Canticle*, stanza 13, p. 75.

10. *Complete Works* III, Peers translation, *Living Flame of Love*, stanza 4, § 4, p. 106.

11. *Collected Works*, Kavanaugh-Rodriguez translation, *The Ascent of Mount Carmel*, bk. I, chap. 13, § 11, pp. 103–4.

12. *Collected Works*, Kavanaugh-Rodriguez translation, *Ascent Mount Carmel*, bk. II, chap. 7, § 11, p. 125.

13. *Collected Works*, Kavanaugh-Rodriguez translation, *Ascent Mount Carmel*, bk. II, chap. 7, § 11, p. 125.

14. *Collected Works*, Kavanaugh-Rodriguez translation, *Spiritual Canticle*, stanza 29, § 3, pp. 523–24.

## Johann Arndt—pages 257–61

1. *Johann Arndt: True Christianity*, trans. Peter Erb (New York, NY: Paulist Press, 1979), foreword, p. 21.

2. *True Christianity*, III, 20, quoted by Peter Erb, p. 11.

3. *True Christianity*, V, 7, p. 257.

## Benet of Canfield—pages 262–68

1. *Renaissance Dialectic and Renaissance Piety: Benet of Canfield's Rule of Perfection*, trans. Kent Emery, Jr. (Binghamton, NY: Medieval & Renaissance Texts & Studies, 1987), III, 13, p. 216. All references are to this volume.

2. II, 3, p. 163.

3. II, 4, p. 165.

4. III, 3, p. 181.

5. III, 4, p. 183, my emphasis.

6. III, 20, p. 253.

7. III, 17, p. 235.

8. III, 19, p. 244.

9. III, 20, p. 253.

10. III, 11, p. 210.

11. III, 20, p. 248.

## Francis de Sales—pages 269–74

1. Francis de Sales, *Treatise on the Love of God*, trans. John K. Ryan (Rockford, IL: Tan Books, 1975), vol. II, bk. 7, chaps. 6–7, pp. 30–33.

2. Quoted by Francis Power, "Francis de Sales, St.," *New Catholic Encyclopedia*, second ed., V, p. 866.

3. Francis de Sales, *Introduction to the Devout Life*, trans. John K. Ryan (Garden City, NY: Doubleday, 1972), p. 31.

4. *Devout Life*, V, § 18, p. 291.

5. *Treatise on the Love of God*, I, bk. 6, chap. 2, p. 272.

6. *Treatise on the Love of God*, I, bk. 6, chap. 2, p. 275.

7. *Treatise on the Love of God*, II, bk. 7, chap. 1, p. 17.

8. *Treatise on the Love of God*, II, bk. 9, chap. 4, p. 107, my emphases.

## Pierre de Bérulle—pages 275–79

1. *Bérulle and the French School: Selected Writings*, ed. William M. Thompson, trans. Lowell M. Glendon, S.S. (Mahwah, NJ: Paulist Press, 1989), *Discourse on the State and Grandeurs of Jesus*, 2, 13, p. 126. All references are to this one work, unless otherwise noted.

2. 1, 6, p. 113.

3. 2, 2, p. 116.

4. 2, 13, p. 126.

5. 2, 10, p. 124.

6. 2, 10, p. 125.

7. 28, 1, p. 160.

8. 29, 1, p. 166.

9. 29, 1, p. 166.

10. 28, 1, p. 163.

11. *Elevation of Jesus Christ our Lord Concerning the Conduct of His Spirit and His Grace Toward Mary Magdalene: Selected Writings*, 1, 5, p. 174.

12. *Elevation of Jesus Christ*, 12, p. 179.

## Marie of the Incarnation—pages 280–85

1. *Marie of the Incarnation: Selected Writings*, ed. and trans. Irene Mahoney, O.S.U. (Mahwah, NJ: Paulist Press, 1989), *The Relation of 1654*, 9th state of prayer (= 9th S), XXXIX–XLI, pp. 112–16. All references are to this work.

2. 7th S, XXIX, p. 92.

3. 8th S, XXXII, p. 98.

4. 9th S, XXXIX, p. 113.

5. 9th S, XLI, p. 116.

6. 12th S, LI, p. 142.

7. 12th S, LII, p. 142.

8. 12th S, LII, p. 143.

9. 13th S, LVIII, p. 156.

10. 13th S, LXV, p. 171.

11. 11th S, XLVII, p. 130.

## Blaise Pascal—pages 286–90

1. *Blaise Pascal—Pensées*, trans. A. J. Krailsheimer (New York: Penguin Classics, 1966), § 468, p. 179.

2. *Pensées*, § 149, p. 76.

3. *The Essential Pascal*, ed. Robert W. Gleason, S.J., trans. G. F. Pullen (New York: New American Library, 1966), §§ 626–27, p. 195.

4. Blaise Pascal, *Pensées and Other Writings*, trans. Honor Levi (New York: Oxford University Press, 2008), p. 178.

5. *Pensées*, § 449, p. 169.

6. *The Essential Pascal*, "Religious Writings," pp. 207–10.

## Angelus Silesius—pages 291–93

1. *Angelus Silesius: The Cherubinic Wanderer*, trans. Maria Shrady (Mahwah, NJ: Paulist Press, 1986), bk. 5:339, p. 124.

2. Bk. 3:11, p. 72.

3. Bk. 6:173, p. 134.

4. Bk. 1:108, p. 44.

5. Bk. 5:259, p. 119.

6. Bk. 5:239, p. 117.

7. Bk. 6:1, p. 129.

8. Bk. 6:1, p. 129.

9. *The Cherubinic Wanderer*, trans. Willard R. Trask (New York: Pantheon Books, 1953), bk. 6:263, p. 61.

## George Fox—pages 294–97

1. *The Journal of George Fox*, ed. Rufus M. Jones (Richmond, IN: Friends United Press, 1976), p. 101.

2. *Journal*, p. 66.

3. *Journal*, p. 68.

4. *Journal*, p. 79.

5. *Journal*, p. 78.

6. *Journal*, p. 82.

7. *Journal*, p. 84.

8. *Journal*, p. 101.

9. *Journal*, p. 97.

10. *Journal*, p. 120.

11. Walt Whitman, "Essay in November," *The Collected Writings of Walt Whitman* I, ed. Gay Wilson Allen and Sculley Bradley (New York: New York University Press, 1977), p. 276.

## Crises in Mysticism—pages 298–304

1. Pope Innocent XI, "Coelestis Pater," Bull of November 20, 1687, trans. Bernard McGinn, *The Essential Writings of Christian Mysticism* (New York: Modern Library, 2002), p. 503. Referred to as McGinn, *Essential Writings*.

2. McGinn, *Essential Writings*, p. 491.

3. McGinn, *Essential Writings*, p. 494.

4. McGinn, *Essential Writings*, p. 507.

5. Montanus, a second-century self-proclaimed prophet, identified himself as the "Paraclete," announced the imminent end of the world, and viewed the prophets in his group as the first manifestations of the definitive coming of the Spirit. The prophetesses, Priscilla and Maximilla, are his most well-known followers in the rigorously ascetical movement they initiated.

6. McGinn, *Essential Writings*, p. 508.

## Viscount Charles-Eugène de Foucauld—pages 305–6

1. *Meditations of a Hermit*, trans. Charles Balfour (Maryknoll, NY: Orbis Books, 1981), Nazareth, 1897, p. 131.

2. *Charles de Foucauld*, writings selected by Robert Ellsberg (Maryknoll, NY: Orbis Books, 1999), letter of August 14, 1901, p. 31.

3. *Charles de Foucauld*, June 1896, witness 51–53, p. 85.

4. *Charles de Foucauld*, p. 9.

5. *Meditations of a Hermit*, Nazareth, 1897, p. 131.


## Thérèse of Lisieux—pages 307–12

1. *Story of a Soul: The Autobiography of St. Thérèse of Lisieux*, trans. John Clark, O.C.D. (Washington, DC: Institute of Carmelite Studies, 1976), p. 194. All quotations in this chapter duplicate the emphases, capitalization, and punctuation found in Thérèse's texts.

2. *Story of a Soul*, p. 194.

3. *St. Thérèse of Lisieux: Her Last Conversations*, trans. John Clarke, O.C.D. (Washington, DC: Institute of Carmelite Studies, 1977), p. 135.

4. *Story of a Soul*, p. 265.

5. *Saint Thérèse of Lisieux: General Correspondence* (1877–1890) I, trans. John Clarke, O.C.D. (Washington, DC: Institute of Carmelite Studies, 1973), Letter 85, her emphasis. In her letter to her sister Céline (Letter 65), she writes, "What a grace when, in the morning, we feel no courage, no strength to practice virtue; that is the moment to put the axe to the root of the tree. . . . We are tempted to leave all behind, but in one act of love, even *unfelt* love, all is repaired."

6. *Her Last Conversations*, p. 134.

7. *Her Last Conversations*, p. 88.

8. *Her Last Conversations*, p. 77.

9. *Story of a Soul*, p. 266.

10. *Story of a Soul*, p. 213.

11. *Story of a Soul*, p. 219.

12. *Her Last Conversations*, p. 217.

13. *Her Last Conversations*, p. 205.

14. *Story of a Soul*, p. 271.


## Gemma Galgani—pages 313–17

1. Father Germanus of St. Stanislaus, Passionist, *The Life of the Servant of God Gemma Galgani: An Italian Maiden of Lucca* (St. Louis: B. Herder Book, 1913), trans. A. M. O'Sullivan, O.S.B., chap. XXV, p. 287. All references are to this volume.

2. Chap. XXII, p. 235.

3. Chap. XVI, p. 164.

4. Chap. XXV, p. 282.

5. Chap. XXIII, p. 252.

6. Chap. XII, p. 116.

7. Chap. XIV, p. 137.

8. Chap. VII, p. 59.

9. Chap. XIX, p. 198.

10. Chap. XXX, p. 345.

11. Chap. XXX, p. 347.

## Elizabeth of the Trinity—pages 318–21

1. *Elizabeth of the Trinity. Complete Works*, II: *Letters from Carmel*, ed. Conrad de Meester, O.C.D., trans. Ann Englund Nash (Washington, DC: Institute of Carmelite Studies, 1995), letter 269, pp. 264–65.

2. *Reminiscences of Sister Elizabeth of the Trinity, Servant of God, Discalced Carmelite of Dijon*, trans. a Benedictine of Stanbrook Abbey (Westminster, MD: Newman Press, 1952), p. 11.

3. Conrad de Meester, O.C.D., *Light, Love, Life: A Look at a Face and a Heart*, trans. Sr. Aletheia Kane, O.C.D. (Washington, DC: Institute of Carmelite Studies, 1987), p. 13.

4. *Elizabeth of the Trinity. Complete Works*, I, ed. Conrad de Meester, O.C.D., trans. Sister Aletheia Kane, O.C.D. (Washington, DC: Institute of Carmelite Studies, 1984), p. 184.

5. *Complete Works*, I, *Heaven in Faith*, § 43, p. 112.

6. Letter 169, p. 110.

7. Letter 131, p. 60.

8. *Light, Love, Life*, p. 137.

9. Letter 335, p. 360.

10. *Light, Love, Life*, p. 139.

## Pierre Teilhard de Chardin—pages 322–29

1. Pierre Teilhard de Chardin, *Writings in Time of War*, trans. René Hague (New York: Harper & Row, 1968), "The Mystical Milieu," p. 148.

2. Jean Pierre Dumoulin, ed., *Let Me Explain* (New York: Harper & Row, 1970), p. 152.

3. Henri de Lubac, *The Religion of Teilhard de Chardin* (Garden City, NJ: Doubleday, 1968), "Science et Christ," February 27, 1921 lecture, p. 16.

4. Pierre Teilhard de Chardin, *Letters from a Traveler*, trans. unidentified (San Francisco: Harper & Row, 1962), p. 86.

5. "The Universal Element," *Writings in Time of War*, pp. 299–300.

6. *Writings in Time of War*, p. 119.

7. Pierre Teilhard de Chardin, *How I Believe*, trans. René Hague (San Francisco: Harper & Row, 1969), p. 3.

8. *The Heart of the Matter*, trans. René Hague (New York: Harcourt Brace Jovanovich, 1979), p. 41.

9. *The Activation of Energy*, trans. René Hague (New York: Harcourt Brace Jovanovich, 1979), p. 381.

10. "The Heart of the Matter," *Heart of the Matter*, p. 43.

11. *Lettres intimes à Auguste Valensin, Bruno de Solanges, Henri de Lubac, André Ravier (1919–1955)* (Paris: Aubier-Montaigne, 1974), p. 312.

12. Pierre Teilhard de Chardin, "Introduction to the Christian Life," *Christianity and Evolution*, trans. René Hague (New York: Harcourt Brace Jovanovich, 1971), p. 159.

13. *Journal*, February 24, 1918 entry, p. 281.

14. *The Divine Milieu*, no translator given (New York: Harper & Row, 1960), p. 117.

15. *Journal*, July 18, 1920 entry.

16. "Christianity and Evolution," *Christianity and Evolution*, p. 181.

17. "Some General Views on the Essence of Christianity," *Christianity and Evolution*, p. 135.

18. *Hymn of the Universe*, no translator given (New York: Harper & Row, 1965), p. 23.

19. *Divine Milieu*, p. 125.

20. *Divine Milieu*, p. 102.

21. *Divine Milieu*, p. 104.

22. *Human Energy*, trans. J. M. Cohen (New York: Harcourt Brace Jovanovich, 1969), preface.

23. *Divine Milieu*, p. 133.

24. *Letters from a Traveler*, pp. 99–100.

25. *Science and Christ* (New York: Harper & Row, 1968), p. 104.

26. *Letters from a Traveler*, p. 216.

27. *Lettres intimes* (Paris: Aubier-Montaigne, 1972), p. 25, my translation.

28. *Science and Christ*, p. 106.

29. *Lettres intimes*, p. 273.

30. *Divine Milieu*, p. 116.

31. *Divine Milieu*, p. 119.

32. *Science and Christ*, p. 112.

## Edith Stein—pages 330–31

1. *Self-Portrait in Letters*, quoted in *Edith Stein: Essential Writings*, ed. John Sullivan, O.C.D. (Maryknoll, NY: Orbis Books, 2002), letter of March 23, 1938, p. 91.

2. *Self-Portrait*, letter of March 23, 1938, p. 91.

3. *Edith Stein: Essential Writings*, letter of the 2nd day of Christmas, 1932, p. 60.

4. Letter 287, quoted in *The Collected Works of Edith Stein, Volume Six: The Science of the Cross*, trans. Josephine Koeppel, O.C.D. (Washington, DC: Institute of Carmelite Studies, 2002), p. xix.

5. *Science of the Cross*, quoted in *Edith Stein: Essential Writings*, p. 26.

6. *Edith Stein: Essential Writings*, p. 158.

## Maria Faustina Kowalska—pages 332–37

1. *Divine Mercy in My Soul: The Diary of the Servant of God Sister M. Faustina Kowalska, Perpetually Professed Member of the Congregation of Sisters of Our Lady of Mercy* (Stockbridge, MA: Marian Press, 1987), § 60, pp. 30–31. All references are to this work.

2. § 40, p. 21.
3. § 148, p. 83.
4. § 60, p. 31.
5. § 1670, p. 591.
6. § 1020, p. 389.
7. § 1056, p. 399.
8. § 824, p. 323.
9. § 98, p. 55.
10. § 98, p. 55.
11. § 137, p. 76.
12. § 1767, p. 627.
13. § 604, p. 254.
14. § 1556, p. 552.

## Karl Rahner—pages 338–44

1. "Christian Living Formerly and Today," *Theological Investigations VII*, trans. David Bourke (New York: Herder and Herder, 1971), p. 15. References to the *Theological Investigations* will be abbreviated as *TI*, followed by the volume number.

2. "Teresa of Avila: Doctor of the Church," in Karl Rahner, *Opportunities for Faith*, trans. Edward Quinn (New York: Seabury, 1970), p. 125.

3. Paul Imhof and Hubert Biallowons, eds., *Karl Rahner in Dialogue* (New York: Crossroad, 1986), p. 211. The Whitsunday, 1961, entry in Dag Hammarskjöld's well-known work, *Markings* (trans. Leif Sjöberg & W. H. Auden [New York: Vintage Spiritual Classics, 2006], p. 205), is a striking example of what Rahner means by the mystical experience of God in everyday life becoming more explicit. "I don't know," Hammarskjöld wrote, "Who—or what—put the question. I don't know when it was put. I don't even remember answering. But at some moment I did answer *Yes* to Someone—or Something—and from that hour I was certain that existence is meaningful and that, therefore, my life, in self surrender, had a goal."

4. *Karl Rahner in Dialogue*, p. 182.

5. "Mysticism," *Encyclopedia of Theology* (New York: Seabury Press, 1975), pp. 1010–11.

6. "Christian Living Formerly and Today," *TI* VII, p. 15.

7. "Why Become or Remain a Jesuit?" *Madonna* (Jesuit publication, Melbourne, Australia) (April 1987): p. 11.

8. "Why Become or Remain a Jesuit?" p. 11.

9. Karl Lehmann and Albert Raffelt, eds., *The Practice of Faith* (New York: Crossroad, 1983), "Experiencing the Spirit," p. 81.

10. "Experiencing the Spirit," *The Practice of Faith*, p. 81.

11. "Religious Enthusiasm and the Experience of Grace," *TI* XVI, trans. David Moreland, O.S.B. (New York: Seabury Press, 1979), pp. 35–51.

12. *Karl Rahner in Dialogue*, pp. 329, 297, my emphasis. "Sober Christianity" is a phrase that often showed up in his lectures and writings.

13. Albert Raffelt and Harvey D. Egan, ed., *The Great Church Year* (New York: Crossroad, 1993), "Teresa of Avila: Doctor of the Church," p. 362.

14. "Mystical Experience and Mystical Theology," *TI* XVII, trans. Margaret Kohl (New York: Crossroad, 1981), p. 92.

15. "Mystical Experience," *TI* XVII, pp. 362–63.

16. "Experience of Transcendence," *TI* XVIII, p. 175.

17. Klaus P. Fischer, *Der Mensch als Geheimnis* (Freiburg im Breisgau: Herder, 1974), "Brief von P. Karl Rahner," trans. Daniel Donovan, p. 406.

18. "Experience of the Holy Spirit," *TI* XVIII, p. 208.

19. "Mysticism," *Encyclopedia of Theology*, pp. 1010–11.

20. *Visions and Prophecies*, trans. Charles Henkey and Richard Strachan (New York: Herder and Herder, 1963), p. 14, note 12.

21. *Schriften zur Theologie: Wissenschaft und Christlicher Glaube* XV, "Rede des Ignatius von Loyola an einem Jesuiten von heute" (Züruch, Einsiedeln, Köln: Benziger Verlag, 1983), pp. 384–85. My translation.

## Bernard Lonergan—pages 345–49

1. Bernard J. F. Lonergan, S.J., *Method in Theology* (New York: Seabury Press, 1979), pp. 105–6.

2. Harvey D. Egan, S.J., *What Are They Saying About Mysticism?* (Ramsey, NJ: Paulist Press, 1982), chap. 9, "A Future Mystical Theology," pp. 109–16.

3. *Method in Theology*, p. 105.

4. *Method in Theology*, p. 115.

5. *Method in Theology*, p. 115.

6. William Johnston, S.J., *The Mysticism of the Cloud of Unknowing* (New York: Desclée Co., 1967).

7. *Method in Theology*, p. 113.

8. *Method in Theology*, p. 273.

9. *Method in Theology*, p. 105.

10. In an undeservedly neglected study, "Complacency and Concern in the Thought of St. Thomas" (*Theological Studies* vol. 20, nos. 1–3 [March, June, and September 1959]: pp. 1–39, 198–230, 342–95), Lonergan's disciple Frederick E. Crowe, S.J., does for Aquinas's understanding of *complacentia* what Lonergan did for Aquinas's understanding of *verbum*. Unfortunately, the English term "complacency" is misleading.

11. *Method in Theology*, p. 343.

## Simone Weil—pages 350–51

1. Simone Weil, *Waiting for God* (New York: Harper Perennial, 2009), trans. Emma Craufurd, letter IV, p. 38.

2. *Waiting for God*, letter IV, p. 28.

3. *Waiting for God*, letter IV, p. 27.

4. *Waiting for God*, letter IV, p. 31.

## Henri Le Saux—pages 352–56

1. Abhishiktananda, *Saccidananda: A Christian Approach to Advaitic Experience* (Delhi: I.S.P.C.K., 1974), p. 176.

2. *Saccidananda*, p. 172.

3. Abhishiktananda, *Guru and Disciple*, trans. Heather Sandeman (London: SPCK, 1974), pp. x–xi.

4. *Saccidananda*, p. 66.

5. *The Eyes of Light* (Denville, NJ: Dimension Books, 1983), p. 52.

6. *Eyes of Light*, p. 53.

7. *Guru and Disciple*, pp. x–xi.

8. *Eyes of Light*, p. 95.

9. *Eyes of Light*, p. 32.

10. *Eyes of Light*, p. 118.

## Thomas Merton—pages 357–63

1. Preface to the Japanese edition of Thomas Merton, *The Seven Storey Mountain*, quoted by Monica Furlong, *Merton—A Biography* (San Francisco: Harper & Row, 1980), p. 267.

2. *Seven Storey Mountain* (New York: Harcourt Brace, 1948), p. 123.

3. *The Climate of Monastic Prayer* (Spencer, MA and Kalamazoo: Cistercian Publications, 1969), p. 121.

4. Thomas P. McDonnell, ed., *A Thomas Merton Reader*, rev. ed. (Garden City, NY: Doubleday, 1974), p. 325.

5. *The Ascent to Truth* (New York: Viking Press, 1951), p. 197.

6. *The Ascent to Truth* (New York: Harcourt Brace, 1951), p. 257.

7. "The Inner Experience: Kinds of Contemplation (IV)," *Cistercian Studies* XVIII, 4 (1983): p. 161.

8. *New Seeds of Contemplation* (New York: New Directions, 1961), p. 152.

9. "The Inner Experience: Kinds of Contemplation (IV)," p. 294.

10. "First Christmas at Gethsemani," *Catholic World* 170 (December 1949): p. 30.

11. *The Asian Journal of Thomas Merton*, edited from his original notebooks by Naomi Burton, Brother Patrick Hart, and James Laughlin (New York: New Dimensions, 1973), pp. 312–13.

12. *Asian Journal of Thomas Merton*, p. 312.

13. *Conjectures of a Guilty Bystander* (Garden City, NY: Doubleday, 1966), p. 21.

## William Johnston—pages 364–67

1. William Johnston, *The Mirror Mind: Spirituality and Transformation* (San Francisco: Harper & Row, 1981), p. 9.

2. New York: Desclée Co., 1967.

3. Garden City, NY: Doubleday, 1973.

4. *Mirror Mind*, p. 9.

5. *The Inner Eye of Love: Mysticism and Religion* (San Francisco: Harper & Row, 1978), p. 20.

6. *The Still Point: Reflections on Zen and Christian Mysticism* (San Francisco: Harper & Row, 1970), p. 138.

7. *Mirror Mind*, p. 59.

8. *Still Point*, p. 4.

9. *Silent Music: The Science of Meditation* (San Francisco: Harper & Row, 1974).

## Mother Teresa—pages 368–72

1. *Mother Teresa: Come Be My Light: The Private Writings of "the Saint of Calcutta,"* ed. Brian Kolodiejchuk, M.C. (New York: Doubleday, 2007), letter of March 8, 1962 to Father Joseph Neuner, S.J., p. 230. All references are to this volume.

2. General letter of January 31, 1980 to Missionaries of Charity, p. 315.

3. Letter of December 3, 1947 to Archbishop Ferdinand Périer, S.J., p. 99.

4. Undated letter between 1957–60 to Lawrence Trevor Picachy, S.J., p. 83.

5. Letter of April 1961 to Joseph Neuner, S.J., p. 83.

6. Letter of July 29, 1956 of Archbishop Périer to Mother Teresa, p. 168.

7. Letter of November 17, 1964 to Missionaries of Charity Superiors, p. 248.

8. Notes of "the copy of the Voice since September 1946," p. 44.

9. Letter of May 6, 1962 to Joseph Neuner, S.J., p. 230.

10. Letter to Joseph Neuner, S.J., probably April 1961, p. 211.

11. Letter of December 1, 1967 to Patty and Warren Kump, p. 262.

12. Letter of December 21, 1969 to Archbishop Lawrence Trevor Picachy, S.J., p. 266.

13. Letter of July 14, 1967 to Joseph Neuner, S.J., p. 14.

14. Retreat notes, pp. 195, 351.

15. Speech at Regina Mundi Institute, Rome, December 20, 1979, quoted in Kolodiejchuk, p. 286.

16. Testimony of Sister Margaret Mary, p. 331.

# Index of Subjects

# Index of Names